Life and Letters in Tudor and Stuart England

FIRST FOLGER SERIES

QUEEN ELIZABETH

*From a painting at Longford Castle, Wiltshire, reproduced by
kind permission of the Right Honourable the Earl of Radnor.*

LIFE AND LETTERS
IN TUDOR AND
STUART ENGLAND

FIRST FOLGER SERIES

Edited by Louis B. Wright

and Virginia A. LaMar

PUBLISHED FOR

THE FOLGER SHAKESPEARE LIBRARY

BY CORNELL UNIVERSITY PRESS

ITHACA, NEW YORK

CORNELL UNIVERSITY PRESS

First collected edition 1962

Library of Congress Catalog Card Number: 62–21552

PRINTED IN THE UNITED STATES OF AMERICA

BY THE MERIDEN GRAVURE COMPANY

PREFACE

THE Folger Shakespeare Library of Washington, D.C., a research institution administered by the Trustees of Amherst College, has an extraordinary collection of books, pamphlets, manuscripts, engravings, and other materials useful for the study of Western civilization from about 1485 to 1715. Although the primary purpose of the Folger Library is to encourage advanced research in history and literature, the Library also recognizes an obligation to the nonspecialist who wants to know more about the civilization of western Europe in the sixteenth and seventeenth centuries, particularly the civilization of the Tudor and Stuart periods, when the English-speaking people were beginning their first expansion overseas and were laying the foundations of new realms abroad.

The Folger Library is publishing a series of booklets designed to describe various aspects of the history of the sixteenth and seventeenth centuries. These booklets, illustrated with contemporary pictures, for the most part from the Folger's own collections, and equipped with selective bibliographies, have proved helpful to students and general readers in search of concise introductions to a variety of topics in social and intellectual history. For the further convenience of readers, we have planned to bring the booklets together in a series of bound volumes. This is the first of such volumes.

It is particularly fitting that we can begin this series with an essay on Queen Elizabeth I by Sir John Neale, the distinguished biographer of the great Queen and one of the most eminent historians of the period. This essay, delivered as a lecture at the Folger Library on the four hundredth anniversary of the Queen's accession, attracted much attention at the time and deserves to be made available to the general public.

These essays, bibliographies, and illustrations were not designed for specialists and scholars familiar with the field. They were prepared with the hope of interesting a larger group in a period of history that is vitally important to a proper understanding of the civilization that we have inherited.

For students and readers who may wish to acquire photographic reproductions of illustrations and documents suggested by these essays, the Folger Library is prepared to supply microfilm and photographs.

Louis B. Wright

July 1, 1962

CONTENTS

England's Elizabeth

A LECTURE DELIVERED AT THE FOLGER SHAKESPEARE
LIBRARY ON NOVEMBER 17, 1958, THE FOURTH
CENTENARY OF THE ACCESSION OF ELIZABETH I

By Sir John E. Neale

THIS is November 17, 1958. Four hundred years ago today, Queen Elizabeth "of glorious memory"—Good Queen Bess, as she was affectionately known to generations of Englishmen— ascended the throne of England. And here are we—you of the New World, where the name of Virginia establishes your interest in the occasion, and I from the Old World, unable to resist the call to the ghost to go west—here are we met to commemorate the day. In the words of the simple ballad writer, composed in 1600:

> Now let us pray
> and keep holy-daye
> The seaventeenth day of November;
> For joy of her Grace
> in every place,
> Let us great prayses render.

But why should we? you may ask. It is my business to supply the answer.

3

First of all, we are associating ourselves with an old English tradition that lasted for two centuries. It was about ten years after Elizabeth's accession that villagers and townsmen in England took to ringing their church bells and rejoicing on November 17. The custom began spontaneously. So far as I know, there were no precedents, though in Catholic England there had been saints' days galore. After a few years, the Anglican Church adopted this popular innovation, making a Protestant holyday of November 17; and as the cult of the Queen intensified, the day was celebrated throughout the land in a pleasing variety of ways, ranging from elaborate tilts at Westminster, where the royal Court assembled, to the simple service, bell ringing, and bonfires of the rural village.

Like its origins, the history of the day is unique. The death of the Queen naturally brought the November holiday to an end, and her successor, James I, cashed in on the idea by transferring the celebration to his Accession Day in March. But soon the people of England, growing disgusted with the Scots, losing confidence in the government, and renewing their old fear of Catholicism, began to feel that England's golden age was in the past, and consequently revived their celebration of November 17 with the ringing of bells and public joy and sermons in commemoration of Queen Elizabeth's Day. The dynamic of a people —which is to exult in the present—turned to the nostalgia of memory and regret; witness the title of a tract published in 1642 and devoted to praise of Elizabeth's virtue and her government —*The humble petition of the wretched, and most contemptible, the poor Commons of England, to the blessed Elizabeth of famous memory.*

In the second half of the seventeenth century, when the later Stuart sovereigns in their folly flouted the prejudices of the nation and brought the Protestant establishment into apparent danger, a new intensity was imparted to the celebration of Queen Elizabeth's Accession Day—the Birthday of the Gospel, as it was often called. With the aid of Opposition politicians, the annual festival in London was turned into an occasion for fantastic antipapist processions, ending in the burning of effigies on a huge bonfire. Guy Fawkes Day—that other Protestant festival, held on November 5, the anniversary of the Gunpowder Plot, and still celebrated by English children with fireworks and "guys"—was completely outclassed by the rejoicings and ceremonial of Queen Elizabeth's Day. "The feast the factious rabble keep," Dryden termed it. London maintained its day of bigotry into the eighteenth century, while in the countryside the more restrained and appropriate practice of bell ringing continued on this day, certainly to the end of the third decade of that century. Gradually, however, the atmosphere changed and the fame of Queen Bess dwindled, leaving Guy Fawkes in command of November. By the early nineteenth century, the vestigial remains were a day's holiday at two of London's ancient schools and also—oddly enough—at the national Exchequer.

We are no longer stirred by the crude passions that roused the London mob in the seventeenth and eighteenth centuries. But the instinct of a people which made a Thanksgiving Day of November 17: that surely interests us. Posterity has never wavered in regarding the Elizabethan period as one of the golden times of history. How indeed could it, when the age gave birth to such immortal names and achievements as those of Sidney, Spenser, Bacon, and Shakespeare; Hawkins, Drake, and Raleigh? What a people's instinct did was to associate this astounding flowering of an age with a single event—the accession of Elizabeth Tudor to the throne of England.

The people were right. Consider the alternative: imagine that Queen Mary Tudor, Elizabeth's sister, had lived the normal span of life and produced an heir to the throne. Tied to Spain and Catholicism, England's story—Europe's and America's as well— would have been very different. The enterprising minds and personalities of high Elizabethan days were associated with the fresh ideology of that age—Protestantism. In the circumstances we have envisaged, it seems certain that the energies of such men would have found an outlet and been absorbed in civil dissension. As it was, Mary's brief reign hovered on the brink of civil war, and the gloom cast on the nation by subordination to a foreign king, along with the priestly cruelty of burning heretics at the stake—it would have been less offensive to call heresy treason and use the gallows—all this was tolerable only because Mary was childless and ailing, and a bright future seemed at hand in the person of Elizabeth. Otherwise, England, not France, would probably have inaugurated the Religious Wars of the second half of the century, and under a Catholic government they would have been as prolonged as the French Religious Wars. How could the literary achievements of the period have come out of such a setting? How could its maritime saga have been enacted with the King of Spain still King of England? How could Virginia and New England have been what they were and are without the Elizabethan background? What would have been the story of Francis Drake or Walter Raleigh? Would Shakespeare have written his plays?

Let us broaden our speculation to include the continent of Europe. Had premature death and childlessness not brought the rule of Philip and Mary to so abrupt an end, the Council of Trent would still have met, the Catholic Church would still have shed its uncertainties, and the Counter Reformation would still have been launched on the strong basis of renewed confidence. But official England—Scotland, too, for the Reformation could not have prevailed there without Elizabeth's assistance—would have been on the Catholic side, instead of opposed to it. What difference that would have made, it is perhaps hard to say; but the difference would certainly have been considerable. As this profound struggle between the rival ideologies of those days developed, the leaders of the Counter Reformation came to think of Queen Elizabeth as their prime enemy, while to Protestants throughout Europe she was their principal protector. She intervened diplomatically, financially, and militarily in support of the Protestant cause in France and the Netherlands, as well as in Scotland. One may doubt whether the revolt of the Netherlands could have prospered without her, or the Huguenots in France have continued their struggle to win in the end the Edict of Nantes. And if she had not so engaged the attention and resources of the Counter Reformation, could Geneva have cocked a snook with such effrontery and undermined the French state with its genius for subversive practices? There is a moral as well as a material side to Elizabeth's influence. Her fame and fortune were in themselves of incalculable survival value for the cause of Protestantism in Europe.

We should not be misled by the peaceful and uneventful accession of Queen Elizabeth into thinking of November 17, 1558 as an ordinary transfer of the throne from one dead monarch to her natural successor. The exiles returning to England after their flight abroad from the Catholic regime of Mary Tudor, the citizens of London in their welcome to the new Queen, and the majority in the House of Commons when the first Parliament of the reign assembled—all these, and many more, saw the occasion as the overthrow of one ideology and the victory of its rival: we might almost say, a revolutionary *coup d'état*. And, in fact, there is evidence to suggest that Elizabeth was organized to fight for her throne, if the need had arisen.

To ardent Protestants, the miraculous preservation of their Queen from all the perils of her sister's reign was the admirable work of God's own hand. In an oration, written for the accession, John Hales imagined God saying to Englishmen: "Ye see, my people, what I have done for you. . . . I have not only discovered mine, yours, and my land of England's enemies . . . but I have also taken away their head and captain, and destroyed a great number of them, that ye should not be troubled with them; and some of them I have left, that ye may make them spectacles and examples, to the terror and fear of their posterity." Addressing Elizabeth, Hales told her that if she fulfilled her destiny, carrying out the revolution fully and quickly, then all men would confess that she was "of God specially sent and ordained. And as the Queen of Sheba came from afar off to see the glory of King Solomon—a woman to a man—even so shall the princes of our time come—men to a woman—and kings marvel at the virtue of Queen Elizabeth."

Here, in this elation of spirit after a depressing reign, lay the potential dynamic of the new age. I have said "potential." If it were to be a case of replacing one persecuting ideology by the fanatical impulses of another—if, in the words of John Hales, the Elizabethan government were to make of Catholics "spectacles and examples to the terror and fear of their posterity"—what chance would there be of national unity? The rule of the saints is not conducive to common happiness. And yet from these godly men—supremely from them—could come a new inspiration. To harness this to the broader emotion of patriotism; to nurse the ardor of men like Hales and yet restrain their harmful fanaticism; to cultivate the Puritan sense of a divine purpose guarding and promoting the welfare of England, as God in the Old Testament had watched over Israel—to do this and at the same time qualify that exclusive spirit by tolerance, here was the problem of statecraft.

It called for exceptional ability and a genius for leadership; and since that leadership, in a period of personal monarchy, had to come from the sovereign, and the sovereign was a woman, ruling men who believed the regiment of women to be monstrous, it also called for extraordinary will power. Happy fortune too was needed: a combination and succession of accidents, not least of which was the long life of the Queen. Elizabeth's reign might be interpreted as a gamble, a gamble of hers with time. She preferred to run the gravest risks rather than act against her deeper promptings. "Safety first" was not her motto. Her ministers—

all of them, including the ablest and most trusted—wrung their hands in despair over her. "To behold miseries coming and to be denied remedies!" moaned Lord Burghley. "Our remedy," wrote Sir Francis Walsingham, "must be prayer, for other help I see none." "If we prosper," echoed another Councillor, "it must be, as our custom is, by miracle." In such a situation, what wonder, when peril after peril was successfully avoided and the reign progressed with resounding fortune, if that biblically minded generation, which in 1558 regarded Elizabeth as the ward of Providence, perceived God's eternal vigilance in the preservation of his servant Elizabeth and his chosen Englishmen? Her enemies were just as impressed; but they thought her the daughter of the Devil. The sober fact is that if she had died twenty years sooner she would probably have left a name of infamy in history; and she knew it. Our generation, which watched Sir Winston Churchill's leadership of England during the late war and has read Lord Alanbrooke's diary, can appreciate all this.

The harnessing of the revolutionary spirit began almost at once with the religious settlement made at Elizabeth's first Parliament. It was a Protestant settlement, but with comeliness and tradition preserved and fanaticism excluded. We know too little about its story, but all that little shows that it was the personal policy of the young Queen, stubbornly forced through a reluctant, radical House of Commons. The Anglican Church, now four hundred years old and venerable, was uniquely the creation of this woman. Though not so conservative as she wished, it has certainly proved, what she wanted it to be, amazingly comprehensive. At all times it has harbored high, low, and also moderate churchmen. It might be regarded as the symbol of her rule. The Deborah of the revolutionaries certainly failed them. Rather than be a party leader, she chose to lead the nation. In so doing she created a left wing of discontent.

The paradox of the Elizabethan age is that its flavor and dynamic came from this left or Puritan wing, and came through

9

a romantic attachment between them and their Queen. It was an attachment for which I think the closest parallel in our history is that between Englishmen and Winston Churchill in our own time.

What is the explanation? As in the case of Winston Churchill, undoubtedly the supreme art and deliberate policy of the Queen. But there were more specific reasons—reasons of an accidental character. The first was the Queen's failure to marry, the consequent lack of an heir, and the uncertainty about the succession to the throne. If no religious problem had existed, Mary Queen of Scots would have been the obvious heir apparent; but she was a Catholic, the spearhead of the opposing ideology, and English Protestants would on no account tolerate the prospect of her succession. The future of Protestantism therefore continued as it had during Mary Tudor's reign, linked indissolubly with the life of Elizabeth. Whatever her shortcomings, she remained the Deborah of the saints: they had no other choice. If she had married and borne a child, the radicals would almost certainly have transferred their hopes to the heir, and the romance would have turned sour. Everyone knows that Elizabeth was the Virgin Queen; it is not often realized how vital to her success that role was.

The second reason for the romantic attachment of Queen and people was the mounting concentration of the Catholic Counter Reformation against Elizabeth and her England—the cold war of the two rival ideologies of that age, with its hot spots. The crucial event was the flight of Mary Queen of Scots to England in 1568, after her lurid tale of misadventure in her own country. Thenceforward, until her execution in 1587 put an end to this frightful danger, the alternative, Catholic Deborah was in England, a focus—though captive—for every plot and scheme of the counter revolution. Granted a similar revolutionary climate and a similar life-or-death struggle, who could be confident that, even in our modern civilized days, a bloody end would not be put to such an intolerable situation in less than twenty hazardous years? Elizabeth's statesmen, Parliament, and people exerted their utmost pressure to exact that solution, and exact it rapidly, from their Queen. Her obstinate refusal was an even more personal policy than her religious settlement. She pursued the *via media* in politics as well as religion, gambling with her own life and the country's apparent welfare for the sake of rooted principles and instincts. We may doubt whether any masculine ruler would have shown such compunction.

Even before the arrival of Mary Queen of Scots in England, an attack of smallpox, from which it was feared that Elizabeth would not recover, had reminded English Protestants of the slender thread upon which their world depended. As the cold war developed and Catholic missionaries penetrated into England, undermining the ideology of the nation and recruiting what their militant leaders abroad regarded as a potential fifth column to be called into action on the day the cold war became a hot one, and as plot succeeded plot, with the purpose of killing the Queen and replacing her by Mary Queen of Scots, the reaction of Protestant England, quite understandably, was passionate in the extreme.

Increasing danger imparted a new and peculiar intensity to the bond of affection between Elizabeth and her people. She herself cultivated the relationship with consummate art, playing her part, on set occasions, with the skill of a born actress. She was as sensitive to public relations as any modern publicity agent. She wrote her own speeches for Parliament, fining and refining her phrases like the most finicky stylist. When, for example, at the final crisis over Mary Queen of Scots, two of these speeches were needed for propaganda purposes at home and abroad, she secretly worked over the printer's text herself rather than permit a mere report to be printed. Her courtly progresses through the countryside—her summer holidays—were episodes in publicity, marked by most elaborate and artificial entertainments and relieved by innumerable touches of the unconventional. "Stay thy cart, good fellow! stay thy cart, that I may speak to the Queen," cried a worthy lawyer to the royal coachman, holding up the long, courtly train on progress in Huntingdonshire. "Whereat," we are told, "her Majesty laughed as she had been tickled," and gave the good man "great thanks and her hand to kiss." She wooed her Londoners unceasingly, on set occasions and as numberless minor opportunities presented themselves.

> The people flocked there amain,
> The multitude was great to see;
> Their joyful harts were glad, and fain
> To view her princely majesty,
> Who at the length came riding by,
> Within her chariot openly;
> Even with a noble princely train
> Of lords and ladies of great fame.
> Her Majesty was glad to see
> Her subjects in so good a case,
> Which then fell humbly on their knee,
> Desiring God to save her grace.
> And like a noble prince that day
> For them in like sorte did she pray;
> And curteously she answered still,
> I thank you all for your good will.

Her court was a community in itself, thronged with visitors, especially on Sundays, come to see the Queen, perhaps to catch her eye and be spoken to.

For their part, the people admired her qualities of mind and heart—her "magnanimity," as they often termed it, using that word in its etymological sense, which, alas, it has now lost.

> The peerles pearle of princes all,
> So ful of pitty, peace, and love,
> Whose mercy is not proved small,
> When foule offendors doo her moove,

> A phenix of moste noble minde,
> Unto her subjects good and kinde;
> A moste renowned virgin queen,
> Whose like on earth was never seen.

Patriots felt profound content in the thought that their country was personified in her, much as Englishmen, in our time, felt about Winston Churchill. As their mutual perils were overcome and their enemies confounded, the conviction deepened that God had indeed chosen her as his handmaiden and her people as his people. In the Parliament of 1587, Job Throckmorton—who may have been that pamphleteering genius, Martin Marprelate— told the story of a Frenchman, who, hearing of a vital English success, rapped out an oath and said, "I think God be sworn English: there is nothing will prosper against the Queen of England." "With what affection that wretched man spake it," commented Throckmorton; "I know not. But sure, we that have lived in the eyes of all men, so choked, as it were, with blessings of God beyond desert, we that have lived to see her Majesty's life, so dear unto us, pulled out . . . even out of the lion's jaws in despite of Hell and Satan, may truly—not in any pride of heart, but in humbleness of soul to our comforts—confess that indeed the Lord hath vowed himself to be English." All such emotions led Englishmen to worship Elizabeth this side of idolatry and to make of her a cult, which, with its feminine ingredient, was converted into a patriotic romance.

The cult of the Queen was expressed in the literature of the age, in courtly pageantry, and by artists in her portraits. Much, of course, was highly artificial, though that does not mean that it was necessarily false, and the ballads were usually simple enough. The parliamentary debates of the high Elizabethan period—from the arrival of Mary Queen of Scots to the post-Armada years—throb with the pride of Englishmen in their sovereign. Even the most obstreperous Puritans—indeed, they above all—rejoiced in her. "It makes my heart leap for joy to think we

13

have such a jewel," declared one of them in the House of Commons. "It makes all my joints to tremble for fear when I consider the loss of such a jewel." Job Throckmorton pictured, in apocalyptic mood, England's supreme bliss: that, if it so pleased God, the last day of Queen Elizabeth's life might be the last day of this earth, and "that when she fleeteth hence . . . we may then behold . . . Jesus sitting in his throne of judgment, to our endless and everlasting comfort."

In 1585, when England was horror-stricken by the assassination of William the Silent and its own Catholic plots, a Sussex Puritan lawyer, who had sat in Parliament, recorded similar sentiments in a draft will, written on the flyleaf of the family's Wycliffe Bible:

I heartily pray the Almighty God to send a long, prosperous and happy life and reign to our good Queen Elizabeth, and to send us all grace that we may all live in his fear as good and dutiful subjects to our said gracious Sovereign Lady and Queen, and all die before the sorrowful days of England shall come, if God should take her from us before the end of the world. And that if for our sins he shorten her days, as he did the days of good King Edward [VI], that yet he will grant me the grace to die at her feet before her, and that at the end of all things, which is at hand, we may joyfully rise again to life everlasting, with perpetual joy and felicity. Amen. Amen.

Thus, there was this cult of the Queen as the symbol of patriotism and the Protestant ideology. The other aspect of England's reaction to its perils was the desire to promote political security by penal laws, increasingly drastic as the danger became more acute. The State in those days was inevitably ideological. How far it went along the totalitarian road depended on policy. Quite early, Elizabeth's Councillors and Parliament wanted to enforce attendance at Communion in church by statute, in order, as one Puritan Member said, that "the very secrets of the heart in God's cause . . . must come to a reckoning, and the good seed [be] so sifted from the cockle that the one may be known from the other." The Queen vetoed that bill, and when in a later Parliament an attempt was made to revive the measure, she interfered to stay its course. Though requiring outward conformity to the law, she abhorred all inquisitional practices and would open no windows into men's souls.

By 1580 the cold war was hotting up, and the infiltration of Catholic missionaries was reinforced by the beginning of Jesuit missions. The menace had to be dealt with, and when Parliament met statesmen and both Houses drafted what they regarded as the necessary legislation. They wanted to stop the missionaries by making their work treasonable and their converts traitors, to prohibit saying or attending Mass under the severest penalties, and to bar Catholics from entry into the professions. With these and other proposals they would have imposed (or tried to impose) orthodoxy in their ideological State as ruthlessly as the totalitarian regimes of our contemporary world. The Queen intervened to prohibit many of their proposals, scale down the penalties of others radically, and insert a secular instead of a doctrinaire principle into the Act.

As the drama unfolded, the pattern remained the same. In 1584, for example, after the assassination of William the Silent, the people of England, knowing that papal approval had been given for the murder of Elizabeth, joined in a Bond of Association, devised by Privy Councillors, the avowed intention of which was to use lynch law against the Catholics' prospective Queen, Mary of Scots, in retaliation for plots to kill their own Queen. In the following Parliament, when it was planned to give statutory sanction to this lawless agreement, Elizabeth interfered to amend both statute and Bond of Association in the interests of decency.

Liberal-minded historians of the past—not so imaginative as we necessarily are about the passions aroused by a prolonged ideological struggle—have deplored the anti-Catholic penal

15

legislation of the Elizabethan period. By enlightened nineteenth-century standards it was indeed shocking, though the critics seldom realized that the crucial question for those days was how the law was administered. All the same, this legislation was mild —astonishingly mild—compared with the penalties that Privy Councillors, Lords, and Commons did their utmost to secure. Their obstacle was always the Queen.

It was the same at the other extreme. In the passionate atmosphere of the time, doctrinaires of the left—the Puritans—acquired an authority and following out of proportion to their number or their gospel. In the name of Truth and Patriotism they wanted to reform the Anglican Church root and branch, to obtain what had been denied them in the Settlement of 1559, and even to go the whole hog in Protestant ideology. It is the perennial story of revolutions, except in the sequel. In the name of patriotism, if not of truth, they generally found a majority of fellow travelers in the House of Commons ready to back them, and substantial sympathy for many items of their program in the House of Lords and among Privy Councillors. After all, what surer defense was there against the enemy than a nation legislated into Protestant godliness? The saints seemed to have the right answer to the country's grave political problem.

Elizabeth would not budge an inch. Always at hand, always vigilant, she argued, threatened, sent prohibitory messages, imprisoned offenders in the Tower, and wielded her legislative veto. Then, when the doctrinaires, having secretly built up a subversive Presbyterian movement within the Church itself, tried to legislate the revolution into existence, she disciplined them with rigor and put up her best orators in the House of Commons to expose their conspiracy. It was deliberate, consistent, and personal action, and undoubtedly saved the Church of England.

What does all this amount to? Surely that in a period of passion Elizabeth prevented the ardor of fanatics, the vengeful indignation of patriots, and the panic of fear of many from running away with policy. She resisted even the ruthless logic of her statesmen. Lord Burghley was probably the most moderate of her Councillors, as he was the most responsible and the one she trusted most. Drawing up the pros and cons of problems, as was his habit, he found himself supporting many of those parliamentary measures that the Queen vetoed or amended. "The Queen's Majesty," he told Walsingham in 1571, "hath been always a merciful lady, and by mercy she hath taken more harm than by justice, and yet she thinks that she is more beloved in doing herself harm. God save her to his honor long among us." Doubtless there were those near Elizabeth who whispered advice against the majority opinion of Council and Parliament; but we know enough about some of the most striking instances to be sure that the overwhelming weight of authority was against her. In this sense she may often be said to have gambled with the fate of the kingdom. It is worth asking how this could be.

In the first place, the constitution of the country was personal monarchy. The sovereign received counsel or advice, but all decisions were hers. One of the remarkable features of Elizabeth's rule is the extent to which she kept both major and minor decisions in her own hands. Again, she chose her own Councillors. Their superlative quality is equally remarkable. Even her "favorites" were men of parts and were made to work hard. Legend and history have been wrong about one of these favorites, Sir Christopher Hatton, and I think we are due for a reassessment of another, the famous Earl of Leicester. She was an almost infallible judge of men, and if with her temperament and perversity she gave her servants many headaches, she was loyal to them and won their genuine devotion. "She is our God in earth," wrote Lord North in 1575. "If there be perfection in flesh and blood, undoubtedly it is in her Majesty. For she is slow to revenge and ready to forgive. And yet . . . she is right King Henry, her father. For if any strive with her, all the princes of Europe cannot make her yield. Again, whoso humbly and lovingly submitteth himself to her desire, she doth and will so graciously receive and recompense him, as every [person] that knoweth her doth honor and entirely love her." Elizabeth did not discard her statesmen, much less ruin or execute them, as her father did. In this she set a new, a civilized example to princes.

It is an interesting reflection that masters who have the faculty of choosing servants of outstanding ability usually remain nonetheless masters. To diagnose why this was the case with Elizabeth is easy. A person of exceptional intelligence and studious, inquisitive temperament, she was educated in the rigorous manner of the Renaissance by the finest scholars of the time. She was a cultured woman, the intellectual peer or superior of her advisers, and had the requisite linguistic and historical knowledge to keep even foreign policy in her hands. Moreover, in her youth she had passed through a school of experience where everything —even her life—depended on her wit and intelligence. Her political instinct was already mature when she came to the throne at the age of twenty-five, and over the years, judging solely by results, she made so few blunders that time could only confirm and justify her trust in it. Her greatest statesman, Lord Burghley, who was inclined at first to share contemporary prejudice against a woman ruler, was brought at length to acknowledge her surpassing wisdom. The divergences of policy between him and his mistress seem often to have been divergences between logic and instinct. Perhaps her greater trust in instinct was a feminine trait, though experience, as so often can be said of instinct, was a predominant ingredient. She worked hard and conscientiously at her job and lived for it, with mind and emotion. She had every reason for self-confidence except that of sex, and her masterful nature and birth compensated here. Tradition has portrayed her as unprincipled. It is a superficial judgment, bred of ignorance. In fact, no sovereign or statesman has clung more obstinately and daringly to certain fundamental principles, though in small things few women have tantalized men more frequently by their mutability.

It was principle, deep-rooted in instinct, that led Elizabeth to restrain the passion of an angry nation against Catholics and stand adamant against the dreams of doctrinaires. For this, surely all who in any degree owe something to English civilization still remain indebted to her. Our tradition is one of tolerance. In England the fanatic has never got his way. We have had a Civil War: it did not go to the extremes normally experienced in such strife. We have had our revolutions: that in 1688 is always known as "Glorious," it was so bloodless and respectable; and the one we are going through now is so good-tempered that only when we stop to think do we know that we are in it. For explanation, we need not, like our Elizabethans, invoke God's Englishman. I suppose we might agree that the Bible and the English Common Law largely deserve the credit. But with the Bible, it is the New and not the Old Testament. Elizabethan Parliaments, in their bloody moods against Catholics and Mary Queen of Scots, quoted the Old, not the New, Testament and got the bishops and ecclesiastical lawyers to fortify their petitions to the Queen with precedents and vengeful injunctions from it. As for the Common Law—which, like the Bible, is an American as well as a British heritage—two of its great principles are the rule of law and the rights of individuals. "The King is under the law," said the medieval Bracton; and his successors have echoed him. The Bond of Association of 1584 against Mary Queen of Scots was the negation of law, and if the legal system, by this and other devices, had been prostituted to the use of passion, what a precedent would have been set! In its nature, passion does not endure; but laws and the way political institutions are used tend to have a prolonged existence and far-reaching effects. It is alarmingly easy to inject poison into the body politic. Recovery may be slow, and no one can foretell when it will be complete.

"Nothing in the world," complained the Earl of Leicester to Sir Francis Walsingham in 1582, "grieveth me more than to see that her Majesty believes this increase of Papists in her realm can be no danger to her. The Lord of his mercy open her eyes." That the Queen, at this critical time in our history, remained sensitive to civilized feelings and resisted her advisers is surely cause for us to salute her memory on this, her day. Politically it was folly. She was much too intelligent not to grasp the force of the advice she was given and success alone could justify the responsibility she assumed. By the mercy of God and the devotion of her people success was granted her.

The devotion of her people! Inevitably I return to that theme. It was as Gloriana, Belphoebe, and other conceits of the Elizabethan imagination; it was as an orator who in her great Armada speech spoke these words, "I know I have the body of a weak and feeble woman, but I have the heart and stomach of a King, and of a King of England too"; who, later, in her Golden Speech told her Commons, "Though God hath raised me high, yet this I count the glory of my crown, that I have reigned with your loves"; it was also as one whose impromptu dressing-down of an insolent Polish ambassador, spoken in Latin, thrilled that generation and remained a memory in early Stuart Parliaments; and finally it was as one who, in her last State address to the Realm, rendering a final account of her stewardship, could phrase her peroration in words magical and moving in their simplicity, "This testimony I would have you carry hence for the world to know: that your Sovereign is more careful of your conservation than of herself, and will daily crave of God that they that wish you best may never wish in vain"—it was as such a person, a great woman in a great office, with an unsurpassed gift for romantic, intrepid leadership, that she won the adoration of her subjects and conjured from individuals and the nation as a whole their utmost genius. She was, wrote Francis Osborne some fifty years later, "the choicest artist in kingcraft that ever handled the sceptre in this northern climate."

Let two of the supreme minds of all time, both Elizabethan, both in reflection after the Queen's death, when sycophancy cannot be thought to have smirched their praise; let these two— William Shakespeare and Francis Bacon—speak her panegyric.

Shakespeare wrote his panegyric in the form of a prophecy by Archbishop Cranmer at Elizabeth's christening:

> Let me speak, sir,
> For heaven now bids me; and the words I utter
> Let none think flattery, for they'll find em truth.
> . . . She shall be—
> But few now living can behold that goodness—
> A pattern to all princes living with her,
> And all that shall succeed her: Saba was never
> More covetous of wisdom and fair virtue
> Than this pure soul shall be: all princely graces,
> That mould up such a mighty piece as this is,
> With all the virtues that attend the good,
> Shall still be doubled on her; truth shall nurse her;
> Holy and heavenly thoughts still counsel her;
> She shall be lov'd and fear'd; her own shall bless her;
> Her foes shake like a field of beaten corn,
> And hang their heads with sorrow; good grows with her.
> In her days every man shall eat in safety
> Under his own vine what he plants; and sing
> The merry songs of peace to all his neighbors.
> God shall be truly known; and those about her
> From her shall read the perfect ways of honor,
> And by those claim their greatness, not by blood.

Here is Francis Bacon's encomium:

Elizabeth, both in her nature and her fortune was a wonderful person among women, a memorable person among princes. . . . The government of a woman has been a rare thing at all times;

21

felicity in such government a rarer thing still; felicity and long continuance together the rarest thing of all. . . . A womanish people might well enough be governed by a woman; but that in England, a nation particularly fierce and warlike, all things could be swayed and controlled at the beck of a woman, is a matter for the highest admiration. . . . There are some times so barbarous and ignorant that it is as easy a matter to govern men as to drive a flock of sheep. But the lot of this Queen fell upon times highly instructed and cultivated, in which it is not possible to be eminent and excellent without the greatest gifts of mind and a singular composition of virtue. . . . To crown all, as she was most fortunate in all that belonged to herself, so was she in the virtue of her ministers. For she had such men about her as perhaps till that day this island did not produce. But God, when he favors kings, raises also and accomplishes the spirits of their servants. . . . As for her memory, it is so strong and fresh, both in the mouths and minds of men, that now death has extinguished envy and lighted up fame, the felicity of her memory contends in a manner with the felicity of her life. . . . The only true commender of this lady is Time, which, so long a course as it has run, has produced nothing in this sex like her, for the administration of civil affairs.

"The only true commender of this lady is Time"; and Time— to adapt a remark made by Elizabeth during her Coronation procession—"Time hath brought us hither."

The Life of William Shakespeare

By Giles E. Dawson

WILLIAM SHAKESPEARE was recognized in his own time as the best of the dramatists supplying plays for London's half dozen theatres. *Romeo and Juliet, Richard III,* and *Hamlet* were among the most popular productions on the Elizabethan stage. Still, if the first audience at one of these plays could have been polled after the performance was over, it is not inconceivable that half of them would have been unable to name the author. A generation not blessed with newspapers, magazines, public relations offices, advertising campaigns, or women's clubs neither knew nor cared much about the men who wrote the plays, however excellent the plays might be. No youths pursued Shakespeare with autograph albums; no collector would have given a shilling to acquire the original manuscript of *Hamlet.* Autographs and autograph manuscripts were not valued and not collected. Yet men did talk about Shakespeare and held opinions about him and his writings, and some fifty or sixty persons commented on him or alluded to him in print during the poet's lifetime. Most of these printed allusions, however, are concerned with one or another of Shakespeare's plays or poems; few speak of the poet himself; none furnish details about his private life. This is just what we should expect. People were interested in plays, and to some extent in actors, but not in playwrights.

This characteristically Elizabethan attitude has had the effect of denying to us much knowledge of Shakespeare's personality and his private activities which we might have had if men had written reviews, articles, and books about him. In this kind of biographical obscurity Shakespeare is like all other Elizabethan dramatists and, for that matter, nearly all of his contemporaries, apart from those who achieved great distinction in church or state. Personal letters, diaries, and account books sometimes supply detailed information, but even these are more concerned with business than with personalities. And private papers have been preserved, as a rule, only in the great country houses occupied generation after generation by families of the ruling class, whose private and official affairs had to be recorded and who had ample room for storing old papers. Elizabethan dramatists did not belong to such families, and any private papers they owned or produced have not, with the most trifling exceptions, survived. Those papers that had the best chance of survival were official records of governments, cities, towns, parishes, and corporations. It is mainly from these that our scanty knowledge of the activities and movements of Elizabethan individuals is derived. Parish registers, deeds, tax records, court records, government orders, fiscal documents, wills —all these possessed an obvious value for the future, and provision was made for their preservation. When a private person is married, when he pays his taxes, when he sues his neighbor or is sued by him, when he runs afoul of the law, when he buys or sells real property, when, finally, he dies and is buried—then his name enters the permanent record.

It is so with Shakespeare. What we know about him comes largely from records of the kinds just mentioned. The most important of these are listed below:

1) Stratford-upon-Avon parish register, recording baptisms, marriages, and burials (see Plate 3).

2) The Register of the Bishop of Worcester, containing documents relating to a license for Shakespeare's marriage, 1582.

3) The grant of arms, by the official College of Arms, to John Shakespeare, 1596.

4) A writ of attachment addressed to the sheriff of Surrey, bringing charges against Shakespeare and others, 1596.

5) Documents connected with taxation in London, 1597–1599.

6) Documents connected with the purchase and repair of New Place, 1597–1616.

7) Letters written by or addressed to Richard and Adrian Quiney, mentioning Shakespeare, 1598.

8) A document relating to the holdings of grain by residents of Stratford, including Shakespeare, 1598.

9) Several documents which name Shakespeare as an actor or as a member of the Lord Chamberlain's Men (later the King's Men), the acting company to which Shakespeare belonged.

10) Several documents relating to the joint ownership, by Shakespeare and others, of the Globe and Blackfriars playhouses.

11) Documents concerned with the buying of real property in or near Stratford in 1602.

12) Wills of Thomas Pope and Augustine Phillips (1605), actors and shareholders in the King's Men.

13) Stratford Court of Record documents concerned with the collection by Shakespeare of money owed to him by two fellow townsmen, 1604 and 1608.

14) Documents concerning the lease of Stratford tithes by Shakespeare, 1605.

15) Shakespeare's deposition (Court of Requests) in the suit of Belott *v.* Mountjoy, 1612.

16) Deeds of the purchase by Shakespeare of a house in Blackfriars, London, 1613.

17) Shakespeare's will, 1616.

The first pertinent entry in the parish register tells us that William, son of John Shakespeare, was baptized on April 26, 1564, a Wednesday. We do not know the date of his birth. The Prayer Book of 1559 urges parents not to defer baptism beyond the Sunday or holy day following the baby's birth. If this was intended to suggest that Sundays and holy days should be preferred for baptisms, no preference for any particular day is observable in the Stratford register in the 1560's. All we can assume about the custom there is that baptism would normally follow birth by no more than a few days. The anniversary of Shakespeare's birth has for some two centuries been celebrated on April 23, a date suggested only by unreliable late tradition, perhaps influenced by the odd but irrelevant fact of his death on April 23, fifty-two years later. It is as likely a date as any other.

John Shakespeare, glover or leatherworker, was a burgess of Stratford—one of the substantial tradesmen elected to the town council. About 1558 he had married Mary, daughter of Robert Arden, a landowning farmer of Wilmcote, not far from Stratford. Of this union were born eight children, of whom William was the third child and the first son.

On Shakespeare's boyhood there is no documentary evidence. His plays and poems abound with passages that might be taken as recollections of the Warwickshire countryside, such as this description of a hunted hare:

> Then shalt thou see the dew-bedabbled wretch
> Turn and return, indenting with the way;
> Each envious brier his weary legs doth scratch,
> Each shadow makes him stop, each murmur stay.

Much of this sort of thing may well reflect in some way Shakespeare's stored-up memories of childhood; it would be remarkable if the experiences of his childhood were not reflected in innumerable ways in his mature work. But it is impossible to read this record now, and we cannot reasonably say that any particular passage had its origin in the recollection of the years in Stratford. We are entitled to suppose that the young Shakespeare spent these years in the usual activities of boyhood. Other boys in Stratford outwardly not very different from him went to school, for the town was fortunate enough to have an endowed school (Plates 5 and 6). No register of the boys who attended it survives, and we cannot with certainty name a single one of the pupils. But since the school was there and the headmaster was paid, the easy and natural inference is that William Shakespeare was a pupil in it for some years—the easier because his father would have been at no expense for his tuition, for it was free for the sons of burgesses. The main subject at schools like Stratford's was Latin. By the time they had spent six or seven years there boys would have a pretty fair familiarity with considerable parts of Ovid, Virgil, Cicero, and Horace, and some acquaintance with other classical writers. The study of rhetoric and of religion and morals, mostly conducted in the Latin tongue, was considered indispensable. A smattering of Greek was not uncommon. The supposition that Shakespeare's education was of this kind receives some support from the statement of Ben Jonson, a friend and fellow playwright, that he had "small Latin and less Greek"—an expression that must be judged in the light of Jonson's own extensive knowledge of the ancient languages, and in the light, too, of his well-known arrogance. The knowledge of Latin and of classical literature demonstrated in Shakespeare's plays and poems is not incompatible with the kind of education that an unusually bright boy might be expected to have acquired at the Stratford school.

The Stratford parish register contains no entry of Shakespeare's marriage, and from this we must suppose that it took place elsewhere. Ordinarily banns of matrimony were published in the parish church of the bride on three successive Sundays before a marriage. Marriage without banns or with one publication required a license from the bishop. Apparently Shakespeare, or someone on his behalf, applied to the Bishop of Worcester (in whose diocese Stratford lay) for such a license to marry Anne Hathaway. The record is not now complete: all that survives are an entry in the bishop's register stating that a license had been issued on November 27, 1582, and a bond, also in the bishop's registry and dated November 28, by which two sureties (both Stratford men) undertook that there was no legal impediment to the marriage, that it would not be carried out without the consent of the bride's relatives, and several other points. The bond stipulates one publication of the banns. Much puzzlement has been caused by the fact that in the entry the bride is called "Anna Whately of Temple Grafton" (a village near Stratford), while in the bond she is called "Anne Hathwey of Stratford." Careless confusion of two names by the clerk is the best explanation. William Shakespeare is named as the bridegroom in both documents. Anne—as we know from the inscription on her grave in Stratford—was eight years older than her husband.

The parish register supplies the next two dates. Under May 26, 1583 (six months after the date of the marriage license), is recorded the baptism of "Susanna daughter to William Shakespeare." The baptisms of two more children, twins, are recorded under date of February 2, 1585: "Hamnet & Judeth sonne and daughter to William Shakspere."

This is the last date for which there is any record of Shakespeare's being in Stratford until his return there some years later. We next hear of him as an actor and probably a playwright about 1592, when we can safely assume that he was living in London. Where was he in the interval of seven years or so? Many answers to this question have been proposed, all highly speculative, none supported by substantial evidence. The only possible answer is and must remain until new evidence is found, that we do not know. At some time after about the middle of the year 1584 Shakespeare left his native town and made his way, directly or indirectly, to London. As to the date of his departure we have not even the faintest clue. He may well have been, and indeed probably was, in London for a year or more before 1592, and there is no reason to suppose that he did not continue living in Stratford for some years after 1585.

Late in the year 1592 Robert Greene, a popular writer of plays, romances, and pamphlets, refers to Shakespeare in a pamphlet called *Greene's Groats-worth of Wit*. The passage as a whole is ambiguous, but in it Greene unmistakably quotes part of a line from 3 *Henry VI* and speaks of Shakespeare as an actor. This play is not probably Shakespeare's first, and we must suppose that he did not become both actor and playwright overnight. Which play was his first is not known. Among the earliest were the three parts of *Henry VI, Richard III, The Comedy of Errors*, and *Titus Andronicus*. The last named of these was, in 1594, the first to appear in print—in a small unbound pamphlet, on the title-page of which the author is not named. His name was not, in fact, printed on the title-page of any play until 1598, when *Love's Labor's Lost* was said to be "By W.

Shakespere" and both *Richard II* and *Richard III* "By William Shake-speare." In this same year, 1598, a man named Francis Meres published a book called *Palladis Tamia: Wit's Treasury*, where, in a discussion of recent and living poets, he speaks of Shakespeare as enriching the English tongue with "rare ornaments and resplendent abiliments"; as "mellifluous and honey-tongued Shakespeare"; as "among the English . . . the most excellent in both kinds"—both comedies and tragedies, he means, of which he names six each and thus provides a valuable gauge of the poet's early dramatic activity.

Meres also mentions Shakespeare as the author of *Venus and Adonis* and *The Rape of Lucrece*. By publishing the first of these in 1593 Shakespeare had established a reputation as a nondramatic poet. He dedicated it to Henry Wriothesley, Earl of Southampton, signing the dedication "William Shakespeare." *Lucrece* appeared in the following year, and the fact that it too is dedicated to the same nobleman suggests that the first dedication, as well as the first venture in nondramatic poetry, was well received. Beyond the existence of these two dedications nothing further is known about the relationship between the poet and his noble patron.

As actor and playwright Shakespeare was a member, at different times, of two or three acting companies. Every troupe of players had a patron—a nobleman, an important government official, or at least a man of influence. Bands of men wandering uncontrolled about the country were considered dangerous and were regarded with official suspicion. Since most troupes of actors subsisted by traveling from town to town and producing their plays in innyards and town halls, they fell under this suspicion and therefore required, on the one hand, the influence and protection effected by the license of a powerful patron and, on the other hand, his occasional restraint or discipline. London of course afforded the biggest audiences and the biggest profits, and it is natural that the best companies should have spent as much time there as possible. Before Shakespeare arrived on the scene, several of these companies occupied, and in some cases controlled, newly erected permanent playhouses in London, the first ever built in England.

The years 1592 to 1594 are an obscure time in the history of the London stage. Severe outbreaks of the plague and other unsettling influences resulted in the dissolution of old acting companies and, in due course, the formation of new. Existing records are neither sufficiently complete nor sufficiently clear to throw much light on the dates or the composition of the several companies that operated in and out of London in the early nineties. With how many of these Shakespeare was connected as actor or as writer or both we cannot know. Two almost certainly were the Earl of Pembroke's company and the Earl of Sussex' company—commonly known for short as Pembroke's Men and Sussex' Men. It is possible too that during these years Shakespeare underwent at least one period of dramatic inactivity, which may have provided the opportunity or created the need for nondramatic writing. In 1594 the Lord Chamberlain's company was formed, and there is ample evidence of Shakespeare's connection with it from that year onward until his retirement, perhaps until his death. A record of a dramatic performance at the court of Queen Elizabeth in December 1594 names William Kemp, William Shakespeare, and Richard Burbage, "servants to the Lord Chamberlain." In the earlier companies to which he had been attached it is not unlikely that Shakespeare occupied a lowly position as a hired man, but there is some reason to believe that upon formation of the Chamberlain's Men he was from the first one of the sharers, or, as we should now put it, partners or stockholders. This is suggested by the inclusion of his name, as we have seen, with two of the chief members of the new company in its first recorded appearance at court.

So rapid a rise to prominence and importance in one of the leading theatrical companies must presumably mean that he was recognized by his fellows as possessing talents that would be of value to them. There being no testimony to his having shown any notable superiority as an actor, we can only conclude that Shakespeare's services as a playwright were what the company valued. It is also possible that he was able to buy his share. A late tradition (Nicholas Rowe, 1709) has it that the Earl of Southampton rewarded him with £1,000 for the dedication of the two poems shortly before the formation of the Chamberlain's Men; the amount is utterly incredible (being the equivalent of something roughly like $50,000 today), but rich patrons were expected to give rewards, and a possible £100 would explain his ability to buy into the company. But this is conjecture: all we know is that Shakespeare appears to have been a leading member of the company from 1594 onward. In 1603 his name stands second in a list of nine sharers, a number which gradually increased in succeeding years of prosperity. In 1599 some seven of the sharers, Shakespeare being one, had built the Globe (Plates 8 and 9), the largest and most splendid of London playhouses, and in 1609 they expanded with the acquisition of a second house, a "private" indoor theatre, the Blackfriars. For this company, and only for it, Shakespeare wrote plays from the time of its foundation. Whether in addition he long continued as a regular actor it seems impossible to determine. Little significance can be attached to the fact that his name heads a list of the "Principall Actors in all these Playes" prefixed to the First Folio edition of his plays (1623).

Soon after James I came to the throne in 1603 the king himself took the company under his patronage, after which it was known as the King's Majesty's Servants, now usually the King's Men. The members were made Grooms of the Chamber, an honorary position in the royal household without fee, subsistence, or lodging. Ordinarily no duties were involved, but the Wardrobe accounts show the issue of scarlet cloth for liveries to "The Chamber," with the nine members of the acting company listed, Shakespeare's name first, in order that they might take part in a royal progress through London on March 15, 1604, to honor the Spanish Ambassador.

Shakespeare's position as a shareholder in the Lord Chamberlain's company must be taken to explain the evidences of prosperity which begin to appear about 1596. It was in this year that his father—or he in his father's name—made a successful application to the College of Arms for the grant of a coat of arms. Such a grant constituted a step up in the world, one for which a minimum requisite was the possession of an income appropriate to the rank of gentleman, which rank, in theory at least, the grant conferred. John Shakespeare, who thirty years earlier had been mayor of Stratford and a man of worship and substance, had in recent years been suffering a steady decline in his business and his fortunes, connected, no doubt, with a general decline in the commerce of Stratford. Therefore it has usually been assumed, as in fact it was then by at least one man in a position to know, that the application for arms was actually initiated by the prosperous son. So long as the father was living the customary formalities of heraldry required that any grant of arms be to him rather than to a son.

Of Shakespeare's life in London aside from his plays and the theatre we have a few clear facts. From subsidy rolls we learn that he was assessed in October 1596 as a resident of St. Helen's parish, lying within the city wall in the north. Not far distant— just without the wall, through Bishopsgate—stood The Theatre, the playhouse principally occupied by the Chamberlain's Men during that period (Plate 9). Only a month or so later, on November 29, 1596, he had moved across the river to the Southwark side, where the Chamberlain's Men may now have occupied the new Swan playhouse. This information comes to us from a writ of attachment addressed to the sheriff of Surrey, charging William Shakespeare, Francis Langley, and two women with threatening bodily harm to one William Wayte. The sheriff of Surrey could attach only persons who lived in that county. Langley was the owner of the Swan, which stood on the south bank of the Thames, across the river from London proper and in Surrey. We do not know the precise nature of the quarrel between Wayte and the four persons of whom he demanded bonds requiring them to keep the peace, but the writ of attachment well illustrates the way in which official archives can yield up biographical information. From another document, a deposition made by Shakespeare in a lawsuit of 1612, we learn that he, "William Shakespeare of Stratford upon Aven in the Countye of Warwicke gentleman of the age of xlviii yeres or thereaboutes," was, about 1602 and perhaps until 1604, lodging at the house of one Christopher Mountjoy, a French Huguenot tiremaker (a maker of fancy headdresses), in Cripplegate Ward, on the north side of the city. The fact that he is "of Stratford upon Aven" may be taken to indicate that he then had no London address but was settled in his native town.

It has usually been supposed that when Shakespeare went up to London he left his wife and children behind in Stratford. Though not improbable, this is not demonstrable, for all that we know with any degree of certainty is that Mrs. Shakespeare is never heard of in London, that the twins of 1585 were the last children known to have been born to her, that Hamnet, the only son, was buried in Stratford in 1596, and that the two daughters eventually married Stratford men. Shakespeare's *Sonnets*, probably written during the 1590's, have been thought to suggest a passionate attachment of the poet to a lady now unidentified. But this is guesswork, not fact, and the facts known hardly warrant the assumption of an estrangement between the poet and his wife. Shakespeare may from the beginning of his London career have kept in close touch with Stratford and his family, making frequent journeys thither.

Only after Shakespeare attained prosperity should we expect to find him buying real property and otherwise investing substantial sums, and this could scarcely have been before 1596, some two years after the formation of the Chamberlain's Men with Shakespeare as a sharer. The buying of New Place, one of the principal dwellings of Stratford, in 1597 certainly implies his presence in Stratford. From 1598 we have several letters which provide a glimpse of relations between Shakespeare and his fellow townsmen. Abraham Sturley, writing from Stratford to Richard Quiney (whose son was in a few years to marry Shakespeare's daughter Judith), speaks of property near the town which Shakespeare was considering buying and hopes he will also buy some of the Stratford tithes. In October of the same year Richard Quiney writes to Shakespeare from London, asking him to lend the considerable sum of £30 on security, and during the following month three other men of Stratford write to Quiney about this same money, apparently required for some important project. Shakespeare may have been in London at the time, but he was no stranger to his Stratford neighbors. From this time onward a number of investments and business transactions in and about Stratford suggest frequent visits there. In view of the inherent unlikelihood that all such transactions would be matters of record, it will be safe to assume that there were many more of them than we know of. In 1598 we find him dealing in malt—a common form of investment at that period in Warwickshire. In 1604 and again in 1608 he brought suit in the Stratford Court of Record for the recovery of money debts.

The purchase of New Place and other Stratford property suggests that even before the turn of the century Shakespeare began to think of the days when he might retire from the hurly-burly of city life to quiet domesticity among the rural scenes of his childhood. Not for some years yet was he to take such a step. Indeed in the first decade of the new century he was to reach his greatest dramatic activity and write his greatest plays. *Twelfth Night, Hamlet, Othello, King Lear, Macbeth,* and several others all belong to this period. This is the decade, too, in which the King's Men, now established in the new Globe, attained the first place among London acting companies. Prosperity came to Shakespeare about 1596; before his retirement he may have enjoyed some degree of wealth.

It was about 1610 or 1611 that he retired. Various reasons have been proposed by biographers: poor health, a yearning for a quiet life, a desire to be with his family, an inability to accommodate himself to the changing tastes of the playgoing public, who were beginning to demand novelty and psychological curiosity, to prefer tragicomedy to tragedy and comedy of manners to romantic comedy. We cannot know what motivated Shakespeare's decision—probably one of the considerations just mentioned, or a combination of them. There is reason for thinking, since they are not mentioned in his will, that he disposed of his shares in the King's Men and in their playhouses when he retired or soon after. His retirement from full participation in the company's affairs was not a clean break with London and the stage. He was pretty certainly in London on March 10, 1613, when he signed an indenture by which he bought a dwelling house there—formerly the gatehouse of what had been the Blackfriars Monastery. The price, £140, shows it to have been a rather substantial property. In June of the same year Shakespeare's company produced his last play, *Henry VIII* (thought by some authorities to have been written with a collaborator). What moved him to take up his pen again after a break of something like two years since he had written *The Tempest*, we do not know. An unhappy accident provided an ironic period to Shakespeare's stage career: during what may have been the first performance of *Henry VIII*, the shooting of a small cannon set the Globe playhouse on fire, and it burned to the ground.

On March 25, 1616, Shakespeare executed his will, the original of which, bearing his three signatures on its three sheets, has fortunately survived (Plate 10). The bulk of his estate, including New Place, the Blackfriars gatehouse, and other real property in and about Stratford, he left to his elder daughter Susanna. For his other daughter, Judith, who had married Thomas Quiney less than two months before the date of the will, he made provision by a substantial bequest of money. In addition he left several small bequests to other relatives and to a number of neighbors and friends—among the latter his "fellows" of the King's Men, John Heminges, Richard Burbage, and Henry Condell. These last bequests are of interest as demonstrating Shakespeare's close and lasting friendship with his professional associates, and especially the bequests to Heminges and Condell, because it was they who were, in 1623, to be in some way responsible for the editing and publishing of Shakespeare's collected plays in the volume now commonly known as the First Folio (see Plate 14). This they did, they say, "only to keep the memory of so worthy a friend and fellow alive as was our Shakespeare." The will mentions Shakespeare's wife only in a single bequest inserted between the lines as if it were an afterthought, leaving to her his "second best bed." No significance is to be attached to this. With or without a will, she was by common law protected in her rights of dower to a life interest in any portions of the estate not specifically exempted, and these would have given her a comfortable income and the right to occupy New Place during her life. Both the substance and the form of the bequest may be plausibly accounted for by supposing that Mrs. Shakespeare asked for the bed.

Just under a month later, on April 23, 1616, Shakespeare died, probably within a day or two of the birthday on which he would have been fifty-two years old. The shortness of the interval between Shakespeare's will and his death has naturally led to the assumption that illness and the expectation of an early death led to the making of the will. Some persons have claimed to see further evidence of illness in the signatures. While such illness cannot be regarded as altogether improbable, there is in fact no evidence of it. There is nothing odd about the signatures; they were originally quite firm and are now as clear and legible as the state of the paper permits. The timing of the will is sufficiently accounted for by Shakespeare's desire to make suitable provision for his daughter Judith in view of her recent (and belated) marriage. We can safely assume that it was for this reason that a new will was substituted for one made much earlier. The only seventeenth-century account of Shakespeare's death suggests that it was sudden. John Ward, vicar of Stratford from 1662 to 1681, wrote in a notebook, "Shakespear, Drayton, and Ben Jhonson had a merry meeting, and itt seems drank too hard, for Shakespear died of a feavour there contracted." This John Ward kept notes on many subjects, chiefly medical and theological, in calf-bound notebooks, of which sixteen have survived (and are now in the Folger Library). He had studied medicine and appears to have been a cautious and intelligent man much interested in Stratford antiquities. Though his report is hearsay, still it is hearsay well founded: Ward was in a position to know the truth, for the facts would have been widely talked about at the time of the poet's death, and many persons who might have attended the funeral must still have been alive in Stratford when Ward made his entry in a volume dated 1661–1663. Nevertheless, we can accept the story only with reservations, as a plausible account which conflicts with no other evidence.

Shakespeare's remains were interred under the floor of the chancel of Holy Trinity Church, the parish church of Stratford, just inside the altar rail. The well-known epitaph carved in a floor stone (Plate 12) has been attributed to Shakespeare himself, and, rude doggerel though it be, there is no serious bar to our accepting this attribution. The obvious purpose of the epitaph is to frighten off anyone planning to disturb the grave, and it is not difficult to conceive that Shakespeare, who always knew how to suit poetic style to his auditory and his purpose, would here pitch his verse to the level of gravediggers and the like. In any case, the epitaph has been successful, for the grave has never been opened or disturbed. At some time between 1616 and 1622 a monument was erected on the north wall of the chancel, not far from the gravestone (Plate 13). Executed by Garratt Janssen, a Flemish tomb maker of Southwark and one of the best of his trade, the monument is of superior workmanship and is characteristic of the artist and of the time. In spite of its obviously conventional and stylized portraiture, M. H. Spielmann, the leading authority on the subject, thinks it probable that it was based on a life mask. However this may be, the "Stratford bust" must be regarded as an informed attempt to represent the poet's appearance with some fidelity. The 1623 First Folio edition of the plays contains a copperplate portrait, probably made from a drawing or miniature and probably showing Shakespeare at an early age (Plate 14). It is crudely designed and has generally been regarded with disapproval, but it is quite evidently a portrait of the same man represented in the Stratford monument. Except for these two, executed soon after Shakespeare's death, no other portrait can be shown to have originated before about 1675 or to possess the slightest authority as a faithful delineation of Shakespeare's face.

He was survived by his two daughters and one granddaughter. Susanna had married Dr. John Hall, a Stratford physician, and they had a daughter Elizabeth, born in 1608. Judith was but newly married to Thomas Quiney. In his will, as we have seen, Shakespeare left all of his real property, the bulk of his estate, to his elder daughter, putting into the will an entail apparently designed to ensure the descent of this considerable estate in the male line of the Hall family. If he saw himself as the progenitor of a long line of substantial propertied descendants, his dream was destined to be thwarted. Elizabeth was the Halls' only child, and she, though twice married, died childless in 1670. The Quineys made a better start with three sons, but they died young and unmarried, the last in 1639. But if Shakespeare was denied a line of descendants, he left, in his plays, a progeny which will keep his memory fresh while civilization lasts.

SUGGESTED READING

Sir Edmund K. Chambers, *William Shakespeare: A Study of Facts and Problems* (2 vols., Oxford, 1930) is the most complete and reliable biography, containing transcripts of all the important documents but because of its closely compressed style is not easy reading.

Joseph Quincy Adams, *A Life of William Shakespeare* (Boston and New York, 1923), though now somewhat out-of-date, is both readable and accurate and is reliable except where more recent scholarship has superseded it.

Hazelton Spencer, *The Art and Life of William Shakespeare* (New York, [1940]) is an excellent life with emphasis on the plays, reliable when dealing with fact, weak in criticism and interpretation; it contains valuable information on stage history, Spencer's specialty.

Marchette Chute, *Shakespeare of London* (New York, 1949) is a biography both easy and pleasant to read, the best of its kind, in which accuracy is not sacrificed to the desire to produce a popular work.

F. E. Halliday, *Shakespeare: A Pictorial Biography* (London, [1956]) contains scores of excellent and well-chosen pictures of Stratford, London, the playhouses, the early books, the manuscripts and records, with brief text.

F. E. Halliday, *A Shakespeare Companion, 1550–1950* (London, [1952]) is a useful dictionary of concise information on Shakespeare's life, his environment, his plays, and the publication, criticism, and production of his plays.

Shakespeare's England: An Account of the Life and Manners of His Age (2 vols., Oxford, 1917) consists of chapters (each by a different authority) on the court, education, agriculture, law, the sciences, the fine arts, sports and pastimes, and other subjects; though now somewhat out-of-date, it is an extremely valuable storehouse of information.

Sir Edmund K. Chambers, *The Elizabethan Stage* (4 vols., Oxford, 1923) presents an exhaustive study of the playhouses and acting companies, 1550–1616, with valuable appendixes listing plays, dramatists, etc.; it is superseded at some points by more recent scholarship and is not easy reading.

Virgil K. Whitaker, *Shakespeare's Use of Learning* (San Marino, Calif., 1953) consists of a thorough examination of Shakespeare's sources and the reading which influenced him; Chapters 1 and 2 contain valuable discussion of his education.

Marion H. Spielmann, *The Title-page of the First Folio of Shakespeare's Plays: A Comparative Study of the Droeshout Portrait and the Stratford Monument* (London, 1924) presents the most authoritative discussion of the early portraiture of the poet.

William Jaggard, *Shakespeare Bibliography* (Stratford, 1911) achieves a remarkable degree of success in an attempt to list every edition (in English) of Shakespeare's writings and every work about him or related to him up to 1910.

Walther Ebisch and Levin L. Schücking, *A Shakespeare Bibliography* (2 vols., Oxford, 1931) lists important works on Shakespeare, arranged under subject headings.

Plate 1. Shakespeare's Birthplace. According to well-founded tradition, Shakespeare was born in this room. Like other upstairs rooms in the house, it is now fitted up with furniture of the sort likely to have been found in the house of a prosperous tradesman such as John Shakespeare in the late sixteenth century.

43

Plate 2. Shakespeare's Birthplace. In this half-timbered house, built in the early sixteenth century, Shakespeare was born and spent his earliest years. It was then two separate structures, John Shakespeare's dwelling and his shop. Since 1857, when it was restored, it has been a shrine visited by many thousands of tourists every year.

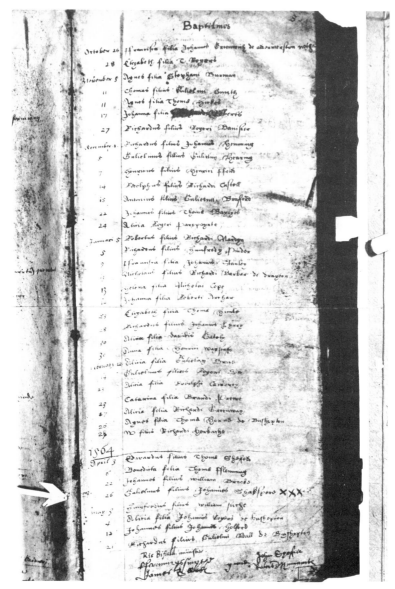

Plate 3. The Parish Register. Under date of April 26, 1564, is the entry of Shakespeare's baptism: "Gulielmus filius Johannes Shakspere." On other pages are entries of his burial and of the baptisms, marriages, or burials of his parents, his brothers and sisters, his wife, his children, his grandchildren. The Register may still be seen in the parish church.

Plate 4. Holy Trinity Church, Stratford. When William Shakespeare was carried to the baptismal font here on April 26, 1564, the church looked essentially as it now does, in its beautiful setting close beside the Avon. The central tower was built about 1200, the rest mainly a century and a half later.

Plate 5. The Grammar School. The upper room of the building on the left was used as the grammar school after the middle of the sixteenth century. Built about 1418, the building was originally the guildhall, and in Shakespeare's time the town council met in a room on the ground floor.

Plate 6. The Grammar School. This room has been in use as a schoolroom for some four hundred years. Here Shakespeare very probably learned his Latin.

Plate 7. Clopton Bridge. In Roman times an important road, or "street," forded the Avon at Stratford, which got its name from that fact. Much later a wooden bridge was built here, and about 1500 Sir Hugh Clopton (the builder also of Shakespeare's house, New Place) built the present many-arched bridge of stone.

Plate 8. The Globe Playhouse. This model was made by Dr. John Cranford Adams after exhaustive study of all the evidence. The nature of the evidence does not permit authoritative reconstruction of small details. Still, this model reliably represents the important features of the stage on which many of Shakespeare's plays were performed.

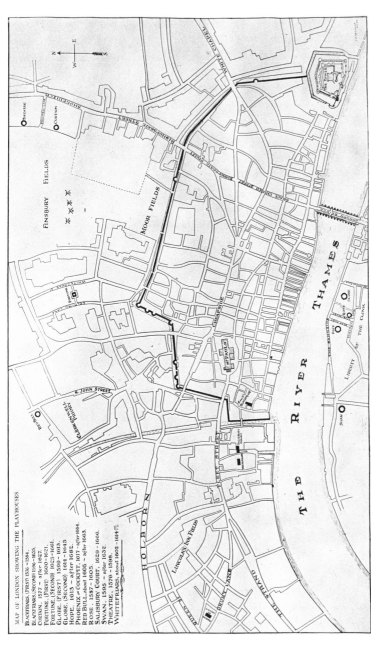

MAP OF LONDON SHOWING THE PLAYHOUSES

BLACKFRIARS, (FIRST) 1576 – 1584.
BLACKFRIARS, (SECOND) 1596 – 1655.
CURTAIN, 1577 – after 1627.
FORTUNE, (FIRST) 1600 – 1621.
FORTUNE, (SECOND) 1623 – 1661.
GLOBE, (FIRST) 1599 – 1613.
GLOBE, (SECOND) 1614 – 1645.
HOPE, 1613 – after 1682.
PHOENIX or COCKPIT, 1617 – after 1664.
RED BULL, about 1605 – after 1663.
ROSE, 1587 – 1605.
SALISBURY COURT, 1629 – 1666.
SWAN, 1595 – after 1632.
THEATRE, 1576 – 1598.
WHITEFRIARS, about 1605 – 1614 (?).

Plate 9. London. This rough map shows the positions of the playhouses—the Theatre (the first playhouse) north of the city on Bishopsgate Road, the Globe south across the Thames on the Bankside, and the others. The heavy black line represents the old city wall, the limit of municipal authority.

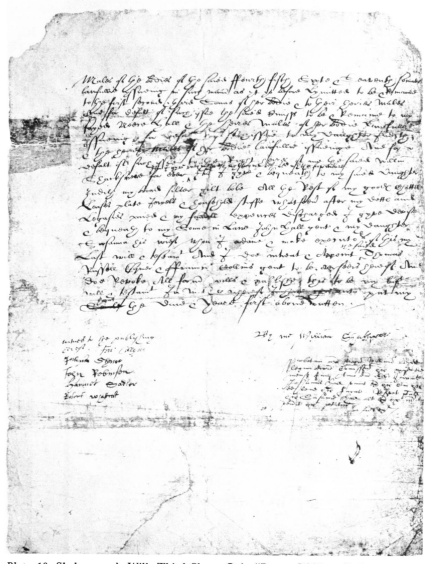

Plate 10. Shakespeare's Will, Third Sheet. Only "By me William Shakespeare" is in his own autograph. Sheets 1 and 2 are also signed, and these and three signatures on other documents are the only remaining specimens of Shakespeare's handwriting of which we can be perfectly sure. The will is in Somerset House, London.

Plate 11. Holy Trinity Church, the Chancel. Shakespeare's remains lie buried under the floor of the sanctuary, inside the altar rail. Above, on the wall and in the window, just right of the door, is the memorial bust. This part of the church is perpendicular gothic of the late fifteenth century.

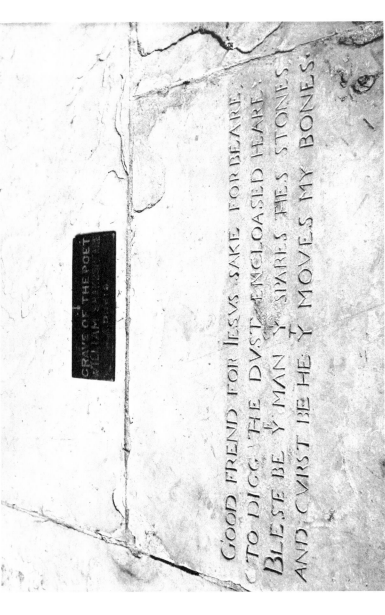

GOOD FREND FOR IESVS SAKE FORBEARE,
TO DIGG THE DVST ENCLOASED HEARE:
BLESTE BE Y MAN Y SPARES THES STONES,
AND CVRST BE HE Y MOVES MY BONES.

GRAVE OF THE POET
WILLIAM SHAKESPEARE
Died 1616

Plate 12. Shakespeare's Epitaph. This floor slab marks the grave in the chancel of Holy Trinity Church. Tradition has it that Shakespeare composed the crude epitaph, and this, if not probable, is at least possible.

54

Plate 13. The Memorial Bust, Holy Trinity Church. This monument, of painted limestone, almost certainly executed by Garratt Janssen, a London tomb maker, was erected before 1623. It is of stylized design conventional in that period and of good quality. The trouble and expense thus willingly incurred by a survivor are some guarantee that pains would have been taken to obtain a reasonable likeness of the poet.

MR. WILLIAM
SHAKESPEARES
COMEDIES,
HISTORIES, &
TRAGEDIES.

Publifhed according to the True Originall Copies.

LONDON
Printed by Ifaac Iaggard, and Ed. Blount. 1623.

Plate 14. The First Folio Title-Page. The first edition of Shakespeare's collected plays was prepared with the assistance of two of his friends and fellow actors. The engraved portrait, if somewhat crude, is clearly a representation of the same man shown in the memorial bust at Stratford and must have been approved by his friends.

The Authorship of Shakespeare

By James G. McManaway

"Hamlet. Why look you there. . . . My father in his habit as he lived."

EVERY writer who wishes to write about the man William Shakespeare longs, but longs in vain, to see him "in his habit as he lived," to tell his story with the wealth of intimate detail that is expected in the biographies of famous men. Nowadays literary men and people of the theatre are idolized. Their voices are on the radio, their faces on television and in the movies. Their goings and comings are reported as news, and the public knows, or thinks it knows, their tastes in breakfast food, beverages, cigarettes, and women (or men, as the case may be). They are public characters, lionized and, on occasion, mobbed by ecstatic admirers.

To imagine a society in which there were no actresses, in which actors were scarcely respectable, and in which literary men were for the most part either wealthy amateurs or impoverished professionals—to imagine, in a word, the kind of society in which Shakespeare lived—is difficult indeed.

For a playwright of his time, Shakespeare's life is well documented. He was christened on April 26, 1564, in Holy Trinity Church, Stratford-upon-Avon, the eldest son to John and Mary (Arden) Shakespeare; he died on April 23, 1616, and was interred in the chancel of Holy Trinity Church. We know his wife's name and origin, the dates of christening and burial of their three children, as well as many facts of their later lives. The elder daughter married the well-known Dr. John Hall and in 1643 was hostess to the Queen of England, who spent two nights and parts of three days at New Place, which Susanna

Hall had inherited from her father. Susanna's daughter, Elizabeth, took for her second husband John Bernard, who was knighted by Charles II in 1661.

From the time that he began to enjoy prosperity—about 1596 —William Shakespeare's financial dealings are recorded in some detail. He bought and restored New Place, the imposing house built about 1483 by Sir Hugh Clopton, mayor of Stratford. With his son's support, John Shakespeare secured the grant of arms for which application had been made earlier; thenceforth, each was *generosus*, a propertied gentleman. There were purchases of real estate in and about Stratford and, in 1613, in London. The London property was the Blackfriars Gatehouse, a logical purchase for a man whose company of actors had been performing in an adjacent Blackfriars building since 1609.

William Shakespeare, gent., of Stratford-upon-Avon, gave a deposition in a suit brought in 1612 by Stephen Belott to gain possession of the dowry promised Belott's wife, Mary Mountjoy, at the time of their marriage about 1603, when Shakespeare was lodging with the Mountjoys. His signature identifies him with the purchaser of the Blackfriars Gatehouse (two related documents bear his signature) and with the man who in the spring of 1616 signed the three pages of his will, bequeathing, among other things, twenty-six shillings and eight pence to his "fellows" Richard Burbage, John Heminges, and Henry Condell, to buy memorial rings. These men had been his fellow actors and friends since about 1594, and in 1623 Heminges and Condell brought out the First Folio edition of his plays "without ambition either of self-profit, or fame; only to keep the memory of so worthy a friend, and fellow alive, as was our Shakespeare."

Men of Shakespeare's age had a very different set of values from our own. Plays written for the public stage were not considered to be literature. *Nos haec novimus esse nihil:* "We know these things to be nothing," appears on the title page of one play quarto. The Latin motto expresses the opinion of many of the playwrights, who turned out scripts to be used by actors in the entertainment of a not always discriminating public.

The actors themselves led a precarious existence. A few gifted players who had business ability and prudence managed to become sharers in the ownership or operation of a playhouse and thus to acquire property and recognition as substantial citizens. Edward Alleyn, the great tragic actor of the Lord Admiral's Men, became wealthy enough to found Dulwich College. Heminges and Condell were churchwardens of St. Mary Aldermanbury in London. There is probably envy of their economic success mixed with scorn of their aspirations to gentility in the words that, about 1600, Ben Jonson puts into the mouth of one of his characters: "They [the actors] forget they are i' the statute, the rascals, they are blazoned there, there they are tricked, they and their pedigrees; they need no other heralds, I wis" (Tucca in *Poetaster* [I.ii.53 ff.]). The statute is that of 39 Elizabeth (1597–1598), ch. 4, where it is required that

[2]   All fencers, bearwards, common players of interludes and minstrels wandering abroad (other than players of interludes belonging to any baron of this realm, or any other honorable personage of greater degree, to be authorized to play, under the hand and seal of arms of such baron or personage) . . . shall be taken, adjudged, and deemed rogues, vagabonds and sturdy beggars, and shall sustain such pain and punishment as by this Act is in that behalf appointed.

The initial punishment was that the culprit be

[3]   stripped naked from the middle upwards and shall be openly whipped until his or her body be bloody [Sir Edmund Chambers, *The Elizabethan Stage* (Oxford, 1923), IV, 324].

Prosperity among actors was the exception. From the earliest times, minstrels, jugglers, and such entertainers of the public had been very low in the social scale, and it was with difficulty that they managed to rise in public esteem. A forceful character like Edward Alleyn or Richard Burbage might be sought after by certain of the young gentlemen of the Inns of Court and celebrated in verse at his death. But their Bohemian way of life, the uncertainty of regular employment that was not lessened by frequent recurrences of the plague, which closed all places of entertainment, and the discomforts of taking to the road kept most actors outside the pale of respectability. This state of affairs continued until David Garrick proved later, in the eighteenth century, that an actor could live on terms of intimate friendship with the nobility. In the reigns of Elizabeth and James no one thought actors worthy of biographical notice.

Poets fared little better. Edmund Spenser, recognized by his contemporaries as the greatest nondramatic poet since Chaucer, writes that London was his "most kindly nurse," but the year of his birth is unknown, and although he claimed kinship with the great Spencer family of Althorpe, no one has discovered the nature of the relationship. His father's baptismal name is unknown; his mother's name is known only because the poet's praise of his second (or perhaps third) wife, Elizabeth Boyle, mentions the fact that Queen, mother, and wife shared the one name. There is no absolute certainty about the identity of Spenser's first wife. His early love, "Rosalind," is a mystery. There is only conjecture about what dashed his hopes of quasi-diplomatic service on the Continent. In Ireland, to which he seems to have been rusticated, he acquired property and became Clerk of the Council of Munster; but in 1581 he is also, mysteriously, prebendary of Effin. As clerk to Lord Grey, and in other official capacities, Spenser wrote many letters and documents, at least fifty-nine of which have been identified. They are written in three distinct hands: two for English (secretary and italic) and one for Latin. No personal letter to or from him has come to light and not one line of poetry in his handwriting.

John Milton, who was born in 1608 a few years before Shakespeare's death and who lived till 1674, was famous as a poet and political writer. He was the first great English poet to have his biography written by his contemporaries, but the first life of Milton to appear independently was composed by one of his adopted nephews (Edward Phillips) not because Milton was a poet but because he had written a violent political book while serving as Latin secretary during the Commonwealth period. Yet with all the autobiographical publicity that accompanied Milton's bitter pamphlet war with foreign critics of England, the cause of his rustication from Cambridge is unknown, and the facts of his unhappy first marriage are still a mystery. It was to be expected that Milton would lose his life, along with the regicides, when Charles II came to the throne in 1660; but while his friends spirited the blind poet away from London, Andrew Marvell interceded for him in Parliament, and the Royalist Sir William Davenant (whom Milton is reported to have saved from execution about 1651) obtained his release. "The details," writes a recent biographer, "remain obscure."

It is instructive to note that in William Winstanley's *England's Worthies* (1660) the two Elizabethan poets Sir Philip Sidney and John Donne are included because the first was the flower of chivalry (there is a brief reference to the *Arcadia* and to the *Astrophel and Stella*) and the second was dean of St. Paul's (there is one reference to a religious poem).

That blazing star, Sir Walter Raleigh, illustrates well the indifference of his age to biography and to literary manuscripts. A well-known editor of his poems writes of him:

Raleigh was born about 1552, at Hayes Barton in Devonshire. . . . Some time in his teens he went up to Oriel College, Oxford, where it is not recorded that he took a degree. . . . Of the next ten years, the formative years of his life, we know very little beyond the fact that he fought in the French Wars of Religion and in the Irish campaigns of Lord Grey. . . . There is more than one story that professes to account for his sudden rise to favour, but they are fairy-tale chances and lean on the logic of day-dreams [Agnes M. C. Latham, ed., *The Poems of Sir Walter Raleigh* (London, 1951), p. xv].

The date of his birth is uncertain; the name of the school he attended is unknown. There is a decade of which research has discovered almost nothing. This is the man who for ten years was a reigning favorite at Court, a great sea captain, the adventurer who sank £40,000 of his private fortune in attempts to colonize Virginia, the man who is credited with introducing tobacco into England and the potato into Ireland. He was envied and hated by the greatest in England. His *History of the World,* written while he was a prisoner in the Tower, went through ten editions between 1611 and 1700. Some autograph letters survive, but not one manuscript page of *The History of the World.* Of his poetical works, a fragment of *Cynthia,* 522 lines, in his handwriting, is among the Cecil Papers at Hatfield House; and the late W. A. White is reported to have had a two-page autograph manuscript of "The Lie." No one troubled to preserve the original manuscripts of anything else that he is known to have written.

The author of the Jacobean tragedies that rank nearest to Shakespeare's was John Webster. Here is a biographical note about him published in 1941:

Of the Elizabethan dramatists there is not one concerning whose life we know less than John Webster's. Hitherto antiquarian research has failed to bring to light any biographic data of any consequence. We do not know when or where he was born or died, who his parents were, what sort of education he received, whether he really was a tailor by trade, whether he was married, how he earned his living, and so forth [S. A. Tannenbaum, *John Webster (A Concise Bibliography)* (New York, 1941), p. vii].

The other playwrights of the time are little better known to us, with the exception of Christopher Marlowe and Ben Jonson, and there are special reasons why so much is recorded about them. The parish registers and school records of Canterbury, where Marlowe, the son of a shoemaker, was born, have been preserved. He won a scholarship and matriculated at Corpus Christi College, Cambridge, from which he received the degree of Master of Arts in mysterious circumstances. Something of his later life is recorded because of a killing in

which he became involved, because of his outspoken, unortho-
dox opinions about religion, but most of all because of his violent death. About Jonson, whose stepfather was a bricklayer,
considerably more is known, but even of this pugnacious man's
biography many details are in question. He was born in 1572,
possibly on June 11. His father was probably a clergyman,
but his baptismal name is unknown; neither the baptismal
name nor the surname of the mother is recorded. In 1589
Jonson was withdrawn from Westminster School, to which he
had been sent by "a friend," and "put to another craft." And
in July, 1597, "he makes his sudden appearance in Henslowe's
employ." In the "lost years" he had service (dates unknown)
in the wars in the Low Countries, where he won a duel and
stripped his dead foe. Of his long-suffering wife, the one recorded fact is that she and her husband were subject to "correction" in 1606 for habitually absenting themselves from service and communion in the parish church. The couple had at
least two children, Mary, who lived only six months, and Ben,
who died in 1603 at the age of seven. Jonson fought another
duel, with a fellow actor, and escaped execution only by plead-
ing benefit of clergy. (In medieval times the clergy were permitted to plead exemption from sentence for having committed certain felonies; later, this privilege—not abolished
until 1827—was extended to any first offender who could read.
The test passage, often called the neck verse, was usually a
Latin version of Psalm 51 printed in black letter.) Most of
the known details of his later life have been preserved because of his irregularity in religion, his association with the
nobility while writing court masques, and his aggressiveness
in every relationship. His part in writing a play, *The Isle of
Dogs,* landed him in prison in 1597, and he was in prison again
in 1604 for his part in *Eastward Ho.* Jonson was at the center
of the War of the Theatres in 1599–1602; he quarreled with
Inigo Jones about court masques; and he was contemptuous
in criticism of contemporary writers and dictatorial in stating
his own literary theories. In short, Marlowe and Jonson had

color; they made news. Their lives were filled with actions that brought them in conflict with authority and thus into the kinds of official records that have been preserved.

The other playwrights of the time led less violent lives and, consequently, are shadowy figures. Of John Lyly, Thomas Lodge, George Peele, Thomas Dekker, Robert Greene, Samuel Daniel, George Chapman, and Thomas Heywood, for example, the year of birth can only be guessed. No autograph of Robert Greene has been discovered. Of the others named, there are a few signatures, an autograph letter or two, but no literary autographs except a scrap from Marlowe, a fragment of a poem of Daniel's, an autograph poem by Peele, and lines in *Sir Thomas More* in Dekker's hand. These men are better known to us than Webster, less known than Marlowe and Jonson.

Shakespeare lived quietly, unobtrusively, for the most part—there are many contemporary references to "gentle" Shakespeare. He fought no duels, had no religious difficulties, served no time in jail for debt or violence, avoided dogmatism in literary matters, wrote no court masques. He did not make news or get into official records in the same way that Marlowe and Jonson did.

The first English playwright to have a formal biography written to be published with his *Works* was William Shakespeare. For his edition of the plays in 1709, the first modern edition of an English playwright, Nicholas Rowe collected what data he could in London and then sent the famous Shakespearean actor Thomas Betterton (1635?–1710) to Stratford to look at records there, such as the parish registers, and to collect local traditions of Shakespeare. Betterton began acting *Hamlet* in 1660 and continued to play the title role and other Shakespearean roles until 1709. His career began while William Beeston and the younger William Cartwright were still active in the theatres. Pepys saw Cartwright play Falstaff in 1667. Both Beeston and Cartwright had been actors before the Puritans closed the playhouses in 1642. The elder William Cartwright was an actor with the Lord Admiral's Men, chief rivals to

Shakespeare's company; and Beeston's father Christopher was a fellow member of Shakespeare's company in 1598. They knew Shakespeare, and their sons knew of him. About 1681 William Beeston told John Aubrey, among other things, that Shakespeare had been a schoolmaster. He was also Aubrey's authority for the statement that Shakespeare was "the more to be admired *quia* [because] he was not a company keeper; lived in Shoreditch; wouldn't be debauched. And if invited to, wrote [that] he was in pain." In other words, Shakespeare did not care for drunken riots and, if invited, pleaded a headache. He could put into Falstaff's mouth the praise of sherry sack, but his own opinion seems to have been more like that of Cassio: "O God, that men should put an enemy in their mouths to steal away their brains! That we should, with joy, pleasance, revel, and applause, transform ourselves into beasts!"

Another man from whom Betterton learned about Shakespeare was Sir William Davenant (1606–1668), who was writing plays in 1634 and managed the Duke's Company after 1660. He it was who instructed Betterton in how Shakespeare had taught Burbage to play Prince Hamlet. Davenant was godson to Shakespeare and, in his cups, suggested that the relationship might be closer. His elder brother, Robert, who became an eminent divine, said in Aubrey's hearing that when he was a small boy (he was born in 1603) Shakespeare "gave him a hundred kisses." For a hundred years after Shakespeare's death there was an unbroken tradition among playwrights and theatre people, who knew him "indirectly, and directly too." These were the people in the best position to know the facts, and they accepted without question the fact that Shakespeare the actor was the poet and playwright.

Against this background of Shakespeare's biography and reputation it is desirable now to place some of the particular details of his life, beginning with his education and following with some of the recorded facts of his life in London and of his literary career.

The law of the universe seems to be that everything changes.

Men establish new forms of government—republics instead of absolute monarchies; scientists prove that the earth moves around the sun and then relate our galaxy to the countless other galaxies in space; biologists and psychologists discover some of the marvels of the human body and mind; and the new learning displaces the old. Systems of education are revolutionized. Latin, the universal language, once the most important subject for study from primary school to the university, is now read with pleasure by very few people, and spoken by still fewer. Literary classics written in former times seem difficult and a little strange. The plays of Shakespeare have suffered this fate. The ideas about physiology and psychology current in his day seem quaint. Stories that he borrowed from Ovid, his references to characters in classical myth, give his lines now an appearance of erudition. How amazed he would be to hear a modern ten-year-old prattle about jet propulsion and trips to the moon! Other times, other customs; the commonplaces of one age are marvels to another.

What appears to modern readers as great learning in Shakespeare was more justly appraised by his contemporaries and by those in succeeding generations who attended similar grammar schools and had, besides, the advantages of university education. In *The Progress to Parnassus,* a play written by Cambridge students about 1601, the character called "Kempe" (after Will Kempe, the comic actor in Shakespeare's company) says to "Burbage": "Few of the university men pen plays well, they smell too much of that writer Ovid, and that writer Metamorphoses, and talk too much of Proserpina and Jupiter. Why here's our fellow Shakespeare puts them all down, I [aye] and Ben Jonson too." Ben Jonson told the Scotch poet William Drummond that "Shakespeare wanted art." Francis Beaumont's poetical letter from the country to Jonson is more explicit:

> Here I would let slip
> (If I had any in me) scholarship,
> And from all learning keep these lines as clear

As Shakespeare's best are, which our heirs shall hear
Preachers apt to their auditors to show
How far sometimes a mortal man may go
By the dim light of Nature.

Thomas Fuller, in his *Worthies, Warwickshire* (1662), compares Shakespeare to Plautus, "who was an exact comedian, yet never any scholar," and adds boldly: "Indeed his [Shakespeare's] learning was very little." A paragraph in Nicholas Rowe's "Life" that prefaced his edition of Shakespeare in 1709 puts the matter admirably. Rowe was poet laureate, a writer of successful plays, a friend of Addison and Pope, and a beneficiary of the Prince of Wales's generosity. Among the bits of information he gleaned about Shakespeare, probably through Betterton's inquiries at Stratford, is a direct statement about Shakespeare's schooling.

His father, who was a considerable dealer in wool, had so large a family, ten children in all, that tho' he was his eldest son he could give him no better education than his own employment. He had bred him, 'tis true, for some time at a free school, where 'tis probable he acquired that little Latin he was master of; but the narrowness of his circumstances, and the want of his assistance at home, forc'd his father to withdraw him from thence, and unhappily prevented his further proficiency in that language. It is without controversy that he had no knowledge of the writings of the ancient poets, not only from this reason, but from his works themselves, where we find no traces of anything that looks like an imitation of 'em; the delicacy of his taste and the natural bent of his own great genius, equal, if not superior to some of the best of theirs, would certainly have led him to read and study 'em with so much pleasure that some of their fine images would naturally have insinuated themselves into and been mix'd with his own writings; so that his not copying at least something from them may be an argument of his never having read 'em. Whether his ignorance of the ancients were a disadvantage to him or no may admit of a dispute; for tho' the knowledge of 'em might have made him more correct, yet it is not improbable but that the regularity and deference for them which would have attended that correctness might have restrain'd some of that fire, impetuosity, and even beautiful extravagance which we admire in Shakespeare: and I believe we are better pleas'd with those thoughts, altogether new and uncommon, which his own imagination supplied him so abundantly with, than if he had given us the most beautiful passages out of the Greek and Latin poets, and that in the most agreeable manner that it was possible for a master of the English language to deliver 'em. Some Latin without question he did know, and one may see up and down in his plays how far his reading that way went. In *Love's Labor's Lost,* the pedant comes out with a verse of Mantuan, and in *Titus Andronicus,* one of the Gothic princes, upon reading

> *Integer vitae scelerisque purus*
> *Non eget Mauri jaculis nec arcu—*

says, "Tis a verse in Horace," but he remembers it out of his grammar, which, I suppose, was the author's case.

What is known of Shakespeare's education comes, then, largely from the poems and plays themselves. The Stratford of his boyhood was blessed with a good grammar school refounded under the charter of 1553 from Edward VI. Its master was paid £20 a year and provided with a house. This equaled the salary of the master of Eton and enabled the borough to employ first-class men. Thomas Jenkins, for example, who was master from 1575 to 1579, the years when young William should have been in the upper school, was fellow or scholar of St. John's College, Oxford, B.A. April 6, 1566, M.A. April 8, 1570. A high-school principal of equivalent education today would be a Ph.D. of Harvard.

The registers of the school are not extant, but it is incredible that William Shakespeare was not one of the pupils. His father was an energetic and ambitious man. A relative newcomer to Stratford, he was chosen a member of the borough council in 1557. Five years later he served two years as one of the two chamberlains, and upon the expiration of his term he was charged with preparing the borough accounts during the two-year term of the men who followed him in office. In 1568 he was elected to the highest municipal office, that of high bailiff. His application for a grant of arms in 1576 shows his aspirations. Such a man would never deny his first-born son the privilege of schooling to which his father's position entitled him.

Passages in several of the plays show intimate knowledge of the books that were used in the lower and upper schools of England. The hornbook, from which the children learned their letters, is twice referred to (*Love's Labor's Lost* [V.i.48]; *Richard III* [I.i.54–57]). Next came the *ABC with the Catechism*, alluded to in *King John*, "And then comes answer like an Absey book" (I.i.196), and *The Two Gentlemen of Verona* (II.i.22). There are frequent quotations from the Psalms, regularly in the version found in the Book of Common Prayer, which in some schools replaced the usual primer. From each of these, boys learned selections from the services of the church, certain prayers, and passages from the Scriptures. These books were the chief texts of the petty school; when committed to memory, as they had to be, they stored the pupils' minds with the best English prose, the great poetry of the Psalms, and the fundamentals of Anglican religion.

At the age of about six William should have entered grammar school, where he would have been expected to learn to read and write Latin easily and to speak it. The important text was Lily's *A Short Introduction of Grammar*, printed largely in Latin. It is named in one of the earliest plays, *Titus Andronicus* (IV.ii.20–23), where two lines are quoted from Horace. In the *Sententiae pueriles* of Culmannus and the *Disticha moralia* of Cato with notes by Erasmus a boy found moral maxims and explicit warnings against vice. Other maxims were committed to memory from the *Adagia* and *Apopthegmata*, in which were found many of the best lines from the Greek and Roman writers. *Aesop's Fables*, a play or two from Terence and Plautus, Mantuan's *Eclogues* (see reference in *Love's Labor's Lost* [IV.ii.95–96], the *Zodiacus vitae* of Palingenius, and Nowell's *Catechism*, which was studied in English, Latin, and Greek, gave the grammar-school boys more and better Latin than all but a few college students now possess. And the intensive method of teaching fixed the religious and profane texts indelibly in young memories. The oral and written exercises imparted skill in rhetoric and stretched the imagination, as the boys practiced writing letters and delivering orations, taking care always to choose sentiments appropriate to the given situation and words suitable to the writer or speaker. Ovid, Virgil, Cicero, Horace, and Juvenal gave schoolboys a familiarity with classical mythology that in these days, when even the modern languages are studied with reluctance, would be expected only in college courses in Latin. The textbooks of the petty and the grammar school were the ones that Shakespeare knew. The curriculum of the universities was a closed book to him.

Shakespeare's education was one of the topics about which John Aubrey questioned William Beeston, and this is his memorandum: "Though as Ben Jonson says of him, that he had but little Latin and less Greek, he understood Latin pretty well: for he had been in his younger years a schoolmaster in the country." Such a youthful occupation is entirely compatible with scenes in several early plays. Holofernes in *Love's Labor's Lost* is described as a pedant, who teaches the *ABC*, and there is much schoolboy punning on Latin words. In *The Taming of the Shrew* Lucentio disguises himself as a tutor so that he may court Bianca, and there is a short burlesque of a Latin lesson ([III.i]; Tranio has already quoted Lily's *Grammar* at I. ii.167). Another tutor, Sir Hugh Evans, is introduced in *The Merry Wives of Windsor*, and when William recites his elementary Latin there is much laughter at Mistress Quickly's ignorance (IV.i). The good humor with which pedagogues are treated shows that though Shakespeare may have crept unwillingly to school he had vivid—and fond—recollections of his experiences.

Once the limits of Shakespeare's formal education are recognized, it is easier to see the qualities that make his writings immortal. He read books in London, read them avidly and efficiently, taking from them stories for his plays and ideas for his characters, but he was not bookish. "Small have continual plodders ever won," says Biron in *Love's Labor's Lost,* "save base authority from others' books." A main part of Shakespeare's genius lay in his possession of a quality that his Julius Caesar attributes to Cassius: "He is a great observer, and he looks quite through the deeds of men." Not for him the simplicity of King Duncan, who reflects sadly, "There's no art to find the mind's construction in the face." Better than any other poet, Shakespeare could listen to a voice, regard a face, and, in imagination, conjure up the thoughts and emotions of all kinds of people, low and high. The other part of his genius was in his ear for the rhythms of speech and his matchless use of words.

The year of Shakespeare's arrival in London is unknown, as are the circumstances that brought him. Whether he was a private tutor, as Beeston reported, or simply a young man with a family to support and the consciousness of a gift of poetry, he must shortly have become an actor and a playwright. For by 1592 he was vilified in a posthumous book by Robert Greene for his presumption in writing plays. When powerful friends came to his defense, Henry Chettle, Greene's literary executor, published an apology: "My self have seen his demeanor no less civil than he excellent in the quality he professes: Besides, divers of worship have reported his uprightness of dealing which argues his honesty, and his facetious grace in writing, that approves his art." This means that Shakespeare was thus early a good actor ("the quality he professes") and a successful writer, that he conducted himself like a gentleman ("uprightness"; "honesty"), and that he had won the favor and friendship of people of high station ("divers of worship").

When the plague closed the playhouses in 1592–1594, he had time to write—or at least to publish—two narrative poems, *Venus and Adonis* (1593) and *The Rape of Lucrece* (1594), the only books he saw through the press. Each of these is dedicated to the young Earl of Southampton, who may plausibly be identified as one of the "divers of worship."

The popularity of Shakespeare's plays that made Greene envious led publishers to buy his play manuscripts whenever they could. *Titus Andronicus* appeared in print in 1594. Unauthorized texts of *Henry VI, Part 2* and *Part 3*, were published in 1594 and 1595 as *The First Part of the Contention of . . . York and Lancaster* and *The True Tragedy of Richard Duke of York.* By 1598 publishers began to put Shakespeare's name on title pages: *Richard II* (quartos 2 and 3), *Love's Labor's Lost,* and *Richard III* (quarto 2). Before this time the public had paid little attention to the authorship of plays.

In this same year 1598 Londoners could read in *Palladis Tamia, Wits Treasury,* a description of the state of English poetry. The author, Francis Meres, probably taking a hint from Richard Carew's *The Excellence of the English Tongue* (ca. 1596), in which Shakespeare had been compared to Catullus, names the important English writers beginning with Chaucer and equates each with one of the classical authors. Meres's purpose was to proclaim that the English language was a suitable medium for good writing and that England had poets equal to the best of other lands. Incidentally, he names twelve plays by Shakespeare.

Meres lists Shakespeare as a distinguished writer of many kinds of literature: he names him along with Sidney and Spenser as an enricher of the English language; with Spenser and Daniel as a lyric poet; with Lord Buckhurst, Dr. Legge, Dr. Edes, and Marlowe as a writer of tragedies; with the Earl of Oxford, Dr. Gager, Rowley, and Lyly as a writer of comedies; and with the Earl of Surrey, Sir Thomas Wyatt, Sir Philip Sidney, Spenser, and Drayton as "the most passionate among us to bewail and bemoan the perplexities of love." "The Muses," he writes, "would speak with Shakespeare's fine filed phrase, if they would speak English." As for drama in general, "As Plautus and Seneca are accounted the best for Comedy and Tragedy among the Latins; so Shakespeare among the English is the most excellent in both kinds for the stage."

This testimony of Meres is invaluable, not only because it names twelve of Shakespeare's plays then in existence and mentions that his sonnets were circulating in manuscript among his private friends, but because it represents the knowledge of a hack writer, familiar with all the gossip of literary London. A master of arts of both universities, Meres came to London and began a literary career. Between 1595 and 1602 he published a sermon, translated a devotional book, and had a share in the production of a series of anthologies. In 1602 he was named rector of Wing in Rutland and removed from London.

Three things make Meres's record important: (1) he names the poets in each group in order of social rank: earls, barons, knights, doctors, gentlemen, common people; (2) writing while most of the men were still living, he mentions both the Earl of Oxford and Shakespeare in one group: "The best for Comedy amongst us be, Edward Earl of Oxford, Doctor Gager of Oxford, Master Rowley once a rare scholar of learned Pembroke Hall in Cambridge [of which Meres was B.A.], . . . Lodge, . . . Shakespeare . . . "; and (3) Meres moved in the same circles as many of the poets. Nicholas Ling, who collected the first volume of the series of anthologies to which Meres contributed the second, was the publisher of the first and second quartos of *Hamlet* (1603, 1604/1605), and James Roberts, the printer of Volumes I and III of the series and also the first quarto of *The Merchant of Venice,* quarto 2 of *Titus Andronicus,* and quarto 2 of *Hamlet,* had a contract with the Lord Chamberlain's men, Shakespeare's company, to print their playbills; he also made a series of staying entries for them in the Stationers' Register. Roberts, Ling, and, consequently, Meres were in a position to know Shakespeare personally, both as actor and playwright.

Shortly after his arrival in London to ascend the throne of England, King James took under his protection the Lord Chamberlain's Men, who were thenceforth known as the King's Men. The license, dated May 19, 1603, begins thus: "We . . . do license and authorize these our servants Lawrence Fletcher, William Shakespeare, Richard Burbage, Augustine Phillips, John Heminge, Henry Condell . . . to use and exercise the arts and faculty of playing comedies, tragedies, histories . . . during our pleasure." And pursuant to this appointment Shakespeare was one of those to whom four yards of red cloth were issued by the Master of the Great Wardrobe, to walk (or ride) in procession with the King through London on March 15, 1604. This is only one of the documents that link Shakespeare and Heminges and Condell.

The fortunate discovery in the Public Record Office of some of the documents in a suit brought in 1612 by Stephen Belott against his father-in-law, Christopher Mountjoy, a Huguenot refugee, provides a positive link between Stratford and London. The details of the suit are relevant only to the extent that they prove Shakespeare's acquaintance with the Mountjoy family in 1602 and his dwelling in their house, at least for a time, in 1604, where he might have improved his knowledge of French. One of the documents is a deposition by William Shakespeare of Stratford-upon-Avon, gentleman, of the age of forty-eight years or thereabouts, the signature to which corresponds to those on Shakespeare's will.

On March 10, 1613, Shakespeare bought of Henry Walker a house in Blackfriars known as the Gatehouse. The conveyance, bearing Shakespeare's signature, is in the Guildhall Library, London; the counterpart, signed by Walker, is in the Folger Shakespeare Library. Shakespeare is identified as a gentleman of Stratford-upon-Avon. Associated with him in the transaction were John Heminges, gentleman, William Johnson, vintner, and John Jackson, gentleman, all of London. Heminges, Jackson, and Johnson were trustees for Shakespeare. The purchase price was £140. Heminges is the fellow actor named in the King's warrent of 1604 who would help bring out the Folio of 1623. William Johnson has been identified as the owner of the famous Mermaid Tavern in Bread Street. John Jackson, gentleman, was a well-to-do Londoner from Kingston-upon-Hull, who in 1599 had acted as a trustee for Shakespeare and the other members of his company in distributing the shares in the ground lease of the Globe. Another document relating to the property, a mortgage deed now in the British Museum, was executed on the following day. This, too, is signed by Shakespeare, Johnson, and Jackson. Heminges was again a participant. The mortgage was to ensure that Walker would receive a balance due of £60. Without possibility of question, the actor at the Globe and the gentleman from Stratford were the same man.

Shakespeare's will provides still more links with London. Each page is signed by him, and in it he makes bequests to three of his long-time friends of the London stage: "to my fellows John Heminge, Richard Burbage and Henry Condell twenty-six shillings, eight pence apiece to buy them rings." To Thomas Russell, Esq., he bequeathed £5 and entreated and appointed him to be one of the "overseers" of the will. Russell was a gentleman of good estate, who had inherited manors at Alderminster and Broad Campden, both within a few miles of Stratford-upon-Avon. He married, as his second wife, the widow of the great and wealthy scientist Thomas Digges, whose fine house was in the parish of St. Mary Aldermanbury in London. John Heminges was a fellow parishioner and later a churchwarden of St. Mary's. Russell came of an ancient family and had important relatives and friends. The younger of his stepsons, Leonard Digges, an Oxford graduate and a poet, was often at Stratford. His two poems in praise of Shakespeare take on greater importance from having been written by a man with every opportunity to know the dramatist personally. The shorter one, printed in the First Folio, gives the earliest reference to the memorial bust of Shakespeare in Holy Trinity Church.

To the Memory of the Deceased Author,
Master William Shakespeare.

Shakespeare, at length thy pious fellows give
The world thy works: thy works, by which outlive
Thy tomb thy name must; when that stone is rent,
And time dissolves thy Stratford monument,
Here we alive shall view thee still. This book,
When brass and marble fade, shall make thee look
Fresh to all ages.
  .   .   .   .   .
Be sure, our Shakespeare, thou canst never die,
But, crown'd with laurel, live eternally.
L. Digges

The longer poem, which was first printed with Shakespeare's *Poems* (1640), gives additional proof of personal knowledge of "never-dying Shakespeare":

First, that he was a poet none would doubt
That heard the applause of what he sees set out
Imprinted; . . .
Next Nature only helped him; for look thorough
This whole book, thou shalt find he doth not borrow
One phrase from Greeks, nor Latins imitate,
Nor once from vulgar languages translate,
Nor plagiary-like from others glean,
Nor begs he from each witty friend a scene
To piece his acts with; all that he doth write
Is pure his own. . . .

At Shakespeare's death it was thought that he should be buried in the Poets' Corner in Westminster Abbey alongside Chaucer, Spenser, and Francis Beaumont. One of the widely circulated poems of the time begins thus:

On Mr. Wm. Shakespeare he died in April 1616

> Renowned Spenser, lie a thought more nigh
> To learned Chaucer, and rare Beaumont lie
> A little nearer Spenser, to make room
> For Shakespeare. . . .
>
> William Basse

John Milton realized that burying Shakespeare in Westminster Abbey would not have increased his fame. His poem "W. Shakespeare" in the Second Folio (1632) opens with these lines:

> What needs my Shakespeare for his honor'd bones,
> The labor of an age, in piled stones
>
> .   .   .   .
>
> Thou in our wonder and astonishment
> Hast built thy self a lasting monument.

Milton is echoing Jonson's poem in the First Folio:

> I will not lodge thee by
> Chaucer or Spenser, or bid Beaumont lie
> A little farther, to make thee a room:
> Thou art a monument, without a tomb,
> And art alive still, while thy book doth live.

But the actual "monument," the portrait bust in the chancel of Holy Trinity, has great importance. Erected before 1623, it was executed by the younger Gerard Johnson, son of the Dutch immigrant Gheerart Janssen, who carried on his business in London. Below the bust an inscription names Shakespeare and praises his writings. Above the cornice is a square block bearing the arms of Shakespeare. The inscription on the monument, in Latin and English, is itself a positive identification of Shakespeare as a poet.

Iudicio Pylium, genio Socratem, arte Maronem:
Terra tegit, populus maeret, Olympus habet.

Stay, Passenger, why goest thou so fast?
Read, if thou canst, whom envious Death hath plast [placed]
Within this monument; Shakespeare, with whom
Quick nature died, whose name doth deck this tomb
Far more than cost. Sith all that he hath writ
Leaves living art but page to serve his wit
                    Obiit Anno Domini 1616
                    Ætatis 53, Die 23 April

The Latin verses may be rendered thus: "Him who was a Nestor in wisdom, in intellect a Socrates, in art a Virgil, the earth encloses, the people mourn, and Olympus holds."

The arms on the monument are depicted according to the grant of arms issued on October 20, 1596, by the College of Heralds. William Dethick, Garter Principal King of Arms, drew up the document, of which two copies are in the official files of the College of Heralds. In the upper lefthand corner, opposite his first words, Dethick wrote Shakespeare's motto: *Non sanz droit*, and made a drawing of his arms:

Gold, on a bend sables, a spear of the first steeled argent. And for his crest or cognizance a falcon, his wings displayed argent, standing on a wreath of his colors, supporting a spear gold, steeled as aforesaid, set upon a helmet with mantles and tassels as hath been accustomed and doth more plainly appear depicted on this margin.

The arms on the Stratford monument agree in every detail with Dethick's grant. They appear again on the seal of Susanna Hall. There is no possibility that the family of the actor-poet was not the recipient of the grant, because in the course of a quarrel in 1602 among the heralds a paper was written which names Shakespeare and gives a sketch of his arms; in the margin, apparently in the hand of Ralph Brooke, York Herald, are the words: "Shakespeare the player." Another officer of the College of Heralds, the learned William Camden, author of the *Britannia* (1586) and of the *Annals* (1615) of Queen Elizabeth, and Clarenceux King of Arms, wrote as follows:

These may suffice for some poetical descriptions of our ancient poets; if I would come to our time, what a world could I present to you out of Sir Philip Sidney, Ed. Spenser, Samuel Daniel, Hugh Holland, Ben Jonson, Th. Campion, Mich. Drayton, George Chapman, John Marston, William Shakespeare, & other most pregnant wits of these our times. . . . [*Remains*, "Poets," 1605].

Within a few years of his death Shakespeare was bringing fame to Stratford. The unknown author of *A Banquet of Jests or Change of Cheer* (1630) begins a mildly amusing joke with words that illustrate the growth of Shakespeare's reputation: "One traveling through Stratford-upon-Avon, a town most remarkable for the birth of famous William Shakespeare . . ." A more detailed statement was written by a Lieutenant Hammond in 1634:

In that day's travel we came by Stratford-upon-Avon, where, in the Church in that town, there are some monuments; which Church was built by Archbishop Stratford; those worth observing and of which we took notice were these . . . a neat monument of that famous English poet, Mr. William Shakespeare, who was born here [*A Relation of a Short Survey of 26 Counties . . . By a Captain, a Lieutenant and, an Ancient, All three of the Military Company of Norwich*].

In the year 1662 the Reverend Mr. John Ward, M.A. of Oxford in 1652, became rector of Holy Trinity Church. Upon leaving the university, Ward had taken lodgings in London near Barber Surgeon's Hall so that he might attend lectures on anatomy, for he was almost equally interested in the cure of the body and the cure of souls. His notebooks, now in the Folger Shakespeare Library, are filled with memoranda about medicine and theology and contain many references to events in his life and to people he met or heard about. They show that upon his arrival in Stratford he did what every prudent, conscientious clergyman does: he inquired about the important parishioners. One family name would interest him, for whenever he went into the chancel of Holy Trinity Church there was the monument to William Shakespeare, and there were the burial places of Anne his wife, Susanna his elder daughter, and her husband, the prominent physician Dr. John Hall.

Hall, the physician, a selection from whose casebooks had been translated into English and published in 1657, Ward would know about. Hall's daughter Elizabeth's first husband, Thomas Nash, was also buried in the chancel; she was in 1662 the wife of Sir John Bernard of Abingdon. Elizabeth had inherited New Place, one of the finest houses in Stratford, and, as all Stratford remembered, she and her mother had been hostesses in 1643 to Queen Henrietta Maria and her attendants when they occupied New Place en route from London to join King Charles in the North. Ward's notebooks contain four entries about Shakespeare and his family:

Shakespeare had but two daughters, one whereof Mr. Hall the physician married and by her had one daughter, to-wit the Lady Bernard of Abingdon:

I have heard that Mr. Shakespeare was a natural wit, without any art at all. He frequented the plays all his younger time, but in his elder days lived at Stratford; and supplied the stage with two plays every year, and for that had an allowance so large that he spent at the rate of a £1000 a year, as I have heard:

Remember to peruse Shakespeare's plays and be versed in them that I may not be ignorant in that matter:

Shakespeare, Drayton, and Ben Jonson had a merry meeting and it seems drank too hard, for Shakespeare died of a fever there contracted. [It has been conjectured that he caught pneumonia, for drinking does not cause a fever.]

The testimony of the Reverend Mr. John Ward is unimpeachable. The most famous names in recent Stratford history were Shakespeare and Hall. The most exciting event in recent memory was the visit of Queen Henrietta Maria. Shakespeare's granddaughter was now Lady Bernard, and the family home was one of the show places of the town. Of course the new rector must read Shakespeare's plays, so as not to show ignorance of them, for apparently they were part of the subject of conversation among the best people.

There are two authentic likenesses of Shakespeare. One of these is the engraving by Martin Droeshout, printed on the title page of the First Folio (1623). Since the artist was only about twenty-two when the book came from the press, he must have worked from a portrait; at the age of fifteen, as he was when the poet died, he was too young to have formed a trustworthy impression. The identity of the portrait he copied is unknown. Possibly it was that now in the National Portrait Gallery in London. This has been attributed to Richard Burbage, who is known to have painted portraits; it has also been attributed to Joseph Taylor, an actor with the King's Men (or to John Taylor, a contemporary artist). According to early tradition, Taylor bequeathed it to Shakespeare's godson, Sir William Davenant. From him it passed to Thomas Betterton. From Betterton it went to his long-time associate on the stage, Mrs. Barry. The record of its ownership continues unbroken until it became the property of the Duke of Chandos, from whom it passed to the National Portrait Gallery. Whatever faults of execution Droeshout may have committed in his engraving, it is certain that Shakespeare's friends provided him with an authentic portrait to copy.

The portrait bust in Stratford was erected in 1622. Gerard Johnson the Younger carved it, possibly from a life mask or a death mask. Its acceptance and erection in Holy Trinity Church are reasonable assurances that the family considered it a reasonable likeness. About 1748 it required minor repairs and repainting. Later, in 1793, it was painted stone color to give it a classical appearance. And still later, in 1861, the original colors were restored as faithfully as might be. Because of differences in detail in the engraving printed in William Dugdale's *Warwickshire* (1656), there has been controversy about the reliability of the bust as it is now seen. This need not be taken seriously, for many of the monuments depicted by Dugdale, unchanged from his day to this, differ markedly from the engravings in *Warwickshire*. It may be remarked that Dugdale shows the arms of Shakespeare, as granted by Dethick in 1596, and the inscription below the bust which names the poet.

When interest in Shakespeare caused collectors to buy early quartos and folios at ever higher prices, it was natural that a search should be made for early portraits. Some of those brought to light may be genuine likenesses, painted in his lifetime, but not one has an unbroken pedigree, and so all are suspect. Others, when subjected to close study, have proved to be clumsy or skillful alterations of early portraits of subjects unknown. The market for Shakespeare portraits was brisk, buyers were not always critical, and false claims were made. This kind of shady business has nothing to do with the authorship of Shakespeare; it is simply proof that a painting called "Shakespeare" would fetch a higher price than a "portrait of a gentleman unknown."

The Elizabethan indifference to playwrights extended to their manuscripts. Manuscript plays had value only for actors, who might want to perform them, or publishers, who might want to have them printed. There were no Elizabethan collectors of literary autographs. When Francis Bacon arranged with Humfrey Hooper to publish his *Essays* in 1597, Hooper delivered the manuscript to John Windet the printer, and when the job was finished, this manuscript was discarded. No one treasured it, not even the author. By 1625 the number of Bacon's essays had increased in successive editions from ten to fifty-eight. If Bacon had been a man of relatively small importance in 1597, he had risen meteorically under King James until he became Baron Verulam, Viscount St. Alban, and Lord Chancellor; then meteorlike he had fallen. Had Elizabethans been collectors of literary autographs, surely the manuscripts of the successive revisions of and additions to the *Essays* should have been a prize worth striving for. But no one was interested, and in consequence Bacon's manuscripts of the *Essays* perished. In just the same way Shakespeare's holograph copies of *Venus and Adonis* and *The Rape of Lucrece* were discarded as waste paper as soon as Richard Field had set them in type.

As a matter of fact, paper was an expensive commodity and was seldom wasted. Almost all the paper was imported, and people used it until it went to pieces. The bindings of Elizabethan books are filled with scraps of manuscript and pieces of printed matter that accumulated in the shops of printers and bookbinders. All that is left of the first edition of Shakespeare's *King Henry IV, Part I*, is a single sheet, now in the Folger Shakespeare Library, that someone used in making a binding for a copy of Thomas' *Rules of the Italian Grammar* (1567). As late as 1700 a favorite way to insult a poet was to suggest that his verses would be good for lighting a fire or wrapping a fish, or for some humbler use.

Very few of the plays written in Tudor and early Stuart times were printed. The actors believed that popular plays should be kept out of print, for if people could buy and read them they might be less eager to pay to see performances in the theatre. Another danger was that rival companies of actors might use them for giving performances, for there was no law to prevent such competition.

Then, as now, a playwright sold his new play to a producer, who was in Shakespeare's age a company of actors. The modern playwright may, if he wishes, retain publishing, radio, television, and moving picture rights. Not so in Elizabethan times. When a company of actors bought a play, it acquired all rights. The company could perform the play as written or employ someone to revise it; it could even lock up the play without performance; it could, at its discretion, sell the play to a publisher. The publisher, in turn, acquired absolute copyright to himself and his heirs forever. When he had the play printed, it did not occur to him to ask or permit the author to read proofs, for in selling his play to the actors the author had disposed of all his rights in it. In Shakespeare's case he sold his plays, after 1594, to the company of which he was a sharer. The manuscripts went into what may be called the company library, and there the licensed promptbooks presumably remained until Parliament closed all playhouses in 1642 and the King's Men distributed their assets among the then sharers.

The other companies of actors may be presumed to have parceled out their play manuscripts in the same way in 1642. Several promptbooks, such as Philip Massinger's *The City Madam,* were sold to publishers or published by their unemployed actor-owners. By 1653 Humphrey Moseley, the publisher, had bought up from the actors a quantity of manuscript plays that had never been printed and entered them in the Stationers' Register. Only a few of these were printed, because the London of the Commonwealth period had little love for the stage; many of the manuscripts have disappeared. Probably the Great Fire of 1666 took a heavy toll of unprinted plays as it swept through London and destroyed untold quantities of bookshops and their contents. (Copies of the Third Folio of Shakespeare of 1663/1664 are scarce for the probable reason that many of the unsold copies were burned.)

It was not until about 1660 that private collectors appear to have developed an interest in unprinted plays. A letter from the Lords Somerset, Cavendish (later the Duke of Devonshire, builder of Chatsworth), Gerard, and Roscommon contains greetings to a wealthy fellow collector, Abraham Hill. Cavendish, along with the Earls of Oxford, Pembroke, Winchilsea, and Sunderland and others of lower station, made regular Saturday excursions to the shops in quest of rare books and manuscripts. And about 1678 Hill copied down the titles of more than fifty manuscript plays he had come upon. Only three plays are now extant in manuscript with titles corresponding to those in Hill's list; no manuscripts of the other plays are traceable.

There is no reference to Shakespeare's play manuscripts in his will for the obvious reason that he no longer possessed them. As written, each had been sold to the actors.

During Shakespeare's life approximately half of his plays were put into print in one way or another; sometimes from unauthorized manuscripts, as in the case of the first quartos of *Romeo and Juliet, Hamlet, Henry V,* and others; sometimes from copies that seem to have been in Shakespeare's own handwriting, as *The Merchant of Venice* or the second quarto of *Romeo and Juliet.* When the printer finished his job, the manuscripts were regarded as worthless. The same thing happened after Jaggard had finished printing the Folio of 1623; the printer's copy was thrown away. This tossing out of printer's copy was not peculiar to Shakespeare. Of all the hundreds of plays put in print up to 1700, there is not one surviving example of a manuscript that went through a print shop. Obviously the nonsurvival of Shakespearean literary manuscripts has no bearing on the subject of authorship.

Letters and private papers, except the real estate documents referred to above, have all disappeared. At Shakespeare's death they would have remained in New Place in the care of his widow Anne and his elder daughter Susanna Hall. After the death of the widow in 1623 Dr. John Hall and his wife remained at New Place. Hall's will, probated in 1636, provided that his "Study of Books" (these may or may not have included volumes belonging to Shakespeare) should be disposed of as his son-in-law Thomas Nash might wish: "As for my manuscripts . . . you may, son Nash, burn them or do with them what you please." In consequence of a lawsuit against Dr. Hall and his heirs, a charge was filed in 1637 by Susanna Hall, her daughter Elizabeth, and the latter's husband, Thomas Nash, that in August, 1636, Baldwyn Brookes, mercer of Stratford, with the assistance of the undersheriff and some of the Stratford officers, broke into New Place and "there did take and seize upon the ready money, books, goods, and chattels of the said John Hall deceased . . . to the value of one thousand pounds at the least and have converted the same to their or some of their own uses without inventorying or appraising the same." No further documents in the suit have been discovered, and so it is not known whether Mistress Hall recovered anything.

At the death, in 1670, of Shakespeare's last lineal descendant, his granddaughter Elizabeth, it may be supposed that any surviving books and papers remained at Abingdon, the residence of her second husband, Sir John Bernard.

There are several books in which Shakespeare's name is written. Some of the signatures may be genuine, but others are obvious forgeries.

As Shakespeare's plays gained ever wider popularity, some of their admirers expressed their admiration in extravagant terms. Idolaters professed to find technical knowledge about law, medicine, military science, and the like that is ordinarily possessed only by professionals, together with familiarity with foreign lands betokening wide travel, and erudition and elegance suitable to university-educated members of the nobility. No human ever possessed all the qualities that were in sum attributed to Shakespeare. In reaction against these absurdities, first one and then another writer began to point out the discrepancies between the biographical facts then known and the supposed accomplishments. The next stage was to propose that someone else wrote the plays.

Reduced to simplest terms, the process was as follows: The plays must have been written by a learned man, an intimate of the court, who had traveled extensively. Who had these qualifications? The first name to be proposed was that of Francis Bacon, who in youth had "taken all knowledge to be [his] province." Other people, dissatisfied with this candidate, suggested Edward de Vere, seventeenth Earl of Oxford, or Henry Wriothesley, third Earl of Southampton, or William Stanley, sixth Earl of Derby, until twenty or more rivals were in the field, including Queen Elizabeth I and Anne Hathaway. When each of these, in turn, was proved by opposed partisans to be ineligible, it was argued that a coterie wrote the plays and poems, or that the works had been parceled out to a number of people. In no case has it been possible to produce a shred of evidence that anyone in Shakespeare's day questioned his authorship. And not one fact has been discovered to prove that anyone but Shakespeare was the author.

It may be well to classify the objections to William Shakespeare and consider them apart from the claims advanced for any of the proposed authors.

The bitter attacks on Shakespeare often begin by calling Stratford-upon-Avon a mean, dirty, bookless town, incapable of producing a great man. The facts are that Stratford was a prosperous borough town with an ancient charter, where citizens were not merely renters but were the owners of their homes. The charge that Stratford was dirty proceeds out of a single item in the borough accounts: the record of a fine levied upon John Shakespeare for permitting a heap of refuse to collect before his house in 1552. The commendable zeal of the authorities in enforcing their regulations is the best evidence that Stratford had standards of sanitation and took vigorous measures to uphold them. The grammar school had been conducted for two hundred years before the Reformation and customarily employed Oxford and Cambridge graduates at high salaries. This "proper little market town," as William Camden the historian described it, was capable of producing important men. John de Stratford, who enlarged the parish church and founded a college of priests nearby, rose to the Archbishopric of Canterbury in the reign of Edward III, and his brother Robert became Bishop of Chichester and Chancellor of England. Another son of Stratford, Sir Hugh Clopton, was Lord Mayor of London in the year Columbus discovered America. Sir Hugh built the stone bridge that is still used by traffic crossing the Avon; he also built the nave of the Guild Chapel, still a landmark in Stratford; and the house he erected in 1483, New Place, became in due time the residence of William Shakespeare. Clopton's will provided funds for what would now be called five-year scholarships to six poor boys, three at Oxford and three at Cambridge.

The second charge brought against Shakespeare is ignorance. He has been called, among other things, "the mean, drunken, ignorant and absolutely unlettered rustic of Stratford," who could neither read nor write a line. Some people, after trying to decipher the signatures to Shakespeare's will and other legal documents have, in their own ignorance, called him illiterate. The usual hand written in England from about 1500 until long after Shakespeare's death bears the name of English or secretary. The "fine Italian hand" that Shakespeare mentions was introduced in the sixteenth century and by 1700 it had almost completely displaced the secretary hand. English or secretary letters resemble those used in German script, and most of them are totally different from the familiar italic letters of the modern cursive hand. Once the secretary forms are learned, Elizabethan manuscripts are no more or less difficult to read than modern hands. It is just as proper to call Goethe illiterate for writing German script as to say that Shakespeare was illiterate because he wrote English or secretary script.

The nature and extent of Shakespeare's schooling has already been described, as has the extent of formal education exhibited in the plays. The poet laureate John Dryden, a "learned" poet of the reign of Charles II, sums up the situation neatly in his *Of Dramatic Poesy, An Essay:*

To begin, then, with Shakespeare: he was the man who of all modern, and perhaps ancient poets, had the largest and most comprehensive soul. All the images of nature were still present to him, and he drew them not laboriously, but luckily: when he describes anything, you more than see it, you feel it too. Those who accuse him to have wanted learning, give him the greater commendation: he was naturally learn'd; he needed not the spectacles of books to read nature, he look'd inwards, and found her there.

A third objection to Shakespeare is that he could have had no opportunity to hear the conversation of royalty and nobility and, consequently, could not have written the dialogue of the plays. But just how did royalty and the nobility talk? Where are the transcripts of councils, private conversations, and amorous courtship? A modern poet (Don Marquis in "Pete the Parrot and Shakespeare") has a manager hand Shakespeare a "mouldy old script" and demand that he prepare at once a manuscript filled with some of his usual hokum: fat men making love, "and kings talking like kings never had sense enough to talk." The fact is that Shakespeare's court scenes are psychologically convincing, and we assume that people in the Renaissance actually talked in this way. If it were true that only courtiers could write dialogue like that, John Webster, the son of a London merchant tailor, must have been an Italian courtier to write the effective dialogue of his plays *The White Devil* and *The Duchess of Malfi.*

Several of Shakespeare's plays include details that have not yet been traced in source books and appear to suggest firsthand observation of foreign places and customs. Thus *Love's Labor's Lost* shows more than casual familiarity with French names. *The Two Gentlemen of Verona* has unusual geographic details. Some knowledge of Elsinore is supposed to be revealed in *Hamlet* and possession of then unprinted historical details in *Macbeth.* Now Bacon or the Earl of Derby might be proposed as the authors of *Love's Labor's Lost* because of their travels in France. The Earl of Rutland had an embassage to Denmark, a fact not overlooked by those who would assign *Hamlet* to him. A reputed journey to Italy by the Earl of Southampton encourages some writers to think he wrote *The Two Gentlemen of Verona.* Plays have been attributed on similar grounds to the Earl of Essex, Sir Walter Raleigh, and others. Even if one single piece of evidence could be found to support any or all of these various ascriptions, the results would be chaotic, for it would be necessary to believe that a coterie composed of these, and perhaps other, people wrote the plays.

That is, of course, absurd. Some of these men were the bitterest rivals and at times deadly enemies. It is inconceivable that for a period of about twenty-five years (1588–1612) they could have collaborated to produce the plays at the dates they are known to have appeared on the stage. To hold such opinions is to shut one's eyes to the many sources of information open to a playwright. Even an island-bound poet could talk to travelers, who brought back stories from France and Italy and vivid accounts of their cities and customs. News pamphlets taught Londoners the names of the principal leaders in the French Wars, if only because English treasure was invested in the cause of Henry of Navarre and because the outcome of that religious struggle was of vital importance to every Englishman. English actors, reputed to be the best in Europe, performed frequently in Denmark, as well as in Germany and the Netherlands, and they reported their observations and experiences to all who would listen. Shakespeare's Romans are as truly Roman as his Renaissance Italians are Italian. No one, on this account, would suggest that the author of *Julius Caesar* must have lived in ancient Rome. The truth of the matter is that poetic genius overleaps both space and time.

The author of the plays was not a formally trained lawyer—or doctor, or soldier, or sailor—however vividly and appropriately technical terms are often used. Research has shown that Shakespeare uses legal terms and situations less frequently than some of the other playwrights, and often less accurately. It was a litigious age. People haled each other into court upon small provocation, and a certain number of legal terms made up a part of every man's vocabulary. So with war and navigation. A sword or dagger was never very far from an Elizabethan's hand. The citizenry were expected to know something of the use of weapons. And the average Londoner was much closer to the sea in those days of Drake and Hawkins and Frobisher than today. What a poet needed was a quick eye, a keen ear, a sensitive imagination, and a retentive memory—

and, in Dryden's words, "the largest and most comprehensive soul of all modern, and perhaps ancient poets."

Most of the objections to Shakespeare as the author of his plays have originated in ignorance of theatrical conditions and of the records that have survived. Frequently it is stated, for example, that Shakespeare could not have been a playwright because his name does not appear in the records of Philip Henslowe. Henslowe was a London businessman with a variety of interests. He engaged in pawnbroking, invested in real estate, was active in bearbaiting, and held minor court appointments; but his name lives because of the contents of his theatrical account books. Between 1592 and his death in 1616 he owned or financed several playhouses (the Rose, the theatre at Newington Butts, the Fortune, the Hope) and had financial dealings with, or was banker for, several companies of actors (chiefly the Admiral's Men, 1594–1604; then Worcester's, the Lady Elizabeth's, etc.) His *Diary* and *Papers,* as the account books are called, are among the most detailed and valuable records of the Elizabethan theatre. They contain, among other matters, many entries of payments to Jonson, Dekker, Hathaway, Drayton, and others for writing plays. Shakespeare's name is not mentioned. Why? The answer is easy. In the early 1590's theatrical people were in a turmoil. Acting companies formed, disintegrated, and reformed, with much shifting about of actors and sale and resale of promptbooks. The plague closed the playhouses for much of the time between 1592 and 1594, with occasional brief intervals of theatrical activity. Several titles of Shakespearean interest appear in Henslowe's business records for these years: *Henry VI, Titus Andronicus, Taming of the Shrew, Hamlet.* But at this time Henslowe did not name the authors of plays, and so it is not possible to match plays and poets.

In the autumn of 1594 relief from the plague permitted the resumption of theatrical activity in London. And just at this time the Lord Chamberlain took under his protection a newly organized company of actors that included William Shakespeare. From 1594 until the playhouses were closed in 1642 this company had a continuous history, with a succession of noble patrons until 1603, when King James chose them to be the King's Men. During the long years from 1594 to 1642 this company was, almost without interruption, the strongest, best, and most successful in London, as the record of payments to them for performances at Court clearly demonstrates. Not once in these years did Shakespeare's company have any financial connections with Philip Henslowe or with any of the acting companies dependent upon him. Since after 1594 Shakespeare acted and wrote only for the company of which he had become a sharer, his name could not appear in Henslowe's records, any more than the president of General Motors could be named on the payrolls of Chrysler or Ford.

Much ingenuity has been expended in the attempt to find in Shakespeare's works hidden messages about their authorship, and there is a voluminous literature on the subject. This has all been subjected to impartial scrutiny by two eminent cryptanalysts, William F. and Elizebeth S. Friedman, who in *The Shakespearean Ciphers Examined* (1957) prove conclusively that no crypto-system hitherto used by anti-Shakespeareans meets the basic tests of cryptology. Determined to avoid partisanship, they refuse to make a search for codes or ciphers, but they give assurance that none of the supposed discoveries thus far reported has any validity.

Shakespeare's artistry, unique in its perfection, did not develop in a vacuum. The Shakespeare of the early plays sounds, for lines on end, like Marlowe or Greene or Kyd or Peele, because these men had slightly preceded him in the field and had something he could learn by imitation. Then Heywood and Middleton and a dozen others, slightly younger, began to learn from Shakespeare. Theatrical London of those years was an exciting, intoxicating little world, somewhat like New York and Hollywood in the early days of radio and television. Everyone tried to improve on everything that had succeeded for anyone else, and then to invent something new. Writers imitated, they borrowed, each man learning from the others and, with luck, doing something original that the rest would try to copy. At the same time they ridiculed and criticized each other, so that the exact date of a play can sometimes be arrived at by a study of the plays it imitates or borrows from and those that, in turn, imitate or satirize it. These things were true of diction and metrics, as well as of incident, character, and plot. So it is relatively easy to write the history of English drama from, say, 1585 to 1642. The events hang together, with a place for everyone and everyone in his place. In such a scheme the observed development of Shakespeare as theatrical writer and poet is credible and logical. The chronology of his works meshes perfectly with the chronology of the whole literature of the age.

There is no problem of authorship for those who have read Elizabethan drama in a setting of Elizabethan literature and history. Those who find difficulty do so because they attempt to treat Shakespeare as a special case, without proper reference to contemporary writers and the customs and attitudes of his age. Read Shakespeare's works in chronological order of composition, and it will be obvious that they are the product of a single intellect. Metrical devices, characteristics of expression, qualities of mind that are present in the earliest writings, are traceable throughout. But as the poet develops, his early exuberance changes to skillful mastery and ripens into mature profundity. The early comedies tinkle with rhyme and sparkle with wordplay as the poet revels in the discovery of his talent. The golden comedies and the late histories reveal a writer who has mastered his craft and is free to contemplate the vanities of "Man, proud Man." The next stage of development is to investigate some of the complexities of the human spirit and to grapple with the timeless problems of evil and death. At length come the romances, in which the poet is concerned with forgiveness and reconciliation and the renewal of life. Throughout, there is the same mind at work, revealing itself in

95

the careful architecture of the plays. Throughout, there is the same sensitive spirit, able to enter perfectly into the mind and heart of every character in every situation. And throughout, there is the same incredible mastery of language, so that each character always has the right words to express his particular thought or emotion.

> Nature herself was proud of his designs,
>   And joy'd to wear the dressing of his lines! . . .
> Yet must I not give Nature all, Thy art,
>   My gentle Shakespeare, must enjoy a part.
> For though the poet's matter, Nature be,
>   His art doth give the fashion. . . .
> For a good poet's made, as well as born.
>   And such wert thou.

> [Ben Jonson, "To the Memory of My Beloved, the Author Mr. William Shakespeare: and What He Hath Left Us," prefixed to the First Folio, 1623].

SUGGESTED READING

The life of Shakespeare may be studied in great detail in Sir Edmund Chambers' *William Shakespeare: A Study of Facts and Problems* (2 vols., Oxford, 1930), an encyclopedic presentation of biographical and literary documents and criticism, with a good bibliography of each topic. A much more readable account will be found in *A Life of William Shakespeare* (Boston, 1923) by Joseph Quincy Adams. Marchette Chute's *Shakespeare of London* (New York, 1949; reissued as a paperback in 1957) is a lively story of Shakespeare as a human being, particularly valuable for its account of other members of Shakespeare's company, such as Heminges and Condell. Excellent short biographies will be found in Giles E. Dawson's *The Life of William Shakespeare* (Folger Booklets on Tudor and Stuart Civilization, Washington, 1958) and the sections entitled "The Author," "The Publication of His Plays," and "The Shakespearean Theatre" by Louis B. Wright in the Introductions to the several volumes of The Folger Library General Reader's Shakespeare (New York, in progress).

The borough accounts of Stratford-upon-Avon contain the records of John Shakespeare and give a fair picture of the status of that busy market town (Edgar I. Fripp, editor, *Minutes and Accounts of the Corporation of Stratford-upon-Avon and Other Records, 1553–1620,* transcribed by Richard Savage (4 vols., Oxford, 1921–). Levi Fox has written a readable, well-illustrated history of Stratford, *The Borough Town of Stratford-upon-Avon* (Stratford-upon-Avon, 1953).

A brief account of education in Shakespeare's time will be found in Craig R. Thompson's *Schools in Tudor England* (Folger Booklets on Tudor and Stuart Civilization, Washington, 1958). *The Education of Shakespeare* (London and New York, 1933) by George R. Plimpton gives an account of some of the important schoolbooks of that period. Detailed discussions of the school curriculums and the influence of schoolbooks on Shakespeare will be found in T. W. Baldwin's *William Shakspere's Petty School* (Urbana, Ill., 1943) and his *William Shakspere's Small Latine and Lesse Greeke* (Urbana, Ill., 1944). Virgil K. Whitaker's *Shakespeare's Use of Learning* (San Marino, Calif., 1953) deals with the reflections of Shakespeare's reading in some of his works. And Sister Miriam Joseph's *Shakespeare's Use of the Arts of Language* is a technical treatise on the rhetorical devices Shakespeare learned in school.

The best source of information about play manuscripts and theatrical documents is the generously illustrated *Dramatic Documents from the Elizabethan Playhouses; Stage Plots; Actors' Parts; Prompt Books* (2 vols., Oxford, 1931) by Sir Walter Greg. "Where Are Shakespeare's Manuscripts?" (*New Colophon,* no. 8 [1950], pp. 357–369) by James G. McManaway, is a popular description of some of the conditions in which an Elizabethan playwright worked. There is a mine of information about Elizabethan theatrical conditions in *Henslowe's Diary* (2 vols., London, 1904–1908) and *Henslowe Papers* (London, 1907), both edited by Sir Walter Greg. R. A. Foakes and R. T. Rickert have just published a new edition, *Henslowe's Diary . . . with Supplementary Material* (Cambridge, Eng., 1961), from a fresh transcription of Henslowe's manuscripts. An excellent idea about how plays were licensed before performance is given in Joseph Q. Adams' *The Dramatic Records of Sir Henry Herbert, Master of the Revels, 1623–1673* (New Haven, 1917). This is brought up to date in Adams' essay, "The Office-Book of Sir Henry Herbert, Master of the Revels" (in *To Doctor R.* [Philadelphia, 1953], pp. 1–9). The most extensive collection of literary autograph material is Sir Walter Greg's *English Literary Autographs, 1550–1650* (Oxford, 1932, issued in three parts), which reproduces specimens of the handwriting of poets and playwrights, with transcripts, and lists all the examples known to him in 1932 to have survived. This is invaluable for learning what manuscripts written in English secretary look like. A slightly earlier study, without facsimiles, describes the scarcity of writing in the hands of Elizabethan playwrights, "Extant Autograph Material by Shakespeare's Fellow Dramatists" (*The Library*, ser. 4, X [1930], 308–312) by Henrietta C. Bartlett. The most detailed study of Shakespeare's handwriting and of his probable part in *Sir Thomas More* is *Shakespeare's Hand in "Sir Thomas More"* (Cambridge, Eng., 1923) by Alfred W. Pollard, Sir Walter Greg, E. Maunde Thompson, J. Dover Wilson, and R. W. Chambers. This reproduces portions of the manuscript play supposed to be in Shakespeare's handwriting and each of the six signatures of Shakespeare preserved on legal documents.

The early allusions to Shakespeare as an actor, poet, and playwright and the hundreds of imitations or echoes of his lines and references to his dramatis personae are collected in *The Shakspere Allusion Book: A Collection of Allusions to Shakspere from 1591 to 1700* (reissued, 2 vols., Oxford, 1932). In a preface to the reprint Sir Edmund Chambers adds a few important allusions discovered in recent years. He gives a judicious selection of the allusions in appendixes to his *William Shakespeare*. Gerald E. Bentley adds a number of allusions in *Shakespeare and Jonson: Their Reputations in the Seventeenth Century Compared* (2 vols., Chicago, 1945) and points out that references tend to praise the learning and art of Jonson at the expense of Shakespeare, the natural genius.

The most careful study of Shakespeare portraits is that of M. H. Spielmann, *The Title-Page of the First Folio of Shakespeare's Plays: A Comparative Study of the Droeshout Portrait and the Stratford Monument* (London, 1924).

R. C. Churchill, *Shakespeare and His Betters* (Bloomington, Ind., 1958), and Frank W. Wadsworth, *The Poacher from Stratford* (Berkeley, Calif., 1958), have collected information about the history of anti-Shakespeareanism and the chief anti-Stratfordians. "The Anti-Shakespeare Industry and the Growth of Cults" by Louis B. Wright (*Virginia Quarterly Review*, XXV [1959], 289–303) is a spirited attack upon faddist speculation. James G. McManaway discusses the matter from a different point of view in "Shakespeare and the Heretics" (*To Doctor R.* [Philadelphia, 1953], pp. 136–153). And there is a considered account by Giles E. Dawson in "The Anti-Shakespearean Theories" (*Encyclopaedia Britannica*, XX [1960–], 457–458).

The claims of those who have sought acrostic or code and cipher messages in Shakespeare's works are considered and rejected as illusory by Colonel William F. Friedman and Mrs. Friedman in *The Shakespearean Ciphers Examined* (Cambridge, Eng., 1957).

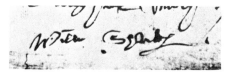

Plate 1(a). Shakespeare's signature to his deposition of May 11, 1612, in the Belott-Mountjoy lawsuit. From the original in the Public Record Office, London.

Plate 1(b). Shakespeare's signature to the conveyance of the Gatehouse in Blackfriars, March 10, 1613. From the original in the Guildhall Library, London.

Plate 1(c). Shakespeare's signature to the mortgage deed of the Gatehouse in Blackfriars, March 11, 1613. From the original in the British Museum.

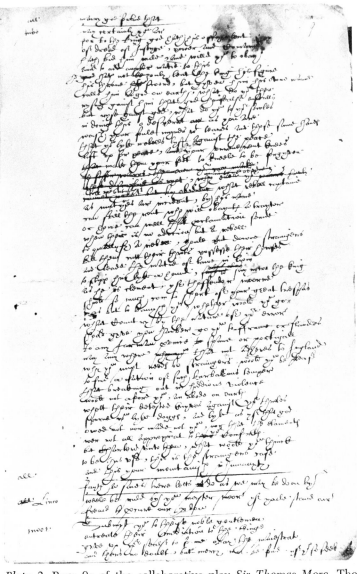

Plate 2. Page 9a of the collaborative play *Sir Thomas More.* The verses on pages 8a, 8b, and 9a are thought by many to be in the handwriting of William Shakespeare. From the original in the British Museum (Harl. MS. 7368).

Plate 3. A sketch of the coat of arms of "Shakespeare the player" as granted by William Dethick, Garter King of Arms, in 1596. Probably in the hand of Ralph Brooke, York Herald, about 1602. Folger MS. V.a.156.

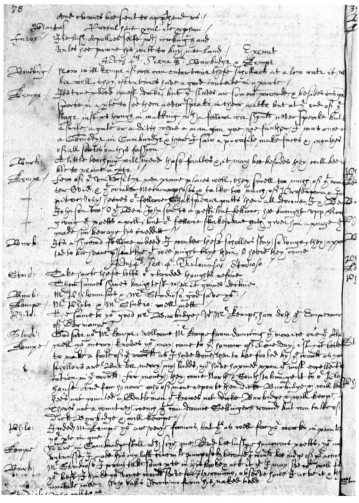

Plate 4. A page of *The Progress to Parnassus*, "as it was acted in St. John's College in Cambridge, Anno 1601." An anonymous play, written and performed by students at Cambridge. Folger MS. V.a.355. The cross in the margin is opposite the reference to Shakespeare quoted on page 68.

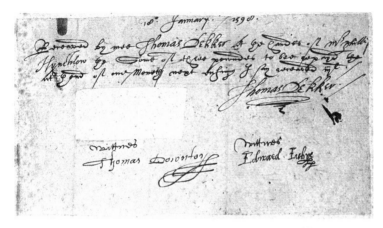

Plate 5(a). A note, written and signed by Thomas Dekker, for £3 loaned to him by Philip Henslowe on January 18, 1598. Thomas Downton and Edward Juby, two actors, sign as witnesses. One side of Folger MS. X.d.319.

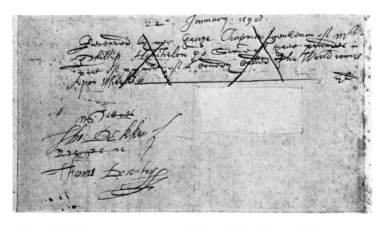

Plate 5(b). A receipt written and signed by George Chapman on January 22, 1598, for £3 from Philip Henslowe, in part payment— in advance—for writing a play called *The World Runs upon Wheels*. Chapman's signature has been cut out by an autograph collector. Thomas Dekker and Thomas Downton sign as witnesses. The other side of Folger MS. X.d.319.

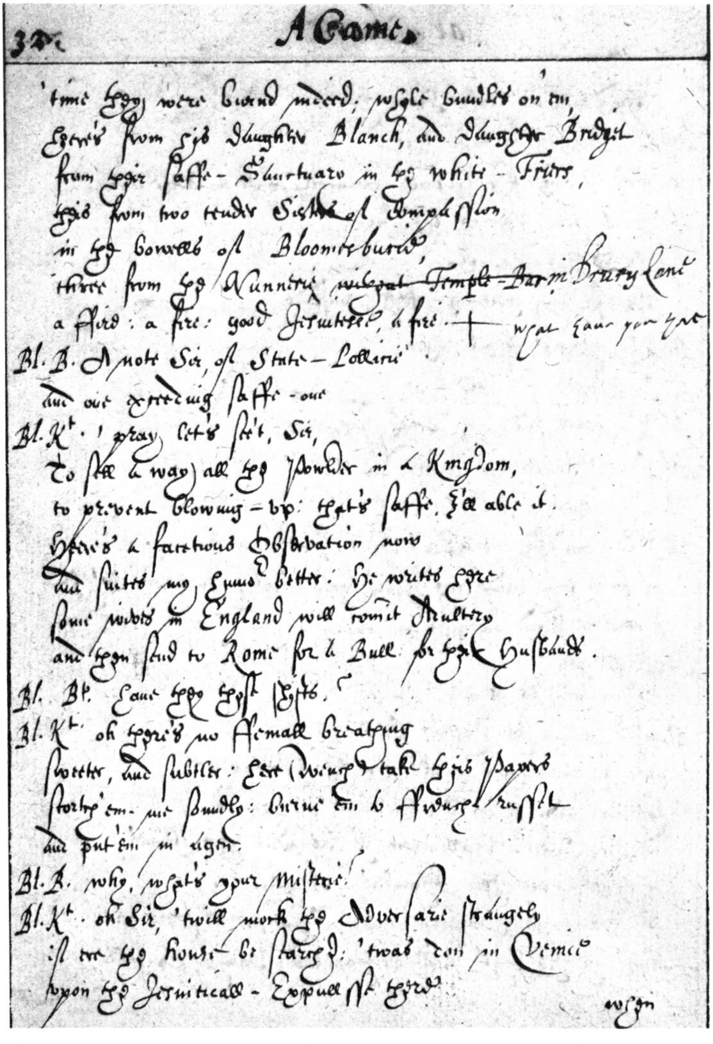

Plate 6. A page of Thomas Middleton's *A Game at Chess* (1624), in the handwriting of Ralph Crane, who did professional copying for the King's Men. In lines 6 and 7 the author, a younger contemporary of Shakespeare, has made corrections in the text. Folger MS. V.a.231.

Shakespeare's Theatre and

the Dramatic Tradition

By Louis B. Wright

108

FOR many years the characteristics of Shakespeare's stage have excited the interest of scholars. In thousands of pages of learned commentary they have discussed the history of Elizabethan theatres, the physical conditions of the stage, the composition of the companies of actors, the influence of the physical nature of the stage upon the quality of the drama, and scores of related topics. In an area where precise documentary evidence is scanty, many topics have aroused controversies that cannot be resolved dogmatically. For example, blueprints for the original construction of the Globe playhouse do not exist, and our knowledge of it is based on a variety of evidence, much of which is inconclusive.

Though scholars may not agree on every detail of stage construction, they have accumulated enough evidence to permit the reconstruction of a characteristic theatre in its essential outlines. The public theatres were not exact replicas of each other, of course, and the so-called "private" theatres showed many differences. We would do well to remember that, then as now, individual theatres varied considerably in their appointments and equipment, and a generalization about the staging of a play in one theatre may not precisely fit conditions in another. Nevertheless the conditions of staging in all of the public playhouses had a general similarity and certain theatrical practices were common to them all.

Traditionally the English had found pleasure and delight in

dramatic entertainment. For centuries before the development of Elizabethan drama, folk games, pageantry, and processions had been a part of English life. Wandering entertainers had been a familiar sight in both manor houses and town halls. Jugglers, sleight-of-hand artists, acrobats, rope dancers, bear leaders, and fortunetellers, who belong to an ancient profession antedating recorded history, roamed the English countryside and regularly turned up at fairs and festivals. When performers of rude dramatic skits first appeared in England, no man can say. Mimes and clowns performing impromptu roles probably date from the Roman occupation. Certainly the clown has an ancient if not an honorable lineage. In the country, the mummers play and other types of folk drama go back to an early date.

The theatre proper, however, traces its origins back to the Church, even to the most solemn part of the liturgy, the Easter Mass. Between the ninth and the eleventh centuries throughout Europe the Easter Mass acquired richness and variety. In some churches, a brief text, or "trope," attached itself to the beginning portion of the Mass called the *Introit* and served as a kind of dramatic introduction to the service. In the Easter Mass this trope began, "*Quem quaeritis in sepulchro, O Christicolae?*" [Whom seek ye in the sepulchre, O followers of Christ?], and when the three Marys replied that they sought Jesus of Nazareth who had been crucified, the angel responded that he was not there, that they should go forth and say that he had risen as it had been prophesied. This bit of liturgical decoration gave rise to other dramatic episodes, notably to a similar playlet attached to the Christmas Mass. Liturgical drama of this type was acted throughout the European Church until the middle of the fifteenth century, by which time religious plays had already become secularized and had passed from the church into the streets and market place.

Precisely when or how this secularization came about, no one knows. A summer feast day, that of Corpus Christi, first established by the Church in 1264 and revived in 1311, provided an ideal time for an outdoor celebration and was soon the occasion for the performances of secularized Biblical plays. Since Corpus Christi Day falls on the Thursday after Trinity Sunday (the eighth Sunday after Easter), the performers could count on a long summer's day with a chance for good weather. In many towns throughout England on Corpus Christi Day associations of tradesmen known as guilds made themselves responsible for the presentation of cycles of plays based on the Bible, beginning with the Creation and ending with the Last Judgment. When possible, particular guilds chose plays that suited their callings. At Newcastle, York, and elsewhere, for example, the Shipwrights were responsible for the play concerned with building Noah's Ark. Corpus Christi Day was not the only occasion for the performance of guild plays. At Chester, for example, the plays were given during the week following Whitsunday. Although in some places the plays might be performed on stationary platforms, the general practice was to use "pageant wagons" —which in America would be called "floats"—platforms or structures on wheels which could go from place to place about the town until the whole cycle had been seen in sequence at several stations. When an entire cycle was given in one day, the performances had to start early and end late. The York cycle numbered at one time at least fifty plays, forty-eight of which have survived. If the audience tired of them, the records do not show it, and the cyclic plays, given in the language of the people, continued in popular esteem in some places until Shakespeare's time. Plays were acted at Chester in the 1570's and at Coventry, only a few miles from Stratford, until 1580.

These cyclic plays performed by the trade guilds are usually called miracle or mystery plays (the latter probably from an old French word for trade). Literary historians have sometimes tried to make a distinction between mystery and miracle plays. They would restrict mystery plays to those based on the Bible and miracle plays to those based on episodes in the lives of the saints, but the distinction has not gained currency, and both terms are used to describe the guild plays. Saints plays were never so popular in England as in France and elsewhere on the Continent.

The significant fact about the guild plays in the growth of the dramatic tradition in England is their popularity over a great span of years and their dissemination throughout the country. As late as the mid-sixteenth century, even many small towns had a summer festival of drama in which large numbers of citizens participated. Gradually non-Biblical material crept into the stories, particularly in certain roles that offered possibilities for comedy. Noah had trouble getting his wife into the Ark, for instance, and had to beat her "black and blue" to the jollification of the spectators. The raging of King Herod became a comic scene, and the devils in the Last Judgment made much comic by-play as they snatched urchins from the street and carried them off to Hell Mouth. Finally, in a sheep-stealing episode in the Second Shepherds' Play in the Towneley (or Wakefield) Cycle, we have a fully developed comedy taken from the folklore of the countryside.

Still another type of drama, also religious in its beginnings, flourished in the fifteenth century. This was the morality play, an allegorical drama in which the characters are personified abstractions such as Envy, Pride, Mercy, Repentance, and the like. The conflict in this type of drama is between Good and Evil for the Soul of Man, with a variety of situations precipitated by such characters as the Seven Deadly Sins, who are opposed by the Seven Virtues.

The longest morality play (more than 3600 lines) and one of the most comprehensive in theme is *The Castle of Perseverance*, extant in a manuscript now in the Folger Library. Dating from about 1425, it exemplifies most of the situations found in this type of play. Human Kind, the hero, tempted by the World, the Flesh, and the Devil, takes refuge in the Castle of Perseverance, where he is besieged by the Seven Deadly Sins and defended by the Seven Virtues. Having grown old during a long war of words, Human Kind is tempted to leave the Castle by Covetousness, the sin peculiar to old age, but he soon repents, and after

Mercy, Truth, Justice, and Peace have delivered sermons, God the Father pardons Human Kind, and the play closes with advice to the audience to "think on your last ending."

The manuscript contains an interesting diagram showing the method of staging. A rough drawing of the Castle occupies the center of an arena with fixed scaffolds at intervals around the circumference for other scenes as they would be required. This multiple-set type of staging was common in the medieval drama and persisted to the Elizabethan period, particularly in plays at court. The audience conveniently forgot the other sets while action was taking place on the one required at the moment.

Despite the unpromising subject matter of the morality plays, they were popular in the second half of the fifteenth century and they continued in favor down to the accession of Queen Elizabeth. Indeed some belated moralities were acted during her reign, and morality play elements occasionally appear in the fully matured Elizabethan drama.

One reason for the popularity of the moralities was the amount of comedy that the actors managed to introduce. Even in so early a play as *The Castle of Perseverance* the personified abstractions were qualified slightly by the comic appearance of Belial, a devil equipped with bizarre fireworks. In the somewhat later play of *Mankind* (ca. 1475), the chief interest is in the clownery of Titivillus, the great devil, and his cohorts. At one point the comic characters Nought, New Guise, and Now-A-Days sing a travesty of a Christmas carol that must have delighted unsqueamish audiences, though a modern editor simply prints a series of dots and says, "The song is unprintable."

Mankind also illustrates the development of a professional class of actors. No longer is drama left to the auspices of clerks attached to religious establishments, to trade guilds, or to any other amateurs. As early as the last quarter of the fifteenth century town records in many parts of England show that professional actors were strolling from town to town with amusing plays in their repertories. In *Mankind* even the collection of money is made a scene of comedy as Titivillus passes his hat and solicits the audience to pay. The most popular characters in the morality plays were the devils and their assistants. From an early date these comedians were responsible for the enduring popularity of theatrical performances throughout the country. During the half-century after *Mankind* professional troupes of actors multiplied, and during the reign of Henry VIII the country swarmed with players who acted out of doors or in manor houses, castles, and town halls to the increasing delight of the spectators.

A new type of play generally called an interlude developed in this period and gained popularity. The term is not precise and scholars debate about its meaning. Interludes were usually short dramatic pieces, frequently corresponding in length to a one-act play, and were often performed in the halls of great houses, sometimes as part of the entertainment offered at a dinner for some visiting dignitary. They were secular in tone, though some interludes continued to use personified abstractions of a sort. In one of the most curious of the type, *A New Interlude and a Merry of the Nature of the Four Elements*, attributed to John Rastell and written soon after the accession of Henry VIII, we are treated to a long dramatized lesson in science.

The more popular interludes, however, abandoned teaching in favor of sheer entertainment; the best of the writers in this kind was John Heywood, who provided short comic plays and farces for Henry VIII and his noblemen. Although Heywood was not an innovator and was content to borrow from Chaucer and to adapt French farcical stories to dramatic form, his interludes have a freshness and a vitality not found in morality plays with which they competed for favor. Among the better known of Heywood's interludes is the *Play of the Weather*, in which Jupiter decides to let people choose their own weather but has to return to arbitrary methods when no two can agree on what they want. Another of his interludes, the *Four P's*, exemplifies an ancient but still popular comic device, the contest to see who can tell the biggest lie.

Many interludes and belated morality plays on a wide variety of themes survive from the first half of the sixteenth century. They include political satires like John Skelton's *Magnificence* and Sir David Lindsay's *Satire of the Three Estates*, dramatized tracts concerned with religious controversy like John Bale's *God's Promises* and other works from his vitriolic pen, and plays entirely for entertainment like those of Heywood and such embryonic comedies as *Tom Tyler and His Wife*. The secular interludes made a significant contribution to the comic tradition, and the satiric moralities gave a new dramatic purpose to the stage. The somewhat amorphous drama of the early sixteenth century stimulated the continued development of a popular taste for plays.

The players of interludes did not confine their performances to the great halls of the nobility but often took to the road. Entries in the town records of the visits of players increased markedly in the 1530's and continued through the rest of the century. Scarcely a town was too small to have a visit from a group of strolling players, who frequently described themselves as the servants of some noble lord. This designation merely meant that the nobleman had consented to become the patron of the company of players and thus to lend them his name as a measure of protection against harassment from local authorities, for players occupied a low position in the social scale and were frequently classified in civic regulations with vagabonds and sturdy beggars, a situation that prevailed until Shakespeare's lifetime.

Although relics of the old types of drama cropped up now and then throughout the sixteenth century, by the early years of Elizabeth's reign mature secular drama had come into being. The earliest type to develop was comedy, partly because of a strong native tradition of comic stage situations and partly because the new learning of the Renaissance had familiarized academic audiences with Roman comedy. It was not mere chance that one of Shakespeare's earliest plays, *The Comedy of Errors*, was an adaptation from the *Menaechmi* of Plautus, for he may have remembered the Roman dramatist from his grammar school studies. As early as 1553 Nicholas Udall, a former headmaster at Eton, composed a play on a Roman model and gave it the title of *Ralph Roister Doister*. Though it owes much to Plautine comedy, it is recognizably English in spirit. Sometime about 1553–1554, the students of Christ's College, Cambridge, saw performed in their college hall another English comedy, *Gammer Gurton's Needle* by an unidentified "Mr. S., Master of Arts." This play is still amusing enough to gain an audience.

On January 18, 1562, two years before Shakespeare was born, the young gentlemen of the Inner Temple, one of the Inns of Court where law students received their training, presented before Queen Elizabeth the first fully developed English tragedy of which we have record, *The Tragedy of Gorboduc*. The authors, Thomas Sackville, later Earl of Dorset, and Thomas Norton, modeled their play after the style of the Roman writer Seneca but they also showed a familiarity with Italian dramatists. Though Elizabethan drama had not yet reached full maturity, the forms of both tragedy and comedy were now established and the development of both types would show rapid progress during the next three decades to culminate in the work of Shakespeare and his contemporaries.

The growing demand for plays and the development of full-length drama had created such a need for professional playhouses by the late 1570's that in 1576 a cabinetmaker-turned-actor named James Burbage erected the first building in London designed exclusively for the use of players. To it he gave the descriptive name, The Theatre. Its site was east of Finsbury Fields, a park area to the northward of the city proper, on land leased from one Giles Alleyn. Burbage had been careful to choose a site just outside the jurisdiction of the city authorities yet close enough to be accessible to playgoers. Within a year another playhouse called the Curtain (from the name of the estate on which it was located) opened nearby. London now had two professional public playhouses, both outside the city's jurisdiction. It was important to be beyond the reach of the aldermen of London, for they maintained an inveterate hostility to the players on the grounds that they caused disturbances, brought together crowds that spread the plague, lured apprentices from their work, and were generally ungodly.

An early attempt to open a playhouse within the city was made by Richard Farrant, Master of the Children of Windsor Chapel. For a long time the choirboys of Windsor Chapel, like the choirboys of the Chapel Royal and St. Paul's Cathedral, had been accustomed to performing plays and to taking part in other entertainments at Court. Farrant conceived the notion of renting a hall in part of the old Blackfriars Monastery and of fitting it up for a playhouse on the pretext of rehearsing plays to be performed before the Queen. Although the Blackfriars property was within the walls of the city of London, not far from St. Paul's Cathedral, it retained its ancient exemption from the jurisdiction of the city's aldermen. Even so, Farrant did not dare try to open a public theatre but announced that it would be a "private" house though open to paying customers. This distinction between "public" and "private" theatres would persist throughout the Elizabethan period. Farrant's subterfuge worked and he opened his playhouse late in 1576 or early in 1577. Despite trouble with his landlord his theatre was a modest success until his death in 1580. The Blackfriars Theatre operated for another four years under the direction of William Hunnis, Master of the Children of the Chapel Royal, with the help for a time of John Lyly, a young novelist and dramatist. There Lyly's own plays were performed by the boy actors.

From the time of the opening of the earliest formal theatres, the public and the private houses differed widely in physical characteristics and methods of staging. The public theatres, for all we know, may have been influenced in their shape and construction by the circular arenas, like those on the Bankside across the Thames, which were used for bull- and bear-baiting. A more significant influence on their architecture, however, came from the inns. Long before the erection of regular theatres, players had used the yards of inns, and in London certain inns like the Cross Keys, the Bell, and the Bull were noted as playing places for professional actors. At the inns, the players had been accustomed to set up a stage at one end of the open courtyard and to accommodate spectators in the courtyard, which was open to the weather, and in the surrounding galleries.

The public theatres for many years retained this open-court-yard feature. There the "groundlings" for the price of a penny could stand while more opulent spectators could pay a higher fee for the privilege of sitting in the galleries. Plays were performed in the daytime, beginning in the early afternoon, for the stage had no means of artificial lighting. The public theatres could not be used in the worst weather or in the dead of winter. The private houses were enclosed halls in which plays could be given at night. They could be used in winter and in all weathers. The stage was lighted by candles, lamps, or torches. The private houses were not private in the sense of restricting audiences to any special groups but prices were higher than in the public playhouses, a fact that may have given the private houses a somewhat more select audience.

A place of recreation long popular with the citizens of London was the Bankside, an extensive area on the Southwark side of the Thames and west of what is now Southwark Cathedral. Much of this territory consisted of land that had formerly belonged to the Church or the Crown, and the aldermen of London had no authority over certain areas like the Manor of Paris Garden and the Liberty of the Clink. These and other localities beyond the jurisdiction of the city became the sites for a variety of amusements.

To the Bankside, Londoners went to witness bear- and bull-baitings at arenas erected for the purpose. After one of the old arenas collapsed in 1583 with some loss of life, a polygonal amphitheatre called the New Bear Garden was erected. Other even less savory enticements brought Londoners to the Bank-side. This area by the 1580's was attracting the interest of theatrical entrepreneurs. One of these was Philip Henslowe, a semi-literate but shrewd businessman, who in 1587 was instrumental in building the Rose playhouse, not far from the Bear Garden. Henslowe has earned the gratitude of literary historians because he kept an account book, usually described as his "Diary," which preserves much theatrical and dramatic history. His son-in-law Edward Alleyn was one of the most famous actors and stage managers of the day.

The popularity of Henslowe's Rose stimulated another businessman, Francis Langley, goldsmith, to purchase the Manor of Paris Garden, west of the site of the Rose and the Bear Garden. There he erected in 1595 a new theatre which he called the Swan. This playhouse is of interest to historians because in 1596 a Dutch priest, Johannes de Witt, saw a performance at the Swan and described the stage to a friend, Arend van Buchell, who made a drawing that is the earliest visual representation of an Elizabethan stage in use.

Because of its association with Shakespeare, the best known of the Bankside theatres is the Globe. The Globe was erected in 1599, in part from timbers of The Theatre, which the lessees, Cuthbert and Richard Burbage, moved across the Thames on December 28, 1598, to a site in Maiden Lane which they had chosen when their landlord made trouble over the lease of The Theatre. To be owners of the new playhouse, the Burbages organized a stock company consisting of themselves and four actors including Shakespeare and John Heminges, who was later to be one of the editors of the 1623 collection of Shakespeare's plays. The theatre owners, or "house-keepers" as they were then called, received half the receipts from the galleries. The acting company received the other half and all the receipts taken at the door. Thus Shakespeare, who was a house-keeper, a member of the acting company, and a dramatist, received income from all three sources. The Globe was completed in 1599 and lasted until 1613, when it burned down after a piece of wadding from a cannon fired during a performance of *Henry VIII* ignited its thatched roof. A second Globe was soon erected to take its place. The first Globe is usually pictured as octagonal on the outside, but despite the octagonal pictures in seventeenth-century views of London, some evidence points to a circular shape. The interior may have been circular. The Globe was the model for the Fortune Theatre, which Henslowe and Alleyn erected in 1600 north of the city on the opposite side of Finsbury Fields from the site of The Theatre and the Curtain. In only one essential did they change the design. The Fortune was square. The builder's specifications for the Fortune, which have survived, provide the best existing information about Elizabethan theatrical construction.

A playhouse that combined the functions of a theatre with those of an arena for bear- and bull-baiting was the Hope, erected in 1613 on the site of the Bear Garden, which had fallen into decay and was torn down to make way for the new building. The owners of the Hope were Philip Henslowe and a partner, Jacob Meade. The contract which the partners signed with the carpenter-contractor exists and throws some light on its construction. The Hope had a portable stage which could be removed when the building was required for other purposes. Over the stage area was a permanent canopy. But details of the construction of the stage and the entry doors that we would like to have are omitted. The contract specifies that the contractor is to build the Hope "of such large compass, form, wideness, and height as the playhouse called the Swan."

One other public theatre needs to be mentioned. This was the Red Bull, built about 1605 in the upper end of St. John's Street, Clerkenwell, about a mile from the old Curtain. This theatre was a favorite with London apprentices and was the place where some of the more boisterous of Elizabethan plays were performed.

Almost as important as the Globe in the history of Shakespeare's company was the second Blackfriars Theatre. In 1596 James Burbage purchased a portion of the Frater building in the rambling old Blackfriars Monastery and remodeled it for a theatre. Like the earlier Blackfriars, it was a covered hall, but it was more elaborately designed, with galleries for spectators and a better equipped stage at one end. The precise construction of the stage we do not know. Burbage leased the theatre for several years to the managers of the boy actors of the Chapel Royal, but in 1608, when the lease expired, a syndicate of seven actors, including Shakespeare, took it over. Henceforth Shakespeare's company operated the Blackfriars as a "private" theatre, but in actuality it was the playhouse regularly used by the company in winter.

Both the Blackfriars and the Globe stages, like other Elizabethan stages, were platform stages without the familiar proscenium arch of the modern theatre and of course without a curtain to come down between the acts and at the end of the play. These stages also lacked painted and movable scenery, though Elizabethan theatres made considerably more use of stage properties than we have been led to believe. The question that has aroused the greatest controversy concerns the use of an inner stage and the location of entry doors and balconies in the back of the stage. The Swan drawing shows a projecting platform stage with two doors flat against the rear wall. People, presumably spectators, are shown in the balcony over the rear stage doors. The Swan drawing also shows a canopy supported by columns over a portion of the stage and a room above that. The canopy and room above were characteristics of the public theatres. The upper room, called the "tiring house," was used for dressing and storage. From a trap door in the canopy, called the "heavens," gods and angels might descend when the action required it.

Most modern reconstructions of the stage of the Globe provide an inner stage, useful for bedroom or "study" scenes, with an upper stage above it. Both of these are closed with curtains. Stage doors open obliquely on each side with boxes or balconies above. This type of construction would best suit a scene like the balcony scene in *Romeo and Juliet*. Some scholars insist that the inner stage was too deeply recessed to permit many in the audience to see properly and that bedroom scenes must have been staged farther forward on the platform, with properties brought into use as they were required. There is no convincing evidence that the regular Elizabethan theatres were designed for performances in the round. There is much evidence for the use of an inner and upper stage with entry doors set either flat against the back or diagonally on the sides. It should be pointed out, however, that the text and directions of many plays seem to indicate the use of the main stage for scenes that editors like to relegate to an inner stage. Such use of the main stage suggests that necessary properties and equipment could be set up in advance and ignored by the audience until time for their use, as in the simultaneous-stage settings in medieval drama.

Where there are so many suggestions of both types of staging, one cannot escape the conclusion that usage varied and that stage construction in the theatres may have differed in some important details. Actors have always been skilled in improvising, and Elizabethan players had to be unusually adroit in this respect in order to adapt their plays to a wide variety of conditions: performances in the great hall at Court, in a public theatre in the daytime, in a private theatre at night, or on some makeshift stage in a country town when the plague closed the London theatres and sent them strolling through the provinces.

During Shakespeare's lifetime the principal theatres were occupied by companies of actors organized under the patronage of various titled personages. The company with which Shakespeare was associated for most of his active career had for its earliest patron, Henry Carey, Lord Hunsdon, the Lord Chamberlain. Hence they were known as the Lord Chamberlain's Men. After the accession of James I, the King became their patron and they were known as the King's Men. They were the great rivals of the Lord Admiral's Men, managed by Henslowe and Alleyn. Competitors with all the adult companies were the child actors drawn from the choirboys of the Chapel Royal, Windsor, and St. Paul's. These actors are referred to in *Hamlet* as "an aery of children, little eyases, that cry out on the top of question, and are most tyrannically clapped for't." The adult companies recruited some of their best impersonators of female roles from the children's companies, for the Elizabethan stage never employed women as players. That innovation had to wait until the Restoration.

Elizabethan acting must have been skillful and effective. To hold the attention of a restless and unruly audience in close proximity, the actors had to speak their lines well and simulate their parts to perfection. The impersonation of women's roles by boys seems to us the least satisfactory element in Elizabethan acting, but there is ample evidence that youths succeeded in these parts. No Elizabethan complained that a boy spoiled the role of Juliet.

Elizabethan audiences were not accustomed to the conventions of modern staging and did not expect realistic stage sets and colorful scenery in the professional playhouses. At Court, it is true, the masques were mounted with magnificent splendor —and at great cost—but these were spectacles for royalty, and few who witnessed plays in the theatres ever saw a masque. We have perhaps overemphasized the bareness of the Elizabethan stage and we may forget that Elizabethan producers made adequate use of stage properties. Nevertheless we are correct in insisting that Elizabethan plays were written primarily for the ear rather than the eye. It was not always necessary to stick up a board reading "The Forest of Arden" or other locale. The poetry frequently conveyed the description adequately for the audience to comprehend both the place and the atmosphere that the dramatist wanted to suggest. In the age of Shakespeare poetic drama reached its greatest height, and one can speculate as to whether Shakespeare would have written so vividly if he could have left to the carpenter and the scene painter the effects that he achieved in words.

SUGGESTED READING

Detailed discussion of the development of the English stage in the periods covered may be found in the following monumental works: E. K. Chambers, *The Medieval Stage* (2 vols., Oxford, 1903); E. K. Chambers, *The Elizabethan Stage* (4 vols., Oxford, 1923); and Gerald E. Bentley, *The Jacobean and Caroline Stage* (5 vols., Oxford, 1941–1956). Detailed treatment of the drama will be found in Karl Young, *The Drama of the Medieval Church* (2 vols., Oxford, 1933) and F. E. Schelling, *Elizabethan Drama, 1558–1642* (2 vols., Boston, 1908). Hardin Craig, *English Religious Drama of the Middle Ages* (Oxford, 1955) will be serviceable to the specialist rather than to the general reader. A sound and scholarly work is Wilhelm Creizenach, *The English Drama in the Age of Shakespeare* (London, 1916). Brief but useful are F. S. Boas, *An Introduction to Tudor Drama* (Oxford, 1933), C. F. Tucker Brooke, *The Tudor Drama* (Boston, 1911), and F. S. Boas, *An Introduction to Stuart Drama* (Oxford, 1946). E. K. Chambers, *The English Folk-Play* (Oxford, 1933) provides an excellent summary of information on this subject. Informal and readable is W. Bridges-Adams, *The Irresistible Theatre: Vol. I. From the Conquest to the Commonwealth* (London, 1957). Information about the status of actors and the organization of actor companies may be found in T. W. Baldwin, *The Organization and Personnel of the Shakespearean Company* (Princeton, 1927).

The most complete history of the Elizabethan theatres is Joseph Q. Adams, *Shakespearean Playhouses* (Boston, 1917). A useful survey of theatrical history with helpful illustrations is Allardyce Nicoll, *The Development of the Theatre* (London, 1927). Valuable for its discussion of the English heritage from the classical past is Lily B. Campbell, *Scenes and Machines on the English Stage During the Renaissance: A Classical Revival* (Cambridge, 1923). Valuable information on theatrical practices is available in George F. Reynolds, *The Staging of Elizabethan Plays at the Red Bull Theater, 1605–1625* (New York, 1940). An elaborate discussion of the construction of the Globe Theatre will be found in John C. Adams, *The Globe Playhouse: Its Design and Equipment* (Cambridge, Mass., 1942). A model of the Globe made by Mr. Adams and Mr. Irwin Smith is on exhibition in the Folger Library, and a description with scale drawings and pictures is available in Irwin Smith, *Shakespeare's Globe Playhouse: A Modern Reconstruction* (New York, 1956). Another scholar's conception of the construction of the Globe is C. Walter Hodges, *The Globe Restored: A Study of the Elizabethan Theatre* (London, 1953). Students interested in the practical aspects of staging a play on an Elizabethan type of stage will find helpful Richard Southern, *The Open Stage and the Modern Theatre in Research and Practice* (London, 1953).

The literature on the physical aspects of the Elizabethan theatres and the influence of structural features on the drama is extensive and some of it is controversial. An informative book is W. J. Lawrence, *The Physical Conditions of the Elizabethan Public Playhouse* (Cambridge, Mass., 1927). Mr. Lawrence was the author of various articles and monographs giving his views of stage construction. Useful also is Thornton Shirley Graves, *The Court and the London Theatres During the Reign of Queen Elizabeth* (Menasha, Wis., 1913). Collateral information is available in Alfred Harbage, *Shakespeare's Audience* (New York, 1941); Arthur C. Sprague, *Shakespeare and the Audience* (Cambridge, Mass., 1935) and *Shakespearian Players and Performances* (Cambridge, Mass., 1953). Further bibliographical clues to a study of the theatres are available in Allardyce Nicoll, "Studies in the Elizabethan Stage Since 1900," *Shakespeare Survey I* (1948), 1–16.

One of the most concise and helpful discussions of the vexed problems concerning the Elizabethan stage is to be found in a lecture by F. P. Wilson, delivered at the University of Amsterdam and published in *Neophilologus* as No. 28 of the Allard Pierson Lectures under the title of "The Elizabethan Theatre" (Groningen, 1955).

A Note on the Views of London and the Theatres

The question of the validity of the various contemporary "Views of London" by engravers and map-makers is too complicated for discussion in such a brief space. The matter is treated in detail in I. A. Shapiro, "The Bankside Theatres: Early Engravings," *Shakespeare Survey I* (1948), 25–37, and by Irwin Smith, *Shakespeare's Globe Playhouse*, (New York, 1956), pp. 14–28. Mr. Shapiro argues from the evidence in the engravings that the Globe was round on the outside. Mr. Smith, from similar evidence in addition to other evidence presented by J. C. Adams, argues that the Globe was octagonal. Some views show it as an octagonal structure; others show a round exterior. Since artists and engravers were free in their interpretation of topographical details and borrowed from one another, one can never be certain of the accuracy of these illustrations.

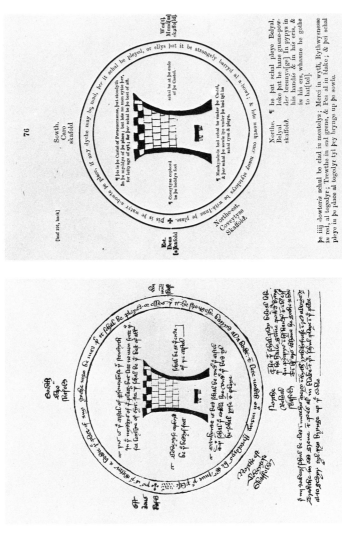

[leaf 191, back]

Sowth.
Caro
skafold

West. Mundus[us] skafold.

¶ This is þe Castel of Perseueraunce, þat stondyth In þe myddys of þe place; but lete no men sytte þer, for lettynge of syt; for þer schal be þe best of all.

schal be at þe ende of þe Castel.

þat it schal be pleyed, or ellys þat it be strongly barryd al a-bowt; & lete nowth ouer-many stytelerys be with-inne þe place.

¶ Þis is þe watyr a-bowte þe place, if any dyche may be mad, þer it schal be pleyed;

¶ Coueytyse copbord be þe beddys feet

¶ Mankynde is bed schal vnder þe castel, & þer schal þe sowle lye vnder þe bed tyl he schal ryse & pleye.

Est. Deus [us]kafold.

Northe-est. Coveytyse. Skafold.

Northe. Belyal skafold.

¶ He þat schal pleye Belyal, loke þat he haue gunne-powder brennynge[1ge] In pypys in his handis & in his eris, & in his ers, whanne he gothe to bat[tel].

þe iiij dowteris schul be clad in mentelys; Merci in wyth, Rythwysnesse in red, al togedyr; Trewthe in sad grene, & Pes al in blake; & þei schal pleye in þe place al togedyr tyl þey brynge vp þe sowle.

Plate 1. (Left) A fifteenth-century sketch showing the stage sets for *The Castle of Persever-ance.* From a manuscript in the Folger Library. *(Right)* Manuscript notes of *The Castle of*

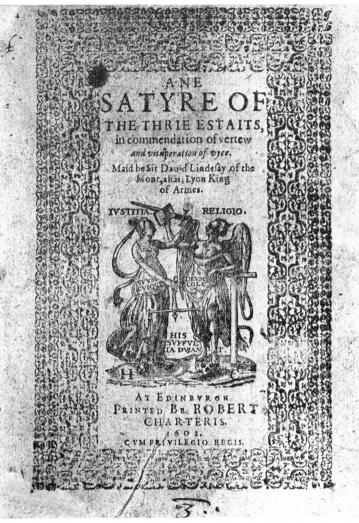

ANE
SATYRE OF
THE THRIE ESTAITS,
in commendation of vertew
and vituperation of vyce.

Maid be Sir Dauid Lindesay of the
Mont, alias, Lyon King
of Armes.

IVSTITIA.   RELIGIO.

SVVM
CVIQVE   DEVM
COLE

HIS
SVFFVL
TA DVAN

AT EDINBVRGH
PRINTED BE ROBERT
CHARTERIS.
1602.
CVM PRIVILEGIO REGIS.

Plate 2. Title page of the 1602 edition of Sir David Lindsay's *Satire of the Three Estates.* Courtesy of the Huntington Library.

THE
TRAGEDIE OF GORBODVC,
whereof three Actes were wrytten by
Thomas Nortone, and the two laste by
Thomas Sackuyle.

Sett forthe as the same was shewed before the
Q*VENES* most excellent Maiestie, in her highnes
Court of Whitehall, the.xviij.day of January,
Anno Domini. 1561. By the Gentlemen
of Thynner Temple in London.

IMPRYNTED AT LONDON
in Fleteftrete, at the Signe of the
Faucon by *William Griffith*: And are
to be sold at his Shop in Sainde
Dunftones Churchyarde in
the West of *London*.

Anno, 1565. Septemb.22.

Plate 3. Title page of the earliest English tragedy.

Plate 4. Portrait of Richard Burbage.   From an engraving in the
Folger Library of the painting in Dulwich College.

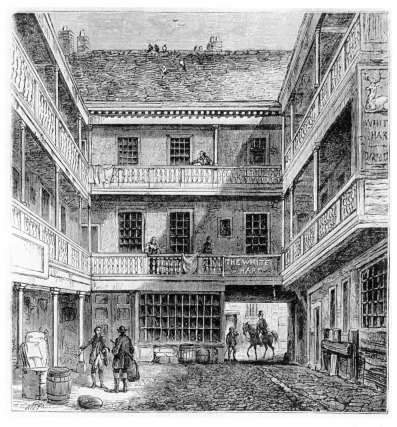

Plate 5. The yard of the White Hart Inn. Before the erection of professional playhouses, the courtyards of inns like this provided a place where
actors could set up temporary stages. Spectators stood in the yard or sat in
the galleries.

Within the image, the following labels appear:

tectum

porticus

mimorum ædes

orchestra

ingressus

proscænium

planities siue arena.

quntum sed dispari et structura, bestiarum romuctab.
oni destinatum, in quo multi ursi, tauri, et stupenda
magnitudinis canes, diuersis cautis et septis aluntur, qui
ad

Plate 6. An interior sketch of the Swan playhouse, made by Arend van Buchell from information supplied by Johannes de Witt in 1596.

133

Plate 7. An Elizabethan playhouse stage as reconstructed in the Folger Library by the architect, Paul Cret. This stage is supposed to simulate the characteristic construction in the public theatres but it does not attempt to imitate any particular playhouse. Details of the balconies, inner stage, and the placement of entry doors are controversial.

134

Plate 8. The Bear Garden, the Rose, and the Globe. A detail from
the background of an equestrian portrait of King James by Delaram.
The view of London was supposed to represent the city as it was
when James came to the throne in 1603.

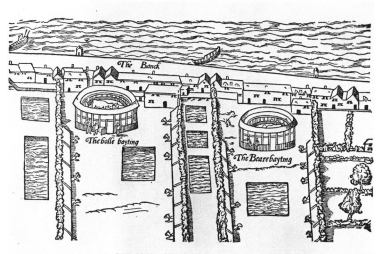

THE BEAR- AND BULL–BAITING RINGS

These "rings" later gave place to the Bear Garden. (From Agas's *Map of London*, representing the city as it was about 1560.)

Plate 9. Bear and Bull Rings. From Agas' *Map of London* as reproduced in J. Q. Adams, *Shakespearean Playhouses* (Boston, 1917), p. 123.

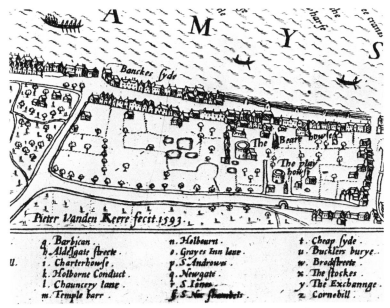

Pieter Vanden Keere fecit 1593

	q. Barbican.	*n. Holbourn.*	*t. Cheap fyde.*
	h Aldefgate ftreete.	*o. Grayes Inn lane.*	*u. Bucklers burye.*
u.	*i. Charterhoufe.*	*p. S. Androwes.*	*w. Brodftreete.*
	k. Holborne Conduct.	*q. Newgate.*	*x. The ftockes.*
	l. Chauncery lane.	*r. S. Iones.*	*y. The Exchannge.*
	m. Temple barr.	*ſ. S. Nex ſhambets.*	*z. Cornehill.*

Plate 10. John Norden's Map. Reproduced from *Speculum Britanniae* (1593).

Plate 11. Portrait of Edward Alleyn. From an engraving
in the Folger Library of the portrait in Dulwich College.

The Swan

Visscher Delineavit

Plate 12. The Swan playhouse. A detail from Visscher's engraving of 1616, reproduced from the copy belonging to the London Topographical Society.

139

Plate 13. The Bear Garden and the Globe. A detail from Visscher's engraving of 1616, reproduced from the copy belonging to the London Topographical Society.

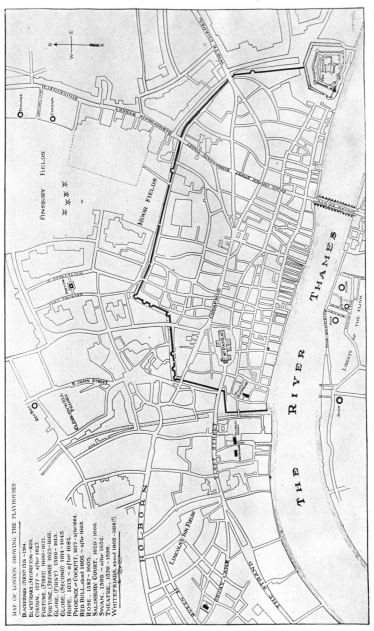

MAP OF LONDON SHOWING THE PLAYHOUSES

BLACKFRIARS, (FIRST) 1576 - 1584.
BLACKFRIARS, (SECOND) 1596 - 1655.
CURTAIN, 1577 - after 1627.
FORTUNE, (FIRST) 1600 - 1621.
FORTUNE, (SECOND) 1623 - 1661.
GLOBE, (FIRST) 1599 - 1613.
GLOBE, (SECOND) 1614 - 1645.
HOPE, 1613 - after 1682.
PHOENIX or COCKPIT, 1617 - after 1664.
RED BULL, about 1605 - after 1663.
ROSE, 1587 - 1605.
SALISBURY COURT, 1629 - 1666.
SWAN, 1595 - after 1632.
THEATRE, 1576 - 1598.
WHITEFRIARS, about 1605 - 1614 (?).

141

Plate 14. Sites of the playhouses. The heavy black line indicates the old wall of the City of London. From J. Q. Adams, *Shakespearean Playhouses* (Boston, 1917).

Plate 15. The stage of the Globe as illustrated in the John C. Adams model.

Plate 16. The title page of William Alabaster's *Roxana* (1632), showing a platform stage with what appears to be a curtained inner stage.

Plate 17. The Swan (39), the Bear Garden (38), and the Globe (37); St. Paul's Cathedral, as it was before the Great Fire of 1666, appears in the background. From Merian's View of London, 1638. From a copy in the Folger Library.

144

Music in Elizabethan England

By Dorothy E. Mason

ANY account of Elizabethan music, however brief, should note the fact that musical development in this age was part of a great intellectual and social movement that influenced the whole of life. The same forces that produced writers like Sir Philip Sidney, Edmund Spenser, William Shakespeare, Ben Jonson, John Donne, and Francis Bacon also produced musicians like William Byrd, Thomas Morley, Orlando Gibbons, Thomas Weelkes, and John Dowland. Artistic greatness was in the very air along with that exciting urge for adventure that was to widen the geographical horizons of the world, and men's spiritual concepts as well.

The great Queen, of course, provided an inspiration for the best efforts of Englishmen, whatever their aims and activities. For music she was the ideal patroness. No mean musician herself—she was an accomplished performer on the virginals—she aided her favorite art immensely in every way possible, bestowing her favors on the singers in chapel and court, on the musicians in public and private theatrical performances. To the great composers of her time she was particularly gracious and helpful.

When Elizabeth died in 1603, there was in England a large and active group of composers (including Byrd, Gibbons, Dowland, Pilkington, Weelkes, and Este among many others) who were destined to continue with brilliance the traditions of the sixteenth century well through the first quarter of the seventeenth. On the other hand, Thomas Tallis, whose music still remains a valuable heritage, had died in 1585, an aged man whose professional life had begun as a gentleman of the Chapel Royal of Henry VIII. Thus, we must keep in mind that the general term "Elizabethan music" is a broad one, covering a full century of distinguished musical activity.

This long chronological span means, of course, that there was no sudden outburst of song or of proficiency in producing or performing it in Elizabeth's age. Singing was an integral part of English life long before the beautifully planned and well-sung madrigals and airs had become a common heritage. We have record of the people, thousands of them, expressing their religious or patriotic fervor in song. In 1560, Bishop Jewel wrote to Peter Martyr:

A change appears more visible among the people; which nothing promotes more than the inviting them to sing Psalms. . . . Sometimes at Paul's Cross, there will be 6000 people singing together.*

Years later, long after the age with which we are now concerned was past, great throngs gathered in York Minster when that city was being besieged during the Civil War in 1644 and, according to Thomas Mace (*Musicks Monument*, 1676),

Always before the sermon the whole congregation sang a psalm, together with the choir and the organ. . . . When that vast concording unity of the whole congregational chorus came, as I may say, thundering in . . . I was so transported, and rapt up into high contemplations, that there was no room left in my whole man, *viz.* body, soul, and spirit, for anything below divine and heavenly raptures.

This glance at a century of communal enthusiasm for expression of devotion in song is presented only to emphasize the brilliance which Elizabeth's own age achieved, when all England was musically awake and literate. It is to this England we now turn.

We shall begin with a very brief survey of the music of the Church. There was a gradual transition from the services of the Roman Catholic Church to the final forms adopted for worship in the Church of England. The Roman plainsong was simplified; the Mass, in adapted form, became the service of Holy Communion. English was substituted for Latin, so that divine service might have meaning for all the people. The music of the Church of England consisted mainly of anthems, morning

---

* The spelling of this and all following quotations has been modernized.

and evening services [Plate 2], musical settings of the responses, and the litany. The anthems, while still contrapuntal in character, became more complex, though gloriously free-spirited and inspiring. Some of the finest of these were written by Christopher Tye, Orlando Gibbons, William Byrd, and Thomas Tallis. The Elizabethan settings of the Psalms which replaced the Catholic hymns were very moving and are still sung. During Elizabeth's reign, at least twenty-two psalters were published based on the metrical versions of the Psalms made by Sternhold and Hopkins alone, the first of them published with music in 1560. Distinguished Elizabethan composers of these settings included Robert Parsons, Thomas Tallis, John Cosyn, and William Damon [Plate 3]. With such inspiring music provided for them, we can understand the satisfaction that psalm-singing must have given Elizabeth's church-going subjects.

The chief glory of Elizabeth's age was, however, the development of its secular vocal music, which reached a high degree of artistry. It did so, of course, because the Elizabethans received perhaps even more enjoyment from singing together socially than they did from singing psalms together in church. An educated person of the time was expected to perform music more than just fairly well. Thomas Morley, "Bachelor of Musicke and Gentleman of Her Majesty's Royal Chapel," in his famous book on music and the teaching thereof, *A Plaine and Easie Introduction to Practicall Musicke* (1597), relates an imaginary conversation which took place at a supper party [Plate 4]:

Among the rest of the guests, by chance, master Aphron came thither also, who falling to discourse of music, was in an argument so quickly taken up and hotly pursued by Eudoxus and Calergus . . . as in his own art he was overthrown. But he still sticking in his opinion, the two gentlemen requested me to examine his reasons, and confute them. But I refusing and pretending ignorance, the whole company condemned me of discourtesy, being fully persuaded that I had been as skillful in that art as they took me to be learned in others. But supper being ended, and music books, according to the custom being brought to the table, the mistress of the house presented me with a part, earnestly requesting me to sing. But when, after many excuses, I protested unfainedly that I could not, every one began to wonder. Yea, some whispered to others, demanding how I was brought up.

We see implied here the prevalent idea that an educated man should not only be able to take his part in a madrigal, but also to know the niceties of musical theory. Moreover, Morley's evidence is supported by that of Henry Peacham, who wrote in *The Compleat Gentleman* in 1622 that one of the fundamental qualities of a gentleman was to be able "to sing your part sure, and at the first sight, withall, to play the same upon your viol, or the exercise of the lute," thus adding instrumental accomplishments to Morley's two earlier requirements.

About the musical interests of these people we have many other authentic reports. Contemporary records of all kinds, from royal account-books to household accounts, public documents, and private inventories, assure us that music, well learned and capably performed, was widespread throughout the land and an important part of everyday Elizabethan life. In addition to the masterpieces left by the greatest composers, we still have extant literally hundreds of catches, glees, ballads, street songs, and vendors' cries. They were sung or hummed on the street and played, with complicated variations, on the virginals by the well-trained sons and daughters of the higher gentry and nobility—all attesting to a land that was highly articulate in music.

The late Canon Fellowes, in his book on *The English Madrigal*, describes one of the great houses, of which there were many in England at this time, Hengrave Hall near Bury St. Edmunds. It was not by any means one of the largest or most beautiful, but it was ample and comfortable, having been built by Sir Thomas Kytson, a wealthy wool merchant who had a great trade with Antwerp. After two generations this family, thanks to shrewd marriages, occupied a place of social prominence and patronized the arts. The second Sir Thomas was particularly interested in music and encouraged performances in his house. Many documents concerning this household have been preserved and shed light on customs that were by no means confined to Hengrave Hall. One of the inventories made after the death of the younger Sir Thomas in 1602 reveals an astonishing music "establishment." There was "the chamber where the musicians play," and in this room were chests of instruments and many song books, English, Italian, and one from Spain. In all, some fifty-four books are listed, mainly of part-songs, for three, four, five, and six voices. There are also a few books of dance music: corrantos, pavans, and galliards. This is a remarkable list, particularly of song books, for most of the English madrigals had not as yet been published. Also on the list we find some forty instruments owned by the family, including twelve viols, seven recorders, four lutes, five virginals, various brasses and woodwinds, and two "great organs."

To have use for such a great number of instruments implies a fairly large group of players resident at the Hall. Their number would be supplemented on special occasions by professionals from the neighboring town of Bury St. Edmunds, by talented retainers, and now and then by guests who might have studied Morley's book.

Master of the music at Hengrave was none other than the famous madrigal composer, John Wilbye, who held his post there for many years. With such a leader, and with the library of at least fifty-four books, a goodly number of them being part-books, there must have been much singing—and good singing, too. Wilbye's music is not easy to perform. Neither were the Italian madrigals which were also there. Much of the music, particularly Wilbye's, was probably in manuscript and written for the Hall [Plate 5]. Wilbye's *First Set of English Madrigals*, published in 1598, was dated from the Austin Friars, the London home of the Kytsons, and dedicated to Sir Thomas Cavendish of Welbeck, who was the husband of Elizabeth, the eldest daughter of Sir Thomas. His second set, published in 1609, was dedicated to Lady Arabella Stuart, another relative of the Kytson family and an occasional visitor at Hengrave, where Wilbye doubtless met her.

This close family intimacy may explain one of the reasons for the charming freshness, the spontaneity, the verve of Wilbye's as well as of other English madrigals, qualities which were lacking in their continental counterpart, the Italian madrigal, upon which the English was modelled. The madrigal, which was a secular, lyrical poem in the native language, was set in the form of an *a capella* song, originally for three voices, and afterwards for four, five, or even more. This contrapuntal form was one which would naturally appeal to the English taste and to the English love for communal performance. The composers adopted what could have become a very artificial and sophisticated style, as it often was across the Channel, but they displayed so much enthusiasm and spontaneity, and were so greatly influenced by the lively spirit surrounding them, that the form became in their hands almost a native expression. Moreover, they seldom followed their Italian and French models in setting the songs to serious poetry, but instead chose popular verse, some of it based on matters of topical interest, such as Weelkes' madrigal called "The Andalusian Merchant," which reflects the common Elizabethan interest in travel and adventure, an eagerness expressed even in song:

> That Andalusian merchant that returns,
> Laden with cochineal and China dishes,
> Reports in Spain, how strangely Fogo burns,
> Amidst an ocean full of flying fishes.
> These things seem wondrous, yet more wondrous I,
> Whose heart with fear doth freeze, with love doth fry.

The later canzonets, airs, and ballads were far more consciously literary, and for these we find verses from England's great poets of the day: Sidney, Spenser, Shakespeare, Jonson, Donne, Raleigh, and others.

The terms "ayre" (air) and "canzonet" we often find used for the same sort of song—a composition for a single voice, with other voices or, later, instruments supporting it [Plate 6]. While the contrapuntal nature of the madrigal made it difficult to set more than one verse of a poem in any one song, the air was sufficiently simple in structure to permit many verses to be sung through without difficulty. For Hengrave Hall and like places, for groups of skilled performers or accomplished amateurs, the madrigal was a highly enjoyable form of entertainment. But at the turn of the century, when many poets were producing lyrics that fairly sang by themselves, it was inevitable that the more simple form of musical expression should become popular.

One of the most famous of the composers of airs was John Dowland, a singer *par excellence* and a lutenist without rival in his day. Of him Richard Barnfield wrote in his sonnet, "To his friend Maister R. L. in praise of Musique and Poetrie":

> Dowland to thee is dear, whose heavenly touch
> Upon the lute doth ravish human sense.

As may be deduced from the list of musical instruments at Hengrave Hall, the most popular ones were probably the lute, virginals, and the family of viols. These had already enjoyed a long popularity, for records tell us that Henry VIII had a large collection of them. The lute was a loved instrument among all classes, either played as a solo instrument for simple affecting airs or used in accompanying or supporting a solo voice. They were of various shapes and sizes, the commonest—the treble lute—being shaped like a large mandolin, with six strings, the five lower attached in pairs, making eleven in all. The strings were fretted and played by being plucked with the fingers of the right hand. The popularity of the instrument lasted until the very end of the seventeenth century [Plate 7].

The viols, too, were used both for solo and accompaniment. A chest of them, about which we read so much, consisted of two treble, two tenor, and two bass viols. If concerted music was played on a family, or chest, of viols, it was called a "consort." If some other instrument, such as a recorder or lute, was brought into the combination, it was known as a "broken consort," or "broken music" [Plate 8]. Viols had six strings, were fretted like the lute, and played with a bow [Plate 7]. The cittern, a kind of country cousin of the lute, usually had four wire strings and was played with a plectrum, or quill [Plate 9].

The virginal, one of the earliest of keyboard instruments, was rectangular in shape and had a keyboard of about four octaves, with strings plucked with a quill instead of being struck with a hammer like our modern piano [Plate 10]. It was queen of instruments during Elizabeth's reign, probably because she was known to be a very accomplished performer. She evidently took great pride in being so, for even in her later years diplomats were sometimes put to it to make the proper flattering remarks about the Queen's performance, even if it meant demeaning their own sovereign ladies.

Finally, we must at least mention the recorders, flutes, flageo-lets, rebecs (three-stringed "fiddles"), tabors (tiny drums), fifes, drums, and sackbuts (trombones)—all popular instruments since early days, and we hear of them repeatedly on the Eliz-abethan stage [Plates 1 and 9].

While much music was undoubtedly written for all these instruments (we still possess much, and over the centuries much more has undoubtedly been lost), yet performers could play from the part-song books just as well. Madrigals for voices often became the music for viols and lutes. Their composers even suggested such arrangements on the title-pages of their com-positions: Michael Este, for example, notes his songs as "apt for viols and voices."

The printing of these part-song books "apt" for various com-binations of voices and instruments should not be overlooked. As shown in Plates 6 and 11, the large folio volumes were so printed, and the parts so arranged, that several persons could sing or play from one book. For example, a work in four parts would usually be arranged thus: On the left-hand page was the cantus part, which, if it was also to be sung to the lute, would have the special lute tablature beneath it. On the right-hand page the three parts were arranged so that the performers could sit or stand at three sides of the table: at the bottom of the page was the tenor part; at the top, facing the other way, the altus; between them, and facing both, was the bassus. In some books, such as Leighton's [Plate 11], alternative instruments were definitely suggested by the composers themselves, making a "broken consort" performance. The polyphony of the part-song easily lent itself to the light-toned instruments of the period, the viols, lutes, and gambas.

In 1599 Thomas Morley published one of the first instrumental ensemble compositions, the *Consort Lessons*, written for six instruments: treble lute, pandora (a kind of lute), cittern, bass viol, flute, and treble viol. Thomas Weelkes, Orlando Gibbons, Tobias Hume, and John Dowland were also among the prominent writers of vocal music who used their polyphonic gifts in the writing of fantasias for instruments and voices.

Weelkes and Gibbons, along with Richard Deering, really had some fun with the form, too, for together they incorporated into one such fantasy more than one hundred and fifty cries and songs of the itinerant vendors on London's streets. All the individual songs concerned themselves with such matters as "New oysters, new mussels, my lily-white mussels," "Hot mutton pies," and "Cherry-ripe, strawberry ripe." Weelkes, amusingly enough, added a rather lugubrious "Alleluia" to all his pieces in this delightful collection.

This could be called "art music" with popular elements, since it was done with consummate skill by England's finest and most accomplished musicians and composers. The real "folk music," performed on the streets along with the cries of the vendors, by ballad-singers, itinerant fiddlers, and others less accomplished, was another thing, no less interesting. Great numbers of ballad texts were printed with directions to be sung to such-and-such an air, "Greensleeves," for example. These ballads were enormously popular, for references to them are constant in all types of written records, from pulpit to theatre. We are reminded of Mrs. Ford in *The Merry Wives of Windsor* [II.i.55 ff.]:

I shall think the worst of fat men as long as I have an eye to make difference of men's liking. And yet he would not swear; prais'd women's modesty, and gave such orderly and well-behaved reproof to all uncomeliness that I would have sworn his disposition would have gone to the truth of his words. But they do no more adhere and keep place together than the Hundred Psalm to the tune of "Greensleeves."

In a manuscript commonplace book once belonging to John Dowland, there is a version of this ballad set for lute, another indication of its popularity amongst all people at the time [Plate 12]. Many ballads and other forms of then-current "popular" music are still accessible to us in Thomas Ravenscroft's collections: *Pammelia* (1609), *Deuteromelia* (1609), and *Melismata* (1611).

Since the printing of complex musical texts had not reached so high an art in England as on the Continent, most of the enormous amount of virginal music written at this time was circulated in manuscript. Two notable exceptions are the *Parthenia, or Maydenhead of the first musicke that euer was printed for the Virginals. Composed by three famous Masters William Byrd, Dr. John Bull and Orlando Gibbons Gentilmen of his Maiesties most Illustrious Chappell,* printed from engraved plates in 1611; and its companion volume, *Parthenia Inviolata or Mayden-Musicke for the Virginall and Bass-Violl. Selected out of the Compositions of the most famous in that Arte by Robert Hole and consecrated to all true Louers & Practicers thereof.* In recent years much more of this interesting music for a very beautiful instrument is being printed for the first time and regaining a deserved admiration.

Music had an important part in the early dramas. The mystery and miracle plays popular in England in the fourteenth century were still being acted occasionally early in Elizabeth's reign and were another means of preserving and continuing the folk-art of the people. Early interludes also continued the tradition, for many of them specifically indicated the use of songs and even particular instruments. John Redford, musician and playwright (*ca.*1485–*ca.*1545), in his position as choir-master of St. Paul's, London, would have been in charge of many of the Latin plays presented by the choir-boys for visiting dignitaries. An extant manuscript of his morality, *Wyt and Science,* contains the words of three different songs. At the end of the play is a further note: "Here come in four with viols and sing 'remembrance,' and at the last quire [verse] all make cur[t]sey and so go forth singing." At the end of another morality play,

Redford again uses music: "Here the[y] sing 'Hey nonny, nonny,' and so go forth singing." We meet that particular refrain long afterwards in Elizabethan ballets.

In 1562 the famous tragedy of *Gorboduc* was acted in the Hall of the Inner Temple on Twelfth Night, and the play was produced with musical effects supplied by viols, cornets, oboes, drums, and flutes. This was no exceptional presentation. Music like this was expected in a play, for it was an important and integral part of everyday life even this early, and actors were already well equipped, musically, to depict that life upon the stage.

With the growth of interest in theatrical performances, with recognized stage practices, there came into being certain accepted standards of stage music as well. The Theatre, built in 1576, and its neighboring houses were repertory theatres, producing a different play each acting day. As we learn from Henslowe's *Diary,* in a typical two-weeks' schedule for February, 1596, the Admiral's Men presented ten plays on twelve acting days, each play employing from ten to twenty musical effects. In the public theatres, music was probably placed in the same category as the stage properties, such as costumes and the machines, to be used whenever required by the dramatic texts. Records show that in 1598 the Lord Admiral's Company owned three trumpets, one drum, one treble viol, one bass viol, one pandora, one sackbut, three tymbrels (small drums), and bells. Considering the demands of the texts of the plays and the instruments in each theatre, there must have been a need for at least eight musicians in each company.

From the play texts themselves we learn that music of certain kinds had specific meanings for the Elizabethan audience. When a king entered or left the stage, hoyboyes (oboes) sounded. A drum beaten on or off stage could indicate a marching army. For each phase of the stage battles there was special music—such as "alarum," "parley," "retreat," played by trumpet and drum, and sometimes even by the flute. Likewise, certain dramatic situations had corresponding musical formulas. It is evident that these were taken from everyday Elizabethan life.

Trumpets and kettledrums were the signs apparent of the approach of Elizabeth and her court and thus heralded the Queen on all state occasions. Parenthetically, it may be stated here that Elizabeth loved the sound of drums and trumpets, and as early as 1571 maintained eighteen trumpeters and six sackbut players in her household. Every day the signal for dinner was given by twelve trumpets and a pair of drums, which "made the hall ring for half an hour together."

Shakespeare, along with his fellow-dramatists, called for much music in his plays. One critic writes: "Shakespeare knew his audience well, and it cannot be coincidence that the two plays whose titles imply that he was giving it what it wanted contain the most songs. *As You Like It* and *Twelfth Night, or What You Will* contain no fewer than six songs each." Two

Plate 13 for Morley's setting of this song; it may have been the version sung in the play]. Ophelia sings in *Hamlet,* Desdemona in *Othello.* Robert Johnson's settings of "Full fathom five" and "Where the bee sucks" from the *Tempest* may have been written for the first performance of the play, although they were not published until 1660 by Dr. John Wilson [Plates 14 and 15]. "What shall he have that kill the deere," a catch sung in *As You Like It* [IV.ii.10–7], comes down to us recorded in a seventeenth century manuscript book of catches [Plate 16].

It must be stressed that all of these songs were not what we now might call incidental music, but that the playwrights used music as a deliberate device to suggest moods, provide atmosphere, prepare the spectators for coming action, and emphasize dramatic situations. Of course, it supplied extraneous entertainment as well.

Our most important generalization to be made about this constant and significant use of music is that the English theatre was musical because the English audience was musically literate, delighted in music, and demanded it. We must remember, too, that the love of music in the plays had received an impetus from the boy choirs, particularly those of the Chapel Royal. It had been customary from early times for the Children of the

Chapel, as they were called, to take part in dramatic entertainment. By the 1570's enterprising Masters of the Chapel Royal were using the boys almost as professional players, and it was logical to emphasize music when the actors themselves were so well equipped to provide such entertainment. Henry VIII and Elizabeth often availed themselves of the talents of the boys of their Chapel, and in many a record we find in the court orders to the Lord Chamberlain the words, "The children of the Chapel to come before the Queen at dinner with a carol."

In 1602 a German visitor, Frederic Gershow, touring England with his master the Duke of Stettin, was greatly impressed by the Queen's Children of the Chapel, and wrote:

The Queen maintains a number of young boys who are required to devote themselves earnestly to the art of singing, and to learn to perform on various sorts of musical instruments, and at the same time to carry on their studies. These boys have their special preceptors in all the various arts, and in particular excellent instructors in music. . . . For a whole hour preceding the play one listens to a delightful musical entertainment on organs, lutes, and flutes.

In addition to these boys, Elizabeth had at her disposal for special occasions, or for special music at theatrical performances at court, many other well-trained London musicians, including the "musicians of the city," or the Lord Mayor's Waits. It is interesting to note that Thomas Morley's *Consort Lessons* (1599), previously mentioned, and one of the few collections of instrumental pieces in print this early, was dedicated to the Lord Mayor and his Waits. They must have been a varied and accomplished group, considering the variety of instruments called for in Morley's score. His dedication is both flattering and significant:

As the ancient custom of this most honourable and renowned city hath been ever to retain and maintain excellent and expert musicians to adorn your Honour's favours, feasts, and solemn meetings; to those your Lordship's Waits, after commending these my labours to your honourable patronage, I recommend the same to your servants' careful and skillful handling, that the wants of exquisite harmony, apparent, being left unsupplied for brevity of proportions, may be excused by their melodious additions, purposing hereafter to give them more testimony of my love towards them.

This means that Morley had indicated the general progressions he wished, and the ornamentation of that very simply indicated melody was left up to the skill and good taste of the various performers. Perhaps they had studied his book, and he felt confident of their ability to do his great work simple justice.

In public theatres music was often performed after the play in addition to such music as may have been a part of the drama. We have an eyewitness, one Paul Hentzner, a Brandenburg jurist, who visited London in 1598 and reported:

Without the city there are some theatres where English actors represent almost every day tragedies and comedies to very numerous audiences; these are concluded with music, variety of dances, and the excessive applause of those that are present.

One of the most popular Elizabethan entertainers was Shakespeare's fellow-actor, Will Kemp, who was famous both in England and on the Continent for his jigs, which were part dance, part pantomime, part songs. Rude things they probably were, but they appealed to the sense of humor of a people who also delighted in bear-baiting and the performances of the dancing horse. After the tours of the English companies on the Continent, many imitations of English plays and jigs appeared there, particularly in Germany. The vogue for them lasted long in England. In one of the late editions (*ca.*1725) of the mid-seventeenth century popular *Dancing Master*, first published by John Playford, there is a dance, with the music, entitled "Kemp's jigg" [Plate 17]. These jigs and suchlike entr'actes gave to the general public the variety of amusement and spectacle which private audiences enjoyed in a far more elegant, rich, and subtle fashion in the masques.

The masque was a form of courtly entertainment which had the characteristics of both play and opera. Its plot was unfolded in song and spoken words, with singing by solo voices and chorus and much intricate dancing, all performed against a gorgeously decorative background, with complicated machinery and effective tableaux designed by the greatest artists of the day. The beginnings of the masque go back to the fourteenth century, but its real development started in the last years of Elizabeth and culminated during the reigns of her two successors. Very little of the music written for the masques has survived in print—probably much of it was never printed, since the performances were given only privately at the court or in noblemen's houses. Thomas Campion's *Description of a Maske: Presented in the Banqueting Roome at Whitehall, on St. Stephens night* . . . (1614) is one of the few printed masques that have come down to us [Plates 18 and 19].

In concluding this brief description of Elizabethan music, it is fitting that we pay tribute to the great Queen who was an ever-constant inspiration to the musicians of her time. We like to think of Elizabeth on one of her "progresses," say the one at Elvetham in 1591, when her host, Lord Hertford, provided music for her pleasure.

On the day of the Queen's departure, there was another "song of six parts with the music of an exquisite consort," to words beginning *Eliza is the fairest Queen.* During this performance, "the Queen of Fairies . . . danced and sang before Her Majesty," who insisted on the performance being repeated three times over, and "called for divers Lords and Ladies to behold it." And finally, "as Her Majesty passed through the park gate, there was a consort of musicians hidden in a bower, to whose playing this ditty of *Come again,* was sung, with excellent division, by two that were cunning. . . . As this song was sung, Her Majesty, notwithstanding the great rain, stayed her coach and pulled off her mask, giving great thanks."

When Elizabeth was old and pathetic and failing, two years before her death, twenty-three of the greatest composers of her realm paid her a touching tribute; together they composed that magnificent set of madrigals in her honor, *The Triumphes of Oriana* (1601), each song ending with the refrain, "Long live Oriana," a lyrical echo of the shouted *vivat's* that had rung in her ears when she ascended the throne forty-three long years before [Plate 20].

SUGGESTED READING

Sir George Grove, *Dictionary of Music and Musicians* (5th edition, ed. Eric Blum, 9 vols., London, 1954) contains invaluable information about music, musical instruments, development of musical forms, and composition, as well as interesting biographical material for the Tudor period.

Morrison Comegys Boyd, *Elizabethan Music and Musical Criticism* (Philadelphia, 1940); an indispensable book for this period with its broad study of the development of Tudor music in all its manifestations.

Edmund H. Fellowes, an authority on Elizabethan music, has written many books on the period, including *English Cathedral Music* (London, 1941); *The English Madrigal* (London, 1925); *The English Madrigal Composers* (Oxford, 1921); *The English Madrigal School* (36 vols., London, 1913–24); *The English School of Lutenist Song Writers* (16 vols., London, 1920–23); *Orlando Gibbons and his Family* (London, 1951); *William Byrd* (London, 1936).

William H. G. Flood, *Early Tudor Composers* (London, 1925); useful for the early years of the sixteenth century (1485–1555).

For music of the theatre, Sir Frederick Bridge, *Shakespearean Music in the Plays and Early Operas* (London, 1923); George H. Cowling, *Music on the Shakespearean Stage* (Cambridge, 1913); Louis C. Elson, *Shakespeare in Music* (Boston, 1901); Fellowes' edition of the *Songs & Lyrics from the Plays of Beaumont and Fletcher* (London, 1928).

William Chappell, *Old English Popular Music* (London, 1893) is still indispensable for folk music.

Information on musical instruments and music written for them may be found in Charles van den Borren, *Sources of Keyboard Music in England* (London, 1915); Francis W. Galpin, *A Textbook of European Musical Instruments* (London, [1946]); Margaret H. Glyn, *About Elizabethan Virginal Music and Its Composers* (London, [n.d.]); Max Kenyon, *Harpsichord Music* (London, 1949); Gerald R. Hayes, *Musical Instruments and Their Music* (2 vols., London, 1928–30).

Gustav Reese, *Music in the Renaissance* (London, [1954]) should be read for its broad knowledge of all Renaissance music, of which the English, however important, was only a part.

An Elizabethan Song Book, the music edited by Noah Greenberg, the text by W. H. Auden and Chester Kallman (London, 1954); a collection of many of the most interesting and beautiful Tudor songs. This is also available in a paper-backed edition, published by Doubleday in 1954.

Musica Britannica (15 vols., 2 still in preparation, London, 1951–   ) is a national collection of British music from the Middle Ages through the eighteenth century. This includes much hitherto unpublished material—music for the early Church and instrumental and vocal collections of the Tudor period, as well as masques, operas, and chamber music of the later period.

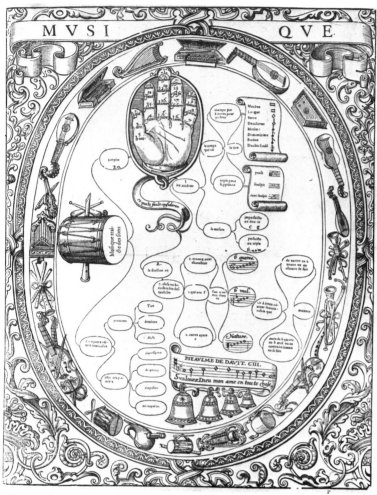

Plate 1. "Musique." From Christophe de Savigny, *Tableaux accomplis de tous les arts liberaux*, Paris, 1587.

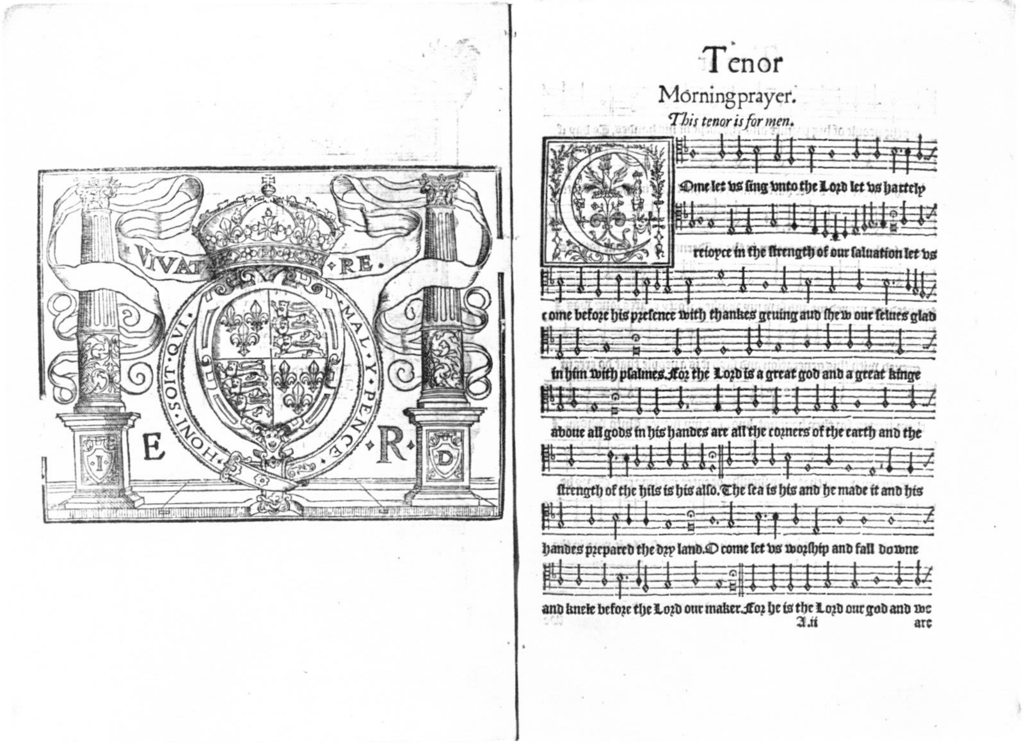
VIVAT
RE.
HONI·SOIT·QVI·MAL·Y·PENCE
E
R
Tenor
Morningprayer.
This tenor is for men.
Come let vs sing vnto the Lord let vs hartely
reioyce in the strength of our saluation let vs
come before his presence with thankes geuing and shew our selues glad
in him with psalmes. For the Lord is a great god and a great kinge
aboue all gods in his handes are all the corners of the earth and the
strength of the hils is his also. The sea is his and he made it and his
handes prepared the dry land. O come let vs worship and fall downe
and knele before the Lord our maker. For he is the Lord our god and we
A.ii
are

Plate 2. Beginning of service from *Mornyng and Euenyng Prayer*, London, 1565.

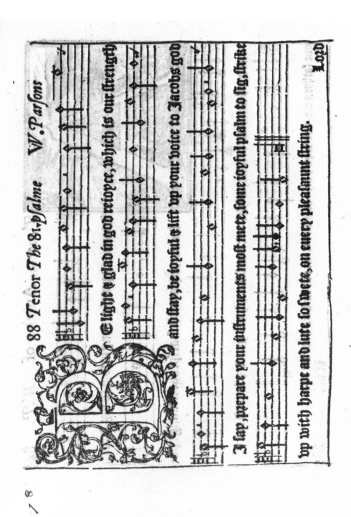

Plate 3. The 81st Psalm from *The Whole Psalmes in Foure Partes*, London, 1563.

Plate 4. Title-page of Thomas Morley's *A Plaine and Easie Introduction to Practicall Musicke*, London, 1597.

Plate 5. A manuscript copy of a song by John Wilbye in a music commonplace book.

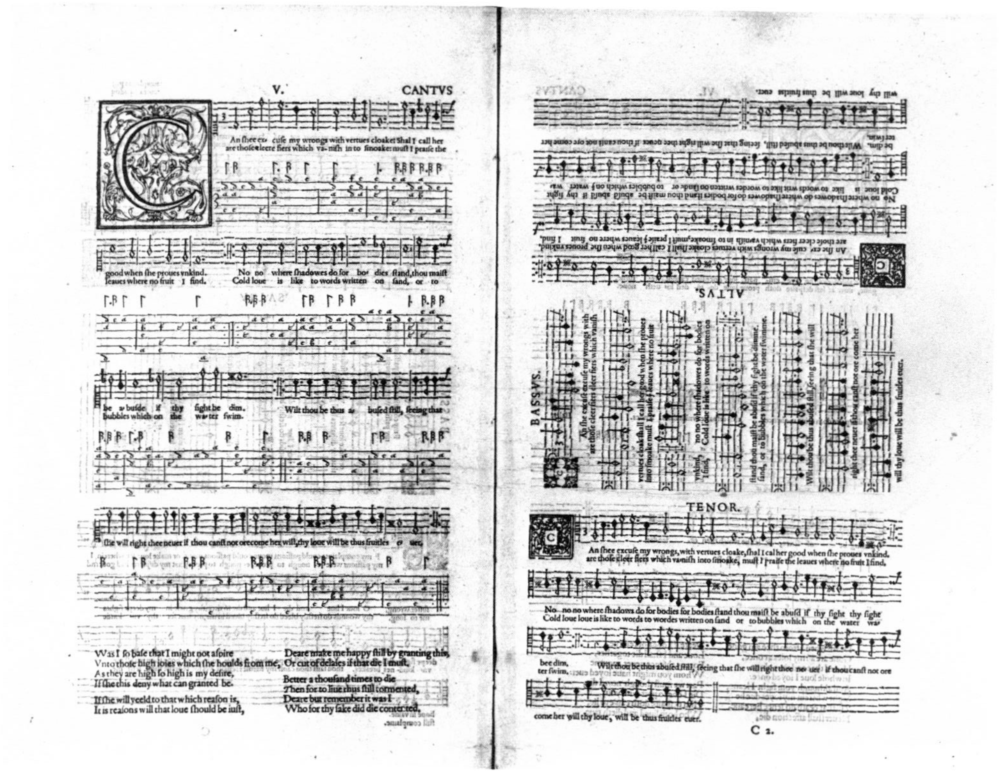

Plate 6. An air from John Dowland's First Booke of Songes or Ayres, London, 1600.

SELECT
Muſicall Ayres
AND
DIALOGUES,
In Three BOOKES.

First Book, contains *AYRES* for a Voyce alone to the Theorbo, or Baſſe Violl.

Second Book, containes Choice *DIALOGUES* for two Voyces to the Theorbo or Baſſe Violl.

Third Book, containes ſhort *AYRES* or *SONGS* for three Voyces, ſo Compoſed, as they may either be ſung by a Voyce alone, to an Inſtrument, or by two or three Voyces.

Compoſed by theſe ſeverall Excellent Maſters in Muſick, *Viz.*

Dr. *John Wilſon,*   Mr. *Nicholas Lanneare,*
Dr. *Charles Colman,*   Mr. *William Smegergill*
Mr. *Henry Lawes,*   *alias Cæſar,*
Mr. *William Lawes,*   Mr. *Edward Colman,*
Mr. *William Webb.*   Mr. *Jeremy Savile.*

LONDON,
Printed by *T. H.* for *John Playford*, and are to be ſold at his Shop, in the Inner Temple, neare the Church doore. 1653.

Plate 7. Lute and viol. From John Playford's *Select Musicall Ayres and Dialogues,* London, 1653.

Plate 8. Dancing in early Venice to the music of a "broken consort" of viols and lute. From Giacomo Franco's *Habiti d'huomeni et donne Venetia,* [1626].

Muſical Inſtruments.   Inſtrumenta Muſica.

C.

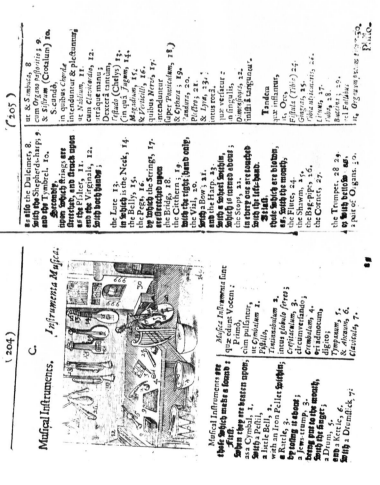

Muſical Inſtruments are
thoſe which make a ſound:
First,
Which they are beaten upon,
as a Cymbal, 1.
with a Peſtil,
a little Bell, 2.
with an Iron Pellet within;
a Rattle, 3.
by toſſing it about;
a Jews-trump, 3.
being put to the mouth,
with the finger;
a Drum, 5.
and a Kettle, 6.
with a Drumſtick, 7.

Muſica Inſtrumenta ſunt
quæ edunt Vocem:
Primò,
cum pulſantur,
ut Cymbalum 1.
Piſtillo,
Tintinnabulum 2.
incus globulo ferreo;
Crepitaculum, 3.
circumvertendo;
Crembalum, 4.
ori admotum,
digito;
Tympanum, 5.
& Ahenum, 6.
Clavicula, 7.

as alſo the Dulcimer, 8.
with the Shepherds-harp, 9.
and the Tymbrel. 10.

Secondly,
upon which ſtrings are
ſtretched, and ſtruck upon
as the Pſalter, 11.
and the Virginals, 12.
with both hands;

the Lute 13.
in which is the Neck, 14.
the Belly, 15.
the Pegs, 16.
by which the Strings, 17.
are ſtretched upon
the Bridg, 18.
the Cithern; 19.
with the right thumb only,
the Vial, 20.
with a Bow; 21.
and the Harp. 23.
with a ſober Scutchin,
which is turned about;
the Stops, 22.
in every one are touched
with the life-hand.
Thirdly,
thoſe which are blown,
as, with the mouth,
the Flute, 24.
the Shawm, 25.
the Bag-pipes, 16.
the Cornet, 27.

the Trumpet, 28 24.
or with bellows as,
a pair of Organs. 30.

ut & Sambuca, 8
cum Organo paſtorio, 9.
& Siſtrum (Crotalum) 10.

Secundâ,
in quibus Chordæ
intenduntur & plectuntur;
ut Nablium, 11.
cum Clavicordio, 12.
utrâque manu;
Dexcerâ tantùm,
Teſtudo (Chelys) 13.
(in quâ Jugum, 14.
Magadium, 15.
& Verticilli, 16.
quibus Nervi 17.
intenduntur
ſuper Ponticulum, 18.)
& Cythara; 19.
Pandura, 20.
Plectro; 21.
& Lyra, 23.
intus rotâ.
quæ verſatur:
in ſingulis,
Dimenſiones, 22.
ſiniſtrâ tanguntur.

Tandem
quæ inflantur,
ut, Ore,
Fiſtula (Tibia) 24.
Gingras, 25.
tibia utriculariis, 26.
Lituus, 27.
Tuba, 28.
Buccina; 29.
vel Follibus,
ut, Organum extra: 16-30.
Finis.

Plate 9. Musical instruments of Elizabeth's age. From Johann Comenius,
Orbis senſualium pictus, 1685.

173

(Playford)

THE
Banquet of MUSICK:
OR,

A Collection of the newest and best SONGS
sung at Court, and at Publick Theatres.

WITH

A THOROW-BASS for the *Theorbo-Lute*,
Bass-Viol, *Harpsichord*, or *Organ*.

Composed by several of the Best Masters.

The WORDS by the *Ingenious Wits* of this Age.

THE FIRST BOOK.

Gui: Vaughan Sculp:

LICENSED,
Nov. 19. 1687.   Rob. *Midgley.*

In the SAVOY:
Printed by E. *Jones*, for *Henry Playford*, at his Shop near the *Temple* Church, 1688.

Plate 10. Virginals and viol. From Henry Playford's *Banquet of Musick*,
London, 1688.

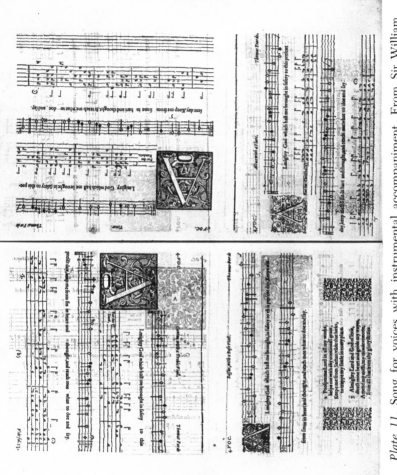

Plate 11. Song for voices with instrumental accompaniment. From Sir William Leighton's *The Teares or Lamentations of a Sorrowfull Soule*, London, 1614.

175

the treble to grén slurs

the ground to gren slurs

Plate 12. A manuscript commonplace book, partly in the hand of John Dowland.

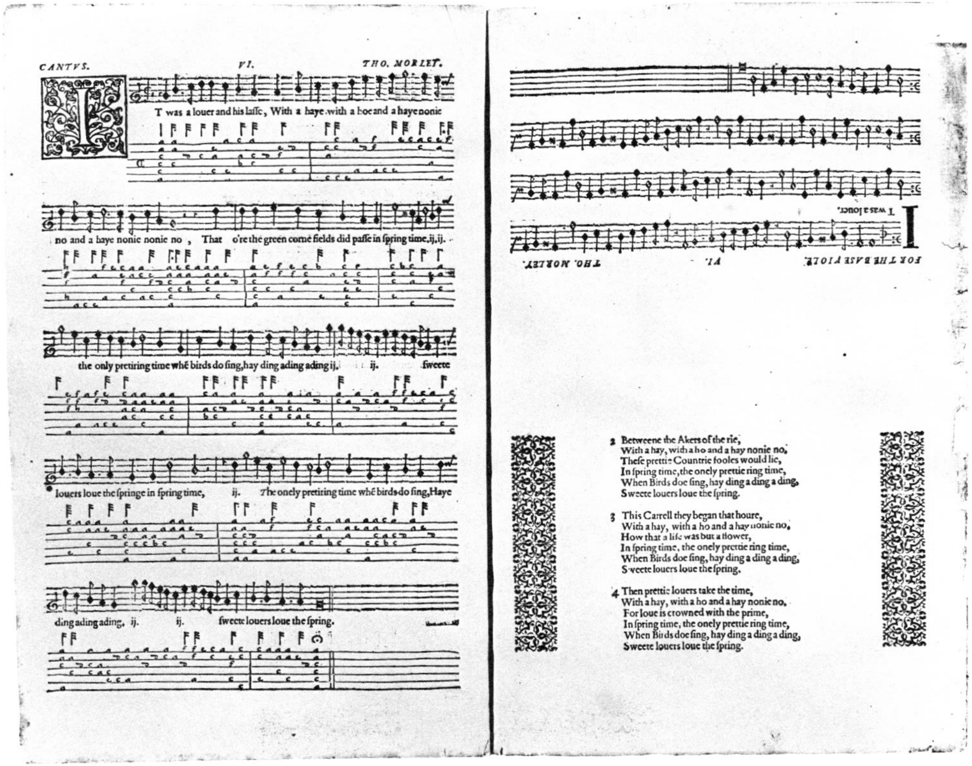

Plate 13. A song from Thomas Morley's First Book of Ayres, London, 1600.

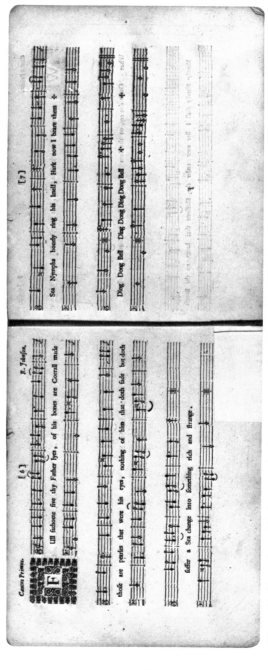

Plate 14. Song from Shakespeare's *Tempest* printed in Dr. John Wilson's *Cheerful Ayres or Ballads*, Oxford, 1660.

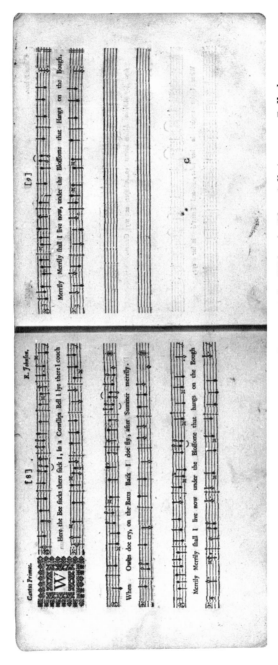

Plate 15. Song from *The Tempest* printed in Dr. John Wilson's *Cheerfull Ayres or Ballads.*

179

Plate 16. A mid-17th-century manuscript commonplace book containing settings of Shakespeare's songs.

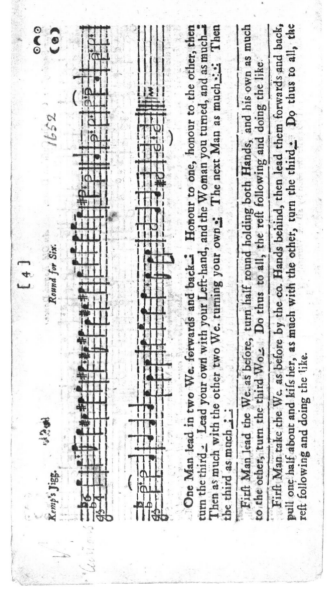

Kemp's Jigg.

Round for Six.

1652

One Man lead in two Wo. forwards and back. Honour to one, honour to the other, then turn the third. Lead your own with your Left-hand, and the Woman you turned, and as much. Then as much with the other two Wo. turning your own. The next Man as much. Then the third as much.

Firſt Man lead the Wo. as before, turn half round holding both Hands, and his own as much to the other, turn the third Wo. Do thus to all, the reſt following and doing the like.

Firſt Man take the Wo. as before by the co. Hands behind, then lead them forwards and back, pull one half about and kiſs her, as much with the other, turn the third. Do thus to all, the reſt following and doing the 'like.

181

Plate 17. A jig from John Playford's Dancing-Master, *18th edition, [ca. 1725].*

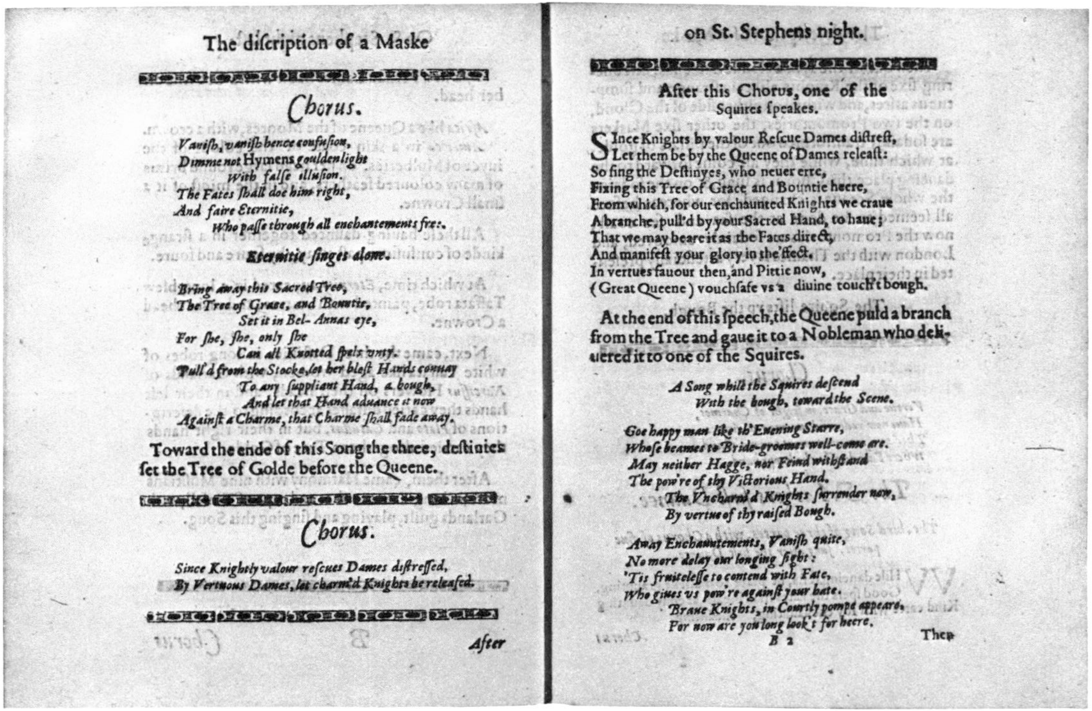

The discription of a Maske

Chorus.

Vanish, vanish hence confusion,
Dimme not Hymens goulden light
    with false illusion.
The Faies shall doe him right,
And faire Eternitie,
Who passe through all enchantments free.

Examine singe dame.

Bring away this Sacred Tree,
The Tree of Grace, and Bountie,
Set it in Bel-Annas eye,
For she, she, only she
Can all Knotted spels vntie,
Pull'd from the Stocke, let her blest Hands conuey
To any suppliant Hand, a bough,
And let that Hand aduance it now
Against a Charme, that Charme shall fade away.

Toward the ende of this Song the three, desiacies set the Tree of Golde before the Queene.

Chorus.

Since Knightly valour rescues Dames distressed,
By Vertuous Dames let charmed Knights be released.

After

---

on St. Stephens night.

After this Chorus, one of the Squires speakes.

SInce Knights by valour Rescue Dames distress,
Let them be by the Queene of Dames releast:
So sing the Destinyes, who neuer erre,
Fixing this Tree of Grace and Bountie heere,
From which, for our enchaunted Knight we craue
A branche, pull'd by your Sacred Hand, to haue;
That we may beare vs the Faees direct,
And manifest your glory in the effect,
In vertues fauour then, and Pietie now,
(Great Queene) vouchsafe vs a diuine touch'd bough.

At the end of this speech, the Queene pulld a branch from the Tree and gaue it to a Nobleman who deliuered it to one of the Squires.

A Song whilst the Squires descend
With the bough, toward the Scene.

Goe happy man like th' Euening Starre,
Whose beames to Bride-groomes well-come are:
May neither Hagge, nor Fiend withstand
The powre of thy Victorious Hand,
The Pearelesse Knights seruant now,
By vertue of his branched Bough.

Away Enchantements, Vanish quite,
No more delay our longing sight:
'Tis fruitelesse to contend with Fate,
Who giue vs you're a going, our late.
Braue Knights, in Courtly pompe appeare,
For now are yonthing look't for heere.

B 2   Then

Plate 18. Two pages from Thomas Campion's The Description of a Maske: Presented in the Banqueting Roome at Whitehall, on Saint Stephens night last, at the Mariage of the Right Honourable the Earle of Somerset: and the right noble the Lady Frances Howard, London, 1614.

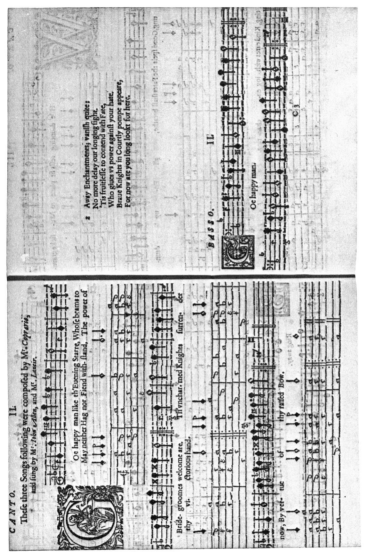

Plate 19. A song from Campion's *Description of a Maske.*

Plate 20. John Wilbye's contribution to Thomas Morley's collection of madrigals, *The Triumphes of Oriana*, London, 1601.

The Bible in English, 1525-1611

By Craig R. Thompson

WITH a few negligible exceptions, Tudor Englishmen, Christians in a realm officially Christian, accepted without question the unique authority of the Bible. Catholic and Protestant might disagree over the relationship between Bible and Church, but both knew the Scriptures were divinely inspired and therefore totally different from all other writings in character and purpose. The Bible is a book—words. As words, it could be treated like other books, copied, sold, illustrated, annotated, translated. As divine revelation, it required to be read, preached, believed, obeyed, for it was the record wherein God spoke to man.

No English translation of the complete New Testament was in print until 1526, none of the complete Bible until 1535. In the next generation, translations became plentiful enough, and in Elizabeth's reign cheap enough, to be within the means of the ordinary man. Printing, Protestantism, and a long series of experiments in translating the Bible made the English "the people of a book, and that book was the Bible." Gradually the phrases and rhythms of the English Bible were absorbed and imitated; they became naturalized, a part of English speech. It is no accident, then, that the most popular version of the world's most popular book is an early seventeenth-century revision of sixteenth-century work. That this "Authorized" or "Royal" or "King James" Bible of 1611 will be the one most widely used half a century from now is not likely, but its place in the religious and literary history of English-speaking peoples is secure.

In the medieval Church, the Bible used was the Latin version now generally called the Vulgate. This was prepared by St. Jerome, who undertook it at the request of Pope Damasus (*ca.* 382). Jerome produced a New Testament and two versions of the Psalms by revising, with the aid of Greek texts, the existing "Old Latin" versions. Later (405) he issued a Latin Old Testament translated from the Hebrew. The Vulgate was not actually made official until the sixteenth century, when the Council of Trent declared it the authentic Bible (1546) and Pope Clement VIII issued a revised and official text (1592).

Partial translations and paraphrases of the Bible had been made in England since Anglo-Saxon times, but no complete translation is known for certain before the late fourteenth century. The first demonstrable version of the complete Bible into English is connected with the name of John Wyclif, the Oxford reformer. Probably little of it is from his pen, but the conception was his. He and his followers, the Lollards, emphasized in their preaching the supreme authority of the Scriptures. But to "search the Scriptures" men needed a Bible in their own tongue. To fill this need the Wyclifites made two translations from the Vulgate. The earlier (*ca.* 1381–1383), by Nicholas Hereford, was a word-for-word rendering; the revision of this, by John Purvey and others (*ca.* 1395), less literal and less Latinate. For example, where the earlier version has in Psalm 23:1–2, "The Lord governeth me and no thing to me shall lack; in the place of leswe [pasture] where he me full set. Over water of fulfilling he nourished me; my soul he converted," the later one reads: "The Lord governeth me and no thing shall fail to me; in the place of pasture there he hath set me. He nourished me on the water of refreshing; he converted my soul."

To appreciate what the Bible in their own tongue meant to sixteenth-century Englishmen, we must recall how long it took to reach them in printed form, approved or unapproved, and how deeply involved with other questions was this one of a vernacular Bible. "Ignorance of the Scriptures is ignorance of Christ," declared Wyclif, quoting Jerome. Yet in 1408 the Synod of Oxford forbade translation of the Bible into English and the expounding of any translation that had not been inspected. No translation, past (Wyclifite) or future, might be read, publicly or privately, unless approved. Disobedience made the offender liable to the charge of heresy. Why this hostility to the vernacular Bible for the laity? Not from bigotry but from principle and conservatism: from the prevalent theory of the Christian Church and of a Christian society and from the habitual resistance of the official mind to innovation. Prelates objected on political and linguistic as well as religious grounds. They quoted from Jerome a familiar passage on the difficulty of translation. When Thomas More cited this same passage against Tyndale in 1528, Tyndale's answer was: Jerome made a translation, "Why may not we also?" Because (went the argument) misunderstanding might result; and this, by producing wrong beliefs, might imperil one's soul and the souls of others. From Wyclif's day to Tyndale's we meet the same argument again and again. In 1542 the Bishop of London refused to have anything to do with a scheme for a new translation, saying, "I will never be guilty to bring the simple people into error." More denounced Tyndale's translation but regretted the lack of a better, confessing he did not know why none had been made. When one should appear, all copies, he thought, ought to be kept by bishops, who would lend them from time to time to respectable persons.

A medieval theologian might know his Bible well, an ordinary priest rarely did, a layman very rarely indeed. Books were scarce and were therefore valuable property—too costly for students, who rented them instead, a quire or so at a time, from stationers licensed and strictly supervised by the universities. Chaucer's clerk of Oxford dreams of someday owning twenty volumes, but it is only a dream. After the middle of the fifteenth century, thanks to printing, such dreams could become realities. Printing revolutionized the book trade, multiplied the number of books and readers, changed reading habits,[1] methods of

---

[1] Before the era of printing, books were commonly read aloud (and therefore much more slowly), even when one read to oneself. The Bible affords an interesting example in Acts 8:26–39. Philip asks the Ethiopian, who is reading Isaiah as his chariot jogs along, "Understandest thou what thou readest?" He knows what the man is reading because he *hears* him. Until printing came, ideas about the nature of literature and criticism were based on the assumption that literature is mainly an auditory art. Printing made it mainly a visual one and gradually transformed conceptions of style, artistic originality, literary property, and so on.

scholarship, and conceptions of literature. Books could now be issued in hundreds or even thousands of copies, each with the same text on corresponding pages; this was not true of manuscripts. Now there could be standard texts to quote from or refer to. (The Bible had no chapters until the thirteenth century, no numbered verses until the sixteenth.) Moreover, the introduction of printing coincided with important developments in philology. Printing and philology together made textual and historical criticism possible and so opened a new epoch in Biblical studies.

The famous 42-line Gutenberg Bible (1456) was the first of many editions of the Vulgate printed in the fifteenth century. A complete Hebrew Bible was printed in 1488; an edition of the Greek New Testament, by Erasmus, in 1516. By 1500 translations of the Bible had appeared in most major European languages except English. In England the unfavorable attitude of ecclesiastical authorities, who were suspicious of anything that smacked of Lollardry, apparently made the venture too risky even for an enterprising publisher like Caxton.

The Reformation did more than anything else to assure a printed Bible in English. In Lutheran and Reformed theology, the Bible was central. Tyndale, a partisan of such theology, sums up the argument for translation as a preference for light instead of darkness: to walk in darkness is to stumble, and "to stumble is the danger of eternal damnation." He translated that poor folk "might also read and see the simple word of God." But is the Bible "simple"? Yes, said the Reformers, in that the Gospels tell us plainly what is needful for salvation. To this their adversaries retorted that since the Bible after all came from the Church, it required authoritative interpretation by the Church. Translation could not be left to unauthorized amateurs.

The Bible makes every demand on the translator made by any ancient text, and more, because he may not take the liberties with a sacred book that he takes with others. Too much is at stake. He must be accurate at all costs, must care more for matter than for style. Still, the Tudor translators were men of their times, dependent on the same stock of language as other men, and anxious to produce translations other men could and would read. The spirit in which they approached their text differed from that of other translators, but their purely linguistic resources were the same.

In addition to close knowledge of his original, the translator needs sympathetic understanding of its spirit, its "atmosphere." His grasp of his own language must be sensitive enough to make his version more than merely reliable. It must also be readable, idiomatic English: dignified but not affected, colloquial without being vulgar. The Rheims New Testament (1582) with its *agnition, comessations, exinanited, prefinition,* its "Give us today our supersubstantial bread" sometimes made unnecessary difficulties. The conservative Bishop Gardiner had once proposed (1542) that translators keep certain essential terms in Latin; these included *Christus, Dominus, Spiritus Sanctus, ecclesia, episcopus, charitas, gratia.* Had this advice been heeded, the ordinary reader would have been little better off than he was before. Cheke, Gardiner's contemporary, tried with some success to make his own version of Matthew as "Saxon" as possible, but his *frosent* for *apostles, freshman* for *proselyte, groundwrought* for *founded, hunderder* for *centurion* have a strange look today. The Englishman needed a Bible in plain, familiar English, not one with crucial words left in a foreign tongue or rendered by newfangled expressions he never heard of. The versions of Tyndale and his followers he could read. Their publication was a triumph for the English language as much as for new ideas.

That the English in the sixteenth century became a Bible-reading people is at once evident from the number of translations printed and reprinted, apart from abundant evidence of other kinds. The Bible of 1611 was only the latest and best of a long line. Its main predecessors may now be briefly described.

Because of its enduring influence on the language of the English Bible, the greatest of these was the first, William Tyndale's. Rebuffed by the Bishop of London whose support he sought for his project of translating the New Testament from Greek, Tyndale went to Germany in 1524. His translation, made from Erasmus' Greek text, Luther's German version, and the Vulgate, was ready to print in 1525 at Cologne. Before Matthew was finished, work was interrupted and Tyndale had to flee. A fragment of a single copy of this Cologne printing of 1525 survives. We hear of a quarto and an octavo edition printed shortly afterward (1526) at Worms. Of the octavo, two copies (one incomplete) survive. Various reprints appeared between 1526 and 1532, an unauthorized revision in 1534, then a revision by Tyndale himself (also 1534). Tyndale's work on the Old Testament was cut short by martyrdom in 1536. His versions of the Pentateuch and Jonah were published in 1530–1531. Other portions of the Old Testament, left in manuscript translation, were printed after his death.

The quality of Tyndale's translations and their place in the development of English prose deserve far more space than can be given to them here. Diction and rhythms of the King James New Testament owe more to him than to any other single translator. Many of its more familiar phrases come from him, but merely to quote some would not, in itself, show the extent of indebtedness. In the following verses (Luke 15:1–7) there are more differences between Tyndale and the 1611 Bible than in some others, yet even here it is obvious that the 1611 version is mostly Tyndale's (1534):

TYNDALE

Then resorted unto him all the publicans and sinners, for to hear him. And the Pharisees and scribes murmured, saying: He receiveth to his company sinners, and eateth with them. Then put he forth this similitude to them, saying: What man of you having an hundred sheep, if he lose one of them, doth not leave ninety and nine in the wilderness and go after that which is lost, until he find him? And when he hath found him, he putteth him on his shoulders with joy: and as soon as he cometh home, he calleth together his lovers and neighbors, saying unto them: Rejoice with me, for I have found my sheep which was lost. I say unto you, that likewise joy shall be in heaven over one sinner that repenteth, more than over ninety and nine just persons, which need no repentance.

Then drew near unto him all the publicans and sinners, for to hear him. And the Pharisees and scribes murmured, saying: this man receiveth sinners, and eateth with them. And he spake this parable unto them, saying: What man of you having an hundred sheep, if he lose one of them, doth not leave the ninety and nine in the wilderness and go after that which is lost, until he find it? And when he hath found it, he layeth it on his shoulders, rejoicing. And when he cometh home, he calleth together his friends and neighbors, saying unto them, Rejoice with me, for I have found my sheep which was lost. I say unto you, that likewise joy shall be in heaven over one sinner that repenteth, more than over ninety and nine just persons, which need no repentance.

Tyndale's language is plain, direct, forceful, more colloquial sometimes than are later translations. The serpent tells Eve, "Tush, ye shall not die"; the Lord was with Joseph "and he was a lucky fellow"; St. Paul sails "after the Easter holidays." It was the language of Tyndale's time, often made eloquent by his earnestness, his sense of urgency. More attacked him for using *seniors* or *elders* instead of *priests, congregation* instead of *church, love* instead of *charity.* This was no pedantic quarrel. In an age when men were burned or beheaded—the fates of Tyndale and More—for their theological opinions, the implications of theological terms were desperately important. Tyndale avoided the customary terms because they were associated too closely with a system and a set of claims he rejected. More thought new terms could only confuse readers and might unsettle their orthodoxy. Likewise he denounced Tyndale's prologues and notes, which were often Lutheran in tone.

Authority reacted strongly to Tyndale's work. Copies of the 1526 New Testament were promptly banned and if found were destroyed by the English government. A few years later a royal injunction (1530) forbade buying or keeping an English Bible. Yet before Tyndale's death a complete English Bible had come out (1535) with official permission. Political winds had shifted: Henry had broken with the papacy, become "Supreme Head" of the English Church, and changed his policy with respect to an English Bible.

The first entire Bible printed in English was the work of Miles Coverdale, a Cambridge graduate whose interest in the Reformers took him abroad. He was grieved, he says, "that other nations should be more plenteously provided for with the Scripture in their mother tongue than we." Archbishop Cranmer had tried in vain to prod the bishops into making a translation. Their failure and the Crown's growing interest in an English version made the time ripe for Coverdale. His Bible appeared in 1535, inscribed to Henry, "our Moses." It was printed somewhere on the Continent. Two editions printed in England were issued in 1537. One announces that the book is "set forth with the King's most gracious license."

Coverdale says he translated out of "Dutch [German] and Latin" and used "five sundry interpreters." One was Tyndale, another Luther. For all but one (Jonah) of the last fourteen books of the Old Testament, Coverdale's was the earliest printed English version. It was likewise the earliest of the Apocrypha. The Pentateuch and New Testament were revisions of Tyndale, but Coverdale changed or omitted Tyndale's offending notes, and unlike Tyndale he did not insist on *congregation* for *church*, *repentance* for *penance*. This restraint was one reason for his success. Coverdale's most lasting legacy to the English Church was the Psalter, for his is the earliest form of the Psalter used in the *Book of Common Prayer*. Both in the Psalter and elsewhere he gave us phrases that became too familiar to replace: "Thou anointest my head with oil," "valley of the shadow of death," "sufficient unto the day," "I am become as sounding brass."

The next translation, "Matthew's Bible" (Antwerp, 1537) consisted of Coverdale's Old Testament from the end of Chronicles, Coverdale's Apocrypha, the 1535 revision of Tyndale's Pentateuch and New Testament, plus a version of Joshua—II Chronicles inclusive which was very likely Tyndale's. More of Tyndale's work appeared in this Bible than in any other. "Thomas Matthew," said on the title-page to be the translator, is regarded by nearly all scholars as a pseudonym for John Rogers, a companion of Tyndale, who prepared the work for the press.

The Matthew Bible had official approval, for since Archbishop Cranmer was unable to interest the bishops in making a translation, he persuaded the King's Vicar-General, Thomas Cromwell, to license this Bible, which he said he liked "better than any other translation heretofore made." Thus Tyndale's work, forbidden during Henry's reign when put forth under Tyndale's name, was transmitted, ironically enough, by a Bible having the government's sanction.

A revision of Matthew's Bible by Richard Taverner was published by the King's Printer in 1539. Taverner was a sound scholar whose work had merit, but his book could not compete successfully with another Bible issued about the same time or shortly afterward.

This other version was the Great Bible, so called because of its size. It was a revision of the Matthew Bible by Coverdale "and divers excellent learned men," who made liberal use also of a new Latin version by Sebastian Münster. Printing began in Paris, was interrupted by the Inquisition, and resumed in London. The first edition bore the date 1539, but there is reason to think that it did not actually appear until 1540; then six more followed before the end of 1541. On its title-page the book had a picture of the King, flanked by Cromwell and Cranmer, his chief administrators, who present copies to his joyous subjects. Because Cranmer contributed a preface included in the April, 1540, and subsequent editions, this Bible is sometimes called "Cranmer's." Because Cromwell had supported it financially and in other ways, it is sometimes named after him too. Cromwell, however, was removed from office and executed shortly after its publication (July, 1540). His coat of arms was omitted from the title-page of the next edition; Cranmer's remained.

The Great Bible had more powerful backing than any other to date. The second edition proclaimed, "This is the Bible appointed to the use of the churches." Before the first edition had appeared, Cromwell ordered the clergy to see that every parish church obtain a copy on publication.

The placing of an English Bible in every church was an exciting event in English religious history; how exciting may be inferred from a royal proclamation (1541) rebuking those who read or discuss it "with loud and high voices" while Mass is celebrated. One writer (1539) tells us that men now read the Bible instead of Arthurian romances. It is true that for a time servants, laborers, and housewives were forbidden by law to read it (1542–1543), even in private, but such restrictions vanished in the next reign, that of Edward VI (1547–1553), when Bibles were printed and circulated freely. Printing of the book stopped during Mary Tudor's reign (1553–1558), but as soon as Elizabeth came to the throne (1558) the Great Bible and Prayer Book were restored to churches, and both printing and translating of the Bible could be resumed.

The first Elizabethan translation was made by a group of Marian exiles in Geneva, chief among them William Whittingham, who was, he says, "moved with zeal, counselled by the godly, and drawn by occasion, both of the place where God hath appointed us to dwell, and also of the store of heavenly learning and judgment, which so aboundeth in this city of Geneva, that justly it may be called the patron and mirror of true religion and godliness." Whittingham's New Testament appeared in 1557; the complete Bible, in which he had assistance from Anthony Gilby and Thomas Sampson, in 1560. This was dedicated to Elizabeth by her "humble subjects of the English Church at Geneva." For the New Testament, Whittingham used, in addition to the Greek text, Latin, French, and English versions; and for the 1560 edition he revised his work of 1557. The Old Testament was a revision of the Great Bible but based on a fresh comparison of the Hebrew. Both Testaments had chapter summaries and marginal notes.

This Geneva Bible was a landmark, rivaled in importance and influence only by the Tyndale and 1611 Bibles. Its roman and italic type, instead of black letter, set new fashions in Bible printing. It was the first English Bible to divide the text into numbered verses. Whittingham took pride in keeping Hebraisms but added explanatory words to make them more intelligible.

By and large the language was clear and unaffected; the translators strove after "propriety of the words and perspicuity of the phrase." Except in the New Testament, where the influence of Tyndale predominates, the Geneva contributed more to the King James Bible than did any other single version. It quickly became the cheap, popular version of the Scriptures; for well over half a century this was the Bible most read by Englishmen and most often reprinted. Because of its connections with Calvinism, it was especially favored by the Puritans. Apparently it was also the version that Shakespeare, no Puritan, knew best.

After Elizabeth's accession, the Great Bible was reprinted (1562). Certain bishops had expressed dissatisfaction with it as early as 1542, when Convocation voted to amend it. Nothing was done until Archbishop Parker, in 1565 or thereabouts, revived Cranmer's project of a translation made by bishops. Accordingly a committee of some sixteen bishops went to work. They were told to follow the Great Bible, change it only where the original was rendered inaccurately, take advantage of recent Latin translations, and avoid contentious notes and coarse or unedifying words. Parker himself prepared Genesis, Matthew, and some of the Pauline epistles as well as the introductory material. As revisers he and his collaborators made many changes in the Great Bible, borrowing frequently from the recent Geneva version. The Psalter in the Bishops' Bible is an interesting and often independent translation.

The Bishops' Bible, issued in 1568 (revised edition 1572) was a magnificent and costly black-letter folio. It included portraits of the Queen (on the title-page) and her favorite advisers, Leicester (preceding the first page of Joshua) and Cecil (on the first page of the Psalms). In the Folger Library is a copy of this Bible covered with crimson velvet and with Elizabeth's arms and initials stamped on the central gold boss, the Tudor rose on the other bosses; the portraits of Leicester and Cecil are colored.

The Bishops' Bible had little chance of rivaling the Geneva version in popular esteem, but its official status as the Bible read in divine service made it familiar to everybody. Any translation heard at least once a week, year after year, is bound to become familiar. If, in addition, the book is used in solemn rites and expounded as revealed truth, its language will soon acquire special authority.

The only Tudor translation of the Bible by and for Roman Catholics, the Rheims-Douai (New Testament, 1582; Old Testament, 1609–1610), came from English priests living in exile in France. It was planned and supervised by William, later Cardinal, Allen, founder of the English College at Douai. He wanted to equip priests—whose training was entirely in Latin—with a knowledge of the Bible in English in order to help them confute their opponents, who, he remarks, had the Scriptures at their finger tips. Gregory Martin, like Allen a former Oxford scholar, did most of the translating. He began late in 1578, translated two chapters a day, and finished in less than four years. He had some help from others, including Allen, who wrote most of the copious and polemical notes.

This Bible differed from all other Tudor ones: it came from Roman Catholics; it originated in a desire to provide for the clergy, whereas Tyndale and the other early translators had been concerned initially about laymen; unlike Tyndale and others who had translated from Hebrew and Greek, Martin used as his basic text the Latin Vulgate, declared by the Council of Trent to be the authentic Scriptures, though he consulted other texts. The preface, in contrast to those of Protestant Bibles, began by denying that "the Holy Scriptures should always be in our mother tongue, or that they ought or were ordered by God to be read indifferently of all, or could be easily understood of every one that readeth or heareth them in a known language." But in these bad times "special consideration" made a vernacular translation desirable. In the good old days, before "heretical" translations abounded, "there was not so much chatting and jangling of God's word, but much more sincere dealing, doing, and keeping the same."

The Rheims New Testament was a well-printed book and a usually accurate, at times admirable, translation of the Latin version, most of it in plain and fairly simple English. But a desire to ensure correctness by keeping as close as possible to the

Latin when rendering technical terms led the translators here and there to use words foreign to English ears. A glossary at the end of the book explains some of these: for instance, *arch-synagogue* (high priest), *azymes* (unleavened bread), *dominical day* (Sunday), *donaries* (temple offerings), *Pasche* (Easter), *loaves of proposition* (showbread). The translators' desire to avoid question-begging terms was surely legitimate, but their Latinate English produced strange results at times. "And if you invoke the Father, him which without acception of persons judgeth according to every one's work, in fear converse ye the time of your peregrination" (I Peter 1:17). "And beneficence and communication do not forget, for with such hosts God is promerited" (Hebrews 13:16). "Or what permutation shall a man give for his soul?" (Mark 8:37). "And a certain young man followed him clothed with sindon upon the bare" (Mark 14:51). Where Rheims-Douai diction was good, it was very, very good; and where it was bad, it was—un-English.

When James VI of Scotland became King of England in 1603, Puritan leaders promptly submitted to him a list of grievances. At the Hampton Court Conference, which met in January, 1604, to consider the condition of the Church, Dr. John Reynolds of Oxford proposed among other things a new translation of the Scriptures. This suggestion attracted James, and he directed that the work should be undertaken. He had no love for Puritans but welcomed a chance to oppose the popular Geneva Bible, which he detested. He "could never yet see a Bible well translated in English," he said, but the Geneva was the worst of all. Some of its notes he found seditious: for example, one to Exodus 1:19, which, he complained, "alloweth disobedience to kings." (The note condemns the Hebrew midwives' deceit but says their disobedience "was lawful"). The King laid down conditions for the new translation (not all of which were kept) and made some elaborate plans.

Fifty-four churchmen, a number later reduced by four or five, were appointed to the task. They worked in six companies or committees, two at Westminster, two at Oxford, and two at Cambridge. Two members of each group, or twelve in all, constituted a board of revision to pass on the work of the rest. A well-known note by the contemporary jurist and scholar John Selden tells what the companies' method was: "That part of the Bible was given to him who was most excellent in such a tongue . . . and then they met together and one read the translation, the rest holding in their hands some Bible, either of the learned tongues or French, Spanish, Italian, etc. If they found any fault, they spoke; if not, he read on." The final editors were Bishops Bilson of Winchester and Smith of Gloucester.

Instructions to the companies made clear that their labor was to be one of revision rather than of fresh translation. They were to follow the Bishops' Bible, altering it only where necessary, but had permission to use the Tyndale, Coverdale, and Geneva versions where these were superior to the Bishops'. The "old ecclesiastical words" were to be kept, marginal notes avoided. That is, the companies were to improve the Bishops' if they could; where they could not, they were to let it alone. "Truly, good Christian reader," affirms their preface, "we never thought from the beginning that we should need to make a new translation, nor yet to make of a bad one a good one . . . but to make a good one better; or out of many good ones, one principal good one." A copy of the Bishops' Bible surviving in the Bodleian Library contains certain manuscript changes which apparently represent an intermediate stage between the text of the Bishops' and that of the King James. This evidence, together with that in a Lambeth Palace manuscript book containing one company's work on the epistles of the New Testament, indicates that the final revisers did more than arrange the materials submitted and scrutinize them for accuracy. They improved style, sometimes rejecting the companies' changes, sometimes making phrases shorter and more direct and giving them their now familiar shape.

This most famous of English Bibles was printed by Robert Barker and issued sometime in 1611, a large black-letter folio, dedicated to the King. Since the first edition did not satisfy the apparently unforeseen demand, a new one was undertaken in the same year, and in 1612 two quartos and two octavos were added. From time to time corrected texts appeared, notably in 1629 and 1638.

James had informed the bishops that the Bible was to be reviewed by them, submitted to the Privy Council, and finally ratified by royal authority. This procedure was not followed, nor was this Bible ever formally "authorized." It was, says the title-page, "appointed to be read in churches," but no proclamation or injunction enforcing this was issued. It soon superseded the Bishops'. To dislodge the Geneva took longer, but even Geneva could not hold out against it longer than a generation.

To appraise the diction of this Bible is not easy. Christians familiar from childhood with its phrases and rhythms treasure the book for its associations but for that very reason cannot always judge it dispassionately. For a long time, uninformed veneration or the substitution of admiration for analysis threatened to put this version above criticism. Probably most readers' preference for one translation over another owes more to associations or denominationalism than to anything else. One who grows up with the Prayer Book Psalter does not, apparently, come to prefer the Psalter in the King James Bible instead, however devoted he may be to the rest of that version. Readers brought up on the Geneva Bible did not change to the King James overnight; nor, in the nineteenth century, did readers of the King James change overnight to the Revised Version; nor have most users of the King James yet abandoned it for the recent Revised Standard Version, a scholarly work but (to those whose ears are accustomed to the cadences of 1611) a blight on public worship.

The King James Bible was a compromise, achieved in auspicious circumstances by conscientious and scholarly men who had a clear conception of their task and felt equal to it. They kept the Hebrew and Greek before them but borrowed from the Geneva, Rheims-Douai, and other versions when they thought they should. The companies followed their instructions with regard to the Bishops' Bible better than did the final revisers, who polished the work, recasting phrases for the sake of clarity or cadence. Thus the result was no sudden miracle but rather the harvesting or refining of the previous century's experience in translating the Bible into English. Tyndale, Coverdale, and their successors stand behind it. The language of the 1611 Bible, particularly in the New Testament, is Tyndale's more than any other man's. All subsequent revisions except the Rheims-Douai were based on his, directly or indirectly, and although many of his words and rhythms were improved by the time they appeared in the King James version, his work remains the most important part of the fabric.

The supremacy of the King James is one of style, not of scholarship. The men who made it did not set out to manufacture a literary classic—classics are seldom made to order. Yet they did produce one: perhaps the only classic ever turned in by a committee, and one of the few books better in translation (at least this is true of the New Testament) than in the original. Whatever one's theories about the connection between great societies and great art, it can hardly be mere coincidence that the King James Bible came near the climax of a splendid epoch in English political and literary history. The English vocabulary was more capacious, the syntax more flexible and mature in every sense, in 1611 than in 1525. These facts alone do not "explain" Elizabethan and Jacobean literature, needless to say, but they helped to make it possible. The Jacobean translators inherited a general tradition of English prose and, within that tradition, another of Biblical prose established by Tyndale. They modified this somewhat. In the interests of dignity and reverence they archaized slightly. Tyndale had not; his translation had greater colloquial vigor. In poetical and prophetical passages their diction is appropriately ornate. They allowed themselves a free hand in the use of synonyms: a crucial decision, for it gave their language variations aesthetically pleasing as well as illuminating. Always to render the same Hebrew or Greek word by the same English equivalent would, they say justly, "savor more of curiosity than wisdom."

An obvious and fundamental characteristic of Biblical style is parallelism and repetition, one element (phrase or clause) being balanced or contrasted with another. This is evident in all translations but never more felicitously than in the King James: "Beareth all things, believeth all things, hopeth all things, endureth all things," "whether there be prophecies, they shall fail; whether there be tongues, they shall cease; whether there be knowledge, it shall vanish away," "strengthen ye the weak hands and confirm the feeble knees," "then the eyes of the blind shall be opened, and the ears of the deaf shall be unstopped." Excessive parallelism is avoided by deliberate variety. If variety is the "secret" of the style, it is a secret whose techniques and effects are analyzable.

Perhaps the best way of appreciating the style is to study its cadences, for its most distinctive virtue is the adjustment of sound to sense. Here too our judgment may be biased by long familiarity with the book, but the judgment is virtually unanimous. The King James men had ears. As Jacobeans they were more sensitive to speech rhythms and more practiced in them, far better trained in rhetoric and more respectful of it, than their modern successors, some of whom (to paraphrase Acts) much learning doth make tone-deaf.

The paradox of the book is that a work abounding in Hebraic and Hellenistic imagery and idiom could become something seemingly so English. Selden, the seventeenth-century writer previously quoted, marveled at its triumph: "The Bible is rather translated into English words than into English phrase," and Selden thought this fact made the Bible less intelligible to the plain reader. Some modern critics, echoing this complaint, have solemnly convicted the King James Bible of being "a very harmful influence on English prose." "Its alien imagery has nothing to do with us. . . . The plain, honest English speech was overwhelmed with ornament. Blunt Englishmen twisted their tongues to speak like Hebrew prophets."[2] This provocative judgment is more applicable to the Old Testament than to the New. That some of the imagery was "alien" is true; that most

<hr />

[2] W. Somerset Maugham, *The Summing Up* (New York, 1938), p. 35; similarly C. V. Wedgwood, *Seventeenth-Century English Literature* (New York, 1950), pp. 15–17.

of it was too alien to be intelligible is hard to believe. The old translators would have been surprised to learn that Biblical imagery "has nothing to do with us." It had everything to do with them, they thought, because the text was sacred. So we return to our starting point: that, with regard to the Bible, questions of scholarship or literary criticism prove inseparable from questions of religion.

"*Scrutamini Scripturas* [search the Scriptures]. These two words have undone the world," wrote Selden; and the Reformation, the Wars of Religion in France, the Thirty Years' War, and the English Civil War must have suggested the same thought to others. To extraordinary numbers of Christians, however, the precept was compulsive, animating, worth any risk. That is why, when printing, religious change, and reasons of State gave them the open Bible at last, the English became the people of a book.

SUGGESTED READING

Works on the English Bible are so numerous that only a few of the most useful guides can be listed here. Good general bibliographies will be found in Ira M. Price, *The Ancestry of Our English Bible* (3d ed. rev. by W. A. Irwin and A. P. Wikgren; New York, 1956), and in C. C. Butterworth, *The Literary Lineage of the King James Bible* (Philadelphia, 1941). The best collection of records is A. W. Pollard, *Records of the English Bible* (Oxford, 1911). On editions see T. H. Darlow and H. T. Moule, *Historical Catalogue of the Printed Editions of Holy Scripture in the Library of the British and Foreign Bible Society,* vol. I (London, 1903). Important sixteenth-century translations of the New Testament are printed in parallel columns and accompanied by the Greek text and the King James version in *The English Hexapla* (London, 1841).

On the background to Tudor translations: Beryl Smalley, *The Study of the Bible in the Middle Ages* (rev. ed.; Oxford, 1952); B. F. Westcott, *A General View of the History of the English Bible* (3d ed. rev. by W. A. Wright; London, 1905); Margaret Deanesly, *The Lollard Bible* (Cambridge, 1920); J. H. Penniman, *A Book about the English Bible* (2d ed.; Philadelphia, 1931); F. G. Kenyon, *The Story of the Bible* (London, 1936); H. Wheeler Robinson, ed., *The Bible in Its Ancient and English Versions* (Oxford, 1954); Luther A. Weigle, *The English New Testament* (London, 1950); Hugh Pope, *English Versions of the Bible* (rev. by S. Bullough; St. Louis, 1952); W. Schwarz, *Principles and Problems of Biblical Translation* (Cambridge, 1955).

W. T. Whitley, *The English Bible under the Tudor Sovereigns* (London and Edinburgh, 1937) is a readable but not always reliable sketch. *William Tyndale* (London, 1937) and *Coverdale and His Bibles* (London, 1953), both by J. F. Mozley, are standard works. S. L. Greenslade, *The Work of William Tindale* (London and Glasgow, 1938) includes an essay on Tyndale's language by Gavin Bone. On the Rheims-Douai version, see J. G. Carleton, *The Part of Rheims in the Making of the English Bible* (Oxford, 1902). James Strachan, *Early Bible Illustrations* (Cambridge, 1957) is an interesting study.

The facsimile edition, in somewhat reduced size, of the King James Bible, edited by A. W. Pollard (London, 1911), has a valuable introduction and contains most of the records printed in his *Records of the English Bible*. Tyndale's 1534 revision of his translation of the New Testament is available in a reprint edited by N. H. Wallis (Cambridge, 1938). Butterworth's book, mentioned above, prints in an appendix selections from many translations and shows what each contributed to the King James. On the intermediate stage of the revision of 1611, consult E. E. Willoughby, *The Making of the King James Bible* (Los Angeles, 1956). On the King James version and the Hebrew text, see David Daiches, *The King James Version of the Bible* (Chicago, 1941).

On questions of literary style in the translations, see R. G. Moulton, *The Literary Study of the Bible* (Boston, 1895); George Saintsbury, *History of English Prose Rhythm* (London, 1912); C. S. Lewis, *English Literature in the Sixteenth Century* (Oxford, 1954).

¶ The figure of John Wycklife.

Kyng Edward the .iii. did Wicklife defēd
Wherbi he did florich in Orford longe while
But Richard ý.ii. Kyng did somthing bend
To papistis bi whom Wickklife was in exile
Yet dyd thys good man neuer alter his stile
But wrot mani volumis whils he was aliue
To extingwich errour, and truth to reuiue
At the last he returnid to his contrei againe
And lyuid at Lutterworth, where his charg
And after his deth he did ther remain (lay
Fourty winter & one, till come was the day
Whē Satā was suffrid to reu without slate
But thʒ did oure clergie set open his graue
And brēt al his bonis, such chariti thei haue

John Wyclif, *ca.* 1329–1384. From *The True Copy of a Prolog Written in an Old English Bible,* London, 1550. This "prolog" is Purvey's introduction to his revision of the English Bible, *ca.* 1395.

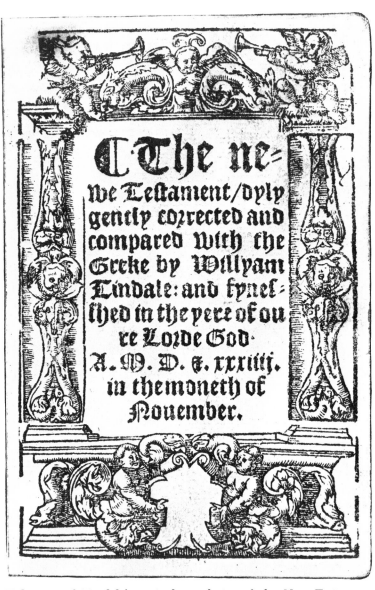

Title-page of Tyndale's revised translation of the New Testament, 1534. (*University of Pennsylvania Library copy.*)

Coverdale's translation, 1535. The first complete Bible printed in English. The woodcuts on this title-page are the work of Hans Holbein. They show, at top left, Adam and Eve hearkening to the serpent; at top right, the Risen Lord; next below, at left, Moses; at right, Christ commissioning the Disciples; below, at left, the reading of the Law; at right, St. Peter preaching; in the center at bottom, King Henry VIII with bishops and nobles; at left, David; at right, St. Paul. (*University of Pennsylvania Library copy.*)

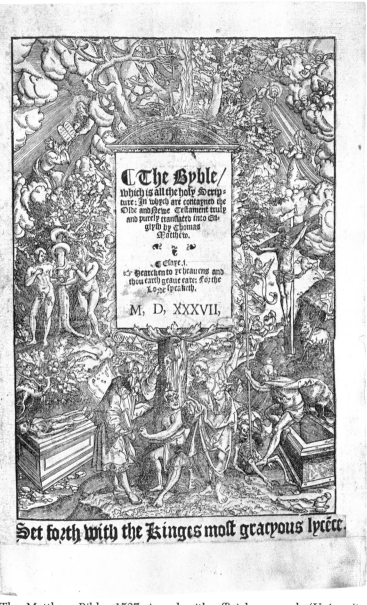

The Matthew Bible, 1537, issued with official approval. (*University of Pennsylvania Library copy.*)

The Great Bible, 1539. King Henry VIII is shown distributing copies of the Scriptures to Thomas Cromwell (on reader's right) and Archbishop Cranmer, who in turn give them to the people. The King's subjects (except those in jail, lower right) hail him with protestations of loyalty. (*Yale University Library copy.*)

The Bishops' Version, 1568, with portrait of Queen Elizabeth on the title-page.

❧ The feconde part of the Byble con-
teyning thefe bookes.

The booke of Iofuah.　　The firft booke of the Chronicles.
The booke of the Iudges.　The feconde booke of the Chronicles.
The booke of Ruth.　　　The firft booke of Efdras.
The firft booke of Samuel.　The feconde booke of Efdras.
The feconde booke of Samuel.　The booke of Hefter.
The thirde booke of the kinges.　The booke of Iob.
The fourth booke of the kinges.

Robert Dudley, Earl of Leicester. Portrait in the Bishops' Bible, 1568.

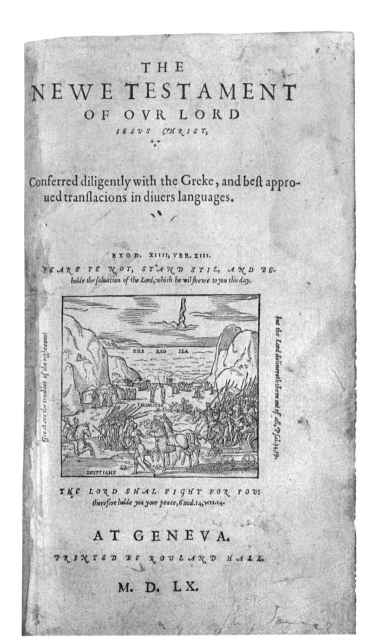

THE
NEWE TESTAMENT
OF OVR LORD
IESVS CHRIST,

Conferred diligently with the Greke, and best appro-
ued translacions in diuers languages.

EXOD. XIIII, VER. XIII.

FEARE YE NOT, STAND STIL, AND BE-
holde the saluacion of the Lord, which he wil shewe to you this day.

Great are the troubles of the righteous:

but the Lord deliuereth them out of all, Psal. 34, 19.

THE RED SEA

ISRAELITES

EGYPTIANS

THE LORD SHAL FIGHT FOR YOU:
therefore holde you your peace, Exod. 14, vers. 14.

AT GENEVA.

PRINTED BY ROVLAND HALL.

M. D. LX.

The New Testament in the Geneva Bible, 1560.

This mappe properly apperteineth to the 33 Chap. of Nombres.

This mappe declareth the way, which the Israelites went for the space of fourtie yeres from Egypt through the wildernes of Arabia, vntil they entred into the land of Canaan, as it is mentioned in Exod. Nomb. & Deuter. It contéineth also the 42 places where they pitched their tentes, which are named Nombers. 33 with the obseruacion of the degrees, concerning the length and the breadth, and the places of their abode set out by nombers.

Map from the Geneva Bible, 1560.

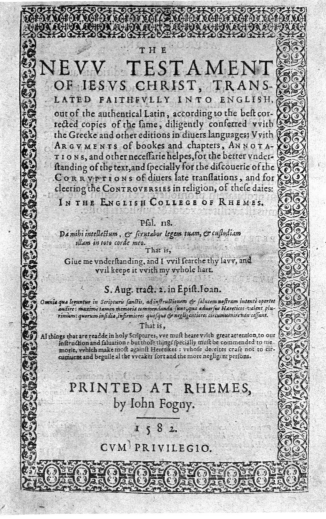

THE

NEVV TESTAMENT

OF IESVS CHRIST, TRANS-
LATED FAITHFVLLY INTO ENGLISH,
out of the authentical Latin, according to the best corrected copies of the same, diligently conferred vvith
the Greeke and other editions in diuers languages; Vvith
ARGVMENTS of bookes and chapters, ANNOTA-
TIONS, and other necessarie helpes, for the better vnderstanding of the text, and specially for the discouerie of the
CORRVPTIONS of diuers late translations, and for
cleering the CONTROVERSIES in religion, of these daies:

IN THE ENGLISH COLLEGE OF RHEMES.

Psal. 118.

*Da mihi intellectum, & scrutabor legem tuam, & custodiam
illam in toto corde meo.*

That is,

Giue me vnderstanding, and I vvil searche thy lavv, and
vvil keepe it vvith my vvhole hart.

S. Aug. tract. 2. in Epist. Ioan.

*Omnia quæ leguntur in Scripturis sanctis, ad instructionem & salutem nostram intentè oportet
audire: maxime tamen memoriæ commendanda sunt, quæ aduersus Hæreticos valent plu-
rimùm: quorum insidiæ, infirmiores quosque & negligentiores circumuenire non cessant.*

That is,

Al things that are readde in holy Scriptures, vve must heare vvith great attention, to our
instruction and saluation: but those things specially must be commended to me-
morie, vvhich make most against Heretikes: vvhose deceites cease not to cir-
cumuent and beguile al the vveaker sort and the more negligent persons.

PRINTED AT RHEMES,
by Iohn Fogny.

1582.

CVM PRIVILEGIO.

The Rheims New Testament, 1582.

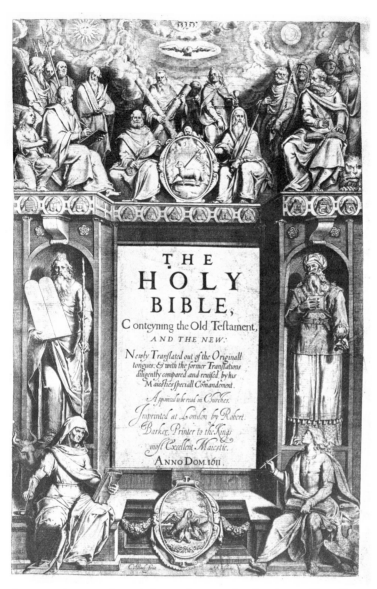

The most famous of English translations, the "Authorized" or "King James" Bible of 1611. (*Yale University Library copy.*)

The fyrst epistle of S. paul

geve most honoure to that parte which lacked / that there shuld be no stryfe in the body:
but that the membres shuld care indifferetly
one for another. And yf one member suffer, all
suffer with him, yf one member be had in honoure, all members be glad also.

Ye are the body of Christ / and members
one of another. And God hath also ordeyned
in the congregation / first the Apostles, secondarely prophetes / thyrdly teachers / then that
that do miracles: after that the gyftes of hea-
lynge, helpers / governers / diversite of tonges.

Are all Apostles? Are all prophetes? Are
all teachers? Are all doars of miracles? Have
all the gyftes of healinge? Do all speake with
tonges? Do all interprete? Covet after the best
gyftes. And yet shewe I unto you a moare excellent waye.

¶ The.xiii. Chapter.

Though I spake with the tonge of men
and angels / yet had no love, I were eve
as soundinge brasse: or as a tynklyn-
ge Cymball. And though I coulde prophesy,
and understode all secretes / and all knowledge:
yee yf I had all fayth, so that I coulde move
mountaynes out of ther places / and yet had no
love, I were nothinge. And though I bestowed all my goodes to fede the poore / and though
I gave my body even that I burned / and yet
had no love, it profeteth me nothinge.

Love suffreth longe / and is corteous. Love
envieth not. Love doth not frowardly / swelleth
not

*Who saye this as moche to saye as so stronge a fayth

Love.

To the Corinthyans. Fo. cc.liii

phil.ij.c.

not disceatfully / seketh not her awne / is not
provoked to anger / thynketh not
evyll / reioyseth not in iniquite: but reioyseth in
the trueth / suffreth all thynge / beleveth all / hopeth
all / endureth in all thynge.

Though that prophesyinge fayle / other
tonges shall cease / or knowledge vanysshe
awaye / yet love fayleth never awaye.

For oure knowledge is unparfect / and oure
prophesyinge is unparfet. But when that which
is parfet is come / then that which is unparfet
shall be done awaye. When I was a chylde /
I spake as a chylde / I understode as a chylde /
I ymagined as a chylde. But assone as I
was a man / I put awaye childesshnes. Now
we se in a glasse even in a darke speakynge:
but then shall we se face to face. Now I knowe
unparfectly: but then shall I knowe even
as I am knowen. Now abideth fayth, hope,
and love / even these thre: but the chefe of these
is love.

¶ The.xiiii. Chapter.

Labour for love and covet spirituall giftes: and most chefly for to prophesye. For
he that speaketh with tonges speaketh
not unto men, but unto god: for no man heareth him / howbeit in the sprete he speaketh
mysteries. But he that prophesyeth speaketh
unto men / to edisyinge / to exhortacion / and to
comforte. He that speaketh with tonges / profiteth him silfe: he that prophesyeth edifieth
the congregation. I wolde that ye all spake
with tonges: but rather that ye prophesied.
For greatter is he that prophisieth then he

Prophesinge is here taken for expo-
undynge / spea.

218

First Corinthians 13. Tyndale version 1534. (Piermont Morgan Library Copy.)

The XII. Chapter.

The XIII. Chapter.

The XII. Chapter.

The XIII. Chapter.

First Corinthians, 13: Coverdale version, 1535. (University of Pennsylvania Library Copy.)

19 For if they were all one member, where were the bodie?

20 But now *are* there manie membres, yet but ᵐ one bodie.

21 And the eye can not say vnto the hand, I haue no nede of thee : nor the head againe to the fete, I haue no nede of you.

22 Yea, muche rather those membres of the bodie, which seme to be ᵐ more feble, are necessarie.

23 And vpon those *membres* of the bodie, which we thinke moste vnhonest, put we more ᵒ honestie on : and our vncomelie *partes* haue more comelines on.

24 For our comelie *partes* nede it not : but God hathe tempered the bodie together, and hathe giuen the more honour to that *parte* which lacked,

25 Lest there shulde be anie diuision in the bodie : but that the members shulde ᵖ haue the same care one for another.

26 Therefore if one member suffer, all suffer with it : if one member be had in honour, all the membres reioyce with it.

27 Now ye are the bodie of Christ, & membres ᵠ for your parte.

28 And God hathe ordeined some in the Church : as first, Apostles, secondly Prophetes, thirdly teachers, then them that do miracles : after that, the giftes of healing, ʳ helpers, ˢ gouernours, diuersitie of tongues.

29 Are all Apostles? are all Prophetes? are all teachers?

30 Are all doers of miracles? haue all the giftes of healing? do all speake with tongues? do all interprete?

31 But ᵗ desire you the best gifts, and I wil yet shewe you a more excellent way.

CHAP. XIII.

Because loue is the fountaine and rule of edifying the Church, he setteth forthe the nature, office and praise thereof.

1 THogh I speake with the tongues of men and ᵃ Angels, and haue not loue, I am *as* sounding brasse, or a tinkling cymbal.

2 And thogh I had the *gift* of prophecie, and knewe all secretes and all knowledge, yea, if I had ᵇ all faith, so that I colde remoue * mountaines and had not loue, I were nothing.

3 And thogh I fede the poore with all my goods, and thogh I giue my bodie, that I be burned, and haue not loue, it profiteth me nothing.

4 Loue suffreth long : it is bountiful: loue enuieth not: loue doeth not boast it self: it is not puffed vp:

5 It disdaineth not: it seketh not her owne things: it is not prouoked to anger: it thinketh not euil:

6 It reioyceth not in iniquitie, but reioyceth in the trueth:

7 It suffreth all things : it beleueth ᶜ all things : it hopeth all things : it endureth ᵈ all things.

8 Loue doeth neuer fall away, thogh that prophecyings be abolished, or the tongues cease, or knowledge vanish away.

9 For ᵉ we knowe ᶠ in parte, and we prophecie in parte.

10 But when that which is perfite, is come, then that which is in parte, shalbe abolished.

11 When I was a childe, I spake as a childe, I vnderstode as a childe, I thoght as a childe: but when I became a man, I put away childish things.

12 For now we se ᵍ through a glasse darkely : but then *shal* we *se* face to face. Now I knowe in parte : but then shal I knowe euen as I am ʰ knowen.

13 And now abideth faith, hope & loue, euen these thre : but the ʰ chiefest of these is loue.

CHAP. XIIII.

1 He exhorteth to loue, commendeth the gift of tongues, & other spiritual gifts, 5 But chiefly prophecying. 34 He comandeth women to kepe silence in the Church, 40 And sheweth what good ordre oght to be obserued in the Church.

1 FOllowe after loue, and couet spiritual *gifts*, and rather that ye maye prophecie.

2 For he that speaketh *a strange* tongue, speaketh not vnto men, but vnto God: for no man ᵇ heareth *him*: howbeit in ᶜ the spirit he speaketh secret things.

3 But he that prophecieth, speaketh vnto men to edifying, and to exhortacion, and to comfort.

4 He that speaketh *strange* language, edifieth ᵈ him self : but he that prophecieth, edifieth the Church.

5 I wolde that ye all spake *strange* languages, but rather that ye prophecied : for greater is he that prophecieth, thē he that speaketh *diuers* tongues, except he expoūde it, that the Church may receiue edificacion.

6 And now, brethren, if I come vnto you speaking *diuers* tongues, what shal I profite you, except I speake to you, ether by ᵉ reuelacion, or by knowledge, or by prophecying, or by doctrine?

7 Moreouer things without life which giue a sounde, whether *it be* a pipe or an harpe, except they make a distinction in the sounds, how shal it be knowen what is piped or harped?

8 And also if the trumpet giue an vncerteine sounde, who shal prepare him self to battel?

9 So likewise you, by the tongue, except ye vtter wordes that haue significacion, how

XX.i.

First Corinthians, 13: Geneva version, 1560.

Math.x.a.
Luk.xi.a.
Ephe.iiii.c.

with it. If one member be had in honour, all the members reioyce with it.

27 Ye are the body of Christe, and members one of another.

28 And God hath ordayned some in the Churche, first *Apostles, secondarely, prophetes, thirdely teachers, then them that do miracles: after that, the giftes of healyng, helpers, gouernours, diuer-

sitie of tongues.

29 Are all, Apostles: are all, prophetes: are all, teachers:

30 Are all, doers of miracles: haue all the giftes of healyng? Do all speake with tongues? Do all interprete?

31 Couet after the best giftes: And yet shew I vnto you a more excellent way.

The.xiij.Chapter.

1 Because loue is the fountayne and rule of edifyng the Churche, he setteth foorth the nature, office, and prayse therof.

(*) If the Angels had tongues, and I had the vse therof, and did not bestowe the to profite my neyghbour, it were nothyng but vaine bablyng.
Luk.xvii.a.

i Cor.x e.
Philip.ii.a.

Hough I speake with the tongues of men and of (*) Angels, and haue not loue, I am [as] soundyng brasse, or [as] a tincklyng Cimball:

2 And though I coulde prophesie, and vnderstoode all secretes, and all knowledge: Yea, & if I had all fayth, *so that I coulde moue mountaynes out of their places, and haue not loue, I were nothyng.

3 And though I bestowe all my goodes to feede the poore, and though I geue my body that I burned, and haue not loue, it profiteth me nothyng.

4 Loue suffreth long, and is curteous: Loue enuieth not, loue doth not frowardely, swelleth not,

5 Dealeth not dishonestlie, *seeketh not her owne, is not prouoked to anger, thynketh none euyll,

6 Reioyceth not in iniquitie: but reioy-

ceth in the trueth:

7 Suffreth all thynges, beleueth all thynges, hopeth all thynges, endureth all thynges.

8 Though p prophesiynges fayle, other tongues ceasse, or knowledge banishe away, [yet] loue falleth neuer away.

9 & For our knowledge is vnperfect, & and our prophesiyng is vnperfect:

10 But when that which is perfect, is come, then that which is vnperfect shalbe done away.

11 When I was a chylde, I spake as a chylde, I vnderstoode as a chylde, I imagined as a chylde : But assoone as I was a man, I put away chyldishnesse.

12 Nowe we see in a (*) glasse, euen in a darke speakyng : but then shall we see face to face. Nowe I knowe vnperfectly: but then shall I knowe euen as I am knowen.

(*) The misteries of God.

13 Nowe abydeth fayth, hope, and loue, these three, but the chiefe of these is loue.

The.xiiij. Chapter.

1 He exhorteth to loue, commendeth the gift of tongues, and other spirituall giftes, 5 But chiefely prophesiyng. 34 He commaundeth women to kepe scilence in the Church. 40 And sheweth what good order ought to be obserued in the Churche.

(*) Vnderstandeth hym.

Olowe after loue, and couet spirituall [giftes] but most chiefelie that ye may prophesie.

2 For he that speaketh with the tongue, speaketh not vnto men, but vnto God: For no man (*) heareth [hym]. Howbeit, in the spirite he speaketh misteries.

3 But he that prophesieth, speaketh vnto men to their edifyng, to their exhortation, and to their comfort.

4 He that speaketh with the tongue,

edifieth hym selfe: *he that prophesieth, edifieth the Churche.

5 I woulde yee al spake with tongues, but rather that ye prophesie: For greater is he that prophesieth, then he that speaketh with tongues, except he expounde it, that the Churche may haue edifyng.

6 Nowe brethren, yf I come vnto you speakyng with tongues, what shall I profite you, except I speake to you eyther by reuelation, or by knowledge, or by prophesiyng, or by doctrine:

7 Moreouer, thynges without lyfe geuing

Rom.xii.b.
Num.xi.g.
* Tongue, is in that place spoken of, which is not vnderstand...

First Corinthians, 13: Bishops' version, 1568.

And you are the body of Chrsit, and members of mem- 16

8 † And * some verily God hath set in the Church first A- 27 postles, secondly prophets, thirdly doctors, next miracles, the graces of doing cures, helpes, gouernements, kindes of tonges. ‡ Are al Apostles? are al prophets? are al doctors? are al miracles? † haue al the grace of doing cures? do al speake vvith tonges? do al interpret? † But pursue the better giftes. And yet I shevv you a more excellent vvay.

Zelous faith. Faith in this same.) This faith is not an other in substance then the common faith in Christ...

Vnitie.

Schisme.

CHAP. XIII.

F I speake vvith the tonges of men and of Angels, and haue not charitie : I am become as sounding brasse, or a tinkling cymbal. † And if I should haue prophecie, and knevv al mysteries, and al knovvledge, and if I should haue al faith so that I could remoue mountaines, and haue not charitie, I am nothing. † And if I should distribute al my goods to be meate for the poore, and if I should deliuer my body so that I burne, and haue not charitie, it doth profit me nothing.

† Charitie is patient, is benigne : Charitie enuieth not, dealeth not peruersly : is not puffed vp, † is not ambitious, seeketh not her ovvne, is not prouoked to anger : thinketh not euil : † reioyceth not vpon iniquitie, but reioyceth vvith

with the truth : † suffereth al things, beleeueth al things, hopeth al things, beareth al things. † Charitie neuer falleth away : vvhether prophecies shal be made voide, or tonges shal cease, or knovvledge shal be destroied. † For in part vve knovv, and in part vve prophecie. † But ‡ vvhen that shal come that is perfect, that shal be made voide that is in part. † Vvhen I vvas a litle one, I spake as a litle one, I vnderstood as a litle one, I thought as a litle one. But vvhen I vvas made a man, I did avvay the things that belonged to a litle one. † Vve see novv by a glasse in a darke sort : but then face to face. Novv I knovv in part : but then I shal knovv as also I am knovven. † And novv there remaine, faith, hope, charitie, these three. but the ‡ greater of these is charitie.

Charitie.) Vvithout Charitie, both tovvard euery particular person, and specially tovvard the common body of the Church, none of al the giftes and graces of God be profitable...

CHAP. XIIII.

6 And there are diuersities of operations, but it is the same God, which worketh all in all.

7 But the manifestation of the Spirit is giuen to euery man to profit withall.

8 For to one is giuen by the Spirit, the word of wisedome, to another the word of knowledge, by the same Spirit:

9 To another faith, by the same Spirit: to another the gifts of healing, by the same Spirit:

10 To another the working of miracles, to another prophecie, to another discerning of spirits, to another diuers kindes of tongues, to another the interpretation of tongues.

11 But all these worketh that one and the selfe same Spirit, diuiding to euery man seuerally as he will.

12 For as the body is one, and hath many members, and all the members of that one body, being many, are one body: so also is Christ.

13 For by one Spirit are we all baptized into one body, whether wee bee Iewes or Gentiles, whether wee bee bond or free: and haue beene all made to drinke into one Spirit.

14 For the body is not one member, but many.

15 If the foot shall say, Because I am not the hand, I am not of the body: is it therefore not of the body?

16 And if the eare shall say, Because I am not the eye, I am not of the body: is it therefore not of the body?

17 If the whole body were an eye, where were the hearing? If the whole were hearing, where were the smelling?

18 But now hath God set the members euery one of them in the body, as it hath pleased him.

19 And if they were all one member, where were the body?

20 But now are they many members, yet but one body.

21 And the eye cannot say vnto the hand, I haue no neede of thee: nor againe, the head to the feet, I haue no need of you.

22 Nay, much more those members of the body, which seeme to bee more feeble, are necessarie.

23 And those members of the body, which wee thinke to bee lesse honourable, vpon these we bestow more abundant honour, and our vncomely parts

24 For our comely parts haue no neede: but God hath tempered the body together, hauing giuen more abundant honour to that part which lacked.

25 That there should be no schisme in the body: but that the members should haue the same care one for another.

26 And whether one member suffer, all the members suffer with it: or one member be honoured, all the members reioyce with it.

27 Now yee are the body of Christ, and members in particular.

28 And God hath set some in the Church, first Apostles, secondarily prophets, thirdly teachers, after that miracles, then gifts of healings, helpes in gouernments, diuersities of tongues.

29 Are all Apostles? are all prophets? are all teachers? are all workers of miracles?

30 Haue all the gifts of healing? doe all speake with tongues? doe all interpret?

31 But couet earnestly the best gifts: And yet shew I vnto you a more excellent way.

CHAP. XIII.

1 All gifts, 2. 3. how excellent soeuer, are nothing worth without charitie. 4 The praises thereof, and 13 prelation before hope and faith.

Though I speake with the tongues of men & of Angels, and haue not charitie, I am become as sounding brasse, or a tinkling cymball.

2 And though I haue the gift of prophecie, and vnderstand all mysteries and all knowledge: and though I haue all faith, so that I could remooue mountaines, and haue not charitie, I am nothing.

3 And though I bestow all my goods to feed the poore, and though I giue my body to bee burned, and haue not charitie, it profiteth me nothing.

4 Charitie suffereth long, and is kinde: charitie enuieth not: charitie vaunteth not it selfe, is not puffed vp,

5 Doeth not behaue it selfe vnseemly, seeketh not her owne, is not easily prouoked, thinketh no euill,

6 Reioyceth not in iniquitie, but reioyceth in the trueth:

7 Beareth all things, beleeueth all things, hopeth all things, endureth all things.

8 Charitie neuer faileth: but whether there be prophesies, they shall faile; whether there bee tongues, they shall cease; whether there bee knowledge, it shall vanish away.

9 For wee know in part, and we prophesie in part.

10 But when that which is perfect is come, then that which is in part, shall be done away.

11 When I was a childe, I spake as a childe, I vnderstood as a childe, I thought as a childe: but when I became a man, I put away childish things.

12 For now we see through a glasse, darkely: but then face to face: now I know in part, but then shall I know euen as also I am knowen.

13 And now abideth faith, hope, charitie, these three, but the greatest of these is charitie.

CHAP. XIIII.

1 Prophecie is commended, 2. 3. 4. and preferred before speaking with tongues, 6 by a comparison drawen from musicall instruments, 12 Both must be referred to edification, 22 as serue for true and proper end. 26 The vse of each in range, 27 and 27 Women are forbidden to speake in the Church.

Follow after charitie, and desire spirituall gifts, but rather that yee may prophecie.

2 For he that speaketh in an vnknowen tongue, speaketh not vnto men, but vnto God: for no man vnderstandeth him: howbeit in the spirit he speaketh mysteries.

3 But he that prophesieth, speaketh vnto men to edification, and exhortation, and comfort.

4 He that speaketh in an vnknowen tongue, edifieth himselfe: but he that prophesieth, edifieth the Church.

5 I would that yee all spake with tongues, but rather that yee prophesied: for greater is he that prophesieth, then hee that speaketh with tongues, except hee interpret, that the Church may receiue edifying.

6 Now brethren, if I come vnto you speaking with tongues, what shall I profite you, except I shall speake to you either by reuelation, or by knowledge, or by prophecying, or by doctrine?

7 And euen things without life giuing sound, whether pipe or harpe, except they giue a distinction in the sounds, how shall it be knowen what is piped or harped?

8 For if the trumpet giue an vncertaine sound, who shall prepare himselfe to the battell?

9 So likewise you, except yee vtter by the tongue words easie to be vnderstood, how shall it be knowen what is spoken? for yee shall speake into the aire.

10 There are, it may be, so many kindes of voyces in the world, and none of them are without signification.

11 Therefore if I know not the meaning of the voyce, I shall be vnto him that speaketh, a Barbarian, and he that speaketh shall be a Barbarian vnto me.

12 Euen so yee, forasmuch as yee are zealous of spirituall gifts, seeke that yee may excell to the edifying of the Church.

13 Wherefore let him that speaketh in an vnknowen tongue, pray that he may interprete.

14 For if I pray in an vnknowen tongue, my spirit prayeth, but my vnderstanding is vnfruitfull.

15 What is it then? I will pray with the spirit, and I will pray with the vnderstanding also: I will sing with the spirit, and I will sing with the vnderstanding also.

16 Else, when thou shalt blesse with the spirit, how shall hee that occupieth the roome of the vnlearned, say Amen at thy giuing of thankes, seeing he vnderstandeth not what thou sayest?

17 For thou verely giuest thankes well, but the other is not edified.

18 I thanke my God, I speake with tongues more then you all.

19 Yet in the Church I had rather speake fiue words with my vnderstanding, that by my voyce I might teach others also, then ten thousand words in an vnknowen tongue.

20 Brethren, bee not children in vnderstanding: howbeit in malice be yee children, but in vnderstanding be men.

21 In the Law it is written, With men of other tongues, and other lippes will I speake vnto this people: and yet for all that will they not heare me, saith the Lord.

22 Wherefore tongues are for a signe, not to them that beleeue, but to them that beleeue not: But prophesying ser-

223

The English Church
in the Sixteenth Century

By Craig R. Thompson

RELIGION, Queen Elizabeth told Parliament in 1585, is "the ground on which all other matters ought to take root." The Christian religion, for most of its adherents at least, implies a Church. As an institution, the Church in England in Tudor times was, as it had always been, the corporate expression of the spiritual life of Englishmen. In another sense it could be regarded as a department of State, subject to control by government even though administered by its own spiritual officers. In the sixteenth century, in England as elsewhere, Church and religion permeated public and private life to a degree not easily grasped by citizens of more secularized societies today.

The material in this pamphlet is selected to illustrate, by means of significant sixteenth-century books, some of the most important aspects of the English Church in its function as spiritual voice of the nation and its character as an institution intimately connected with the State. Only one book—*the* Book, the Bible—affected decisively the Church in Tudor England. The English Bible in the sixteenth century will be treated in a separate Folger pamphlet. The present pamphlet describes other books, some famous, others once famous though now no longer so, but all of them useful as a means of recalling the main events, changes, perplexities, and controversies in the life of the Church of England. Title-pages and woodcuts in the following pages are reproduced from books in the Folger collection; all but three are from first editions.

The sixteenth century was the era of the Reformation, a cardinal episode in the history of organized Christianity and one that had immense effect not only on the Church itself but on social, political, and intellectual life as well. For anyone interested in sixteenth- or seventeenth-century history, institutions, ideas, or art, the Reformation is a central fact: a movement of ideas and experience, mainly but not exclusively religious or ecclesiastical; a dividing line between what textbooks label the "medieval" and "modern" worlds. "Worlds" in this sense do not divide so much as merge into one another. But if guideposts are to be used, certainly the Reformation is one of the more conspicuous in the history of the last five hundred years.

In every land of Western Europe the Church had an ancient and continuous history. Catholic reform in the fifteenth and early sixteenth centuries, the Protestant Reformation, and the Catholic Counter Reformation were efforts to re-form, not to break up or revolutionize, an institution. The Protestant Reformation did prove to be in some fundamental respects a revolution nonetheless, and the cleavage then caused in the Western Church still exists. Yet the reformers did not consider themselves revolutionists at all—reformers seldom do. Henry VIII and most of the English churchmen thought of themselves as Christians who were bringing about, by peaceful means (on the whole), desirable or necessary improvements in the organization of ecclesiastical affairs. Luther, Melanchthon, and Calvin believed they were restorers of Christian theology and of Church order. The Anabaptists, on the other hand, were considered anarchists by the rest of the Protestants, who felt only abhorrence for them.

Viewed in perspective, the story of the Church in England is a part of the general history of the Church, not a chronicle wholly separate and unique. Nevertheless, because the English Church had its distinctive character and traditions; because of the tension between its insularity and its recurrent susceptibility to Continental influences; because of the English Bible; because of Henry VIII, Mary Tudor, Elizabeth, Wolsey, Cromwell, Cranmer, Parker, Whitgift, Burleigh, Walsingham—and finally, because of accident—the reorganization of the English Church took forms differing from those in the lands where Lutheran or Reformed (Calvinistic and Zwinglian) conceptions and practices prevailed.

When Henry VIII came to the throne in 1509, England recognized the papal authority in spiritual matters, as it had done for nine hundred years. Before Henry died in 1547, the English Church had rejected this authority, acknowledged the King as its "Supreme Head," abolished monasticism, and changed the liturgy, all the while continuing to call itself Catholic. In the reign of his son, Edward VI, it became more evidently Protestant. Henry's elder daughter, Mary, set the clock back for a few years. His younger daughter, Elizabeth, restored the Edwardian establishment, then consolidated the position of the Anglican Church, defending it from dissenters on right and left, making further changes in liturgy and administration, but still intending this Church to be Catholic; though after 1570 a sharp distinction began to be made between "Catholic" and "Roman Catholic." Throughout all these changes and reactions, the government had sufficient support from nobility and commons to carry out its ecclesiastical policies.

This does not mean that most Englishmen could be regarded as thoroughgoing Protestants. Until 1560 or 1570 the majority may have favored the old religion. But many changed their views; many others conformed. The government had its way, if sometimes by means of repression, imprisonment, and even bloodshed. For since religion in the sixteenth century was a matter of State as well as a matter of private belief or conscience, it was closely involved with questions of political loyalty, obedience to law, and international diplomacy. This involvement seems remarkable only if we forget how much history repeats itself. Substitute "political beliefs" for "religious beliefs," and some of the deeds of sixteenth-century rulers and governments at once become more intelligible. Societies, through governments, act most drastically in the things that matter most to them. Few people in the twentieth century have been persecuted, let alone killed, for heresy in religion. But the number of persons killed to date in this century (in scientific gas chambers, it is true, instead of on the gallows) for heresy in political faith or for being "non-Aryan" far exceeds the number legally killed in the sixteenth century for their Protestantism or Catholicism. And there are other startling parallels between sixteenth-century and twentieth-century political experience. There are the demands made by a totalitarian regime on private conscience; if the individual does not accede to the demands, he may go to the block, like Thomas More. There is "guilt by association" and the hypothetical question cunningly devised to trap a prisoner—the "bloody question," as it was called by Roman Catholics in Elizabeth's day. "What would you do," government inquisitors asked the Jesuit prisoner John Gerard in 1594, "if the Pope were to send over an army and declare that his only object was to bring the kingdom back to the Catholic allegiance? . . . Whose side would you be on then—the Pope's or the Queen's?" There is the "liquidation" of statesmen whose policy fails—Wolsey and Cromwell, for example. There is even something resembling the familiar propaganda campaign preceding a political action—Cromwell's preparations for confiscating the wealth of the monasteries and then sending his commissioners to find what he wanted them to find. Finally there is the disposition, common to Roman Catholics and Protestants alike in the sixteenth century, to justify one's own atrocities or persecutions and to protest against the horrors committed by others.

Long before the sixteenth century the English government (as Shakespeare's *King John* reminds us) had had serious difficulties with the papacy. By the sixteenth century nationalism was strong enough, and the papacy weak enough, to permit a clever and determined ruler like Henry VIII to challenge the Pope when self-interest prompted him to do so. In England, as in France and Spain, the monarchy had gradually but successfully contested the papacy's exclusive right to appoint bishops and collect ecclesiastical taxes. The Statute of Provisors (1351) prevented the popes from granting English benefices to aliens without royal approval. Another statute, Praemunire (1353), made it treasonable to carry appeals to Rome except with royal consent. In the fourteenth and fifteenth centuries the "Babylonian Captivity" of the popes at Avignon (when France controlled them), the Great Schism (during which two and at one time three men claimed to be Pope), the conciliar movement, the prevalence of simony, and the personal character of certain popes had seriously damaged papal prestige. The moral character of an Alexander VI or a Julius II was not likely to restore it. Julius was a successful warrior, but since the papacy was continually involved in political and diplomatic intrigue, rulers and people had difficulty at times in distinguishing its worldly from its spiritual activities, especially when their own interests were at stake. Pluralism, prolonged absence of some of the bishops from their dioceses on Crown business, clerical laxity, the spiritual decay of monastic and mendicant orders all contributed to an anticlericalism which Henry and Cromwell knew how to exploit when the time came to do so.

Henry prided himself on being a theologian. He was orthodox and devout. When Lutheranism first appeared, he reacted in a typical English way to a new idea: he was sincerely horrified, and wrote a pamphlet. He took steps to prevent the spread of Lutheran doctrines in England. In these actions he had the wholehearted support of bishops and other churchmen.

The Reformation in England had many causes, but unquestionably it was precipitated by the King's desire for a divorce. When refused a divorce, Henry proceeded to abolish the papal power in England and undertook to reconstitute the English Church as a Catholic but nonpapal one.

Henry convinced himself that his marriage to his elder brother's widow, Catherine of Aragon, violated Biblical law. He wanted an heir, and he was infatuated with Anne Boleyn. Cardinal Wolsey's attempts to get the divorce failed. Whatever ecclesiastical objections there may have been, politically the Pope was unable to oblige Henry at the cost of offending Catherine's nephew, the Emperor Charles V. After negotiations had dragged on for three years, the King took matters into his own hands. Through Convocation and Parliament he secured measures ending papal jurisdiction in England. Convocation, the legislative assembly of the Church, was sometimes a willing instrument (in antipapal matters), sometimes a reluctant one (in giving Henry the title of "Supreme Head"). Parliament was more compliant. The King wanted to remain Catholic in doctrine and intended that everybody else should too. But he allowed nothing to stand in the way of his seizing control of the Church. He intimidated the bishops and killed More, Bishop Fisher, and others, both clerics and laymen, who resisted or seemed to resist the royal policy. He closed down the abbeys and monasteries and confiscated their wealth. All this he accomplished in the decade between 1530 and 1540. In 1531, Convocation acknowledged him as "Supreme Head" of the Church in England, "as far as the law of Christ allows." The Supremacy Act of 1534 omitted even this important qualifying clause. In 1532, Convocation made a formal submission, promising it would never enact new canons without royal consent. Parliament strengthened Praemunire by an act (1533) declaring that the English Church was "sufficient and meet of itself, without the intermeddling of any exterior person or persons." This was followed by other legislation to assure ecclesiastical power and revenues to the King.

The Henrician Church, administered by Archbishop Cranmer in accordance with the royal wishes, encouraged Bible-reading; the first complete Bible in English, Coverdale's, appeared in 1535. Though penance, invocation of saints, and purgatory were kept at first, "superstitious" practices connected with them were abolished. Protestant tendencies received a check at the end of the decade, however. Doctrinally the *Six Articles* of 1539, which were imposed on all Englishmen, and the *King's Book* of 1543 were reactionary—much more Catholic than some of the reformers could abide. The *Six Articles* virtually reaffirmed transubstantiation, forbade priests to marry (Archbishop Cranmer had to put away his wife for a time), permitted private Masses, and declared auricular confession to be necessary.

The Church of England, in the last eight years of Henry's reign, was thus "Catholic" in some respects, "Protestant" in others: Catholic, for example, if one agrees with the King and his clergy that a Church without the papacy could be truly Catholic; Protestant if rejection of papacy and monasticism were characteristic of Protestantism, as they were. To most ordinary parishioners, religious life probably continued much as it had before. The monasteries were gone, and one heard less about the Pope; but one heard more English in the service and began to know the Bible better.

Since Edward VI was only nine years old when Henry died, the government was administered by a Council of Regency, dominated at first by the Duke of Somerset, later by the Duke of Northumberland. In general, the seven years' reign was a period of clarification and advancement for Protestantism in England. The two most conservative bishops, Gardiner and Bonner, were imprisoned. A *Book of Homilies* was issued (1547). In the same year royal injunctions ordered the removal of images leading to superstition and the abolition of shrines. Parliament repealed the *Six Articles,* abolished chantries, and ordered that the laity should be given the wine as well as the bread in Communion. Archbishop Cranmer prepared an English service book to replace the Roman ones. This, the first edition of the *Prayer Book,* was published in 1549. It was accompanied by an Act of Uniformity enjoining all clergy to use this book under penalty of imprisonment. The second Act of Uniformity (1552) required use of a revised edition, more Protestant than the one of 1549. This *Book of Common Prayer* of 1552 became the standard text.

By this and other legislation the Church of England became, by 1553, much more Protestant in doctrine and practice than it had been in the latter years of Henry VIII. But when Mary Tudor, a devout Catholic, succeeded Edward in 1553, she tried to sweep away the Henrician and Edwardian innovations and restore the Church and the country to their ancient spiritual allegiance. The old bishops returned; Cranmer, Latimer, and Ridley were arrested and, two years later, executed. Parliament, submissive to the wishes of the Crown (it referred in 1554 to the mission of the new Archbishop of Canterbury, Cardinal Pole, as one "to call us home again into the right way from whence we have all this long while wandered and strayed abroad"), promptly repealed the legislation of the Edwardian reign. Married priests were removed; the Roman liturgy was restored. An Act of Repeal of 1554 canceled all ecclesiastical laws passed since 1528, with one significant exception—that dissolving the monasteries. Thus the Pope was to resume jurisdiction over the English Church, but the laymen who had profited from the sale or gift of monastic properties were to keep what they had gained. Some of the most zealous Protestant divines fled the country. These "Marian exiles" went to Germany or Switzerland, where they absorbed the doctrines and practices of Lutherans, Calvinists, and Zwinglians—a matter of some consequence to the English Church, for when the exiles returned after Mary's death they set to work to bring Anglican doctrine, worship, and polity into line with the Continental models they knew. They were influential, yet less influential, and of course less numerous, than their brethren who had remained in England and risked persecution.

Mary's reign was memorable in English church history not so much because of her reactionary policies as because of the persecutions used to enforce them. Between 273 and 300 persons—the exact number is disputed—were burned in less than five years. About as many Englishmen died for their faith in Mary's short reign as in the forty-five years of Elizabeth's. Nevertheless Mary's life ended in frustration and failure (1558). The English had resented her marriage to Philip of Spain; she was childless; the Pope was hostile, for political reasons; moreover, despite all the legislation and all the burnings, Catholicism was not secure enough. Worst of all, her half-sister, Elizabeth, was not known to share her devotion to the old faith.

Elizabeth, in fact, was not a person of profoundly religious temperament. She held sincere convictions and expressed some decided opinions on spiritual topics, but these did not dictate political and diplomatic policy. Policy came first. This had to be so, because of the urgency of making the country strong and keeping it strong. Elizabeth's ecclesiastical policy is more understandable if we bear in mind the necessity, in the earlier years of her reign, of avoiding war with France, of playing off France against Spain, and of resolving the problem of Scotland. To preserve and strengthen England, the Queen was prepared to adopt whatever ecclesiastical policy seemed most advantageous, to change it when necessary, and to compel uniformity. Her shrewdness, courage, patience, cajolery, and luck gave her opportunities never enjoyed by Mary Tudor. Elizabeth understood her people better, too, and was well served by her ministers. Her policy required, and resulted in, a Church firmly under Crown control, Catholic in doctrine (by Anglican definition, at any rate) but nonpapal. Such a Church must be a compromise, broad enough to have room for those who had been orthodox before Henry's legislation as well as for those who were enthusiastic reformers.

The legal principles of this Elizabethan Church were set forth by two acts of Parliament in 1559. The first, the Act of Supremacy, restored to the Crown the "rights" asserted by Henry VIII but surrendered by Mary Tudor. (Elizabeth was not above appropriating Church revenues.) It repealed Marian legislation and revived the Henrician statutes against the papacy. "All usurped and foreign power and authority, spiritual and temporal" was to be "clearly extinguished"; any "foreign prince, person, prelate, state, or potentate, spiritual or temporal" was forbidden forever from exercising any jurisdiction in the realm of England. Authority over Church affairs was vested in the Crown. Henry's title of "Supreme Head" was not used by Elizabeth, however; instead she was called "Supreme Governor . . . as well in all spiritual or ecclesiastical things or causes as temporal." (In certain *Injunctions*, also of 1559, the Queen assured the clergy that she would never "challenge authority and power of ministry of divine service," that is, would not attempt to exercise strictly spiritual offices.) Consent of Convocation was required before the Crown's commissioners could act in doubtful cases of heresy. All clergy were required by the act to take an "Oath of Supremacy."

The second act of 1559, the Act of Uniformity, restored the *Book of Common Prayer* of 1552 and made the use of it compulsory. Refusal to attend church was made punishable by fine.

Jealous of her prerogatives, the Queen did not often welcome Parliamentary interference in ecclesiastical affairs, though Parliament was usually more than ready to assert its own prerogatives. From time to time Convocation legislated for the Church, but its decisions had to receive royal assent before they became law. A Court of High Commission, appointed by the Crown, had responsibility for maintaining the Acts of Supremacy and Uniformity, and broad powers to enforce ecclesiastical law. Much depended on the subservience or cooperation of the bishops. Cardinal Pole, Archbishop of Canterbury, had died on the same day as Queen Mary. Bishops surviving from Mary's reign were deprived, some imprisoned, for refusing to take the Oath of Supremacy. Some of the men appointed to take their places were returned exiles, Calvinistic in theology. The Church was particularly fortunate in its new Archbishop of Canterbury, Matthew Parker, a patient, moderate, charitable, and scholarly man.

The English Church of Elizabethan times was an institution of ancient traditions but reformed by successive royal programs; Catholic in doctrine, it insisted, but patently Protestant if some of the *Thirty-Nine Articles* are interpreted strictly; Protestant too in its opposition to the papacy and in many changes made in the liturgy since 1547. It was a national Church which, although administered by prelates, was controlled ultimately by government. It demanded uniformity yet sought to be comprehensive. Indeed this was a practical necessity, for when Elizabeth became Queen many of her loyal subjects—how many we do not know, but possibly a majority—adhered to the old religion. Many of these apparently became Anglican, or at least conformed, as the reign advanced; but again we have no reliable statistics to guide us.

Throughout Elizabeth's reign the Anglican Establishment was the object of abuse, and sometimes—as the government and many subjects thought—of plots from two sources, Roman Catholics without and the Puritan faction within. The government dealt severely with these critics when it believed they acted seditiously or treasonably. Every sixteenth-century government made the distinction between "loyal opposition" and sedition a narrow one. Significantly, "loyal opposition" is a nineteenth-century phrase. Tudor government was strongly centralized; Tudor monarchs, like their Continental brethren, sought and kept as much power as possible. To understand the passions and persecutions caused by religious differences in the sixteenth century, we must abandon comfortable nineteenth- or twentieth-century assumptions about toleration; as has already been suggested, the present century is rediscovering how unreliable assumptions about toleration can be. Toleration was a lesson Europe scarcely began to learn before the seventeenth century. Every Church assumed that uniformity was necessary and that nonconformists should be disciplined. All of the larger Churches, by themselves or through government, persecuted at various times. Henry VIII killed Lutherans as well as Carthusians. The Marian government killed Protestants. Elizabeth's government killed some Puritans as well as Roman Catholics. Nearly everybody agreed on killing Anabaptists. The excuse, however dressed up, was always political necessity. Sixteenth-century governments did not believe in allowing an individual to choose his religion freely; such license, they thought, would be certain to produce political disunity and thus imperil the authority of the State.

Elizabeth's government, to its credit, recognized a distinction between heresy-hunting and protecting the State against subversion. It professed a disinclination to harry any subject because of what he thought. But it put the claim of protection very high, and (again like all governments) when convinced that its security was endangered by the prevalence of spies or when goaded by what it considered intolerable extremists, it acted decisively. The times were troublesome. For more than thirty years of Elizabeth's reign, war, the possibility of war, and threats of foreign invasion kept the government in a state of constant alarm. It was not disposed to take chances.

For a time, Roman Catholic laymen were left alone, provided they were above suspicion politically. The clergy were far less fortunate. Before 1570, some had been deprived and imprisoned, but actual persecution did not begin until after that date. The persecution was due to the papal bull, *Regnans in Excelsis* (1570), which excommunicated the Queen and—far worse— absolved her subjects from their allegiance. This decree placed loyal English subjects who were Roman Catholics in the impossible position, if arrested, of having to disobey their temporal or their spiritual sovereign; and some of them suffered cruelly. The bull, the recent (1569) rebellion in the North, and the presence of Mary Queen of Scots in England convinced Parliament that new measures against Roman Catholics were needed. It passed two acts against them in 1571. One made it treason to attempt to deprive the Queen of her title (as the papal bull presumed to do); the other forbade the importation or publication of bulls and made treasonable any attempt to absolve the Queen's subjects from their allegiance. These laws, and later ones supplementing them, were inspired not only by the papal bull and the problem of the Queen of Scots but by the wars of religion in France and the Netherlands and by the threat of Spain. In 1579 or 1580, Jesuit missionaries (following other priests) began to infiltrate England. Their presence led an indignant Parliament to pass a bill (1581) making treasonable the attempt to convert anyone to Roman Catholicism with intent to "withdraw any of the Queen's Majesty's subjects from their natural obedience to her Majesty." To say or hear Mass was made punishable by fine. By a law of 1585, all Jesuits were to be banished and were liable to execution if caught. The English government's fear that Elizabeth might be murdered by partisans of Mary of Scotland—another Protestant monarch, William of Orange, was murdered in 1584—cost Mary her life in 1585. An act of 1593 forbade Catholic recusants to travel more than five miles from home.

Puritanism, on the other hand, was at first more of a nuisance than a danger, for in Elizabeth's reign all but a few Puritans were members of the Church, not Separatists. That separation from the Church of England was the only logical course did not become clear to most until after their long campaign to reform the Church of England had failed.

Puritanism is notoriously hard to define. It has been called a form of idealism. It was at once a state of mind, a program, and a movement within the Church of England. The typical Puritans were Calvinists in theology. They were stern moralists, hated "popery," wanted presbyterian instead of episcopal governance in the Church, and insisted on reducing ceremonialism and liturgy in worship. There were many varieties of Puritanism. It had sympathizers in all ranks of society. It was an ecclesiastical movement, not a social one. The Puritan did not begin with a social theory or a political program. He began with Scripture. Worship, polity, order in the Church were always and in all things to be conformable to Biblical precept and example. Some of the earliest and ablest Puritans had been Marian exiles. Of these, some were for an uncompromising Genevan reform of the English Church; others were more conservative. The former continued to be very responsive to Continental precedent and doctrine and kept in close touch with Continental Protestants.

In 1563 a proposal was made to Convocation to abolish certain practices tending to "superstition": the priest's praying with his face turned from the people; his making the sign of the Cross in baptism; communicants' kneeling. A surplice was to be sufficient vestment. This proposal, which lost by a single vote, resulted in a long and loud debate over vestments. Some clergy resigned; others changed the service to suit themselves. They had dedicated and at times fanatical leaders, never averse to plain speech and incorrigibly obstinate. One of these leaders, Edward Dering, could write to Burleigh in 1573: "The lordship or civil government of bishops is utterly unlawful. . . . Is it not the same that springeth out of the pope's breast? What else are officials, commissaries, chancellors, archdeacons, etc., which rule and govern by the common laws? Much worse than the statutes of Omri, and all the ordinances of the house of Achab: which uphold in the midst of us a court of Faculties, a place much worse than Sodom and Gomorrah." The famous *First Admonition to the Parliament* (1572) referred to the *Book of Common Prayer* as "an unperfect book, culled and picked out of that popish dunghill" the Mass-book.

After 1570, Puritan propaganda became more effective, Puritan influence on Parliament more noticeable, attacks on the prelates more violent. Puritan clergy (later joined by laity) began to hold meetings of their own, "prophesyings" or "exercises" as they were called, for discussion of Scripture and prayer. The government had to take a serious view of these activities, especially after attacks on the bishops became so bold. Puritans leaned to presbyterianism, and presbyterianism carried to an extreme meant the end of episcopal authority, which in turn meant the end of the government's supremacy over the Church. Radical Puritanism, that is, began to look like subversion. Consequently the Elizabethan government took steps to repress it. The Act of Uniformity was invoked. Archbishop Grindal was ordered to stop the "exercises." Grindal, who had strong Puritan sympathies, temporized and was suspended. Convocation accomplished little in combating Puritanism. By 1583, when Grindal was succeeded by Whitgift, presbyterianism was becoming more prevalent among Puritans, who were much encouraged by its triumphs in Scotland. They found Whitgift a far more severe and resourceful opponent than Grindal. But they were helped, and he hindered, by Puritan sympathies (for political as well as other reasons) in the House of Commons and among some of the Queen's ministers. Elizabeth herself was always hostile, recognizing as she did the implications of Puritanism, at least of presbyterianism, for the royal supremacy. For many years she had to resist Puritanism without much help from Parliament. After the middle 1580's, though, Puritan propaganda, for example in the Marprelate tracts of 1588-89, became more violent than ever. Finally Parliament passed an act in 1593 against the "wicked and dangerous practices of sectaries and disloyal persons," forbidding attendance at "unlawful assemblies, conventicles, or meetings under pretence of any exercise of religion" on pain of imprisonment, banishment, and even death. A few Separatists were hanged for sedition; some left the country.

Recusancy continued to plague the authorities, but the Church had become too strong to be captured by either rival, Roman Catholics or Puritans. By the last decade of the century, the Establishment could defend itself—and, through Hooker's *Laws of Ecclesiastical Polity*, it did—as a national Church, both Catholic and Protestant, holding the middle ground. It owed much to the Queen's resistance to attacks by partisans of Rome and Geneva. Not deeply religious—certainly not by comparison with Mary Tudor or Philip of Spain—she was determined to uphold the royal supremacy. She was not greatly interested in theological debates. "I see many over-bold with God Almighty," she said, "making too many subtle scannings of his blessed will, as lawyers do with human testaments." Her motives were first of all political, not spiritual. Church and State were closely joined in Tudor England, and in the final analysis, whatever theologians thought or said, political power controlled ecclesiastical. The Church symbolized the spiritual life of the Queen's subjects, but as a religious establishment was protected by the government. Events were to prove, however, that the problems inherent in the Church's relation to the State had not really been solved. The apparent stability achieved by the end of the reign was a lull before new storms that were to rage for years, divide the country, and cost a king his life before they ended.

SUGGESTED READING

Preserved Smith, *The Age of the Reformation* (New York, 1920, 1948) is a standard history. Harold J. Grimm, *The Reformation Era* (New York, 1954) is a good recent account, with up-to-date bibliographies. Shorter surveys of the Reformation are R. H. Bainton, *The Reformation of the Sixteenth Century* (Boston, 1952) and E. H. Harbison, *The Age of Reformation* (Ithaca, N.Y., 1955). Two recent and readable books on the Church of England are J. R. H. Moorman, *A History of the Church in England* (London, 1953) and S. C. Carpenter, *The Church in England, 597–1688* (London, 1954). Important documents concerning the history of the Church of England are collected in H. Gee and W. J. Hardy, *Documents Illustrative of English Church History* (London, 1896). For the Elizabethan period alone, see G. W. Prothero, *Select Statutes and Other Constitutional Documents Illustrative of the Reigns of Elizabeth and James I* (Oxford, 1894 ff.).

On the Reformation in England two good though brief books are F. M. Powicke, *The Reformation in England* (London, 1941) and T. M. Parker, *The English Reformation to 1558* (London, 1950). From the Roman Catholic point of view: Philip Hughes, *The Reformation in England* (London, 1950–54); G. Constant, *The Reformation in England* (London, 1934–41).

Of the many studies of Puritanism, two of the most useful are M. M. Knappen, *Tudor Puritanism* (Chicago, 1939), and William Haller, *The Rise of Puritanism* (New York, 1938 ff).

Histories of Tudor England and biographies of its leading figures are too numerous to be listed here, but a few of the best books in these genres may be mentioned: G. M. Trevelyan, *History of England* (London, 1926 ff.), bk. III; S. T. Bindoff, *Tudor England* (London, 1950)—both available in inexpensive paperback editions; A. L. Rowse, *The England of Elizabeth* (London, 1950), an opinionated but provocative work; G. R. Elton, *England under the Tudors* (London, 1955); A. F. Pollard, *Henry VIII* (London, 1902 ff.), *Thomas Cranmer and the English Reformation* (London, 1904, 1926); J. E. Neale, *Queen Elizabeth* (London, 1934; reprinted in a cheap edition, New York, 1957), *Elizabeth I and Her Parliaments* (London, 1953–57); R. W. Chambers, *Thomas More* (London, 1935); Conyers Read, *Mr. Secretary Walsingham and the Policy of Queen Elizabeth* (Oxford, 1925), *The Tudors* (New York, 1936), *Mr. Secretary Cecil and Queen Elizabeth* (London, 1955).

The *Bibliography of British History, Tudor Period, 1485–1603,* ed. Conyers Read (Oxford, 1933; a new edition is in the press) is the best guide to writings on the period. *Shakespeare's England* (Oxford, 1916), a collection of essays on many important aspects of Tudor life, should be read by anyone who wants a good introduction to the Elizabethan age. H. F. M. Prescott's fine historical novel, *Man on a Donkey* (London, 1952), about the Pilgrimage of Grace, 1536–37, a rebellion against Henry VIII, succeeds better than do many works of erudition in capturing the mind and spirit of the earlier period.

PLATES

Martin Luther, *Ain Sermon von dem Bann*, 1520

The Church in England, as in so many lands, was deeply affected by the controversies that broke out over Luther in Germany. Although the Reformation cannot be dated within precise limits, any more than can most large, complex movements of ideas, 1517 was the year in which its indisputable leader, Luther, first came into public notice. On All Saints' Eve he posted his Ninety-Five Theses on the doors of the Castle Church in Wittenberg. Some of the theses had startling implications about the theory of indulgences, and therefore about the authority of the Church. In the next three years Luther went on to raise more direct and more portentous questions about the sacraments and papal authority; the subject of indulgences receded to a place of minor importance. But indulgences were the reason for his first public criticism of the Roman system.

Ain Sermon von dem Bann, 1520, is a revision and elaboration of an earlier discourse, *Sermo de Virtute Excommunicationis,* 1518. In *Ain Sermon,* Luther denies that bans, excommunications, and the like can bring about a true separation between God and man; they can merely separate, he argues, from the earthly, external fellowship of the Church. To Luther these were no mere theoretical topics, for he himself had long been expecting excommunication. A few months after *Ain Sermon* came from the press, Pope Leo X denounced him in the bull *Exsurge Domine,* threatening excommunication if he did not recant within sixty days. Luther replied by burning the bull, along with the canon law, at Wittenberg, December 10, 1520. He was then excommunicated by a new bull, *Decet Romanum Pontificem,* January 3, 1521.

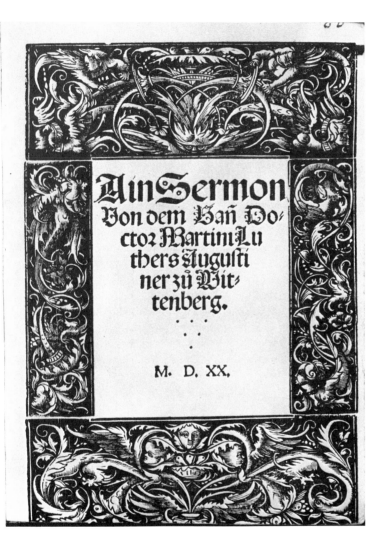

Ain Sermon
Von dem Bañ Doctor Martini Luthers Augustiner zů Wittenberg.

M. D. XX.

King Henry VIII, *Assertio Septem Sacramentorum,* 1521

To the historian, the argument of this thin book is less important than its occasion and authorship. The book is a reply by Henry VIII to Luther's *Babylonian Captivity of the Church,* 1520, which contained a strong attack on the sacramental system of the Church. By 1521, the King and his advisers had become alarmed at the spread of Lutheran ideas and propaganda in England and were taking vigorous countermeasures. In May, 1521, Luther's books were burned in London. Their importation or sale was strictly forbidden. The King, instigated by Wolsey, prepared the *Assertio,* which was published in July, 1521. It did nothing to stem the tide of Lutheranism but gave Henry an agreeable reputation—scarcely deserved, as later events were to show—as a champion of orthodoxy. Pope Leo X praised the book and promptly conferred on its royal author the title of "Defender of the Faith."

How much assistance Henry may have had in the writing of his tract, and from whom, are questions that remain unanswered. He was learned (for a king) and genuinely interested in theology. Persistent rumor credited Erasmus with a part in the composition, but he denied this and said the King was perfectly capable of writing it himself. That the King wrote it entirely unaided is improbable.

The *Assertio* assures its readers that Luther is "a wolf of hell" and "a limb of Satan." Luther retorted with a pamphlet (July, 1522) ridiculing Henry's arguments. A few years later, on hearing that England was receptive to the Reformation, he wrote to the King (1525) in flattering terms. Henry answered with an abusive letter, printed in 1526. (In the Folger Library is a 1528 copy of this booklet stamped with the arms of Henry and his Queen, Catherine of Aragon.) To this Luther wrote a rejoinder.

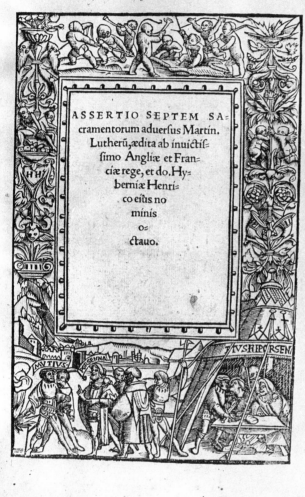

ASSERTIO SEPTEM SA=
cramentorum aduerſus Martin.
Lutherũ, ædita ab inuictiſ=
ſimo Angliæ et Fran=
ciæ rege, et do. Hy=
berniæ Henri=
co eius no
minis
o=
ctauo.

William Tyndale, *The Obedience of a Christian Man*, 1528

As a literary leader of the English Reformation, though he did most of his work from the Continent, Tyndale had many claims to remembrance by the Anglican Church. He popularized Lutheran and Zwinglian teaching for Englishmen; defended these and other Protestant doctrines in a famous controversy with Thomas More; and made probably the most important of all sixteenth-century English translations of the New Testament. This version, the first to be printed in English (1525, 1526), became the basis of later Tudor and Stuart versions, except the Rheims-Douai one. Tyndale did not live to complete his version of the Old Testament.

The Obedience of a Christian Man is an exposition of the obedience owed by children, servants, wives, and subjects. It contains also a defense of the vernacular Bible and a discussion of the different senses of Scripture.

Enemies of the Lutherans charged them with inciting lawlessness and rebellion. This charge Tyndale denies; on the contrary, he says, "it is the bloody doctrine of the Pope which causeth disobedience, rebellion, and insurrection." Tyndale insists on the prerogative of secular rulers: "The king is, in this world, without law; and may at his lust do right or wrong, and shall give accounts but to God only." "All men without exception are under the temporal sword." This was not new doctrine but a restatement or application of the familiar Pauline injunctions in Romans 13:1–6. Tyndale had no intention of exalting tyranny. If rulers themselves do wrong, God will punish them. But they are not answerable to men: "They may not be resisted, do they never so evil; they must be reserved unto the wrath of God." "If they command to do evil, we must then disobey, and say, 'We are otherwise commanded of God,' but not to rise against them."

Henry VIII is said to have remarked, "This is a book for me and all kings to read."

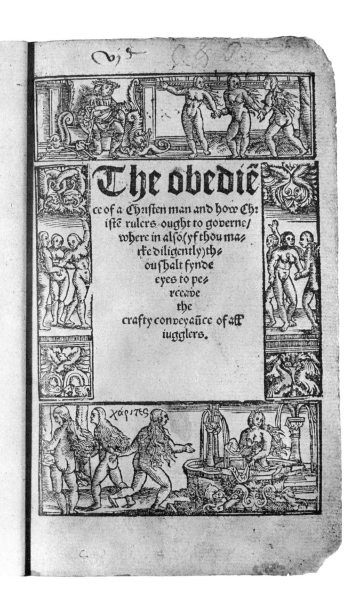

The obediẽ
ce of a Chꝛisten man and how Chꝛ=
iste rulers ought to governe/
where in also (yf thou ma=
rke diligently) th=
ou shalt fynde
eyes to pe=
rceave
the
crafty conveyaũce of all
iuḡglers.

Bilney Ejected from the Pulpit

From Foxe's *Acts and Monuments,* 1563

Thomas Bilney was one of the early Cambridge group of Reformers and a martyr to his religion. He preached against images and prayers to saints, but in other respects was conservative in his views. Convicted of heresy in 1527, he abjured and was imprisoned for a year. In 1531, however, he began to preach more boldly. This time he was arrested as a relapsed heretic and executed.

The incident depicted here occurred in 1527.

Friers pulling Bilney out of the pulpit.

Saint Georges churche in Ipſwich.

253

Latimer Preaching before King Edward VI

From Foxe's *Acts and Monuments*, 1563

Latimer, like Bilney, was one of the Cambridge Reformers and, like Bilney, died a martyr. He became a court preacher in 1530, later a royal chaplain and (1535) Bishop of Worcester. He resigned in 1539. For a time he was under the royal displeasure and imprisoned. After the accession of Edward VI in 1547, he resumed preaching but not his bishopric. When Mary came to the throne, he was arrested and, with Ridley, burned at the stake in Oxford (1555). He was one of the foremost preachers of his day, but his best-remembered words are those he is said to have uttered at his execution: "Be of good comfort, Master Ridley, and play the man; we shall this day light such a candle by God's grace, in England, as I trust shall never be put out."

description of Maiſter Latimer, preaching before Kyng Edward the ſyxt, in the preachyng place at Weſtminſter.

M.Latimer.

Certain Sermons or Homilies, 1547

"Public and continual preaching of God's word is the ordinary mean and instrument of the salvation of mankind," wrote Grindal, the Archbishop of Canterbury, in 1576, when resisting Elizabeth's demand that he discourage preaching. Emphasis on preaching was nothing new (though especially characteristic of the Puritans), nor was complaint about the lack of good preachers. Some of the clergy in Cranmer's time could do little more than read the service books. From the evidence available it is safe to infer that many of them did not, and could not, preach at all. Moreover many parishes, even at the time Grindal wrote, could not afford pastors learned enough to preach.

To provide pulpit discourse where there was none, Archbishop Cranmer edited a volume of twelve sermons, *Certain Sermons or Homilies* (1547), that became a regular part of the service in many churches. He is believed to have written four of them himself. In 1563 a new and larger collection, the *Second Tome of Homilies,* was published. This had twenty discourses, "godly and wholesome doctrine, and necessary for these times," as the *Thirty-Nine Articles* of 1563 affirmed. A significant addition to the collection was made in 1571: a sermon on rebellion, occasioned by the uprising in the North of England in 1569. This sermon was printed separately too.

The rule in Elizabethan times was that parsons were to preach (that is, preach sermons of their own making) if licensed to do so, but not otherwise; if not licensed they were expected to read the *Homilies* to the congregation. The Queen thought the *Homilies* safer than original sermons; Grindal argued that "the reading of homilies hath his commodity but is nothing comparable to the office of preaching."

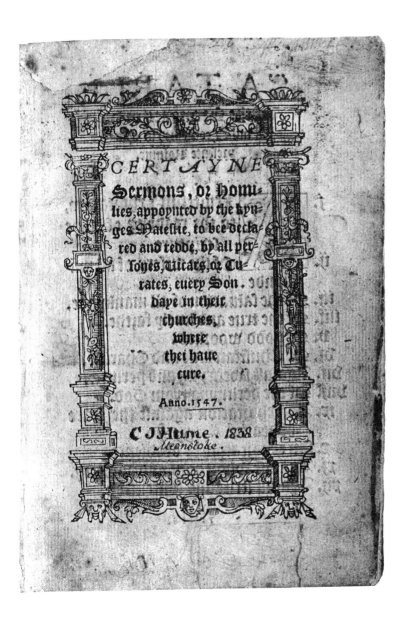

CERTAYNE

Sermons, or homilies, appoynted by the kynges Maiestie, to bee declared and redde, by all persones, Uicars, or Curates, every Sonday in their churches, where thei have cure.

Anno. 1547.

C J Hume. 1838
Megnetoke.

The Martyrdom of Archbishop Cranmer, 1556

From Foxe's *Acts and Monuments*, 1563

Thomas Cranmer's long and troubled career as administrator of the Church of England ended in martyrdom during the persecutions in Queen Mary's reign. He had been a faithful and compliant servant of her father, Henry VIII, from the time of the divorce proceedings until the king's death in 1547. He was appointed Archbishop of Canterbury in 1533 and promptly declared the king's union with Catherine of Aragon invalid. He encouraged the translation and circulation of the Bible; authorities ordered a copy for convenient reading to be placed in every church (1538). He supervised preparation of the *Homilies* issued in 1547 for pulpit use and had copies of Erasmus' *Paraphrases* of the New Testament placed in parish churches. His greatest literary monument is the *Book of Common Prayer* (1549; reissued 1552), part of which he wrote and the rest compiled.

Cranmer guided the Church through the uneasy times of Edward VI, but when the Roman Catholic Mary, daughter of Catherine of Aragon, succeeded Edward, he was doomed. Imprisoned, excommunicated, and deposed from office, he repudiated some of his professed Protestant opinions. From one standpoint this action was logical enough, for he had long accepted the principle that the State may determine the national religion. But in the end conscience compelled him to reaffirm his earlier convictions and take the consequences. In a dramatic scene at St. Mary's Church, Oxford, March 21, 1556, where he was expected to repeat his recantation, he suddenly renounced his earlier action. He declared that his right hand, which had signed the recantation, should be the first to burn. He was hurried to the stake, and when the faggots were lighted he thrust his right arm into the flames.

The burning of Tharchbishop of Cant. D. Tho. Cranmer, in the town dich at
Oxford, with his hand first thrust into the fyre, wherwith he subscribed before.

John Knox, *The First Blast of the Trumpet against the Monstrous Regiment of Women*, 1558

Knox, the patriarch of Scottish Presbyterianism, blew this strident blast from Geneva, where he lived for a time during the reign of Mary Tudor. He directed it against Mary and another Roman Catholic ruler, Mary of Guise, Regent of Scotland and mother of Mary Stuart, the future Queen of Scots. Knox abhorred England's tie to Spain (Mary had married Philip II) and Scotland's to France, for France and Spain were of course the leading Roman Catholic powers.

The opening lines of the preface are typical of Knox's forthright if undiplomatic manner: "Wonder it is, that amongst so many pregnant wits as the Isle of Great Britain hath produced, so many godly and zealous preachers as England did sometime nourish, and amongst so many learned and men of grave judgment, as this day by Jezebel [Queen Mary] are exiled, none is found so stout of courage, so faithful to God, nor loving to their native country, that they dare admonish the inhabitants of that Isle how abominable before God is the empire or rule of a wicked woman, yea of a traitoress and bastard." To allow any woman to rule, he declared, is "repugnant to nature, contumely to God . . . and finally it is the subversion of good order, of all equity and justice."

Elizabeth, who succeeded Mary within a year after the publication of Knox's book, was naturally indignant with such doctrine. Embarrassed by the hostility of a Protestant queen, he sent explanations, but in vain; for he refused to retreat or, as he said, to "call back any principal point or proposition."

Her displeasure notwithstanding, Elizabeth and her government aided Knox and the Protestant party in Scotland in their successful attempt to reform the Church there and in their opposition to Mary Queen of Scots.

THE FIRST
BLAST OF THE
TRVMPET AGAINST
THE MONSTRVOVS
regiment of
women.

✤

Veritas temporis
filia.

M· D· LVIII·

John Calvin, *The Institution of Christian Religion,* translated by Thomas Norton, 1561

Calvinism in England is commonly, and correctly, associated with Puritanism, but the two were not identical. The Puritans were Calvinistic, both in doctrine and in their predilection for presbyterian instead of episcopal rule in the Church. But not all English Calvinists were Puritans. Many Anglicans were also Calvinistic in theology, yet they were unalterably opposed to presbyterianism, as to other features of Genevan polity. Thus, however strongly Elizabethan Puritans and prelates might differ over vestments, liturgy, and the governance of the Church, they could and often did share a Calvinistic bias in theology. Some of the *Thirty-Nine Articles* of the Anglican Church are strongly Calvinistic in tone. Many if not most of the bishops in the 1570s and 1580s—including Archbishop Whitgift, a relentless enemy of Puritanism—belonged to the Calvinistic school of theology. Calvinism appealed to English intellectuals, statesmen, even poets (Sidney and Spenser, for example); it was popular as well as dynamic doctrine.

The translator of the *Institutio,* though his name does not appear on the title-page, was Thomas Norton, a son-in-law of Cranmer. Scholar, poet, member of Parliament, and Puritan zealot, Norton had a remarkably busy career, successfully combining literary, political, and religious interests in a thoroughly Elizabethan way; they were aspects of the same activity, directed towards the same general end. In the literary history of the sixteenth century he has a minor but secure place because of his share in *Gorbuduc* (acted 1562, printed 1565), the earliest English tragedy. He wrote the first three acts.

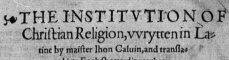

❧THE INSTITVTION OF
Chriſtian Religion, vvrytten in Latine by maiſter Ihon Caluin, and tranſla-
ted into Englyſh according to the authors laſt edition.

❧ Seen and allowed according to the order appointed in the
Quenes maieſties iniunctions.

❧ Imprinted at London by
Reinolde Vvolfe & Richarde Hariſon.
Anno.1 5 6 1·

Cum priuilegio ad imprimendum ſolum.

John Foxe, *Acts and Monuments,* 1563

Foxe was one of the Marian exiles. His huge book, known also as the *Book of Martyrs,* appeared first (in Latin) as a fairly small volume, published at Strassburg in 1554, next in a much expanded Latin edition published at Basel in 1559–63. The English version, a book of nearly 1800 folio pages, is best remembered for its vivid narratives and woodcut illustrations of the persecutions of Protestants during the reign of Mary Tudor, 1553–58.

The conception of history underlying Foxe's book, however limited it seems now, is one that illuminates many aspects of Elizabethan political, religious, and social life. To Foxe, history was to be read as an unceasing struggle between Christ and Antichrist. He believed that the climax of this conflict was the Reformation. And the Reformation would reach a triumphant conclusion in England first of all. It followed that "God's Englishmen" were a chosen people, with a special national destiny.

In 1571, the Convocation of Canterbury ordered that a copy of *Acts and Monuments* be placed in each cathedral church and that every archbishop, bishop, dean, canon, and archdeacon keep a copy in his house.

The illustrations on this title-page show (bottom, left) a Protestant service of preaching and prayer contrasted with (right) what Foxe and his readers thought of as "Romish" pomp and superstition; then (above, left) martyrs and (right) the celebration of the Mass; then (left) the blessed and (right) devils and the damned; at top, the Last Judgment: God the Father, with angels on each side. The kind of worship on the left, the artist implies, leads to heaven; that on the right, to hell.

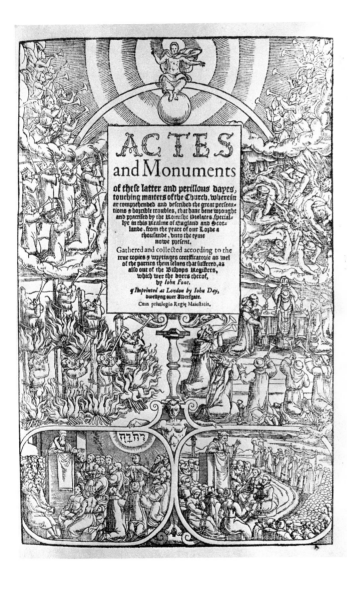

ACTES
and Monuments

of these latter and perillous dayes,
touching matters of the Church, wherein
ar comprehended and described the great persecutions & horrible troubles, that haue bene wrought
and practised by the Romishe Prelates, speciall-
lye in this Realme of England and Scot-
lande, from the yeare of our Lorde a
thousande, vnto the tyme
nowe present.

Gathered and collected according to the
true copies & wrytinges certificatorie as wel
of the parties them selues that suffered, as
also out of the Bishops Registers,
which wer the doers therof,
by Iohn Foxe.

¶ Imprinted at London by Iohn Day,
dwellyng ouer Aldersgate.
Cum priuilegio Regiæ Maiestatis.

John Jewel, *An Apology or Answer in Defence of the Church of England,* translated by Lady Anne Bacon, 1564

Jewel was an Oxford scholar who lived abroad during the Marian troubles. After Elizabeth's accession, he was appointed Bishop of Salisbury (1560) and soon began to distinguish himself as a learned and prolific writer. Like Hooker, his only rival as an apologist for Anglicanism in the Elizabethan reign, he is usually clear, logical, readable; he resembles Hooker also in preferring moderate language and avoiding the angry tone so common in theological disputes in those times.

When Jewel wrote this book, the chief criticism of the Establishment came from Roman Catholics, not (as was true when Hooker wrote) from Puritans. The Elizabethan Settlement was only a few years old, and not yet secure. It needed able defenders and propagandists. The *Apology* helped to fill that need.

Jewel summarizes the doctrines and practices of the Anglican Church, defending them on the basis of Scripture and antiquity, as also by the pragmatic test of success—for the Church, he holds, has justified itself by its achievements. He stoutly maintains the claim of the English Church to be Catholic. "But, say they, ye have been once of our fellowship, but now ye are become forsakers of your profession and have departed from us. It is true we have departed from them. . . . But yet for all this, from the primitive Church, from the Apostles, and from Christ we have not departed."

The *Apology* was first published in Latin in 1562. An anonymous English translation appeared in that year. Another translation, by Lady Anne Bacon, mother of the essayist, came out in 1564. Prefaced to it is a commendatory letter from Archbishop Parker.

An Apologie

or answere in defence of the

Churche of Englande,

with a briefe and plaine
declaration of the true
Religion professed
and vsed in
the same.

Londini, Anno Domini
M·D·LXIIII·

Pope Pius V Issuing the Bull *Regnans in Excelsis* against Queen Elizabeth, 1570

From *A Thankful Remembrance of God's Mercies,*
by George Carleton, Bishop of Chichester, fourth edition, 1630

In this famous and—for Englishmen—fateful document, the Pope excommunicated Queen Elizabeth, "a heretic and an abettor of heretics," declared her deprived of her realm, and absolved her subjects from their duty of allegiance, warning them not to obey her laws. Whoever disregarded the papal command was himself threatened with excommunication.

The bull was not published in the usual fashion and did not become known in England until several months after the Pope had signed it (February 25, 1570).

For some time the Pope had evidently hoped that France and Spain would invade England. Whatever his expectations, issuance of this bull was a political blunder which did serious damage to the papal cause in England. If taken at face value, it placed the Queen's loyal Roman Catholic subjects in an impossible position by making them, or seeming to make them, potential traitors. On the other hand, it rallied Protestants to Elizabeth's support and gave the government every excuse for taking very harsh measures against Romanists on the ground of suspected treason. Parliament replied to the bull in 1571 by passing two acts declaring that anyone who said or wrote that Elizabeth was not the lawful Queen of England, or who imported bulls, or tried to sway subjects from their allegiance should be deemed guilty of treason. Thus these acts mark the final break between England and the papacy. In 1580, Pope Gregory XIII modified *Regnans in Excelsis* by ruling that Catholics might obey the civil law (that is, obey it until the bull could be enforced), but this concession had no effect on the English government's policies.

CHAP. II.

The Rebellion of the Earles of Weſtmerland *and*
Northumberland, *related diſtinctly by* Hieronymus
Catena, *ſo ſtrongly plotted , ſo ſecretly carried, by the*
hand of God diſappointed and broken in pieces. Leon:
Dacres *his overthrow by it. This is the fruit of* Pope-
ry, *and the firſt effect of the* Popes Bull.

In nomine Domini incipit omne malum.   *Fridericus Hulſius*
                                                Invent. & ſculp.

The Popes bull againſt the Queene.

He firſt poyſoned *fruit* of this excommunication was *rotten* before it could
ripen. There was an intention of a great
and terrible Rebellion. The Duke of
Norfolke was excited to ſtirre what Forces hee
could, and to joyne with the Earles of *Weſtmer-*
land *and* Northumberland *:* at the ſame time an Ar-

D   my

Edmund Campion, *Rationes Decem*, 1582

A brilliant scholar at Oxford, Campion left the university in 1569, dissatisfied with Protestantism. In 1571 he went to Douai, then to Rome, where in 1573 he became a Jesuit. He was one of the first Jesuits chosen for the mission to England. After his arrival in England, in June, 1580, he spent the next year ministering to his fellow religionists, secretly of course and often in danger of capture. Finally he was caught (July, 1581), examined—once in the presence of the Queen whom he, as university orator, had welcomed to Oxford in 1566—tortured repeatedly, and executed (December, 1581).

By 1580, when Campion returned to England, the government and public opinion (for the most part) were extremely hostile towards Jesuits and increasingly suspicious of the political loyalty of some of the English Catholic laity. Elizabeth felt confident of the loyalty of her subjects, but the government, considering the Jesuits a "fifth column," took no chances, and introduced new and more severe measures against Roman Catholics. Those convicted of treason were executed. By their defenders they have always been regarded as martyrs for their religion; the Elizabethan government regarded them, and treated them, as traitors.

Rationes Decem presents ten topics, beginning with the Bible, and gives arguments on each. The book carried a Douai imprint but was secretly printed in England. It first appeared a week before Campion's capture. Few copies of the first edition, 1581, are known. The title-page shown here is that of an edition published in the following year at Rome.

RATIONES DECEM

QVIBVS FRETVS,
CERTAMEN

ADVERSARIIS OBTVLIT
in causa F I D E I, *Edmun-*
dus Campianus

E Societate Nominis I ɛ s v Presbyter:
Allegatæ Ad clarissimos viros
nostrates Academicos.

PERMISSV SVPERIORVM.

Romæ, *Apud Franciscum Zanettum.* 1582

William Allen, *A True, Sincere, and Modest Defence of English Catholiques*, 1584

Allen, probably the most notable of English Roman Catholic writers in Elizabethan times, founded the famous English College at Douai in 1568. He wrote important works on Roman doctrines and the priesthood and in 1587 became cardinal. In the year of the Armada, 1588, he wrote an *Admonition* to Roman Catholics in England to rise against Elizabeth when the Spanish landed, and a *Declaration,* to the same end.

In 1583, the Queen's chief minister, Burleigh, wrote a tract, *The Execution of Justice in England,* defending the government's action against "certain stirrers of sedition," that is, those English Catholics (including Campion) arrested and executed for treason. Burleigh bitterly denounced the Jesuit mission to England.

In addition to denying the charge of treason, Allen's *Defence* contains a valuable statement of the Roman Church's position with regard to Elizabeth's government and to the persecution of heretics. "We can prove Queen Mary's doings to be commendable and most lawful; the other [persecution of Roman Catholics by Elizabeth's government] towards us and our brethren, to be injust and impious. . . . As no law of God or man can force us to be Protestants, no more can any reason be alleged nor just excuse made for either young or old, why being baptized or brought up amongst Arians or Calvinists, they may not be forced to return to the Catholic Church and faith again." "When the prince and prelate proceed together against such as by the sentence and law of the Church of Christ are adjudged to be heretics and injurious to God, that is justice." When prince or people rebel against their bishops, he adds, that is persecution.

A TRVE
SINCERE AND MO-
DEST DEFENCE OF ENGLISH
CATHOLIQVES THAT SVFFER FOR THEIR
Faith both at home and abrode: againſt a falſe, ſe-
ditious and ſlaunderous Libel intituled;

THE EXECVTION OF IVSTICE IN ENGLAND.

VVherin is declared, hovv vniuſtlie the Proteſtants doe charge
Catholiques vvith treaſon ; hovv vntrulie they deny their
perſecution for Religion ; and hovv deceitfullie they ſeeke
to abuſe ſtrangers about the cauſe, greatnes, and maner
of their ſufferinges, vvith diuers other matters
perteining to this purpoſe.

Pſal. 62.

Vt obſtruatur os loquentium iniqua.

That the mouth may be ſtopped of ſuch as ſpeake vniuſtlie.

Pſal. 49.

Os tuum abundauit malitia, & lingua tua concinnabat dolos.

Thy mouth hath abounded in malice, and thy tongue hath
coninglie framed lies.

Persecution of Roman Catholics in England

From *Theatrum Crudelitatum Haereticorum Nostri Temporis,* 1592

The caption of the picture blames the persecution on "Protestant Calvinists." Whether the writer means by this phrase that the Puritans were responsible for the government's treatment of Roman Catholics, or that the English Church consisted of Calvinists, is not clear. Neither assertion would be more than half true.

The book from which this picture is taken was first published in Antwerp in 1587. It is said to have been suppressed in Paris on complaint of the English ambassador. Later it was reprinted. The author was Richard Verstegen, who was born in London of Dutch parentage. After attending Oxford he spent the rest of his life on the Continent. He wrote historical and devotional works.

Persecutiones aduersus Catholicos à Proteſtanti-
bus Caluiniſtis excitæ in Anglia.

A Book of Certain Canons, 1571

This canonical legislation, passed by Convocation in 1571, prescribed duties of bishops, deans, churchwardens, and other officials, including schoolmasters. It gives us valuable information about the discipline and standards of the Anglican Church in the first half of Elizabeth's reign. The Queen approved the *Canons,* yet withheld royal assent. They did not have the force of statutory law, therefore, although they became part of ecclesiastical law.

The *Canons* forbid bishops to ordain any men except those who "have been trained up in good letters, either in the university, or some other inferior school, or that doth understand the Latin tongue competently, and hath been well exercised in the Holy Scriptures." An ordinand must be of unblemished reputation and must not be "any that hath been brought up in husbandry, or some other base and handicraft labour."

Parsons are to report yearly to bishops' officers the names of all parishioners over fourteen years of age who do not go to Holy Communion (as by law they were compelled to do). Moreover parsons must see that decorum is kept at divine service and "take heed that young men, especially countrymen (whose nature is more prone to the contempt of godliness and disorder) neither ring bells, neither walk in the churches, nor have idle talk together, nor by laughing or noise or unhonest jesting either let [hinder] the minister or offend the people."

Among the many duties of churchwardens are those of warning tavernkeepers not to allow anyone in their taverns during the hours of divine service, and of preventing peddlers "which carry about and sell pins, points, and other small trifles" from offering their wares in churchyards on Sundays or holidays.

¶ A BOOKE
of certaine Canons,
concernyng some parte
of the Discipline of
the Churche of
England.

In the yeare of our Lord.
1571.

AT LONDON
Printed by Iohn Daye,
dwellyng ouer Al-
dersgate.

¶ Cum gratia & Priuilegio
Regiæ Maiestatis.

John Whitgift, *An Answer to a Certain Libel Entitled "An Admonition to the Parliament,"* 1572

Whitgift's *Answer* is an important document in the early history of controversy between Puritans and prelates in the Church of England. For nearly a decade the Church had been agitated by controversy growing out of a debate over clerical vestments. A new stage in the quarrel was reached with the publication in 1572 of *An Admonition to the Parliament* by John Field and Thomas Wilcox. The authors roundly denounced the shortcomings of the Anglican clergy, rejected rites and vestments which (according to them) were unauthorized by Scripture, and called on Parliament to reform the Church of England on Calvinistic lines. After a second *Admonition* had appeared, Whitgift, then Master of Trinity College, Cambridge, replied for the episcopalians in this *Answer*. Not surprisingly, the *Answer* provoked a strong retort from Thomas Cartwright, a sharp-tongued Puritan leader whose feelings towards Whitgift were not made milder by the fact that Whitgift, as Master of Trinity, had deprived him of his fellowship there a few years earlier. The Whitgift-Cartwright tracts were part of a pamphlet warfare over Puritanism that lasted many years. Puritanism had become an issue for Parliament as well as for Convocation.

Whitgift was a Calvinist in theology but detested Puritanism. In this *Answer* he charged that his Puritan opponent's "unfruitful, froward, and contentious dealing rejoiceth the papist, discrediteth the sound and learned preacher, offendeth the godly, woundeth the weak, invoketh the contempt of magistrates and superiors in the hearts of the hearers, destroyeth that which other men build, and finally doth good to none."

Whitgift went on to become Archbishop of Canterbury (1583–1604). A stern disciplinarian and an unwearied opponent of nonconformists, he was the ablest ecclesiastical statesman produced by the Elizabethan Church.

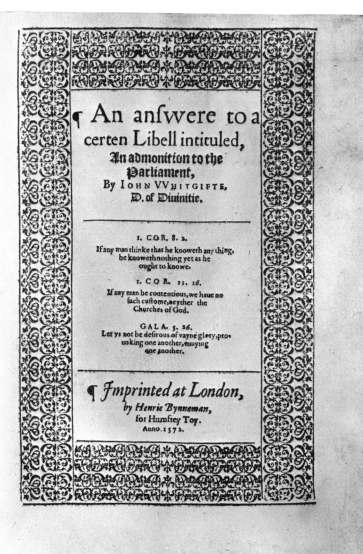

¶ An anſwere to a
certen Libell intituled,
An admonition to the
Parliament,
By Iohn VVhitgifte,
D. of Diuinitie.

1. COR. 8. 2.
If any man thinke that he knoweth any thing,
he knoweth nothing yet as he
ought to knowe.

1. COR. 11. 16.
If any man be contentious, we haue no
ſuch cuſtome, neyther the
Churches of God.

GALA. 5. 26.
Let ys not be deſirous of vayne glory, pro-
uoking one another, enuying
one another.

¶ Imprinted at London,
by Henrie Bynneman,
for Humfrey Toy.
Anno. 1572.

Hay Any Work for Cooper, 1589

This is the fourth of seven Marprelate pamphlets issued from a secret press in 1588–89 during a propaganda campaign waged by certain Puritans against the hierarchy of the Established Church. The quality of these tracts as satire gives them a place in Elizabethan literature, but it was their argument as well as their manner that made them popular in their day. The anonymous author or authors were in dead earnest; they wrote against powerful enemies, most of all the Archbishop of Canterbury, Whitgift; and they were liable to severe punishment if caught.

In 1584 appeared a pamphlet called *A Brief and Plain Declaration* (known also as the *Learned Discourse*), attacking the Anglican bishops and arguing for presbyterian governance of the Church. This was answered by an elaborate *Defence of the Government Established in the Church of England* (1587), by John Bridges. The first Marprelate tract, the *Epistle*, was a reply to this *Defence*. It was issued in the autumn of 1588 and quickly followed by another, the *Epitome*. *Hay Any Work for Cooper* (the title comes from a London street cry of the day) was the fourth of the series. It replies specifically to an *Admonition to the People of England* by Bishop Cooper of Winchester (1589). Government agents finally caught the printers, and "Martin Marprelate" was heard from no more, though the controversy continued to produce pamphlets from both sides.

Anonymous, secretly printed and distributed, the Marprelate tracts caused a brief sensation. Martin was too abusive and perhaps too popular to be ignored by the bishops, too clever and too impudent to be subdued by mere solemn rejoinder. Even some of the Puritans were annoyed by his freedom of speech, which they feared would harm their cause rather than help it.

Hay any worke for Cooper:

Or a briefe Pistle directed by waye of an hublication to the reverende Byshopps/ counselling them/ if they will needs be barrelled vp/ for feare of smelling in the nostrels of her Maiestie & the State/ that they would vse the aduise of reuerend Martin/ for the prouiding of their Cooper. Because the reuerend T.C. (by which misticall letters/ is vnderstood/ eyther the bouncing Parson of Eastmeane, or Tom Coakes his Chaplaine) to bee an vnskilfull and a deceytfull tubtrimmer.

Wherein worthy Martin quits himselfe like a man
I warrant you/ in the modest defence of his selfe and his learned Pistles/ and makes the Coopers hoopes to flye off/ and the Bishops Tubs to leake out of all crye.

Penned and compiled by Martin the Metropolitane.

Printed in Europe/ not farre from some of the Bouncing Priestes.

E 4

Richard Hooker, *Of the Laws of Ecclesiastical Polity,* 1593–97

This treatise is the product of a controversy between Hooker and Travers, a leading Puritan. Hooker was Master of the Temple, Travers a preacher there; we are told that "the pulpit spake pure Canterbury in the morning and Geneva in the afternoon." Books I-IV of *Ecclesiastical Polity* appeared in 1593; book V in 1597. Books VI and VIII were included in an edition of 1648, long after Hooker's death, and book VII in an edition of 1662. The authenticity of books VI-VIII has been questioned, but there is little doubt that they are by Hooker.

Addressed to Hooker's Puritan opponents, the work expounds the Church of England's polity (and doctrine, so far as elucidation of polity requires this), and defends that Church against the assaults of Puritans who wanted to make its order more presbyterian. Hooker likewise defends the Church from certain Roman Catholic attacks.

Against Puritans who insisted that Scripture was not only the principal but the sole authority for Church order, he maintains that natural law and "the light of reason" also give illumination and therefore deserve to be respected. He believed in the value of tradition if tradition is not contrary to Scripture, is seemly, and has proved beneficial to Christians.

Unlike so many sixteenth-century writings on theology or the Church, Hooker's book is charitable and patient in spirit, restrained rather than bitter or intemperate in tone. It is celebrated for style as well as for thought. The dignity, balance, and rhythms of its elaborate sentences are perfectly expressive of the temper of "the judicious Mr. Hooker" and appropriate to his great theme.

OF
THE LAVVES
of Ecclesiasticall
Politie.

Eyght Bookes.

By Richard Hooker.

Printed at London by *Iohn Windet*, dwelling at the signe of the
Crosse keyes neere Powles Wharffe, and are there
to be soulde

Schools in Tudor England

By Craig R. Thompson

> the whining schoolboy, with his satchel
> And shining morning-face, creeping like snail
> Unwillingly to school.
>
> *As You Like It,* II, vii, 145–147

IF we could visit an Elizabethan grammar school, we should find the scene intelligible and at first glance even familiar: teacher and pupils; books, lessons, recitations; rewards and punishments. The "learning process" changes slowly, since education is intensely conservative. So are its victims. Shakespeare's whining schoolboy is typical of all boys, as easily recognizable within the schoolroom as Chaucer's "little clergeon, seven year of age" or Tom Brown or Tom Sawyer, whatever the differences when these worthies are outside.

Closer inspection would reveal some striking contrasts between Tudor secondary schools and our own. Every boy in every grammar school studied Latin then; in fact Latin was his main business as long as he attended school. English literature and modern languages were ignored, physical science unknown, in the curriculum. Grammar schools had no women teachers, of course, and no girls as pupils—Renaissance schools were seldom distracted by co-education. Elizabethans took learning seriously and expected it to be laborious, but they did not believe in universal or compulsory schooling. They accepted unhesitatingly the principle that all schoolmasters should be subject to ecclesiastical jurisdiction. They were not sentimental about children. To Elizabethans, childhood was not a particularly attractive period; it was an unavoidable but trying experience, and the sooner done with the better for everybody. They liked sports now condemned as cruel, believed in stern discipline at home and school, and had never heard of a "child-centered" curriculum, which most of them would have put down as an invention of the devil. Everyone agreed that children who went to school ought to be there eight or ten hours a day, learn their letters properly, and grow up as quickly and quietly as possible into sensible creatures, ready for the station to which it should please Providence to call them.

In the fifteenth century children learned their ABCs from the local priest or in elementary schools that might be separate or joined with a grammar school. If the schools were united, the usher (assistant master), or the master himself if he had no usher, devoted part of his day to the younger pupils. If the elementary school was separate, it might be a song school or an ABC school or a reading or a writing school. In practice the last three amounted to much the same thing sometimes, though we must remember that reading and writing were not equally common attainments. Readers easily outnumbered writers in the fifteenth and sixteenth centuries.

In the later Middle Ages song schools were the most numerous and important kind of elementary schools. As the name implies, these institutions, not all of which were attached to cathedrals or other churches, trained boys as choristers. Pupils learned plainsong and the responses used in the Mass and memorized at least portions of the Psalter—all in Latin, needless to say. Song schools served as elementary schools because they taught the rudiments of reading and writing; some taught also the first part of Latin grammar. They had only slight interest in English, but a boy who could learn something of Latin would have little trouble learning more of English. The school attended by our best-known medieval schoolboy, the clergeon of Chaucer's *Prioress's Tale,* was either a song school or a song school combined with a grammar school. There he and his fellows learn

to syngen and to rede
As smale children done in hir childhede.

It could hardly be a grammar school alone, else the older boy would not be so helpless when asked to construe a Latin hymn. He hints that the request is rather unfair:

> I lerne song, I have but smal grammere.

The higher or grammar schools, sometimes thought of as Tudor inventions, were thoroughly medieval in origin, as much so as the universities themselves. They were of various kinds:

1. Cathedral schools, maintained by cathedral chapters.

2. Collegiate schools, similar to cathedral schools but controlled by secular clergy instead of monks. In medieval England chapters of nine of the seventeen cathedrals were collegiate, the rest monastic. Collegiate foundations could exist without having schools, to be sure, but many colleges kept such schools; at least two, Winchester and Eton, became famous for their schools alone. These schools seem to have had boarders from the start. Of another collegiate foundation, Jesus College, Rotherham (Yorkshire), established in 1483, we know that it had masters of song, grammar, and writing.

3. Monastic and almonry schools. Monasteries had schools, usually very small ones, for their own novices or oblates. In the late Middle Ages some houses also had almonry schools, so called because the almoner, a monk who had the duty of distributing daily alms at the gate, was in charge of the boys. Almonry schools provided instruction for choir boys and charity boys, not for others. The boys studied song with the precentor, who sometimes served as grammar master too. More often a grammarian was brought in to teach them or they went to a grammar school in the neighborhood.

4. "Hospital" schools, connected or formerly connected with almshouses. In early Tudor times the best of these schools were St. Anthony's in London, which John Colet and Thomas More are believed to have attended, and Banbury in Oxfordshire.

5. Guild schools, established by craft or merchant guilds. The guilds appointed chaplains who had the additional duty of keeping schools. Restricted at first to sons of members, these schools later admitted other boys as well. Shakespeare's gram-

mar school in Stratford, built by the Guild of the Holy Cross early in the fifteenth century, was endowed by one of its chaplains as a free grammar school in 1482.

6. Chantry schools, the most common type of grammar school in the fifteenth and early sixteenth centuries. A chantry was a chapel, usually adjacent or attached to a church, endowed for the purpose of having Masses said for the souls of the dead. Founders or benefactors of chantries frequently stipulated that the chantry priest act also as a schoolmaster. Chantry schools could be both song and grammar schools.

7. Grammar schools at the universities. Of these the most important was Magdalen College School, Oxford.

We have no reliable statistics to tell us how the number of schools or pupils in the fifteenth century compared with that in the sixteenth. One eminent historian of education, A. F. Leach, estimates that before the Reformation there was a grammar school to every 5,625 persons in England. When we learn that official figures in 1864 showed only one to every 23,750 persons, the medieval achievement seems more impressive. Two further facts deserve notice: first, that most of the fifteenth-century schools were established to give *free* instruction; second, that many were established by laymen. The founder of Sevenoaks (1432) was a Londoner of the Grocers' Company. Farthinghoe (in Northamptonshire) and Macclesfield (in Cheshire) schools were founded in 1443 and 1503 respectively by a London citizen and a former Lord Mayor; the wife of the latter also established a grammar school. Henry VI not only founded Eton but granted a petition (1447) that four new grammar schools be set up in London.

Grammar schools concerned themselves with the first or "trivial" part of the medieval curriculum, in which the *trivium* consisted of grammar, logic, and rhetoric; the *quadrivium* of arithmetic, music, geometry, and astronomy. Pupils memorized some Latin grammar from the time-honored works of Donatus or Priscian—books standard in schools for a thousand years—or medieval manuals such as the *Doctrinale* of Alexander de Ville-dieu, which, like many grammars, was in verse. For dictionaries a boy of 1475–1510 could resort to the compilations by John of Garland or to the Latin-English vocabularies called *Ortus Vo-cabulorum* and *Promptorium Parvulorum*. When they had a modicum of grammar, the boys proceeded to reading: first Aesop's *Fables* and the *Distichs* of Cato, a collection of versi-fied moral precepts attributed erroneously to Cato the Censor; then to "higher" authors, Terence, Cicero, Ovid, Virgil, Sallust, and some of the Christian Latin writers, of whom Prudentius and Boethius were favorites. Pupils did not read widely but only in extracts, necessarily, for until the second half of the fifteenth century neither master nor pupil had printed texts. Medieval teaching was oral teaching. The master read a text to his pupils and explained it, making them repeat it after him. They parsed sentences, wrote exercises, and recited what they had memorized. The speaking of Latin was emphasized fully as much as the reading and writing of it.

The development of printing brought major changes in edu-cational techniques and materials. Textbooks became plentiful and fairly cheap; consequently visual instruction became as im-portant as oral teaching, reading as hearing. Some of the best new texts for English schools between 1480 and 1525 came from masters or former students of Magdalen College School. John Anwykyll, the first master of this school, produced a grammar and afterward a phrase book excerpted from Terence, with English translation (1483). Another master, John Holt, brought out a Latin grammar, *Lac Puerorum* (ca. 1497 but apparently not printed until a dozen years later), which included wood-cuts to help children learn cases and declensions—an early ex-ample of "visual aids." Vulgaria, collections of English phrases and sentences with Latin equivalents, helped the student to learn self-expression in Latin. One of these vulgaria, prepared probably by yet another Magdalen School master near the end of the fifteenth century but not printed until 1956, presents simply but vividly the contrast between home and school:

The world waxeth worse every day, and all is turned upside down, contrary to the old guise. For all that was to me a pleasure when I was a child, from iij year old to x (for now I go upon the xij year), while I was under my father and mother's keeping, be turned now to torments and pain. For I was wont to lie still abed till it was forth days [late in the day], delighting myself in sleep and ease. . . . But now the world runneth upon another wheel. For now at five of the clock by the moonlight I must go to my book and let sleep and sloth alone. And if our master hap to awake us, he bringeth a rod instead of a candle.

Cardinal Wolsey, a graduate of Magdalen College, was a master at the grammar school for a short time. Later, in his great days, he founded (1528) a short-lived school at Ipswich and wrote a Latin grammar for it. Apropos of masters, it is worth recalling that well into the sixteenth century Oxford and Cambridge offered degrees in grammar for schoolmasters. Candidates for this degree had to prove their competence by lecturing on Priscian. In the fifteenth century Cambridge added a college, God's House as it was called, for the training of grammarians.

An Elizabethan grammar school of 1575 differed from one of 1475 or 1525 chiefly in control, religious instruction, and texts. Masters were still under ecclesiastical authority, and some, like Sir Hugh Evans in *The Merry Wives of Windsor,* were village parsons as well as schoolmasters. But the authority was now that of the Anglican instead of the Roman Church. No English school at any time in the sixteenth century was exempt from ecclesiastical supervision. Religious ideals of education varied but did not diminish after the Reformation, which quickened and enlarged some tendencies already existing and was the cause of certain new ones. Protestant doctrines and polity, exhortations to "search the Scriptures" and to defend the new order against the old, demanded not only a learned ministry but a literate laity. The Reformation did not begin as a lay movement, but its success depended largely on lay support. When Dean Colet refounded St. Paul's School in 1512, he vested control in a body of laymen, the Mercers' Company, and stipulated that the master be a layman. The men who assured the financing and printing of the first English Bibles were laymen, not clergy. In England as on the Continent, the new order emphasized the responsibility of laymen and the need for citizens and the State to do some things formerly left to the Church. In earlier times a wealthy individual might found a chantry and provide that the chantry priest keep a school. In the reigns of Edward VI and Elizabeth I, he founded a school but no chantry, or a town corporation established and endowed the school.

The royal policy of suppressing monasteries and abbeys and confiscating their wealth (1536–1540) was disastrous for many schools. Abolition of monastic schools for novices was no great loss, since there were to be no more monks, but abolition of the almonry schools deprived many boys of grammar-school training. Even if we accept the estimate that there were only about 1500 of these boys, that was a serious loss in the England of 1540. After dissolving the greater monasteries, Henry VIII re-founded eleven important cathedral grammar schools, but some of the smaller schools perished and were not revived. The King's later plan of abolishing chantries was a greater threat to schools, since so many chantries had schools attached. An act of 1545 vested control of chantries in the Crown, but Henry died before the act was enforced.

Edward VI is sometimes credited with having founded many free grammar schools, but in fact his government destroyed more schools than it founded. A second Chantries Act (1547) authorized seizure by the Crown of endowments of chantries and nearly all collegiate churches. Three hundred or more grammar schools belonging to chantries or collegiate churches were affected by this confiscation. Song schools were virtually wiped out. The government promised to use some of the wealth confiscated for the purpose of erecting "diverse and sundry grammar schools" and to give fixed stipends to make up for lost endowments. Had these intentions been carried out, all would have been well; schools would have gone on as before, divorced from chantries. Unfortunately the plans were not carried out. Financial straits, political emergencies, and the cupidity of what would now be called "special interests" interfered. The government restored or re-endowed several dozen schools, but its policies had caused the loss of several hundred.

This misfortune drew loud lamentations from some of the

Protestant leaders, scandalized by what a Protestant government had done to education and fearful of what a dearth of
educated leaders might mean to Church and State. Hugh Latimer, one of the great preachers of the day, appealed to the rich
to spend on education what they had formerly spent on pil-
grimages, chantries, and the like. In the next generation many
of them did so. Thame Grammar School (founded 1559) was
established by a nobleman who had been on the commission
charged with administration of the Chantries Act, Abingdon
(1562) by a mercer, Rugby (1567) by a London grocer, Harrow (1571) by a neighboring yeoman, Merchant Taylors'—
where Richard Mulcaster, one of the greatest of Elizabethan educators, was master and Spenser his pupil—by a London guild
(1561). Sometimes a building was provided by an individual
and the town agreed to pay a master's stipend. The property of
the guild school at Stratford, which had been confiscated by
the Crown, was bought back by the town in 1552. William
Harrison, in his description of England (1577), could boast
that "there are not many corporate towns now under the
Queen's dominion that have not one grammar school at the
least, with a sufficient living for a master and usher appointed
to the same." The evidence available suggests that England had
300 grammar schools in 1530 and at least sixty more than that
number in 1575.

Sixteenth-century schools were of two principal kinds, ABC
or elementary ones—called "petty schools" in Shakespeare's time
—and grammar schools. They were usually though not always
separate; the grammar master did not teach beginners if he
could help it. In some schools older grammar pupils helped to
teach ABC children, but this was not the usual practice. A petition to renew the license of a petty master or "abecedarius" at
Stratford (1604) points out that his school saves the grammar
school the "tedious trouble" of teaching reading. John Brinsley,
in his treatise on grammar schools, *Ludus Literarius* (1612),
expressed what was no doubt the prevalent opinion when he
wrote that it was an unreasonable thing for grammar schools to
be saddled with teaching the ABC. In very small or poor towns,

however, such an arrangement might be unavoidable. Brinsley's further observation that an additional advantage of separate petty schools was the employment they gave to poor men or women otherwise unable to earn a living shows how humble a teacher's calling could be. On the other hand, Holofernes in *Love's Labor's Lost* is hardly a monument of humility. Since he "teaches boys [and girls] the hornbook," he must be a petty teacher, but his Latinity is evidence that he could qualify as a grammar master or usher. A cranky, pedantic fellow, he is evidently a character recognized and enjoyed by Shakespeare's audience.

As a rule, pupils entered petty school at four. Some must have had a start on reading at home, for as Charles Hoole notes in his *New Discovery of the Old Art of Teaching School* (1660), "betwixt three and four years a child hath great propensity to peep into a book." Petty school was not merely kindergarten with a bit of religious instruction thrown in. It was first of all a place for learning the catechism and primer, for setting the child on the road to familiarity with Anglican doctrine. Still, he had to learn his letters before he could do more than memorize the catechism. First he mastered the alphabet from a hornbook, a wooden tablet with a handle, the tablet being covered with a sheet of parchment or paper containing the alphabet and Paternoster in English; over this sheet was a plate of transparent horn. After learning the alphabet and syllables, an Elizabethan child was ready for the elements of reading, writing, and perhaps arithmetic. In his two or three years of petty school he used two principal texts, the *ABC with the Catechism* and then the *Primer*. These were in English and, except for parts of his first Latin grammar, were the only English books he used in petty or grammar school. If he made satisfactory progress in his first two years, he might begin Latin in the third, since knowledge of accidence (declensions and conjugations) before entering grammar school would be an advantage when he finally arrived there.

The ABC book was a pamphlet with texts of the Paternoster, Ave Maria, Creed, and Ten Commandments. Since law and custom required the catechism to be studied next after the ABC materials, the two pamphlets came to be printed together, sometimes with the Psalter added, as the *ABC with the Catechism*. When Shakespeare writes that a lover sighs "like a schoolboy that had lost his ABC" (*Two Gentlemen of Verona*, II, i, 22), it is probably the *ABC with the Catechism* to which he refers.

Paternoster, Creed, and Commandments, often with some graces added, were certain to be found also in the next book studied, the *Primer*. Primers were books of devotion containing some of the liturgical offices, Psalms, and litanies. Such books, parts of which were in English, had long been popular with the educated laity. Every Christian was expected to learn the Paternoster, Creed, and Commandments as soon as he was of age to learn anything; to be able to recite them was commonly a requirement for admission to grammar school. When Henry VIII reformed the Church, he issued new primers, in English and with a preface. A primer of 1535 in the Folger Library has an almanac, calendar, Commandments, Creed, General Confession, Paternoster, Ave Maria, Psalms, and prayers. Another, of 1542, adds the Latin text in the margin. One issued in 1545 was intended as an official text "to give our subjects a determinate form of praying in their own mother tongue." King Henry, "Supreme Head of the Church of England," wanted "one uniform manner or course of praying throughout our dominions." Besides the English text he provided a Latin one for those youths who were learning that language or had already learned it.

The primer of 1545 was prescribed anew under Edward VI in 1547 and reprinted, with revisions, in Elizabeth's reign. With the textual and bibliographical history of primers and catechisms between 1550 and 1600 we need not concern ourselves here, apart from noticing two facts: first, that the *ABC with the Catechism* was sometimes published separately but at other times incorporated with the *Primer;* secondly, that although brief primers continued to be used in petty school in the Elizabethan reign, their place as devotional books for older children and adults was taken over by the Book of Common Prayer.

A Tudor schoolboy received his serious mental training in grammar school, where he spent his seventh or eighth to fourteenth or fifteenth year. After that he was finished with formal education unless he went to a university. What was a grammar school like? We might do well to begin with mention of St. Paul's in London, a school of special interest because of its pre-Reformation origin, its detailed statutes, and its distinctive tone of Christian humanism. St. Paul's was a re-endowment and re-building of a school that had been in the churchyard of St. Paul's since the twelfth century. Its second founder was the dean of the cathedral, John Colet (1466?–1519), a wealthy, scholarly, and influential theologian. He appointed his first high master, William Lily, in 1512. Colet's friend Erasmus praised the school and helped to write an introduction to grammar and a catechism for its use. Through these and numerous other books this great Dutch scholar and writer did as much as any Englishman to set the pattern of humanistic training in English grammar schools of the sixteenth and seventeenth centuries.

Colet's statutes of 1518, which would take many pages to quote in full, provide the best picture we have of the ideals and practices of early Tudor grammar-school education as planned by a Christian thinker who was in some respects a firm traditionalist, in others an innovator. These statutes provided for two masters and for a chaplain, who was to help teach when needed. Pupils were to be received "of all nations and countries indifferently." Under "What Shall Be Taught," Colet wrote:

As touching in this school what shall be taught of the masters and learned of the scholars, it passeth my wit to devise and determine in particular, but in general to speak and somewhat to say my mind: I would they were taught always in good literature both Latin and Greek, and good authors such as have the very Roman eloquence joined with wisdom, specially Christian authors that wrote their wisdom with clean and chaste Latin either in verse or in prose, for my intent is by this school specially to increase knowledge and worshiping of God and Our Lord Christ Jesu and good Christian life and manners in the children.

In the medieval period, school was often held in church, a

custom which lingered here and there until the seventeenth century ("like a pedant that keeps a school i' the church," *Twelfth Night,* III, ii. 82), and when the school acquired a building of its own this was likely to be in or near the churchyard. Some Tudor schools had only one room; others provided quarters for master, usher, and boarders. School work was done in a single large room, not in separate classrooms, though there are examples of this room's division into several by the use of curtains. Even so the schools would have seemed to us noisy, dirty, and, like all Elizabethan buildings, intolerably cold. At one end of the room was the master's chair, at the other the usher's. Pupils sat at benches. They had to furnish their own writing paper, which was expensive in those days, and notebooks, quill pens, a knife for cutting pens, and wax candles in winter.

Until ca. 1540 the majority of schoolmasters were technically "clerks." The Henrician reforms changed their clerical status but not their liability to ecclesiastical jurisdiction. In Tudor society schools and universities were not only dominated by Christian principles but controlled, whether directly or indirectly, by ecclesiastical authority. Until the middle of the seventeenth century the Church had almost a monopoly of formal education in England. Every grammar teacher had to be licensed by his bishop. "It shall not be lawful," say the Canons of 1571, "for any to teach the Latin tongue or to instruct children, neither openly in the schools neither privately in any man's house, but whom the bishop of that diocese hath allowed and to whom he hath given license to teach under the seal of his office." A statute of 1581 directed against papists forbade employment of teachers who did not attend church. Since everyone in Elizabethan England was required by law to go to church anyway, this additional statute, by holding employers responsible, was more of a loyalty test than anything else.

Official documents tell us what qualities were desired in a teacher; what was found is not so clear. The testimony of former pupils or of teachers themselves must be treated with caution, for alumni have notoriously fallible memories and teachers do not always underrate their own attainments—naturally, says one sixteenth-century writer, since they never hear themselves contradicted in school. "Teachers of grammar schools shall be, as far as possible, men of orthodoxy and reputation in addition to being learned." This ordinance of 1529 by the Convocation of Canterbury would have passed as a conventional criterion in 1429 or 1629 as easily as in 1529. Mulcaster tells us that beyond his learning a teacher ought to have

hardness to take pains, *constancy* to continue and not to shrink from his trade, *discretion* to judge of circumstances, *lightsomeness* to delight in the success of his labor, *heartiness* to encourage a toward youth, *regard* to think each child an Alexander, *courteous lowliness* in himself, as if he were the meanest though he were known to be the best.

(This last-named virtue must have come hard to some.) Grammar masters were expected to be university men. A few, William Camden of Westminster for example, were renowned scholars; on the other hand, statutes often add a suspicious "if possible" or "if such may be got" when stipulating the master's qualifications. One set of high-sounding statutes is quoted as requiring a university graduate not under 27, "a man skilful in the Greek and Latin tongues, a good poet, of a sound religion neither papist nor Puritan, of a grave behavior, of a sober and honest conversation, no tippler nor haunter of alehouses, no puffer of tobacco, and above all that he be apt to teach and severe in his government."

A Tudor grammar master had a position of respectability and, in his own province, of authority. Sixteenth-century writers on education stress the duty of parents to look out for their children's welfare, but within the schoolroom the master was, in every sense, *in loco parentis:* he "ought to be to his scholars a second parent and father," says an Elizabethan catechism. Remember, however, that the word "father" implied a degree of authority and strictness now out of fashion. Masters were responsible to the governors of the school and to the bishop of the diocese. Apart from this they had a free hand—and used it. And they had no Parent-Teacher Association to worry about. There may have been Elizabethan counterparts of Mr. Chips, but of these we hear very little. In the literature of the age a school master is more often remembered for his harshness or is presented as an amusing pedant, a cross between an irritable drill sergeant and the absent-minded professor so indispensable to modern cartoonists.

Teachers' salaries varied then as much as they do now. When Canterbury School was refounded in 1541, the grammar master's wage was fixed at £15 2s, the usher's at £6 5s 10d—$42.28 and $17.62 respectively at the current rate of exchange; but to turn these sums into present-day equivalents we might have to multiply them by twenty. Of other laborers in the same vineyard, the dean got £56 13s 4d, a canon £17 6s 8d, a preacher £25, and the choir master £5 7s. The average salary of an Elizabethan grammar master seems to have been about £7 a year. A few got as much as £20, many not above £5; elementary teachers got considerably less. Some received lodgings, gowns, and other perquisites in addition to salary.

Boys and girls attended petty schools together, but beyond that stage a girl was educated at home. A few variations in custom must have existed, else why the stipulation at Harrow (1590) that "no girl shall be received to be taught"? At Bunbury Grammar School, in Cheshire, girls were admitted, but only long enough to learn to read English. We are not to conclude that, because Elizabethans did not believe in "mixed" schools, none of them favored higher education for girls; on the contrary, such training had distinguished advocates and exemplars. The scholarship of Margaret More or of Lady Jane Grey was long remembered. Queen Elizabeth I, who wrote verse, read Greek, spoke Latin well, and translated Boethius, was the supreme paragon of female erudition. But she and the other ladies named were very exceptional. Public opinion considered that in a middle-class girl a decent (but not damaging) amount of learning was appropriate (or at least tolerable), but Elizabethans did not believe in educating women above their station or capacities.

Grammar boys came from all levels of society except the lowest, which had no need for schooling. Except for small entrance fees, most grammar schools were free to all who qualified for admission, their statutes forbidding the master to charge fees. Thus the master at Stratford was bound to "teach grammar freely to all scholars coming to him in the said town, taking nothing of the scholars for their teaching." The principal condition of entrance was competence in elementary reading and writing. This implied knowledge of the catechism and primer. Colet's statutes for St. Paul's instruct the master to say to parents: "If your child can read and write Latin and English sufficiently, so that he be able to read and write his own lessons, then he shall be admitted into the school for a scholar." The requirements at Westminster (founded 1560), Merchant Taylors' (1561), and other schools were similar to those of St. Paul's. Some schools demanded a knowledge of Latin accidence too, and by the end of the century this had become the rule.

Some statutes were equally explicit about the master's duty to get rid of stupid or slothful pupils. The master of St. Paul's was to warn parents: "If your child, after reasonable season proved, be found here unapt and unable to learning, then ye, warned thereof, shall take him away, that he occupy not here room in vain." If, say Canterbury School statutes (1541), a boy should be "of exceptional slowness and stupidity, or of a nature averse to learning," his place should be given to someone of more promise. An Eton memorandum of 1530 reads: "If there be any dullard, the master giveth his friends warning and putteth him away, that he slander not the school." St. Paul's statutes provided that if a boy left to attend another school, he could not be re-admitted; let him go "where his friends shall think there shall be better learning."

The function of a grammar school was clearly defined and understood: it was the teaching of Latin. Greek and Hebrew were added in the sixteenth century, but the main purpose of the seven years' course remained the same—the acquirement, through memorizing of grammar, daily analysis of texts, and incessant practice of composition, of a ready command of the reading, writing, and speaking of Latin. Renaissance theory and practice of education were predominantly and complacently linguistic. "Grammar" should not mislead us. It was almost as inclusive a term as our phrase "language and literature"; a grammarian had as wide a range of activity as a professor of English today. Grammar is defined by a medieval writer as "the art of interpreting poets and writers of history, and of writing and speaking correctly." "Mother and foundation of all the sciences," it is called by Bishop Waynflete, the founder of Magdalen College. And grammar meant Latin grammar. Whatever the language of heaven, asserts a modern philosopher, A. N. Whitehead, it is not Latin. Our forefathers were not so sure. All education was based on Latin. "Here," says the anonymous Magdalen School vulgaria of ca. 1500, "we may drink of the pure well of Latin tongue and eloquence, [than] which is nothing fairer. O gracious children that wetteth their lips therein! . . . Trust ye me, all language is well nigh but rude beside Latin tongue." In the Tudor and Stuart era there could be no doubt that Latin was the language most necessary to learn. It was still an eminently practical subject, the medium of traditional and indeed of much contemporary scholarship, the key that opened the door to careers in the Church, law, medicine, and other professions.

Drilling boys in grammar and teaching them to read, write, and speak a highly inflected language takes time. All masters had the same goal and most traveled to it by the same familiar routes. All boys had the same constant memorizing, reciting, construing, composing to go through. In addition they had to keep notebooks or commonplace books in which to record, and then learn, idioms, quotations, or figures useful in composition or declamation. Not a little of that wide learning and impressive range of quotation adorning Elizabethan literature comes from these commonplace books.

A student began with the eight parts of speech, then went on to accidence proper. Some children learned the accidence in petty school, as we have noted; the rest began it as soon as they entered grammar school. Explanations of the accidence were in

English, everything beyond in Latin. Educators of those times insisted that the accidence be learned slowly and thoroughly. One of them describes what was, with some variations, the common method of teaching it. First, let the master read the lesson aloud, explaining everything. Then quiz the pupils on this lesson, making sure they understand it. Third, have them read the lesson to one another and correct any mistakes the reader makes. Fourth, have them begin to memorize it. Fifth, drill them and examine them frequently.

When Roger Ascham, in his *Schoolmaster* (1570), remarked that "all men covet to have their children speak Latin," he was uttering a truism. Because ability to speak Latin was so important and so esteemed, and because children have such a maddening habit of talking their native language if not watched, speaking English in school constituted a punishable offense for which one was reported to the master by the *custos* or *asinus*, an older boy assigned to this unenviable post of company spy. Canterbury School regulations (1541) say: "Whatever they are doing, in earnest or in play, they must not speak any language but Latin or Greek." At Eton (1530), Latin was required not only in the schoolroom but in the houses where the boys lived. By general agreement the comedies of Terence and the letters of Cicero were the best classical models of conversational Latin, but Tudor writers disagreed on how early the speaking of Latin should begin. A few, including Ascham, thought children began too early and as a result learned barbarous speech instead of the "good clean Latin" so highly prized. Ascham actually forbids children to talk Latin in the earlier stages of study; they will only get it wrong, he says, and should wait until they have a firmer grip on grammar and vocabulary.

After the elements of grammar were mastered, the next stage in many schools was the making of "Latins," that is, putting into acceptable Latin the English phrases and sentences set by the master. For this work the Tudor schoolboy had guidance from some excellent books prepared for just his needs. These were of two kinds, vulgaria and colloquia. Vulgaria contained English phrases and sentences with Latin versions attached; hence a "vulgar" was a sentence in the vulgar tongue, English, assigned for translation. We have already mentioned Anwykyll's little volume of Terentian phrases and an anonymous vulgaria from the end of the fifteenth century. Nicholas Udall, headmaster of Eton and later of Westminster, published a useful phrase book, *Flowers of Latin Speaking* (1533). The most successful vulgaria were produced by John Stanbridge (1508) and Robert Whittinton (1520) of Magdalen School and William Horman (1519) of Eton. These books give us invaluable glimpses of contemporary life, both in the schoolroom and beyond. Undoubtedly they are more agreeable to us than to the schoolboy for whom they were prepared, but even to him they must have had more appeal than the dreary tags of conventional textbooks. Here are a few examples from Stanbridge:

> I was set to school when I was seven year old.
> *Datus sum scolis cum septemnis eram.*
>
> Scholars must live hardily at Oxford.
> *Scholasticos oxonii parce vivere oportet.*
>
> The master hath beat me.
> *Preceptor a me sumpsit poenas.*
>
> Sit away or I shall give thee a blow.
> *Amove sedem sinautem colaphum male addam.*
>
> Sayest thou this in earnest or in game?
> *Ioco an serio loqueris?*

Horman's *Vulgaria* contains 3,000 English sentences, arranged topically, with English translation. Whittinton's book, unlike the other two, first refers to a rule of grammar and then gives an English-Latin illustration.

Beyond vulgaria, and a natural development of them, were colloquies or dialogues. The best of these were written by Erasmus (published 1518–1533), Juan Luis Vives (1538), and Mathurin Cordier (1564). From a short collection of phrases and formulas, Erasmus' book grew into a large volume of witty, vivid, often elaborate dialogues on a variety of subjects. Some of these dialogues are unsurpassed as an introduction to the life and manners of the early sixteenth century. Cordier's colloquies were especially acceptable to many readers because of their author's connection with Calvin and Geneva.

Though long used in certain grammar schools, "making Latins" as a method of composition did not please everyone. Ascham in his *Schoolmaster* rejected it, as did Brinsley in his *Ludus Literarius*. Horman's and Whittinton's books, declared Ascham, taught "an evil choice of words" and "an ill framing of the sentence"; all the pupil cared about in his "butcherly fear of making Latins" was to please the master. Ascham advocated instead a comparative method called "double translation," and, on his assumptions about Latinity, this was a good, foolproof scheme. Equally important, it was essentially a written rather than an oral program of instruction. After the child has learned accidence, the master is to read to the class from the letters of Cicero:

First, let him teach the child, cheerfully and plainly, the cause and matter of the letter; then let him construe it into English, so oft as the child may easily carry away the understanding of it; lastly, parse it over perfectly. This done thus, let the child by and by both construe and parse it over again, so that it may appear that the child doubteth in nothing that his master taught him before. After this the child must take a paper book and, sitting in some place where no man shall prompt him, by himself, let him translate into English his former lesson. Then showing it to his master, let the master take from him his Latin book and, pausing an hour at the least, then let the child translate his own English into Latin again in another paper book. When the child bringeth it, turned into Latin, the master must compare it with Tully's book and lay them both together. . . .

In the more advanced stages of double translation, the pupils come ever closer to original composition. For example, they practice turning into Latin—always aspiring to Ciceronian purity of diction—an English version of some Latin passage whose source is unknown to them. After this they are ready to write, in Latin, something of their own.

In addition to themes, and often in preparation for them, pupils wrote letters. Here again the grand model was Cicero;

after him, Pliny; and good modern handbooks of directions with model letters were easily available. Study of models, practice, and a little judicious cribbing here and there taught the boys how to conduct a correspondence, or at least taught them conventional formulas. The obvious and safest method of procedure was to make an English draft, then turn it into Latin. Under the right teacher this method must have afforded useful practice in English as well as Latin. But the goal was Latinity, not English.

A uniform method of composition was not required, but schools had to use an official grammar, William Lily's. An early booklet consisting of an accidence by Colet (before 1513?) and a syntax by Lily was succeeded by a syntax prepared by Lily and then revised by Erasmus. These works and two short poems on accidence, by Lily, grew into a grammar (1540) which in its 1542 edition carried a royal proclamation forbidding the use of any other grammar in English schools. The proclamation assures teachers of their sovereign's solicitude for youth and exhorts the "tender babes of England" to "shake off slothfulness, set wantonness apart, apply your wits wholly to learning and virtue." In the reign of Elizabeth this injunction imposing Lily's grammar on schools was renewed. If Shakespeare attended grammar school, he studied Lily.

In the upper years of grammar school, rhetoric succeeded grammar as the principal study. The art of rhetoric embraced all the techniques and resources of language. Mastery of this art meant understanding and control of the numerous schemes (figures of arrangement) and tropes (figures of thought, images) essential to every writer and speaker who wished to communicate effectively. What could be more important to learn? Treatises ancient and modern, from Aristotle's to Erasmus', explained the principles and illustrated them. After study of these texts the schoolboy was expected to observe, identify, and appreciate the rhetorical structure and color of everything he read, know how to organize a discourse variously for his purposes, and use schemes and tropes cogently and appropriately.

The nature of Tudor curricula and textbooks may suggest

that the teaching of composition was preoccupied with problems of diction and style to the neglect of substance. This was not necessarily the intention, but it is quite true that teachers and textbooks had more to say about style than content. Readers and writers alike responded to rhetorical art and valued it highly. "Men began to hunt more after words than matter," says Bacon of Ascham and his contemporaries. Yet the subject of composition was so fundamental in Renaissance schools, and Ascham's doctrines so representative, that his views must command respect. His basic principle was *imitatio*, "a faculty to express lively and perfectly that example which ye go about to follow." This "faculty" of imitating compelled patient comparison of approved models, with deliberate and repeated efforts to apply the lessons of such study to one's own writing. Imitation did not strike Ascham or his sympathizers as something stultifyingly narrow or unimaginative or unoriginal. They considered it both liberating and fortifying: "Of itself it is large and wide, for all the works of Nature in a manner be examples for art to follow." Ascham's principles of language study, like the universal cultivation of rhetoric in his age, were expressions of a conviction about the urgency of *form*. How foolish, he says, to protest, "What care I for a man's words and utterance if his matter and reasons be good?" No! Form is part of the meaning, inseparable from it. "Proper and apt words" are to meaning what nourishment is to a body: essential for life. "Ye know not what hurt ye do to learning, that care not for words but for matter and so make a divorce betwixt the tongue and the heart." Form is order. Slovenly writing comes from disorderly thoughts. History shows that when style decays "then also began ill deeds to spring" and evils of every description followed. This conclusion may seem far-fetched but is not peculiar to Ascham or his epoch.

A traditional kind of composition occasionally practiced in school was the disputation or debate, a survival from medieval days when logic or dialectic was a school subject. In Renaissance schools grammar and rhetoric took up so much time that logic received less and less attention and disputation was reserved more and more to the universities. Declamation, on the other hand, remained a standard exercise in grammar schools. At times plays and pageants furnished another and doubtless more entertaining means of practicing Latin speeches. The comedies of Plautus and Terence were natural favorites. Modern Latin dramas on Biblical themes were acted too. If Greek plays were offered, they were likely to be comedies by Aristophanes. We hear also of school drama in English. Nicholas Udall wrote *Ralph Roister Doister* (1553), regarded as the first English comedy, as a school play. Westminster was especially famous for its plays; not surprisingly when we learn that this school's statutes (1560) required a comedy or tragedy in Latin and one in English to be produced in hall at Christmas. Shrewsbury School likewise had a reputation for dramatic performances, including outdoor pageants. In Jonson's *Staple of News* (1626) a censorious character complains that schoolmasters give too much attention to plays and "make all their scholars play-boys."

The making of Latin verses was a standard part of schoolwork. If Renaissance assumptions about the purpose and method of grammar-school training were sound, versifying had much to recommend it. Because it could not be practiced successfully without technical knowledge, it encouraged both exactness and resourcefulness in Latinity. Poetry, specifically neo-Latin poetry, was not habitually regarded as the subtle expression of profound and private emotions or experiences recollected in tranquillity. That is a later and rarefied doctrine. Like music, poetry was largely a matter of techniques which any intelligent person could master if he practiced enough five-finger exercises. As an art, poetry was intimately allied with rhetoric—an additional reason for its presence in the curriculum. Versemaking was a useful exercise in imitation; according to Brinsley, it is merely turning words from a grammatical into a rhetorical order.

A descriptive list of Latin texts read in schools would be useful but far too long to print here. Lily's grammar and the most popular vulgaria and colloquia we have already named. For the youngest pupils, "Cato" and Aesop were prescribed generation after generation. A boy would certainly learn Terence, Cicero, Virgil, Ovid (Shakespeare's favorite, apparently), and Horace;

and if he finished grammar school he would probably have read extracts from Sallust, Caesar, Plautus, Martial, Juvenal, and Livy, to name no others. Modern Latin authors too had a place in the curriculum. Baptista Mantuanus, whose eclogues (1498) had a long vogue, was known to many schoolboys besides Shakespeare. "Good old Mantuan," Holofernes calls him (*Love's Labor's Lost,* IV, ii, 98). The *Zodiacus Vitae* of Palingenius (ca. 1535), a poem of moralized mythology and astronomy, was read in some schools. So were the Latin metrical paraphrases of the Psalms by George Buchanan (ca. 1565), a poet of the highest standing in his time.

Latin was taken for granted as the basis of grammar-school education, but a literature greater in almost every respect— "Cicero only excepted," Ascham warns us!—exists in Greek. No wonder, then, that after the revival of Greek studies in fifteenth-century Italy, ancient Hellenic civilization became an enthusiasm with Western scholars and artists. Known only imperfectly and to very few scholars in medieval England, Greek did not begin to be a subject of university study there until the last quarter of the fifteenth century. At the beginning of Henry VIII's reign a few of the leading English humanists—More, William Latimer, Thomas Linacre, William Grocyn—were known as students of Greek. Colet's statutes (1518) for St. Paul's instruct the governors to appoint as master a man learned in Latin "and also in Greek if such may be gotten," proof that in 1518 such men were not easy to find. Although Colet apparently had something to do with Erasmus' decision to pursue Greek, Colet himself did not know the language. But there is reason to think it was already being taught at Eton and Winchester. Wolsey's statutes for his school at Ipswich omit Greek. Qualified teachers were easier to find toward the end of Henry's reign, yet Greek hardly became a standard study in grammar schools until Elizabeth's time.

Methods of teaching Greek necessarily resembled those used for Latin: patient reading of the grammar and explanation of it by the master, accidence and syntax day after day, memorizing, reading of simple texts as soon as possible, then composition. In

The Governor (1531), Sir Thomas Elyot advised that Greek and Latin be taken up at the same time, when a boy was seven, but ordinarily grammar schools postponed Greek for several years, until the pupil was well along in Latin. Common texts for beginners were Aesop and Lucian, as they are now; then came extracts from Plutarch, Xenophon, Demosthenes, Homer, Isocrates, and Plato. A boy had little incentive to learn to speak Greek, but in many schools he had to write Greek verses. Erasmus notes with admiration that there were English schoolboys who could turn out Greek epigrams. He spares us examples.

Jonson's line about Shakespeare's "small Latin and less Greek" is often misinterpreted by persons who mistakenly believe that "small" Latin in Elizabethan days meant no more than "a little" Latin usually means today. Every Elizabethan who completed grammar school, even the most inconspicuous country grammar school, had studied Latin for seven years and studied it more than anything else. Shakespeare was no profound scholar, not a remarkably bookish man, but he knew Latin well and may have had a smattering of Greek. We have no documentary proof that he went to school at all—schools did not keep many records in those days—but there is every reason to surmise that he attended Stratford Grammar School. Because grammar-school education was largely the same throughout the land, we can be confident that we know the kind of curriculum he encountered, some of the principal texts he studied, and the methods by which the work of the school was carried on. The sort of training outlined in this sketch of schools is what he must have received. His plays, which have many allusions to schools and schoolmasters, prove that he knew Lily's grammar and some of the conventional authors we would expect him to know: Cato, Terence, Virgil, Ovid, and among the moderns Mantuanus and Erasmus. Scholars have demonstrated the probability, in some cases the virtual certainty, of his acquaintance with others and with school rhetorics. His Greek, if he had any, would have been much slighter and is therefore harder to identify; but it would have included portions of the Greek New Testament and catechism.

The third learned tongue, Hebrew, little known and not studied academically in the Middle Ages, found a place in a few Elizabethan schools. The only text of interest was the Old Testament, which some educators, including Milton, believed boys ought to learn to read in the original tongue. Westminster is said to have been the first school to require (1560) that the headmaster be qualified in Hebrew as well as Greek and Latin, and this school became celebrated for its instruction in the three languages. Boys did not attempt Hebrew until they had made some progress in Greek, just as they did not begin Greek until fairly proficient in Latin. Sir Humphrey Gilbert's proposal (1564) for an academy in London "for the education of Her Majesty's wards" provided for Hebrew along with Latin, Greek, French, Italian, Spanish, and German.

What of English? Young children learned the alphabet and started to read English in petty school, using an ABC book and primer for this purpose. English literature was not studied in grammar school, but teachers and pupils could hardly ignore the native language altogether, even though speaking it in the schoolroom was forbidden. A grammarian in 1540 complains that some masters know less English than Latin; that the boys ever did is incredible. The exacting discipline of Latin probably improved their English, since it often happens that the more a person studies a foreign language the more attentive he becomes to the idiom, nuances, and resources of his own. That English was a Germanic language, with a structure unlike that of Latin, did not trouble Tudor educators overmuch.

For a modern reader, one of the most interesting Elizabethan treatments of the place and teaching of English is Mulcaster's *Elementary* (1582). It is not in every respect typical of Elizabethan opinion but is historically important; and because it comes from a successful schoolmaster, it is full of observations based on long experience. Mulcaster was an enthusiastic advocate of English, "a tongue of itself both deep in conceit and frank in delivery." "I love Rome," he wrote, "but London better; I favor Italy, but England more; I honor the Latin, but I worship the English." Cicero had recommended that the study of Greek and Latin be combined. Similarly Mulcaster wanted a child to be able to read both English and Latin "very long before he dream of" Latin grammar. But the child must learn English first:

> While our religion was restrained to the Latin, it was either the only or the oneliest principle in learning, to learn to read Latin. But now that we are returned home to our English ABC, as most natural to our soil and most proper to our faith . . . we are to be directed by Nature and property [propriety] to read that first which we speak first, and to care for that most which we ever use most.

Like many of his countrymen, Mulcaster had his own ideas on spelling and wanted to regularize it. In those times spelling was something a writer or printer usually settled for himself. No official English speller or grammar existed to arbitrate disputes, as Lily's settled those for Latin. Unlike French, English has never submitted to regulation by an academy.

It is a fallacy to suppose that Elizabethans depreciated the English language unduly. On the contrary, their patriotism and provincialism often exalted it. Nevertheless the learned world assumed that English literature, however agreeable as a recreation, lacked the substance, high seriousness, and cultural values of the classics. In 1550 this was hardly an error; by 1650 the story would be different. A knowledge of English literature, as of other modern languages and the fine arts, was something an Elizabethan acquired outside the schoolroom. Who needed formal instruction in the poetry of his own age? The conventional master in Brinsley's *Ludus Literarius* says parents will criticize him because he does not allow time for English. Why not have pupils read daily a chapter of the English Bible? "Now this I cannot possibly do, but they must needs be hindered in their Latin." First things first! Brinsley himself rejects this argument, insisting that there should be exercises in English every day.

Grammar schools existed to instruct in the learned languages. The curriculum was narrow but not so stifling as we might imagine; at any rate, not in the hands of a good teacher. It is hard to believe that the Westminster pupils of Camden, the leading antiquary of his day, learned no British history. And all boys learned something of ancient history from the Greek and Latin texts they spent years in studying. In all fairness to Tudor Englishmen we must allow that their schools recognized the existence of other subjects besides languages and even tried occasionally to teach them if those subjects could be fitted in without disturbing the really important work. Milton advocated the study of politics in order that pupils "may not in a dangerous fit of the commonwealth be such poor, shaken, uncertain reeds, of such a tottering conscience, as many of our great counsellors have lately shown themselves, but steadfast pillars of the state." The Tudors understood as well as Milton or ourselves the uses of political and legal history and modern languages, but they could not find room for these studies in a curriculum filled by Latin and Greek. A boy well grounded in these tongues, which must be taught thoroughly if at all, could —and would if he chose—acquire the other subjects at home or in later years.

Handwriting, a skill the child was expected to get in petty school as a condition of entrance to grammar, was continued in some grammar schools. It was taught by the usher if there was one; if not, by the master. Or it was taught by a writing master in the town. A child was required to learn both the Italian and secretary hands. Sixteenth-century writers on schools are emphatic in their demands that training in handwriting be adequate; and Brinsley's treatise has a long chapter devoted to it. Mulcaster thinks drawing too should be taught in elementary grades.

Francis Bacon observes that if a child "be bird-witted, that is, hath not the faculty of attention, the mathematics giveth a remedy thereunto; for, in them, if the wit be caught away but a moment, one is new to begin." To mathematics as an intellectual discipline, however, Tudor schools paid little regard. The study seldom went further than arithmetic; once in a while it reached geometry. A grammar master simply could not be bothered with this sort of thing when the real business of school, languages, had first call on his time. Here too Mulcaster stands out as an exception, even daring to affirm in an heretical mood, "We do attribute too much to tongues."

"All our teaching is mere trifling unless we be careful to instruct children in the grounds of true religion," declared Hoole in his book on schools. That all education is at bottom religious was considered a self-evident principle. Schoolmasters were expected to avoid disputatious and officious meddling with theological topics but were strictly required to teach the elements of religion from prescribed handbooks. In grammar schools the catechism was regularly taught and recited on Saturdays. By far the most common catechisms in Elizabethan times were those by Calvin and by Alexander Nowell, dean of St. Paul's. Scarcely any book except Lily's Latin grammar was more familiar to English schoolboys for fifty years than Nowell's catechism. In some schools boys also had to sing or recite Psalms daily, using the famous Sternhold and Hopkins metrical versions. Attendance at divine service on Sunday was compulsory. The Canons of 1571 order that children shall be quizzed by their schoolmaster on the weekly sermon. Many children had to take notes on the sermon, an exercise which apparently became a lifelong habit with some.

The Tudor schoolboy had an eight- to ten-hour day and a six-day week in the schoolroom. Normally schoolwork began at six o'clock in summer, seven in winter. At eleven school recessed until twelve or one, then resumed until five or six. Some schools permitted a fifteen-minute break in the middle of the morning and afternoon. At St. Paul's "the children shall come unto school in the morning at seven of the clock both winter and summer and tarry there until eleven and return again at one of the clock and depart at five." At Eton in 1530 "they come to school at six of the clock"; no breakfast until nine, and then only fifteen minutes allowed for it. Dinner was at eleven, supper at five. At Canterbury in 1541 the usher begins work with pupils at six, the master at seven, and boys must return for an hour in the evening. How did they stand it? By not knowing that any other system existed. So far as they were aware, this was the order of

Nature, therefore something to be endured; and those who did not die young had a happy faculty of adjusting themselves to it.

Sufficient timetables of the work in sixteenth-century schools survive to show conveniently the successive stages in the studies we have described. Official accounts can be supplemented or checked by less formal ones; for example, we have a useful sketch of life and work at Winchester in 1550 in a Latin poem by a pupil who survived to become headmaster. For his school at Ipswich (founded 1528) Cardinal Wolsey planned eight forms. In the first the main task was that of learning pronunciation and parts of speech. Latin speaking and translating began in the second, where Cato's *Distichs* were read and Lily's grammar was begun. In the third, the boys had Aesop, Terence, and Lily; in the fourth, more Lily and texts, including Virgil; in the fifth, Cicero's letters; in the sixth, Sallust or Caesar; in the seventh, Horace or Ovid; in the eighth, Valla's *Elegantiae* (a handbook on usage), texts, and essay writing. At Winchester in 1530 the lowest form memorized Stanbridge's *Accidentia* and read Cato and Aesop. In the second form they had more accidence and now some vulgars; in the third, grammar, vulgars, Latin themes, Aesop, and Lucian (these two in Greek, presumably); in the fourth, grammar, prosody, vulgars, compositions, Terence, Ovid, Cicero, letter writing; in upper forms the same sort of thing but more of it, with new authors added. In this and all schools there was "homework" to be handed to the master when school began, and parsing, construing, and reading required at stated hours during the school day. On Fridays a review of the week's lessons was customary.

A weekly timetable of studies at Eton for 1530, drawn up by the master, does not differ significantly from that of Winchester. At Westminster in 1560, however, we find some authors not met at Eton and Winchester in 1530: Justin, Isocrates, Demosthenes, Homer, Plutarch, Vives, Cordier. An anonymous account of life in the sixth and seventh forms at Westminster between 1610 and 1620 shows that grammar-school work in the reign of James I had changed very little from that of 1560.

Not only did Tudor schoolboys spend eight to ten hours a

day, including Saturdays, in the schoolroom, but they had no long summer vacation. On the other hand, they enjoyed many more short holidays than boys do now. Usually every saint's day gave them a day or half-day off. Christmas, Easter, and Whitsuntide provided vacations of a few days each at some schools, a week or so at others. Now and then an extra holiday, called a "remedy," would be granted for some special reason or at the request of an important visitor. Colet must have been annoyed by the custom, for his statutes for St. Paul's forbid remedies except on the personal request of a king, archbishop, or bishop visiting the school; if the master grants any others he is to be fined forty shillings. "Many remedies make easy [*ineruditos,* ignorant] scholars," warns Horman, the Eton master. Milton too deplores the loss of time caused by too many holidays.

No description of Tudor schools would be complete without reference to the sobering topic of discipline, for in no respect did their practices differ more decisively from those in vogue today. Tudor schools were not all alike, but in general the discipline was rigorous and corporal punishment the common method of enforcing it. To teach well and to flog well had been nearly synonymous since antiquity; witness the famous chapter (I, ix) in Augustine's *Confessions* where he tells how desperately and vainly he prayed to escape beating. We read that as part of his final examination a graduate in grammar at Cambridge, in the late medieval period, was required to demonstrate his readiness for the "classroom situation," as it would now be termed, by beating a "shrewd boy." Little wonder that a schoolboy in an Elizabethan play believes that "the devil (I trow) doth make many men hate boys." What is probably the best-known Tudor book on education, Ascham's *Schoolmaster,* was provoked, its author tells us, by a disturbing report that some young Etonians had run away "for fear of beating."

We can easily believe that excessively long hours, an excessively linguistic curriculum, and lack of officially organized games, not to mention normal boyish perversity, made discipline a formidable problem. The problem was faced realistically and solved with classic simplicity, on Scriptural principles: "Foolishness is bound in the heart of a child; but the rod of correction shall drive it far from him." The master's promptness and severity in resorting to the rod are far too commonplace in the writings of the time to leave us in the slightest doubt of the prominence of this mode of chastisement. The following passages in Whittinton's *Vulgaria* bring it closer home:

I played my master a merry prank or play yesterday and therefore he hath taught me to sing a new song today. He hath made me to run a race (or a course) that my buttocks doth sweat a bloody sweat. The more instantly that I prayed him to pardon me, the faster he laid upon. He hath taught me a lesson that I shall remember whiles I live.

My master hath beat my back and sides whiles the rod would hold in his hand. . . . If ever I be a man I will revenge his malice. I trust once to grow able to rid myself out of his danger. And to restore myself in liberty. For the good favor that he showeth me I have kept a comfortative [*antidotum*] for him that shall work this seven year or after.

Both sides take for granted that between teacher and pupil there exists a permanent state of war, ordained in the nature of things.

The time-honored way of keeping boys in order was to strike their outstretched palms with a ferule, a sort of ruler, or flog them with a birch rod, that indispensable instrument of education which the master in Renaissance pictures invariably has in his hand or within easy reach. The method was swift, economical, infallible: what teachers were for and what boys could understand. If beating did not, at the moment, do much to advance their comprehension of Latin syntax, at least it made clear the awful distance between knowledge and ignorance, vigilance and sloth. Tudor schoolmasters would have endorsed the policy of a later brother who warned his class: "Blessed are the pure in heart. Be pure in heart or I'll flog you." Or of another who, vexed when a dullard could not recall the catechism's answer to the question "What is God?" thrashed the offender soundly and then flung him back in his seat with the remark, "*Now* maybe you'll remember what God is. God is LOVE."

Fighting, swearing, truancy, laziness, and theft were common schoolboy vices then as now. We are not surprised to hear of a culprit who "did slide upon the ice, cast snow, fought with his fists and balls of snow, scourge [spin] his top, played for pennies, cherry stones, counters, dice, cards" on his way to school. Clearly such malefactors needed correction. That a day would ever come when teachers not only would refrain from inflicting corporal punishment but would actually be forbidden by law to do so, was something too fantastic for the imagination of Elizabethan masters, pupils, and parents. Important writers on education condemned cruelty and overfrequent use of physical punishment, but they were in the minority. Udall of Eton was remembered for the beatings he inflicted ("for fault but small or none at all," according to one victim) as much as for more agreeable activities. In the next century Dr. Busby, headmaster of Westminster for fifty-six years, won fame as the greatest beater of his time; his name became a proverb. "A great man! He whipped my grandfather; a very great man!" says Sir Roger de Coverley of him in *The Spectator*.

"Whosoever shall consider with any judgment the manner of training up children which we use generally within this realm, cannot but wish that the thing were bettered, as I myself do." With this, the opening sentence of Mulcaster's *Positions* (1581), many thoughtful Elizabethans would have concurred, for schools after all are never satisfactory to sensitive minds and criticism of them never lacking. The subject has a perennial fascination for all concerned, and all seem equally positive of their competence to criticize. Tudor Englishmen were no exceptions. Yet the merits and demerits of Tudor schools raise questions that can be answered only relatively, since the answers depend on our presuppositions about the nature and task of education. We began this essay by pointing out that superficial resemblances between Tudor schools and our own should not obscure the number and significance of the differences. After an examination of those schools we can now perceive that in the lower grades many of the differences were ones of method, equipment, and discipline rather than of aims. In upper forms certain of the fundamental purposes as well as methods have changed or disappeared since the sixteenth century.

"The humble and true teacher meets with more than he expects," wrote William Penn in an exquisitely ambiguous sentence. Humility is not the virtue we should most confidently look for in a Tudor grammar master, but that he met with more than he expected is certainly credible. We may hope that some at least of those masters had the satisfaction of foreseeing the future greatness of their charges, and that many of these were as grateful to their teachers afterward as Jonson was to Camden. Of the vast majority of pupils at grammar school all we know is that they survived it: no slight feat.

SUGGESTED READING

Although books on education are not always lively reading—the "terms of learning" being often "mysteries to the multitude," as Mulcaster complains—anyone interested in Tudor schools will find many rewarding passages in sixteenth- and seventeenth-century works on the subject. Some of the most important treatises available in modern editions or reprints are: Sir Thomas Elyot, *The Governor* (1531); Roger Ascham, *The Schoolmaster* (1570); Richard Mulcaster, *Positions* (1581) and *The First Part of the Elementary* (1582); Charles Hoole, *A New Discovery of the Old Art of Teaching School* (1660). Most of Hoole's topics and conclusions are relevant to the early as well as middle years of the century. Milton's essay on education can be found in many editions. Unfortunately this is not true of certain other writings less famous but more detailed or more representative than Milton's: William Kempe, *The Education of Children* (1588); Edmund Coote, *The English Schoolmaster* (1596); and John Brinsley, *Ludus Literarius* (1612). A slighter book by Brinsley, *A Consolation for Our Grammar Schools* (1622; facsimile edition, New York, 1943) is of special interest because it was written for "all ruder countries and places, namely, for Ireland, Wales, Virginia." Publication was arranged by the Virginia Company, which planned to establish a school and a college in the colony.

Stanbridge's and Whittinton's vulgaria, ed. Beatrice White, are reprinted by the Early English Text Society (London, 1932); Horman's may be read in a sumptuous limited edition by M. R. James (Oxford, 1926). Quotations from the Magdalen School vulgaria are from the edition by William Nelson, *A Fifteenth Century School Book* (Oxford, 1956). A facsimile edition of a 1567 copy of Lily's Latin grammar in the Folger Library, ed. Vincent J. Flynn (New York, 1945) is the most convenient text of that celebrated work. On

Erasmus' educational theory consult W. H. Woodward, *Desiderius Erasmus concerning the Aim and Method of Education* (Cambridge, 1904) and T. W. Baldwin (see below).

Educational Charters and Documents, ed. A. F. Leach (Cambridge, 1911) prints many statutes and curricula of fifteenth- and sixteenth-century schools. The same scholar's *Schools of Medieval England* (New York, 1915) and *English Schools at the Reformation* (London, 1896) are indispensable studies. A good brief introduction to Tudor grammar schools is J. H. Brown, *Elizabethan Schooldays* (Oxford, 1933). Other histories or descriptions will be found in Foster Watson, *The English Grammar Schools to 1660* (Cambridge, 1908) and *The Old English Grammar Schools* (Cambridge, 1916), and A. M. Stowe, *English Grammar Schools in the Reign of Queen Elizabeth* (New York, 1908). Histories of education are too plentiful to require listing here, but W. H. Woodward, *Studies in Education during the Age of the Renaissance* (Cambridge, 1924) ought to be mentioned. There are published histories of Winchester, Eton, St. Paul's, Magdalen School, Westminster, Merchant Taylors', Charterhouse, Rugby, Harrow, Shrewsbury, and other Tudor and Stuart grammar schools. *Letters and Exercises of the Elizabethan Schoolmaster John Conybeare,* ed. F. W. Conybeare (London, 1905), supplies useful evidence of day-to-day practice in the schoolroom. Histories and studies of special topics include *Shakespeare's England* (Oxford, 1916); Louis B. Wright, *Middle-Class Culture in Elizabethan England* (Chapel Hill, 1935); A. L. Rowse, *The England of Elizabeth* (London, 1950); G. M. Trevelyan, *Illustrated English Social History* (London, 1949–1952).

On Shakespeare's schooling there is a short book, with attractive illustrations, by George A. Plimpton, *The Education of Shakespeare* (London and New York, 1933), and a much longer one by T. W. Baldwin, *William Shakspere's Small Latine and Lesse Greek* (Urbana, 1944). This is an exhaustive treatment of sixteenth-century grammar education in England. Baldwin's *William Shakspere's Petty School* (Urbana, 1943) describes elementary schools and texts. See also Virgil K. Whitaker, *Shakespeare's Use of Learning* (San Marino, 1953), chapters 1 and 2. On aims and methods of the rhetorical curriculum as experienced by a later poet, consult D. L. Clark, *John Milton at St. Paul's School* (New York, 1948).

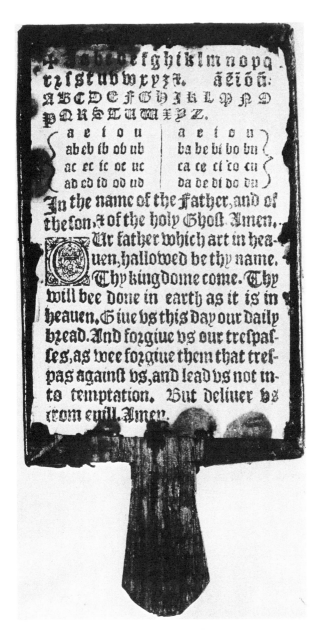

A hornbook of the kind used in Elizabethan petty schools. It is about one fourth as large as this page.

**CRoberti Whittintoni alma in vniuerſi
tate Oxonienſi laureati de octo partib' ora
tionis opuſculū: de nouo recognitum.**

C Auctoris diſtichon.

Grammatice fautrix reliquas dat adire ſozozes.
　Pegaſidum pulſes hac ſine ſcro fozes

C Facūdiſſimi Reinaclī florenatis hexaſtico.

Grammaticen quiſquis magnā aſpernaris auenam
　Nec cupis e tanto grammine principium
Lege itidem parili reliquas poſtpone ſozozes
　Quas tibi Mnemoſines ſancta propago dedit
Prima trahit partus primozdia diua loquendi
　Ad ſocialſcz huius ianua prima patet

Title-page of Robert Whittinton, *De Octo Partibus Orationis*, 1519. An
early edition of a work for beginners in Latin grammar. First printed
ca. 1515.

*omnes omnia decent, id quifque velit, id tentet, quòd pof-
fit . Non fimus id quod Gr æcè fignificantius dicitur
ὄνος λύρας. id eft afinus lyrarum, vel liræ. Sic autẽ Boe-
tius, Afinus ad lyram pofitus. Repugnante natura irri-
tus eft labor. Tu nihil inuita facies dices ve Minerua, te-
fte Horatio.*

DE LEONE ET MVRE. 14

L Eo æftu curfuq; defeffus, fub vmbra fron-
de fuper viridi quiefcebat, Murium au-
tem grege tergum eius pèrcurrrente, ex-
perrectus, vnum è multis comprehendit. Supplicat captiuus, indignum fe effe, cui leo ira-
fcatur: clamitat: reputans ille in nece tantillæ
beftiolæ nihil effe laudis, captiuum dimittit:
Nec verò ita multò poft leo fortè dum per fal-
tum currit, incidit in plagas, rugire licet, exire
non licet. Rugientem miferabiliter leonem
mus audit, vocem agnofcit. repit in cunicu-
los, laqueorum quærit nodos, quæfitos inue-
nit, inuentos corrodit, leo è plagis euadit.

Adfa-

Aesop's *Fables,* a text invariably prescribed for beginners in Greek and Latin. This page from a Latin
edition of 1572 tells the story of the lion and the
mouse.

A scholer, *Scolasticus, vel discipulus.*
*Disco,cis,didici,*To learne.
A micher, or truant, that absenteth him selfe from schole, *Vagus,gi.*
*Vagor garis,*To staye abrode.
Study,*Studium,dij,otium,tij.*
Study by night, *lucubratio,onis.*
To studie by candell lighte, *Lucubro,as.*
A worke done by candell light, *Lucubratum opus.*
*Studeo,des,dui,*To studye.
A lesson,*Lectio,onis.*
*Lego,gis,*To reade.
To reade handsomelye, attentiuelie, & with a gentle iudgement,*Commode, attente,& candido iudicio legere.*
Learninge, *Doctrina, næ,* documentum.
Recordinge,*Meditatio,onis.*
Declaringe, or expounding of a lesson. *Expositio, interpretatio, declaratio,onis.*
A glose, *Glossa, sæ, commentum, ti,glossema,tis.*
Interpretor, taris, Expono, nis, sui,situm. To expounde or declare.
Paper,*Charta,tæ.*
Parchemine,*Membrana,næ.*
A penne made of a quill, *Penna,næ,* But of a reede, *Calamus,mi.*

A penne case,*Pennarium,calaminarium,theca pennaria.*
A penne knife, *Scalprum,vel scalpellum.*
Inke, *Atramentum scriptorium.*
Uermelion to make red inke of,*Minium,nij.*
An ynke horne, *Cornu atramentorum.*
A wryter,*Scriptor,toris.*
Scribo, bis,psi,ptum, To wryte.
A booke, *Liber,bri,codex, ducis, & codicillus.*
The table of a booke, *Index vel elenchus.*
*Titulus,*The title of a booke.
The claspe of a booke,*Fibula.*
A reame of paper,*Summula,læ.*
A quire of a booke, *Volumen,nis.*
A leafe of a booke,*Folium,lij.*
A copie or ensample,*Typus,pi.*
A margene.*Margo,ginis.*
A side of a leafe, *Pagina,næ.*
A part or peece of a leafe, *Scheda,schedula,phylura.*
A parte of a booke,*Tomus,mi.*
A columnne of a leafe,*Columna næ,* Some time it is vsed for a pilour.
A festu,*Festuca,cæ.*
Tables to write in, *Pugillares.*
A pointtell,*Graphia,vel stylus.*
But *stylus,*Is y pointe or pricke of the pointell.
To correcte that which he hath written,*Vertere stylum.*
B,vi,   Orati-

A page from John Withals' English-Latin dictionary for children, *A Short Dictionary Most Profitable for Young Beginners,* revised by Lewis Evans, 1568. First printed in 1553. Words are arranged by subject.

CATECHISMVS,

siue prima Institutio, Disci-
PLINA' QVE PIETATIS
Christianæ, Latinè explicata.

Qui simul eloquio linguam formare Latino,
Et vera mentem Relligione cupis:
Hic liber, atque labor votum dabit vnus vtrunque,
Commoda sic vno bina labore feres.

Londini,
IN OFFICINA REGINALDI
Wolfij, Regiæ Maiest. in Latinis
Typographi.

ANNO DOM. M. D. LXX.
XVI. CALEND. IVL.

Tho: Baker coll: jo: Socius ejectus

Title-page of Alexander Nowell's Latin catechism, 1570. Between 1570 and 1575, Nowell, dean of St. Paul's, produced three catechisms in different sizes. Each was issued in Latin, Greek, and English. This Folger copy once belonged to Thomas Baker (1656–1740), an eminent antiquary, who signed himself "Socius ejectus" because he was deprived of his Cambridge fellowship in 1717.

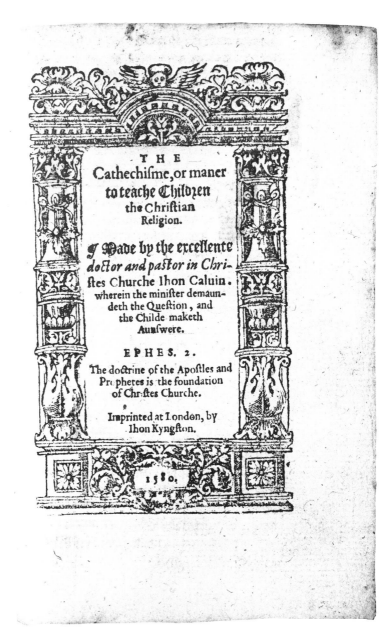

THE
Cathechiſme, or maner
to teache Children
the Chriſtian
Religion.

¶ Made by the excellente
doctor and paſtor in Chriſtes Churche Ihon Caluin.
wherein the miniſter demaun-
deth the Queſtion, and
the Childe maketh
Aunſwere.

EPHES. 2.
The doctrine of the Apoſtles and
Prophetes is the foundation
of Chriſtes Churche.

Imprinted at London, by
Ihon Kyngſton.

1580.

Title-page of Calvin's *Catechism* in English, 1580. This work and Dean Nowell's catechism were the ones principally used in Elizabethan and Jacobean schools.

❡The Minifter.

Hat is the pzincipall and chiefeft ende of mãs life? *1.Sondaie.*

The Childe.

To knowe God.

M. VVhat moueth thée to faie fo?

C. Becaufe he hath created vs, and placed vs in this wozlde, to fet fozthe his glozie in vs, and it is good reafon, that we employ our whole life to his glozy, feing he is the beginning and fountain thereof. *whereunto manne was created and made.*

M. VVhat is then the chifeft felicitie of mã?

C. Euen the felffame, I meane to knowe God, & to haue his glozy fhewed fozthe in vs.

M. VVhy doeft thou call this, mannes chief felicitie?

C. Becaufe that without it, our condition oz ftate were moze miferable, then the ftate of bzute beaftes. *The greateft felicitie that man cã attaine to.*

M. Hereby then we maie euidently fe, that there can no fuche miferie come vnto manne, as not to liue in the knowledge of God.

C. That is mofte certaine.

M. But what is the true, and right knowledge of God?

C. VVhen a man fo knoweth God, that he giueth hym due honour. *The true knowledge of God.*

A.ij. M. VVhiche

Opening page of Calvin's *Catechism*, 1580.

329

Interior of the Grammar School, Stratford. This room has been in continuous use as a schoolroom since the sixteenth century.

Hen the great plage was at London, the yeare 1563. the Quenes Maieſtie Queene *Elizabeth*, lay at her Caſtle of Windſore : Where, vpon the 10. day of December, it fortuned, that in Sir *William Cicells* chamber, hir Highneſſe Principall Secretarie, there dined togither theſe perſonages, M. Secretarie him ſelfe, Syr *William Peter*, Syr *J. Maſon*, D. *Wotton*, Syr *Richard Sackuille* Treaſurer of the Exchecker, Syr *Walter Mildmaye* Chauncellor of the Exchecker, M. *Haddon* Maſter of Requeſtes, M. *Iohn Aſtely* Maſter of the Iewell houſe, M. *Bernard Hampton*, M. *Nicaſius*, and *J*. Of which number, the moſt part were of hir Maieſties moſt honourable priuie Counſell, and the reaſt ſeruing hir in verie good place. I was glad than, and do reioice yet to remember, that my chance was ſo happie, to be there that day, in the companie of ſo manie wiſe & good men togither, as hardly than could haue bene piked out againe, out of all England beſide.

M. Secretarie hath this accuſtomed maner, though his head be neuer ſo full of moſt weightie affaires of the Realme, yet, at diner time he doth ſeeme to lay them alwaies aſide : and findeth euer ſitte occaſion to taulke pleaſantlie of other matters, but moſt gladlie of ſome matter of learning : wherein, he will curteſlie heare the mindc of the meaneſt at his Table.

Not long after our ſitting doune, I haue ſtrange newes brought me, ſayth M. Secretarie, this morning,

First page of Roger Ascham's preface to his *Schoolmaster*, 1570. The "strange news" mentioned at the bottom of the page was a report that some pupils had run away from Eton "for fear of beating." Ascham, a Cambridge scholar, was tutor to Princess Elizabeth, 1548–1549, and Latin Secretary to Queen Mary.

POSITIONS

VVHERIN THOSE PRI-
MITIVE CIRCVMSTANCES

BE EXAMINED, WHICH ARE NE-
CESSARIE FOR THE TRAINING
vp of children, either for skill in their
booke, or health in their bodie.

VVRITTEN by Richard Mvlcaster, *master
of the fchoole erected in London anno.* 1561. *in the parish of Sainct Laurence Povvntneie, by the vvorshipfull
companie of the merchaunt tailers of the faid citie.*

Imprinted at London by Thomas Vautrollier
dvvelling in the blacke Friers by Ludgate
1581

Title-page of Richard Mulcaster's *Positions*, 1581. Mulcaster was headmaster of Merchant Taylors' School (where Spenser was his pupil),
1561–1586, and St. Paul's, 1596–1608. *Positions*, a treatise on the
education of children, was followed by an essay on English spelling and
vocabulary, the *Elementary*, 1582.

& ſtrengtheneth all the vitall actiõs. The litle *handball* is coun-
ted to be a ſwift exerciſe, without violence, and therefore the
rakketters in tennyſe play, if they vſe it in that kinde, which is
thought to be moſt healthfull, muſt ſhew them ſelues nymble
without ſtrayning, & yet it falleth out moſt cõmonly cõtrarie,
while deſire to wynne ſome wager makes the winners looſe a
benefit, which they wiſh for more, & would gladly get to better their health by. This playing abateth groſſenes, and corpu-
lence, as al other of the ſame ſort do: it maketh the fleſh fownd
and ſoft, it is very good for the armes, the greene and growing
ribbes, the back, & by reaſõ the legges are mightely ſtirred ther
by, it is a great furtherer to ſtrength, it quickneth the eyes by
looking now hither, now thither, now vp, now downe, it hel-
peth the ridgebone, by ſtowping, bending and courſing about:
it is verie good for bellies and ſtomakes, that be troubled with
winde or any paine which proceedeth from colde. Now to the
contrary it is not good for ill and bleare eyes, raw ſtomakes,
vndigeſted meat, which haue more neede of reſt then ſtirring,
and for ſuch as will ſoone be turneſicke, which the oft turning
about of the head and eyes cannot but cauſe. The playing at
tennyſe is more coaſtly & ſtraining to aunſwere an aduerſary,
but the playing againſt the wall is as healthfull, and the more
ready, bycauſe it needeth no aduerſary, & yet practiſeth euery
kinde of motion, euery ioynt of the body, and all without danger. Children vſe this ball diuerſly, and euery way healthfully,
in regard of the exerciſe : if accidentarie faultes fall out a-
mong children, in the vſe of the play, the parties muſt beare the
blame, and not the play.

    The ſecond kinde I make the *Footeball* play, which could
not poſſibly haue growne to this greatnes, that it is now at, nor
haue bene ſo much vſed, as it is in all places, if it had not had
great helpes, both to health and ſtrength, and to me the abuſe
of it is a ſufficient argumẽt, that it hath a right vſe: which being
reuoked to his primatiue will both helpe, ſtrength, and comfort
nature: though as it is now cõmonly vſed, with thronging of a
rude multitude, with burſting of ſhinnes, & breaking of legges,
it be neither ciuil, neither worthy the name of any traine to
health. Wherin any mã may euidẽtly ſee the vſe of the trayning
maiſter

A page from a long discourse on games and exercises in Mulcaster's
Positions, 1581. Note his characteristically independent and sensible
comment on football, a rough sport much criticized in Elizabethan
England.

Title-page of William Kempe's *Education of Children*, 1588. Kempe was master of Plymouth Grammar School. The emphasis on discipline which is evident in his Biblical quotations was a favorite theme in Elizabethan writings on education.

Universities in Tudor England

By Craig R. Thompson

AN earlier booklet in this series described elementary and grammar-school training in Tudor England. The present essay attempts to sketch very briefly the organization and work of the two universities, Oxford and Cambridge. It is limited to those institutions as places of teaching and learning; it does not consider such interesting but extraneous topics as college architecture, which is better studied on the site.

Universities were a medieval product, a manifestation of intellectual activity in certain cities in the twelfth century. *Universitas*, a word meaning simply guild or corporation, came to be used of associations of scholars which had curricula, rules of government, recognition by some authority, and power to confer degrees. Oxford and Cambridge were formal associations of this kind. Essentially they were, and still are, corporations of Masters, Fellows, and Scholars engaged in teaching and learning the "arts" (including philosophy) and sciences. As corporations, early universities had two common forms, one typified by Bologna and the other represented by Paris and imitated by British and later by North American universities. Bologna, reputed the oldest university, was organized in the fashion often longed for by modern undergraduates: it was controlled by the students, who even hired and fired professors and prescribed their duties. Paris, on the other hand, was a guild of Masters of Arts, mature scholars who both taught and ruled the younger men.

Medieval university work was professional in aims. Most students were graduate students looking forward to careers in law, medicine, or theology. But since professional studies were not, as a rule, taken up until one became Bachelor of Arts, universities necessarily included undergraduates also. Members of a university had the status of "clerks," an important advantage because of the protection thus afforded against harassment by townsmen or petty officials. We should not conclude, however, that, because students were clerks or because theology as "queen of the sciences" dominated medieval intellectual life, university training was therefore mainly religious. There was little religion in the Arts curriculum. Nor should we suppose that, because of the prestige of theology, a deep sabbath of intellectual tranquillity reigned within the university. A medieval university was no ivory tower. Life in the thirteenth-century University of Paris was probably more turbulent than it is in any university today. Bitter ideological conflicts, with far-reaching consequences, raged within from time to time, while externally the University was often at odds with civil or ecclesiastical authority.

Long before the reign of Queen Elizabeth I, Oxford and Cambridge were venerable homes of learning. They had played a part in every chapter of the national religious and intellectual history since the close of the twelfth century. Like other national institutions, for example Parliament, their condition in 1500 or 1600 was due to accident as well as design, to unexpected and frequently unwelcome changes, to adaptations to new demands. Both universities remained largely medieval in curriculum and customs. Innovations did not always displace inheritances; new and old were adjusted in a manner practicable enough to serve the universities' purposes, flexible enough to respect ancient statutes and ceremonies. Elizabethan university conditions otherwise puzzling, or wholly unintelligible by academic standards or superstitions now prevalent, usually become more clear if examined from a medieval instead of a modern standpoint.

In 1500 Oxford and Cambridge each had ten colleges; by 1600 each had sixteen. At Oxford the oldest were University, Balliol, and Merton, all founded in the thirteenth century. Then came Exeter, Oriel, Queen's, and New College in the fourteenth century, and in the fifteenth Lincoln, All Souls, and Magdalen. The six Tudor colleges were founded between 1512 and 1571: Brasenose, Corpus Christi, Cardinal (afterward Christ Church),

Trinity, St. John's, Jesus. In addition to these colleges, Oxford in 1600 had at least eight halls or hostels: St. Edmund, Broadgates, Magdalen, St. Mary's, Hart, New Inn, St. Alban's, and Gloucester. These were survivors of dozens more that had existed at various times; there had been at least eight named Broadgates, nine named White. Some halls became absorbed by colleges; for example, a White Hall by Jesus College. In the reign of Charles I seven halls still existed; today only one, St. Edmund, remains.

Of Cambridge colleges the oldest was Peterhouse, founded in the thirteenth century. In the next century Clare, Pembroke, Gonville (since the Elizabethan reign called Gonville and Caius), Trinity Hall, and Corpus Christi (commonly called Bene't) were established; in the fifteenth, King's, Queens', St. Catharine's, and Jesus; in the sixteenth, between 1505 and 1596, Christ's, St. John's, Magdalene, Trinity, Emmanuel, and Sidney Sussex. As at Oxford, there had been other colleges and halls, but by 1600 these had disappeared or had been merged with new foundations or absorbed by them; Michaelhouse and King's Hall into Trinity, for example, and God's House into Christ's, Buckingham College into Magdalene. At least twenty sixteenth-century halls are known.

The corporate title of the universities was "The Chancellor, Masters, and Scholars of the University" of Oxford or Cambridge. Each university was a loosely federated republic of colleges. Each college had its own statutes and was governed by a head (Master, President, Provost, Warden, Dean, or Rector) and a body of Fellows. For the present we are more concerned with the university as a whole than with its component parts, for it was the university, not the colleges, that conferred degrees.

The highest dignitary was the Chancellor, elected for life by Masters and Doctors to this honorary, usually nonresidential, but powerful office. He presided on certain ceremonial occasions, intervened on the university's behalf with other influential personages when necessary, looked out for its interests at Court, and sometimes adjudicated internal disputes. His court exercised power, extending even to imprisonment, over all members of the university and over the city of Oxford or town of Cambridge, for the universities had jurisdiction over all local tradesmen.

Tudor Chancellors of Oxford and Cambridge were eminent ecclesiastics or statesmen, great men of affairs. Five of the sixteenth-century Chancellors of Cambridge, as Oxford historians like to point out, were beheaded for treason. One of these, Bishop John Fisher, dominated the University for thirty-five years. He served as Vice-Chancellor in 1501 and was Chancellor from 1504. He was President of Queens' College, 1505–1508, and helped to establish Christ's and St. John's. When his resistance to Henry VIII's ecclesiastical policies brought him to the block in 1535, he was succeeded in the chancellorship by the King's chief minister, Thomas Cromwell, who served until he too was executed (1540). Other Chancellors were Stephen Gardiner, Bishop of Winchester (1540–1547 and 1553–1555); the Duke of Somerset (1547–1552); the Duke of Northumberland (1552–1553); Cardinal Reginald Pole (1556–1558), who was also Chancellor of Oxford; William Cecil, Lord Burleigh (1559–1598); the Earl of Essex (1598–1601); and Sir Robert Cecil, Burleigh's son (1601–1612). Foremost of Elizabethan Chancellors of Oxford was the Earl of Leicester, who held office from 1564 until 1588. He was followed by Sir Christopher Hatton (1588–1591) and Thomas Sackville, Lord Buckhurst (1591–1608).

Presiding over the day-to-day business of the university and representing it in its manifold relations with Chancellor, bishops, and town was the Vice-Chancellor. Unlike post-Reformation Chancellors, he was a resident academician, thoroughly conversant with the university's customs and privileges, all of which it was his duty to maintain against menaces from whatever quarter. By custom the Chancellor nominated the Vice-Chancellor until Elizabethan times. Leicester experimented with election instead of appointment at Oxford in 1566 but was so displeased by the results that he took matters into his own hands again for a time. At Cambridge the Vice-Chancellor was elected by heads of colleges after 1570, and after 1586 every holder of the office was himself head of a college.

Next in importance to Chancellor and Vice-Chancellor were the proctors, elected annually. They had the duty of enforcing university discipline and regulations for town and gown. Because they were also in charge of academic ceremonies and protocol of all kinds, they played a large role in the daily life of the university. Each university had likewise a "high steward," a nonresident officer with certain legal duties. Thomas More served for a few years as steward of both universities. Esquire bedells (whose functions included that of escorting professors to lecture halls and students to degree-taking ceremonies), subproctors, clerks, registrars, and other minor officials need not detain us.

The legislature of each university consisted of its Masters, "regent" and "non-regent," and Doctors. Regents were men who, having lately become M.A., now devoted some time to teaching and to presiding at disputations. In Elizabethan Oxford one's period of regency lasted one or two years; at Cambridge, after 1570, five years.

Oxford had two legislative houses or assemblies, Congregation and Convocation. Congregation, the smaller, was composed of Regent Masters and of Doctors, though Doctors usually left the business to the Masters. Congregation controlled and supervised the routine of lectures and disputations; therefore it controlled the requirements for degrees. Convocation, the more powerful body, included all Non-Regents as well as Regents. At times it delegated powers to Congregation—for example, power to act on requests from students of all grades for dispensations from required periods of residence—but reserved supreme authority for itself. Also it elected the Chancellor and proctors.

Cambridge government in Elizabethan times was vested in a Senate made up of two houses of Regents and Non-Regents. There was also a Caput Senatus, a council consisting of the Vice-Chancellor and five other members, usually heads of houses. Until 1570 the Caput was appointed at the start of each session of the two houses; after 1570, for a year. The Caput became a sort of executive committee. It decided, for instance, whether "graces" (proposals or motions) might be submitted to the Senate.

Westminster and Canterbury kept a close eye on the universities and had many methods, direct and indirect, of making their power felt. This influence was natural, inevitable, in a society in which Church and State were so intimately connected. At the commencement of a new reign it was imperative for the universities to secure a renewal of their rights and privileges. From time to time their fundamental statutes were revised, or new ones imposed, by the Government, ordinarily after investigation of university affairs by a royal commission. This happened, for example, after the death of Henry VIII, when a Government more decisively Protestant came into power. Bishop Gardiner, who was hostile to Reformed doctrine, was replaced as Chancellor of Cambridge by Protector Somerset. A royal commission with broad powers inspected Oxford and Cambridge and afterward issued new statutes. These revised the curriculum and the rules for election of university officers, student dress, worship, and many other matters. In Mary Tudor's reign (1553–1558) England again became officially Roman Catholic. Administrators and candidates for degrees were now required to affirm their Catholicism and acceptance of papal supremacy. Cardinal Pole, Archbishop of Canterbury and Chancellor of both universities, appointed a new commission for university reform. Statutes of Edward's reign were rescinded and new ones, revising university government, were substituted. Since these Marian statutes did not last long enough to make much difference, they do not need description here.

Early in Elizabeth's reign the Edwardian statutes, with slight changes, were reinstituted. A new reign, a new commission: this time to undo the Romanizing of the preceding one. The Edwardian statutes as now restored prevailed at Cambridge until 1570, at Oxford until Archbishop Laud's were issued in 1634–1636. In 1570 Cambridge received another and definitive set of statutes. These purported to improve university organization but in reality were intended just as much to curb the strength and factiousness of young Fellows of colleges, some of whom had strong Puritan sympathies. Ever since 1559 the younger M.A.'s had been the most powerful single group in the University. The statutes of 1570, drawn up by John Whitgift, Master of Trinity, and his friends and clearly based on the Edwardian ones, were approved by Cecil and imposed on the University, despite vigorous protest from many of the Fellows. These new statutes gave effectual control of the University to the heads of colleges, who alone could nominate men for the office of Vice-Chancellor. The Vice-Chancellor's power to imprison members of the University was increased. The Caput was henceforth to be elected by heads and Doctors and to serve for a year at a time. Within each college the Master was to have a veto at all elections of Fellows. To crown Whitgift's victory, he himself was chosen Vice-Chancellor in 1570.

Only the university awarded degrees, but a person had to be admitted to a college before he could become a member of the university. Each college set its own standards for entrance, but all had certain requirements in common. Obviously a freshman had to be competent in Latin, since most lectures and virtually all textbooks were in that language. Every boy who completed grammar school had worked at Latin for seven years and for three or more had studied rhetoric. In addition to Latin, students from the better schools had had a good introduction to Greek. The elements of Christian doctrine, a little history, and less mathematics made up the rest of their school work.

A university's character is determined first of all by its purposes. The Privy Council, in a letter to Cambridge, 1575, affirmed these to be liberal education and the professional study of divinity: the universities "have at the first been instituted principally for the nurture and education of a multitude of youth in good manners, learning, and Christianity, and likewise for the maintenance and sustenation of such as should there teach all liberal sciences and exercise the study and profession of divinity." Going to a university was not then the "thing to do" for everybody who could afford it. Most of those who went had definite professional ambitions in law, medicine, or theology. Not all students took or sought degrees, however. For some it was the residence, not the degree, that mattered. Others were not eligible for degrees and did not matriculate, for they wished to avoid subscribing to the Thirty-Nine Articles of the Church of England. Matriculation, formal registration in the university, was not required at Cambridge until 1544, at Oxford until 1565; admission to a college sufficed.

Universities granted Bachelors', Masters', and Doctors' degrees. Undergraduate studies ended, as they do now, with the B.A. degree. Men with a B.A. degree usually took an M.A. also before proceeding to professional studies, but it was possible to take a law or medical degree without taking an M.A. or even a B.A. degree. To become M.A. was the most important single achievement in academic life. Not only was this degree the most common gateway to professional degrees but by custom it entitled the holder to the *ius docendi ubique:* the right, recognized by the entire academic world, to teach or lecture anywhere. He could instruct undergraduates and preside at disputations, and he could claim a share in the government of the university.

The traditional faculties were Arts, Law, Medicine, and Theology. Men who stayed the full course and met all statutory requirements for a professional degree were in residence for many years. The requirement for an M.A. degree was three years of study beyond the four needed for B.A.; for a Bachelor of Divinity degree, seven additional years beyond the M.A.; for a doctorate in Divinity (then an earned degree, not a gift), four or five years beyond the B.D. Thus a D.D. could take a man almost twenty years, though it must be added at once that residence requirements for advanced degrees beyond M.A. were very often modified or waived. Statutes may have been explicit, but generosity in granting dispensations became habitual. Illness, clerical duties, other studies, travel, schoolmastering, and a hundred other of the usual excuses enabled many men to proceed M.A. or B.D. in much less than the statutory period. Cambridge's new statutes of 1570 endeavored to correct this abuse by forbidding dispensations that permitted a man to omit some exercises or shorten his period of residence, but sabotage by University officers partially thwarted this decree. Oxford too, in the 1570's, made a half-hearted attempt to reduce the number of dispensations.

The Elizabethan Arts course was based firmly on the old medieval *trivium* and *quadrivium*. In his first two years an undergraduate studied mostly rhetoric and Aristotelian logic and some arithmetic and music. In his second year or at the end of it he was admitted to disputations, and in his third and fourth years he had to engage in two of these in his college and two in public. His disputations, lectures, and exercises in the third and fourth years were devoted to the "three philosophies" of Aristotle. Although undeniably conservative, the Arts course did not escape occasional review and adjustment. Royal injunctions of 1535 ordained that students be instructed in logic, rhetoric, arithmetic, music, geography, and philosophy. A royal commission of 1549, however, ruled that the first undergraduate year at both universities should consist of mathematics and that grammar had to be completed before one came to the university. The second year was to be given to logic, the third and fourth to philosophy. How much mathematics the Arts student learned we do not know; certainly it was nothing very advanced. The "mathematicals," as they were called, may have included elements of astronomy, but on the whole we hear little about mathematics in contemporary descriptions of universities.

The ordinances of 1549 were hardly affected by visitorial commissions of the next dozen years, with the important exception that grammar and rhetoric were restored to the freshman year. Cambridge statutes of 1570 contemplate rhetoric in the first year, logic in the second and third, philosophy in the fourth, in addition to participation in two college disputations and two in the "Schools" (the university lecture and disputation halls).

The end and rationale of these studies are obvious. They aimed at an intellectual discipline based on rhetoric and philosophy. One began by mastering the tools of learning, working from simple to complex: first the grammar of language, then its

345

uses as an instrument of thought (logic) and communication or discourse (rhetoric, which included poetry). The logic studied included the predicables, categories, concepts of judgment, deductive and inductive reasoning, and fallacies. A "new" type of logic, that of Peter Ramus (1515–1572), had a vogue for a time, largely because of its supposedly bold independence of Aristotle's and its attractiveness as a short cut to mastery of the subject. The *Dialectica* of Ramus became a popular textbook, especially at Cambridge. For the philosophical studies of the third and fourth years, Aristotle's scientific writings and his *Metaphysics*, *Ethics*, and *Politics* supplied the fundamental texts. Inasmuch as Aristotle's thought was the basis of medieval Scholastic philosophy, we might have expected him to share the disfavor shown to medieval philosophers after the Reformation. Not at all. On many subjects he was still "the master of them that know" in the Tudor curriculum. The old formula for taking the B.A. degree, requesting permission to "read [lecture on] a book of Aristotle's logic," was still in use and still relevant.

Some history and geography found their way into the B.A. course, but the main fare in the sixteenth and seventeenth centuries continued to be grammar and rhetoric, logic and philosophy. Modern languages were studied by some, but these were extracurricular subjects. Greek was the only significant addition to the Arts curriculum in the sixteenth century; in fact Greek was the hallmark of progress in the academic world of the earlier Tudors. To some minds its attractions were literary and philosophical; to others its importance lay in its unique contribution to theological studies and Biblical criticism. Greek was scarcely studied in medieval England. Not until the late fifteenth century did it appear as an interest at Oxford, where for many years it had only a handful of students. During the reign of Henry VIII, Greek became securely established as an academic discipline. Statutes of new colleges provided for it; older colleges added it. Thus Corpus Christi, Oxford, founded in 1515 by a former Chancellor of Cambridge, had from the beginning a lecturer in Greek whose duty it was to discourse daily on Greek grammar, rhetoric, and literature. Lectureships in Greek are said to have been set up at Magdalen, Merton, and Queen's in 1535, and in Greek and Latin at New College and All Souls; students from other colleges also were to attend the lectures. Cambridge's distinctive tradition of Greek scholarship begins with Erasmus, who was invited to the university by Fisher and lived and worked at Queens' College for several years (1511–1514). The royal injunctions of 1535, issued when Thomas Cromwell was both Vicar-General of the realm and Chancellor of Cambridge, ordered every college there to have two daily public lectures on Greek and Latin. But this scheme does not seem to have been carried out at that time in more than a few colleges. St. John's, founded in 1511, was the home of some of the century's best Hellenists: Richard Croke, Sir John Cheke, and Roger Ascham.

We may conclude, then, that the B.A. course in the sixteenth century was mainly traditional, medieval, in content. Academic humanism, best symbolized perhaps by cultivation of Greek and, after 1535, rejection of Scotus, Aquinas, and others of that ilk, broadened the intellectual range of English universities, bringing their studies closer to what later generations would consider a "liberal" education. Within thirty years, wrote Erasmus in 1517, Cambridge had changed from a place where nothing was heard but Scholastic logic, Aristotle, and Scotus to one where literature, mathematics, "a new or at least renovated Aristotle," and Greek now existed. Yet, however much tone and tastes shifted during the century, the formal Arts curriculum changed relatively little. This fact is not surprising nor is it inconsistent with Erasmus' statement, for the most effective or significant intellectual activity in a university is not necessarily visible in the round of studies for the B.A.

Taking the degree at the end of the four-year course involved an elaborate ritual, substantially the same in both universities. At Elizabethan Oxford a student, after first securing permission from his college, "supplicated" or formally asked Congregation for leave to proceed to a degree. Accompanied by a Regent Master of his college, he went to St. Mary's, the University church, where the Regent presented his "supplicat" to Congregation, which voted on it secretly. If the votes were favorable in four successive meetings of Congregation, the candidate received a "grace" or permission to be presented for a degree. On the day preceding his presentation he went through the motions of paying a call on senior officers of the University. After 1580 he subscribed to the Thirty-Nine Articles and took the oath of assent to the Royal Supremacy on degree day. Then the Vice-Chancellor conferred the degree of B.A. upon him. But even now he was not a full-fledged B.A. until he had engaged in certain climactic disputations called "Determinations." This was the arduous part of becoming Bachelor, for he had to stand against all comers who chose to oppose him on logical or philosophical questions; and this he had to do during most of the days of Lent. Similarly at Cambridge, where a student on completing the Arts course was examined by the proctors and Regent Masters and, after this formality, could present his "supplicat" to the Vice-Chancellor and Senate. Now a "questionist," he was interrogated briefly at a ceremony, and after "responding" was ready to "determine."

For an M.A. degree the statutory requirement was still three years of resident graduate study, but this standard was compromised by the universities' liberality in granting dispensations. In the Jacobean reign Cambridge abolished the residence requirement altogether, thus almost inevitably opening the way for the M.A. degree to degenerate to the purely formal one of today, which an Oxford or Cambridge graduate receives simply by staying alive for a stated number of years, keeping his name on the books, and paying a fee. If he had not obtained dispensations, an Oxford or Cambridge B.A. in Tudor times devoted three years to the "three philosophies" as preparation for the M.A. degree. He heard lectures on Aristotle's metaphysics, natural philosophy (physics), and moral philosophy, subjects to which he had been introduced as an undergraduate. He attended disputations regularly, taking part in one or two each year, and gave a few perfunctory lectures on set books. These studies made up the *quadrivium* of arithmetic, geometry, music, and astronomy, or rather had become the recognized substitute for it.

The procedure in taking the M.A. degree was much like that already described for the B.A.: the candidate obtained permission to proceed, "supplicated," and was presented to the Vice-Chancellor, who licensed him to lecture and dispute. He did not actually become M.A. until a year later, after having "incepted" (at Oxford) or "commenced" (at Cambridge). Inception or commencement, which took place in July, meant taking part in certain philosophical disputations called the "Vesperies" and the "Comitia" or "Act"; "act" being a generic term for a thesis defended in disputation. These too were elaborate, traditional ceremonies, though even from these the universities often granted dispensations. Now, if he continued at the university, he became a Regent Master and shared the work of instruction for a few years. After regency he joined one of the higher faculties, Law, Medicine, or Theology.

Except at Paris, law was probably the most popular of professional studies in Continental universities. In Elizabethan Oxford and Cambridge it was less popular than theology, not because the English were less litigious but because of the peculiar organization of legal studies in England and the effects of the Reformation on one important branch of law there. Common law was the province of the Inns of Court in London, not of the universities, which restricted themselves to canon (ecclesiastical) and civil (Roman) law. When the Government abolished the papal prerogative in England and eliminated at a stroke all the vast body of statutes and interpretations so long used in ecclesiastical courts, canon law became a stumbling block and irrelevancy and was accordingly banned. Fellowships for its study were gradually reassigned to students of civil law. The statutes of 1549 fostered civil law as emphatically as they denigrated canon law, but not so effectively. Only eight Cantabrigians became Bachelors of Civil Law between 1544 and 1551, only one Doctor of Laws. The subject had been ruined academically by divorce from canon law. Most political and legal questions raised by the Reformation in England were settled on the basis of common, not civil, law.

An Oxford M.A. seeking to become B.C.L. was supposed to study law for three years. But it was possible to enter the Faculty of Law directly after matriculation, avoiding the B.A. degree entirely. If a man did this, he could get a law degree in four or five years by attending lectures and engaging in disputations. A Cambridge man needed four years beyond the M.A. for a B.C.L. degree; without a B.A. he needed six years in all. By statute an Oxford candidate for the D.C.L. had to be a B.C.L. who had heard lectures for four or five years more before supplicating for the higher degree; but this requirement was frequently dispensed. A Cambridge B.C.L. was expected to study five more years; an M.A., seven more.

Medical education, like legal education, could be obtained at Tudor Oxford and Cambridge, but for prospective physicians or surgeons it became customary to go abroad, to Padua, Montpellier, or elsewhere, for professional training. Moralists might shudder at the dangers of foreign residence to English virtue, but the fact remained that medical education was more advanced on the Continent than in England. In medieval times the study was a medley of traditional remedies, ancient texts (Aristotle, Hippocrates, Galen), and astrology. Anatomy and dissection were uncommon, though not unknown; surgery was considered an inferior branch of the art. Most but not all medical students at Oxford went through the Arts course first. Cambridge allowed no alternative. At the end of eight years' study after matriculation, or four after the M.A. (five at Cambridge), they took the degree of Bachelor of Medicine and could then practice in Oxford or Cambridge. Two years of further study after the M.B. led to an M.D. degree. When we turn from the fourteenth to the sixteenth century, we find that medical students, according to the statutes of 1549, were to view two anatomies in addition to studying for six years and disputing twice before they could become M.B. They were to perform two anatomies and cure three patients before being admitted to surgical practice. For M.D. degrees they had to view two or three more anatomies, hear lectures, dispute, and have been M.B. for four or five years. Besides the degrees of M.B. and M.D., the universities granted licenses to practice surgery anywhere in England. The precise relation between licenses and degrees is not clear. Some Oxford men who supplicated for the license had already been practicing, while others supplicated for the license and the M.B. degree at the same time.

Gonville College, Cambridge, refounded in 1557 by Dr. John Caius, a distinguished physician who had studied with Vesalius in Padua, became a notable home of intending physicians. Two of the three fellowships Caius established were for medicine. Appropriately enough, this was the college of William Harvey, discoverer of the circulation of the blood. After taking his B.A. in 1597, Harvey, like Dr. Caius before him, went to Padua for medical study. Cambridge graduated a total of only thirty-two M.B.'s and M.D.'s between 1570 and 1590, but the number tripled between 1610 and 1640. Some of the topics of medical disputations in Elizabethan and Jacobean universities survive. Here are a few medical problems thought suitable for academic debate: "Whether life can be prolonged by the aid of the medical art" (a real question in those days); "Whether it is better to drink French or red wine than white with meals"; "Whether the frequent drinking of nicotine, commonly called tobacco, conduces to health"; "Whether a man can live more than seven days without food or drink" (did nobody try it?); and that old favorite, now handed over to the psychiatrists, "Whether love is a disease."

Of another degree, that in music, it need only be said that although the Elizabethan age was one of the great periods in English musical history, when the art was universally popular, music attracted very few followers as an academic pursuit. It received no attention in the statutes of 1549. Only about twenty-five men took degrees in music at Oxford between 1583 and 1610. To become Bachelor of Music there one was expected to study music for seven years and to compose and have performed a composition of five parts, described as a "choral hymn." To become Doctor of Music a candidate had to be B. Mus. for five years and compose a song of six or eight parts. Boethius' *De Musica* was still a textbook, and the formula for the degree permitted the candidate to "lecture on some book by Boethius on music."

Supreme among advanced degrees was Theology, and next to Arts it had also the largest number of candidates. In most of the older colleges the Arts course was intended to lead to Theology. Even in sixteenth-century foundations, for example Christ's, Cambridge, and Jesus, Oxford, the Arts course was regarded simply as a steppingstone toward Theology. A B.D. or D.D. degree, as we have learned, exacted long years of study. It presupposed Greek. It required attendance at lectures on the Bible, theology, and Hebrew; engagement in disputations; preaching. The royal injunctions of 1535 had dismissed Peter Lombard, Duns Scotus, and other standard medieval theologians from the curriculum, supplanting them with later authors more acceptable to the new ecclesiastical policies. Statutes of 1549 ordain that B.D.'s shall attend a theological lecture daily, dispute, and preach an English and a Latin sermon in the university church. This Latin sermon, known as the "clerum" because addressed to resident divines, became a public event attended by undergraduates and graduates alike. The clerum was only one of many sermons an undergraduate heard during the year. He was expected to attend university service on Sunday and college chapel on other days of the week. He had no formal courses in religion but was likely to receive informal instruction, in his college, on the Catechism. Theology was inescapable in a Tudor university.

The definitive Cambridge statutes of 1570 require that the M.A. be a "diligent hearer" of daily lectures on theology and Hebrew for seven years (five years sufficed at Oxford, apparently). He is to dispute twice against a B.D. and, after his fourth year, to "respond in Theology." He must preach an English and a Latin sermon in the University church and, within a year after incepting as B.D., preach at Paul's Cross in London. To become D.D. he is expected to study five years more (four at Oxford) according to statute, to dispute, and to preach. In practice this period was very often shortened by dispensation. Some men even received permission to take B.D. and D.D. degrees together, but none could become D.D. without being B.D. The university licensed men to preach anywhere in England. Such a license was independent of a degree and had to be sought separately from it at some stage of the theologian's career; this meant, at Oxford at any rate, after he was M.A. and had preached within the university four times. In the Elizabethan Church no man could preach without a license from university or episcopal authority.

Throughout Elizabeth's reign the universities had difficulties with "popish recusants." Parliament strengthened the Act of Supremacy in 1563, making a second refusal to take the oath punishable as high treason, which meant by death. Papists were subsequently excluded from university degrees, and they remained excluded, as did other dissenters, until 1871. Roman Catholicism did not disappear at once but lingered on here and there in the universities until the 1570's. As late as 1572 the venerable Master of Gonville, Dr. Caius, was accused by his own Fellows of being secretly a practicing papist. His rooms were searched and the vestments and ornaments found there were publicly burned in the college court. Resentment against a papal bull (1570) excommunicating Elizabeth and absolving her subjects from their allegiance, the St. Bartholomew Massacre (1572), the menace of Mary Queen of Scots, and fears of Jesuit plots caused Parliament to pass a series of repressive measures against Catholics between 1571 and 1593. Some university scholars went into exile, as Protestant ones had done under Mary. Legal restrictions on Roman Catholics finally became so severe that no one at a university could openly proclaim sympathy with "popery" without risking serious trouble.

In some respects Puritanism presented a more obstinate problem than Romanism, since the issue between Anglicanism and Romanism seemed clear-cut, whereas Puritans were in the Church of England. They included members of all social classes, commanded the sympathies of many leading scholars in the universities, and had powerful support in Parliament. The intellectual energy of Puritanism, its emphasis on the Bible, hostility to ceremonialism, and, in its more radical adherents, preference for presbyterian over episcopal government were matters that could not fail to agitate the universities. For Oxford and Cambridge were not merely microcosms where debates echoed what went on in the larger world beyond college walls. They supplied that world with ideas and men; they were testing grounds where orthodoxy and dissent met in conflict, where election of a college head or a Fellow might indicate a definite shift in Puritan or anti-Puritan strength.

Academic warfare over Puritanism reached its first climax in 1570 at Cambridge, after a controversy led on the Puritan side by Thomas Cartwright, Fellow of Trinity. His opponent was Whitgift, the Master of Trinity and Regius Professor of Divinity. Whitgift had Cartwright deprived of his academic posts in 1570 and 1571. This affair became a *cause célèbre* in the Church and University. It began an interminable war of words, did much to make Puritanism a concern to Parliament, and finally helped to make Whitgift a bishop and afterward Archbishop of Canterbury. From Canterbury (1583–1604) he opposed Puritans as forcefully as he had done at Cambridge.

Cambridge remained the intellectual center of English Puritanism and of English Protestantism generally in the Tudor and Stuart reigns. This is not to say that Oxford slumbered in conformity and conservatism. It had more Catholics than Cambridge, or at least a reputation for more, but was swept by the same pattern of controversies as Cambridge. Its members read the same books and debated the same questions. Each university had first Catholic and then Puritan recusants and every variety of Anglican. But with two or three exceptions the great names of the Puritan movement were those of Cambridge men. Cecil, who as Chancellor of the University and chief minister of the Crown had power beyond which there was no appeal, found himself compelled to intervene repeatedly in order to mollify or discipline the more refractory brethren. He wrote somewhat testily in 1572 that he preferred to use his authority "for the benefit and preferment of the University than to bestow that little leisure I have from greater affairs in the compounding of your quarrels," but to the end of his life (1598) he heard complaints from and concerning Cambridge.

After this glance at the ecclesiastical setting we may return to university routine. Something must be said about methods of instruction. In medieval universities the teaching consisted of lectures by Regent Masters, each new M.A. being called upon in turn to do his share of the work. In Tudor Oxford and Cambridge the Regents still did much of the teaching, but there were now university professors and college tutors besides. This supplementing of university teaching by collegiate instruction was the most significant and lasting educational development in the Tudor universities. It suited the college system and proved more efficient than university teaching alone. College lectures, given in hall or chapel by lecturers appointed by the college, supplied the undergraduate with topics, arguments, and syllogisms he could use both in college and university disputations. These private lectures did not have the prestige of university ones but were perhaps more useful for that very reason, since they could supplement or continue the other kind or cover the same ground more thoroughly.

Public or university lectures were given by a professor in each faculty. No professorships had more honor than those established by Tudor royalty. Lady Margaret Beaufort, mother of Henry VII, founded with Fisher's advice the Lady Margaret Professorships of Divinity in each university (1502, 1503). Professors on this foundation were to lecture an hour per day on each weekday. Henry VIII founded and endowed Regius Professorships of Divinity, Civil Law, Medicine, Greek, and Hebrew (at Cambridge in 1540, at Oxford in 1546), a benefaction that aroused much enthusiasm. Cambridge statutes of 1570, which in this respect resemble those of 1549, ordain that University lecturers are to lecture four times a week. Theological lectures may deal only with Sacred Scripture. The law lecturer is to take up Roman civil law or the laws of the Anglican Establishment "and no other." In philosophy the lecturer is to discourse on Aristotle's physical, moral, and political works, Pliny *(Natural History)*, or Plato. Lecturers on medicine must expound Hippocrates or Galen. The lecturer on mathematics may explain cosmography by reference to Mela, Pliny, Strabo, or Plato (the curriculum ignores Columbus and Copernicus); arithmetic by works of two modern writers, Tunstall (late Bishop of Durham) or Cardanus; geometry by Euclid; astronomy by Ptolemy. For dialectics Aristotle's *Sophistical Questions* and Cicero's *Topics* are prescribed. For rhetoric the authors are Quintilian, Hermogenes, and Cicero; but these, it is added, are to be expounded in English, so the hearers will understand them. The Professor of Greek must choose Homer, Isocrates, Demosthenes, Euripides, or some other author. His colleague in Hebrew may lecture on no text but the Old Testament; also he is to teach the Hebrew language.

Lectures were "ordinary" and "extraordinary" or "cursory." Ordinary lectures, the more important kind, were formal expositions of particular topics or questions. A cursory lecture consisted of reading through a book and translating it, with comments. B.A.'s studying for M.A. degrees often gave cursory lectures. Ordinary lectures were delivered in the morning, cursory ones in the afternoon. As we have just noticed, a few Cambridge lectures were given in English. Most continued to be given in Latin. Going to a lecture was a serious affair, much more formal than it is now. Scholars escorted the lecturer to the hall. Attendance was compulsory at all lectures in one's faculty and fines were levied for missing them. Students "cut" them nevertheless, and in their ingenuity at thinking up excuses had little to learn from modern undergraduates. Lectures were commonly scheduled at seven or eight in the morning. A course of logic lectures founded at Cambridge in 1611 was to be offered from six to eight and the first hour of each lecture devoted to review and discussion of the previous day's discourse. Before this date we seldom hear of any discussion accompanying lectures. Auditors were expected to take notes.

Equally ancient and honored in university work, but entirely different from lectures in aims and methods, were the disputations. A legacy from medieval Scholasticism, formal disputation survived long after the introduction of printed textbooks and was still the principal mode of academic exercise in Spenser's and Milton's university days, still essentially Scholastic in character, purpose, and often in the very questions debated. If it did little to advance knowledge, it must at least have done much to sharpen wits. As a test of knowledge of logic and of skill in debate, and incidentally of Latin, it could be a crucial demonstration of a man's abilities. It served therefore as a sort of examination, for medieval and Tudor universities had no written tests.

After his second year each student took part in a stated number of disputations in college and in public. He engaged twice as "respondent" (a word recalled by the term still used for the Oxford entrance examination, "Responsions"), twice as "opponent," and his adversaries might be his contemporaries or older students. At Oxford—and Cambridge practice was more or less the same—his first disputation concerned grammatical or logical questions. Three such questions were debated at a disputation, one student acting as respondent and two others as opponents. A Regent Master presided and made an introductory speech. The respondent, who probably spoke first, then defended the affirmative side of the question; his opponents took the negative. Disputations for undergraduates in their third or fourth year and for B.A.'s dealt with philosophical questions, those for more advanced students with topics relevant to their professional faculties.

A man's friends attended his disputations and doubtless tried to encourage him as much as decorum allowed. Each disputant gave arguments, cross-examined the other speaker or speakers, and attempted to refute them, always attacking or defending by means of syllogisms and indeed by any other weapons of logic which he could lay hands on. Much solemn ritual, and some not so solemn, governed these displays. Public and private records preserve a large number of sixteenth- and seventeenth-century questions disputed at Oxford and Cambridge. As we may judge by the following examples from Oxford disputations for the

M.A., many would look quite familiar if we turned them freely into modern idiom. "An ex optimo academico fiat optimus aulicus" (1592) is the ancestor of countless freshman themes on whether a college education will get you ahead in politics. Or how hackneyed seems "An metropolis sit opportunior sedes academiis constituendis quam ignobilius oppidum" (1594): is it better for a university to be in a large city than in a one-horse town? Typical questions for dispute in the Arts faculty at Oxford included: whether the sea is salt (1576), whether women should have a liberal education (1581), whether a comet is helpful or harmful (1584), whether there are more worlds than one (1588), whether there is any certain knowledge of things (1595). At Cambridge in 1597 students in the Faculty of Civil Law debated the proposition: "Despite the judgment of scholars, the power of the sword is the prince's alone." In Theology we find: "The statecraft of Moses should not be binding on Christian commonwealths"; in Philosophy: "All change in the commonwealth is dangerous" and "The senses are not deceived." In all disputations, whatever the questions at issue, skill in argument was what mattered most. Rhetorical resourcefulness, cogency, the tactics of logic and eloquence combined: these carried the day.

The medieval colleges of Oxford and Cambridge had small libraries of chained books, some of which were still chained long after the Elizabethan period. Merton had the oldest college library in England. Oxford had a collection of manuscripts kept in St. Mary's Church, but it did not have a university library until Bishop Cobham of Worcester, in the fourteenth century, built a two-story House of Congregation, the first strictly university building at Oxford. The library occupied the second story. In the fifteenth century the Cobham library was replaced by a new one. This too was in the upper story of a new building, the Divinity School. The new library was a memorial to a great benefactor, Duke Humphrey of Gloucester, a collector who first gave manuscripts to the University in 1435 and continued to do so until his death in 1447.

The foundation of a new library at Oxford by Sir Thomas

Bodley (1545–1613), a diplomat and scholar, may well have been the most important event in the University's Tudor epoch. Bodley began in 1598 by restoring the old Duke Humphrey Library. He built an addition in 1610 and provided in his will for further enlargements. He gave his books to the University and persuaded other persons of means to contribute. He was one of the first of that most useful class of beggars, rich graduates who not only support alma mater generously but solicit others to do likewise and thus make charity fashionable. Use of the library was limited to Doctors, Masters, and Bachelors, but Bachelors had to get permission from Congregation. Bodley wanted no ephemeral productions cluttering up his library. Shakespeare's name does not appear in a Bodleian catalogue until 1635. But by an agreement Bodley fortunately made with the Stationers' Company, which controlled publishing and copyright, the library was entitled to receive on demand a copy of every book printed in England. By Act of Parliament in 1665 Cambridge's library began to share the same privilege.

The Cambridge library dates from ca. 1415 or earlier. The first catalogue listed fifty-two volumes; the second (1473) contained 330. As at Oxford, college libraries grew independently of the University library. Their treasures would take too long to describe, but the incomparable collection of historical manuscripts gathered by Archbishop Parker and given by him to Corpus Christi must not go unmentioned.

At first Oxford and Cambridge had no colleges; students lived wherever they could find lodgings. In time some lodging houses became the halls or hostels so often named in medieval or early Tudor accounts. A hall owned or hired by a Master and occupied by students easily acquired some of the characteristic marks of a college. Finally the universities took control of the halls. In Oxford about sixty came thus under University jurisdiction in the 1480's. At that time there were ten colleges, but the college system was destined to eliminate nearly all the halls. The obvious advantages of collegiate organization, at least from the University's standpoint, and a policy of allowing and finally of requiring undergraduates to live in colleges ended the need for hostels. The earliest colleges, however, were intended for graduates, not undergraduates.

The statutes of Merton, Oxford, were the model for those of Peterhouse, the oldest of Cambridge colleges, and for other early colleges in both universities. Christ Church, Oxford, begun by Wolsey and completed by Henry VIII, had no statutes at all and was governed by a dean and a chapter of canons. All other colleges were governed by a head and a body of Fellows. The Provost of King's and the Master of Trinity, Cambridge, were appointed by the Crown; the Master of Magdalene, Cambridge, by heirs of the founder. In most colleges the head was elected by the Fellows from their own ranks. Fellows of Emmanuel, if they did not choose one of themselves, were supposed to give preference to a member of Christ's; similarly Fellows of Sidney Sussex to a member of Trinity. One Elizabethan Master, James Pilkington of St. John's, Cambridge, who resigned in 1561 to become Bishop of Durham, was succeeded by his brother. On occasion the Crown interfered with elections by recommending a favorite; sometimes with happy results, as when a royal intimation inspired the Fellows of Corpus Christi to elect Matthew Parker in 1544. In the sixteenth century and for a long time afterward all the heads were divines. Early statutes often stipulated that the Master be a B.D. or D.D. or, at the very least, an M.A. studying Theology.

Bishop Pilkington wrote to Cecil in 1561 that, as for the heads of Cambridge colleges, "some be such that I cannot tell whether they do less harm being absent or present, and none or very few do any good." This opinion from a man who had until recently been a Master himself sprang partly from religious quarrels of the day but may also reflect something of that weary cynicism in which harried academic administrators find final relief. Tudor Masters were of all kinds. Thomas Fuller's delineation, in his *Holy State* (1642), of "the good master of a college" portrays one whose learning "if beneath eminency is far above contempt," who "not only keeps the statutes in his study but observes them," "disdains to nourish dissension amongst the members of his house," and "in his elections he respecteth merit." There were also slippery timeservers like Andrew Perne of Peterhouse, notorious for his alacrity in adjusting his religion to the prevalent official doctrines. There were difficult characters like Degory Nichols of Magdalene, who annoyed the Fellows by letting his cows graze in the college court. Some heads were constantly at odds with the Fellows. Dr. Caius of Gonville and Caius punished certain Fellows by putting them in stocks. At one time or another he expelled twenty Fellows from his unruly college. None of the numerous Elizabethan quarrels between Master and Fellows equaled the famous thirty years' war between Richard Bentley and the Fellows of Trinity, Cambridge, in the eighteenth century, but Elizabethan Cambridge witnessed extensive feuds, some of which demanded the combined efforts of Government and Chancellor to end.

Fellows, like Masters, included all the familiar academic types: distinguished scholars, sober divines, conscientious tutors, and on the other hand some whose distinction is not easy to discover. Tudor Fellows do not seem to have been excessively sociable, but perhaps amiability was not considered the highest of academic virtues. They displayed the sensitivity to criticism, zeal for protecting their rights, devotion to principle, and talent for intrigue often found in members of learned societies. Gabriel Harvey of Pembroke, Cambridge, with his grumbling and his genius for making enemies—two other Pembroke Fellows voted against his M.A. degree—may have been more difficult than most, but his very combination of studiousness and irritability renders him an authentic academic type.

Tutors were drawn from Fellows, of course. Medieval Fellows, in the days before the tutorial system, had no teaching duties. Some statutes required or permitted a certain number of Fellows to study law or medicine, but in Tudor as well as in medieval universities most Fellows were in the Faculty of Theology. The number of Fellows at Cambridge increased by a third between 1564 and 1573—there were 320 in 1573—and most of those elected appear to have been in their early twenties. As Regent Masters they held the balance of power in the

University; as young men in a hurry, many of them with forthright opinions on ecclesiastical questions, they sometimes seemed obstreperous to their elders. The new statutes of 1570, drawn up principally by Whitgift, deprived them of their power.

Fellowships, as everyone understood, had to be surrendered if the holders married, but not everyone agreed on how long unmarried Fellows should keep their appointments. Traditionally they had been expected to leave after finishing advanced studies. If they stayed on, as in Elizabethan times became increasingly common, they did not profit the Church. At least this seems to have been the view of the bishops, who in 1584 opposed Puritan suggestions that some Fellows remain in the University. Emmanuel's statutes warn that Fellows must not regard the college as "a perpetual abode." Notwithstanding this explicitness, the Crown nullified the statute. Fellowships came to be looked upon as lifetime appointments or ones to which re-election from time to time was a formality. For a long time there was even a custom of buying and selling fellowships. This abuse required Parliamentary action (1575, 1589) to correct.

"Every college is a little commonwealth in itself," wrote a seventeenth-century Chancellor of Cambridge. Like larger commonwealths, these had constitutional problems and financial crises. Colleges lived off income from their endowments, but as landlords dependent on fixed revenues they suffered from monetary inflation, bad harvests, and other economic woes. They had adopted a practice of granting long leases at low rentals but exacting heavy "fines," payments customarily made when leases were granted or renewed. Parliament in 1571 and 1576 forbade such long leases but decreed (1576) that in all new leases not less than one third of the rent should be paid in grain valued at a price stipulated by the Act; or, in lieu of grain, in money equal to the current market price. This legislation assured colleges of cheap bread if the rent was paid in grain, for the producer's price was fixed and he could not raise it. If he paid in cash, the colleges were assured of more revenue whenever market prices rose. In time this third provided far more income than did the other two thirds and enabled the colleges to grant allowances to Fellows or to increase existing allowances.

Undergraduates were scholars, commoners, or pensioners. In the language of statutes, "scholar" signified a student who, like the graduate Fellows, was "on the foundation," that is, had "exhibitions" or grants or scholarships and received his food and lodging from college funds. Statutes of many colleges specified that a number of commoners and pensioners could or should be received. These were members of a college who were not "on the foundation" and did not always live in college. The name "commoner" implied no invidious social distinctions but merely differentiated students not on the foundation from others. Often the fellow commoners, as they were called, were noble or wealthy youths. "Pensioners," though the term may be of later date than "commoner," had the same relation to a college. Roger Ascham complains in the late 1540's about rich commoners or pensioners who come to the university without serious intellectual purpose and distract the more sober sort. Fellow commoners dined with the Fellows and, if nobles, had enviable privileges, including the convenient one of getting degrees without completing the ordinary requirements. But they were not likely to need or desire degrees. At the opposite extreme were poor students of the kind called "sizars" at Cambridge; menials who performed lowly tasks and ate the leavings from their betters' tables.

Oxford is thought to have had a thousand students at most in 1450. It conferred fewer than a hundred degrees a year. At its low point in the sixteenth century, 1542–1548, it granted only 173 B.A. degrees in six years, according to one account. Cambridge granted 191 B.A. degrees in the same period. In Mary's reign and the early years of Elizabeth's, sixty to seventy men a year supplicated for degrees at Oxford. Cambridge granted only ninety M.A. and 167 B.A. degrees in 1549–1553; in 1557–1558 the totals were 125 and 195. In 1559 only twenty-eight men took the B.A. degree there. William Harrison's description of the universities (1577) says there were about 3,000 students "in them both." During most of the Elizabethan reign Cambridge was the larger. In 1564 it had 1,267 resident members in colleges; in 1569, 1,630; by the end of the century, almost 2,000. In 1560 it gave sixty B.A. degrees; in 1570, 114; in 1583, 277, the largest number in any year of that century. Oxford graduated 157 in the same year. Oxford averaged 270 matriculates annually in 1593–1603. Cambridge in 1597 reported 1,950 students in the colleges and in addition 657 "graduates" (in residence, presumably) and 122 preachers, these last "almost all unprovided for."

Students entered the university as young as twelve, but it is safe to say that the average entering age in the sixteenth century was fifteen, a year higher in the following century. Medieval statutes assumed that freshmen would be fourteen, and the 1570 code for Cambridge ordered that no scholar be admitted unless he had completed his fourteenth year.

Students were bound to be in residence three terms a year (October to Christmas, January to Easter, Easter to July), and some stayed on during the long vacation. They had brief respites after each term and sometimes unscheduled ones when plague broke out. Discipline was naturally paternalistic, partly because of the very youthfulness of undergraduates, partly because of the clerical and semimonastic traditions of the older colleges and the general severity of discipline in medieval and Tudor life. University officers invariably complained that students were going to the dogs, and indeed Elizabethan undergraduates had a reputation for incorrigible unruliness and insubordination. Adults, men twenty years old or over, were formally rebuked, fined, imprisoned, or in extreme cases expelled for delinquencies. For undergraduate malefactors the standard punishment was flogging.

Medieval and Renaissance universities had no official interest in sports or games and assumed no responsibility for amusing undergraduates; paternalism of this kind is an American eccentricity. Statutes strictly forbade most of the recreations naturally attractive to young men, yet the monotonous regularity of these prohibitions proves that they were honored in the breach as well as the observance. Again and again it was necessary to forbid gambling and possession of arms, birds, cards, and hounds. Tobacco was deplored and forbidden. A special object of official displeasure was addiction to silks and fine array. Academic officers seem to have been obsessed by this evil. Oversize ruffs and the wearing of swords and of silks or velvets, unless one's social rank clearly justified this, were specifically forbidden. Even bathing was frowned upon. A decree of the Vice-Chancellor and heads of colleges at Cambridge in 1571, "That No One Go Into the Water," forbade students to enter any river or pond within the county of Cambridge, "either for swimming or bathing, whether by day or by night," on penalty of being severely whipped in the college hall. One of the few forms of exercise condoned was walking, but older statutes stipulated that this was to be done in pairs, never alone. Dr. Caius' statutes (1572) for his college contained the usual prohibitions of idle or corrupting pastimes but were licentious enough to tolerate ball-catching *(pilae reciprocatio)*.

A higher form of entertainment was furnished occasionally by student performances of Greek, Latin, or English plays in college halls. Christ Church, Oxford, appears to have had in its early years two Latin and Greek tragedies and two comedies each year. Sometimes university plays were good enough to achieve a place in literary history. Such, for instance, were the three *Parnassus* plays, English comedies presented at St. John's, Cambridge, 1598–1601. A Cambridge Latin comedy, *Ignoramus*, which was acted before King James and gave him much pleasure, became an academic classic. The supreme English dramatist, Shakespeare, attended neither university, but his Hamlet is the most famous university student in English drama. The title-page of the first quarto edition of *Hamlet* (1603) says that the play was acted "in the two universities of Cambridge and Oxford," but this must mean in the town, not in the college halls. Touring companies succeeded, legally or illegally, in giving performances in the towns, but university authorities were strongly and consistently hostile to such entertainment and objected repeatedly to plays and players in the neighborhood.

Extramural dissipation not only endangered morals but often provoked fighting between students and townsmen. "The relation of the University to the city," as a writer on Elizabethan Oxford observes, "was necessarily antagonistic." Inherent economic and legal conflicts of interest in university towns perpetuated animosities between local residents, especially tradesmen, and members of the university and led to suits, appeals to Government, and disorder. William Harrison, taking the usual academic view, asserts (1577) that the townsmen "are glad when they match and annoy the students by encroaching on their liberties and keep them bare by extreme sale of their wares." No doubt, but the townsmen for their part resented the arrogance and contempt with which they were treated (so they said) by members of the university.

Students kept early hours. Four o'clock was a common hour for rising in the sixteenth century. College gates closed at eight P.M. in winter, nine in summer. That living was uncomfortable by our standards goes without saying. Lecture halls were unheated. Even in college halls or rooms fires were a luxury. In a sermon preached in 1550 a Cambridge divine describes how the scholars there study at night until nine or ten "and then being without fire are fain to walk or run up and down half an hour, to get a heat in their feet when they go to bed." Poor scholars were not so badly off as their medieval predecessors, who begged for a living, but they had a hard enough time. (Oxford, defending itself in 1460 against a charge by friars that fees were too high, indignantly denied that degrees were cheaper at Cambridge.) Fees were paid directly to tutors and lecturers, but there were also miscellaneous charges by university officers that had to be met.

We have noted the active role of Government in academic affairs. Once or twice in a reign royalty itself condescended to visit the universities. Henry VII, accompanied by his mother and his son, Prince Henry, stopped at Cambridge in 1506 on his way to the shrine of St. Mary of Walsingham. Elizabeth paid a visit to Cambridge in 1564 and to Oxford in 1566 and 1592.

James visited Oxford in 1605 and 1614, Cambridge twice in 1615 and again in 1624. For these visits proud but anxious university officers made exhaustive preparations. We have interesting documents describing the plans for Elizabeth's visits to Oxford and equally interesting contemporary accounts of what happened on those visits. The Queen was treated to an interminable round of Greek and Latin greetings, orations, sermons, verses, and plays. Disputations were presented on such edifying topics as "Whether the glory of the blessed will be equal," "Whether air changes bodies more than food and drink do," "Whether astrologers should be banished from the commonwealth." How she endured them all we can only guess. We do know how thoroughly James I, who esteemed himself as a theologian and philosopher, enjoyed a celebrated disputation in Cambridge in 1615. He even intervened in it.

William Harrison, who owed allegiance to both universities, praised Oxford for its larger streets and thought that "for curious workmanship and private commodities" the colleges there were "much more stately, magnificent, and commodious than those of Cambridge." But for "uniformity of building, orderly compaction, and politic regiment," the town of Cambridge exceeded Oxford "many, many a fold." King's College Chapel at Cambridge and the Divinity School at Oxford he considered two of the most beautiful buildings in Europe. "In all other things there is so great equality between these two universities as no man can imagine how to set down any greater, so that they seem to be the body of one well-ordered commonwealth, only divided by distance of place and not in friendly consent and orders." We cannot do better than to accept this judicious Elizabethan appraisal. Other graduates, Francis Bacon among them, could be more critical. But the final word belongs to Chief Justice Coke, Bacon's lifelong rival and, like him, an alumnus of Trinity, Cambridge. The universities of Oxford and Cambridge, wrote Coke, were "the suns, eyes, and minds of the kingdom, from which religion, liberal education, and sound learning are spread most abundantly to every part of the realm."

SUGGESTED READING

Since Oxford and Cambridge were medieval foundations, the best introduction to their Tudor history is made through acquaintance with the nature of medieval universities. This can be obtained from C. H. Haskins, *The Rise of Universities* (Ithaca, 1957), the best short introduction, and from the longer work by Hastings Rashdall, *The Universities of Europe in the Middle Ages*, ed. F. M. Powicke and A. B. Emden (Oxford, 1936). *University Records and Life in the Middle Ages*, ed. Lynn Thorndike (New York, 1944), is a convenient collection of documents, in translation, from and about Continental universities.

Oxford statutes to 1634 are collected in *Statuta Antiqua Universitatis Oxoniensis*, ed. Strickland Gibson (Oxford, 1931). Many valuable works on Oxford history are published in the volumes issued by the Oxford Historical Society; for example, *Elizabethan Oxford*, ed. Charles Plummer (1887); *Epistolae Academicae Oxonienses*, ed H. Anstey (1898); and *Register of the University of Oxford*, vol. II, 1571–1622, pt. 1, Introduction, ed. Andrew Clark (1887), an indispensable work. Anthony Wood's famous *History of the Antiquities of the University of Oxford* first appeared in Latin (1674; English version, 1791–1796). His *Athenae Oxonienses* (1691–1692) is a series of brief biographies of distinguished men educated at Oxford between 1500 and 1690. The standard modern history is that of C. E. Mallet, *A History of the University of Oxford* (London, 1924–1927).

For Cambridge documents see James Heywood (ed.), *Collection of Statutes for the University and Colleges of Cambridge* (London, 1840); George Peacock, *Observations on the Statutes of the University of Cambridge* (London, 1841); James Heywood and Thomas Wright, (eds.), *Cambridge University Transactions During the Puritan Controversies of the 16th and 17th Centuries* (London, 1854). On fifteenth-century Cambridge there is useful information in S. M. Leathes' introduction to *Grace Book A* (Cambridge, 1897); he prints also a Cambridge diary for 1533–1534. Older chronicles of the University were superseded by the writings of C. H. Cooper:

Annals of Cambridge (Cambridge, 1842–1853), *Memorials of Cambridge* (Cambridge, 1858–1866), *Athenae Cantabrigienses* (Cambridge, 1858–1861). For general history of the University there is a three-volume work, *The University of Cambridge,* by J. B. Mullinger (Cambridge, 1873–1888), and a one-volume condensation of this by the same author (London, 1888). W. W. Rouse Ball, *Cambridge Papers* (Cambridge, 1918), includes essays on the Tudor and Stuart periods. Two of the most useful books on Cambridge are also among the most recent. H. C. Porter, *Reformation and Reaction in Tudor Cambridge* (Cambridge, 1958), treats of the place of the University in the ecclesiastical history of the times. William T. Costello, *The Scholastic Curriculum at Early Seventeenth-Century Cambridge* (Cambridge, Mass., 1958), describes disputations and other academic exercises. Both books use unprinted documents from the University and college archives. Another important study, *Oxford and Cambridge in Transition, 1558–1642,* by Mark H. Curtis, is in press.

Published histories of the various colleges in each university are too numerous to list here. They differ a good deal in scope and merit but are always worth consulting.

William Harrison's account of the universities, first published in Holinshed's *Chronicles* (1577), was reprinted by L. Withington (London, ca. 1902). *College Life in the Times of James the First* contains the diary of Simonds d'Ewes. An unpublished set of "directions for a Student in the University," by Richard Holdsworth, d'Ewes' tutor at Cambridge, is quoted by Costello. J. A. Venn, *Early Collegiate Life* (Cambridge, 1913), has material on the sixteenth and seventeenth centuries. The *Parnassus* plays were edited by J. B. Leishman (London, 1949).

Useful studies of special topics will be found in E. G. Rupp, *Studies in the Making of the English Protestant Tradition* (Cambridge, 1947); M. M. Knappen, *Tudor Puritanism* (Chicago, 1939); William Haller, *The Rise of Puritanism* (New York, 1938); C. H. Garrett, *The Marian Exiles* (Cambridge, 1938); *Shakespeare's England* (Oxford, 1916); Louis B. Wright, *Middle-Class Culture in Elizabethan England* (Ithaca, 1958); J. E. Sandys, *A History of Classical Scholarship* (Cambridge, 1903–1908); F. S. Boas, *University Drama in the Tudor Age* (Oxford, 1914) and *Shakespeare and the Universities* (London, 1922); P. S. Allen, *Erasmus* (Oxford, 1934).

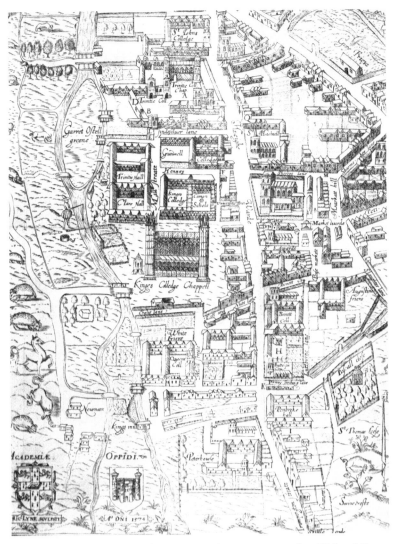

Elizabethan Cambridge. This is part of an engraving by Richard Lyne, 1574, for insertion in John Caius' *Historiae Cantabrigiensis Academiae*, 1574. (Folger Shakespeare Library.)

Elizabethan Oxford. Engraved by Augustine Ryther, 1588, after Ra
the only

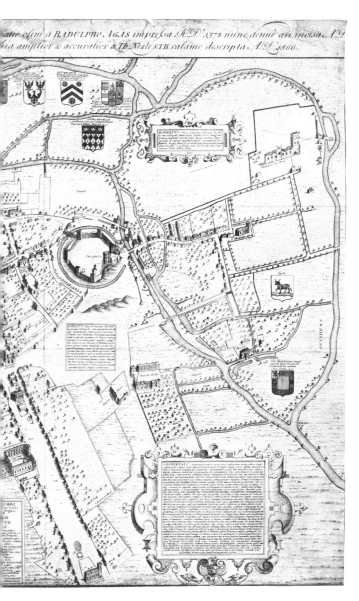

' drawing of 1578. This Folger copy is one of two known and
maged.

St. John Fisher, Bishop of Rochester (1469–1535),
the leading figure in Cambridge affairs in the early
part of the sixteenth century. He was Vice-Chancellor of the University in 1501, President of Queens'
College from 1505 to 1508, and Chancellor from
1504 until his death. (By an unknown sixteenth-
century artist, after Hans Holbein. Courtesy of the
National Portrait Gallery, London.)

William Cecil, Lord Burleigh (1520–1598), Lord
Treasurer and Queen Elizabeth's chief minister;
Chancellor of Cambridge from 1559 to 1598. (En-
graving by an unknown artist.)

Robert Dudley, Earl of Leicester (1532–1588),
High Steward of Cambridge University, 1562, and
Chancellor of Oxford from 1564 to 1588. (Engraving by Willem van de Passe.)

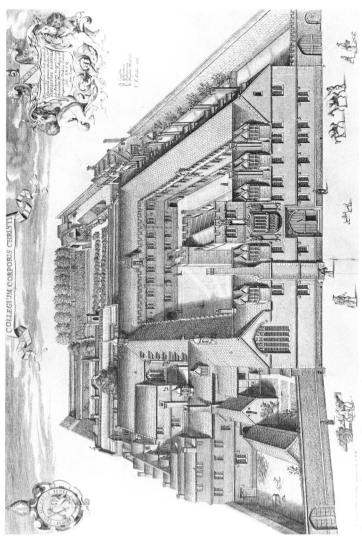

Corpus Christi College, Oxford, in the seventeenth century. It was founded in 1515 by Richard Foxe, Bishop of Winchester, whose statutes provided for public Readers in Latin, Greek, and Divinity. (From David Loggan, *Oxonia Illustrata*, 1675.)

Christ's College, Cambridge. Founded in 1505 by Margaret Beaufort, Countess of Richmond, mother of King Henry VII. (From David Loggan, *Cantabrigia Illustrata*, 1676–1690.)

Christ Church, Oxford. Founded by Cardinal Wolsey in 1518 as Cardinal College and planned on a magnificent scale. It was completed by King Henry VIII. (From David Loggan, *Oxonia Illustrata*, 1675.)

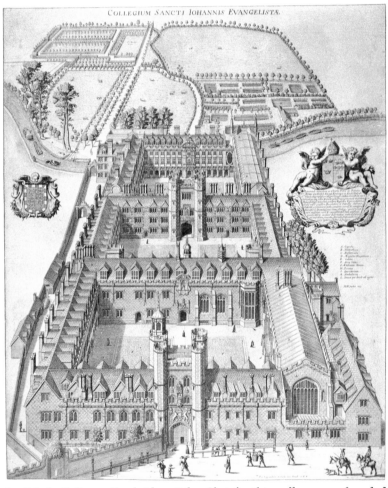

COLLEGIUM SANCTI IOHANNIS EVANGELISTÆ.

St. John's College, Cambridge. Like Christ's, this college was founded (1511) by Lady Margaret Beaufort with the advice of Bishop Fisher. (From David Loggan, *Cantabrigia Illustrata*, 1676–1690.)

Sir Thomas Bodley (1545–1613), founder of the Bodleian Library, Oxford. He was educated abroad and at Magdalen College and was a university lecturer before entering the Queen's service. From 1589 to 1596 he was her representative in the Netherlands. (Courtesy of the Bodleian Library, Oxford.)

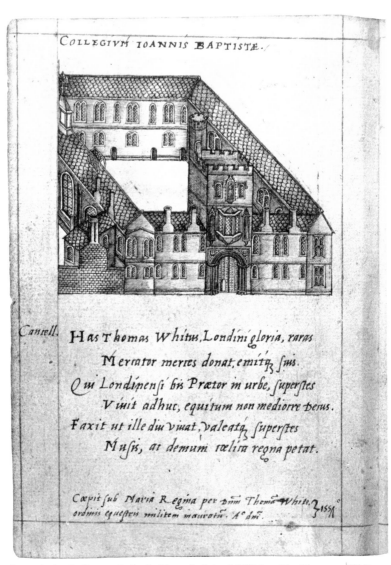

COLLEGIVM IOANNIS BAPTISTÆ.

Cancell.

Has Thomas Whitus, Londini gloria, raras
   Mercator merces donat, emitq́; suis.
Qui Londinensi bis Prætor in urbe, superstes
   Viuit adhuc, equitum non mediocre decus.
Faxit ut ille diu viuat, valeatq́; superstes
   Musis, at demum cœlica regna petat.

Cœpit sub Maria Regina per Dnm Thomã White.
ordinis equestris militem auratū. A° dni.   1557

St. John's College, Oxford. Founded in 1555 by Sir Thomas White, a
London merchant. This drawing is one of a series made by John Bere-
block, an Oxford graduate, in 1566. (Courtesy of the Bodleian Library,
Oxford.)

English Dress in the Age of Shakespeare

By Virginia A. LaMar

ENGLISH dress during the age of Shakespeare reflected the vitality and high spirits of the period. The growth of England as a world power, the increase in trade and prosperity, and the political stability created by Queen Elizabeth's shrewd policies, all helped to develop a spirit of self-confidence. One result of this exuberance was an increase in the taste for fine raiment and an indulgence in magnificent clothing which make the Elizabethan age one of the most gorgeously dressed periods in the island's history.

Although the upper class and even the great merchants of earlier eras had also dressed in rich and colorful fabrics, the sixteenth century saw an elaboration in dress that had not been common. In keeping with the doctrine that everyone was born to a certain station ordained by heaven and should content himself with his lot, however humble, sumptuary laws had traditionally prescribed the degrees of luxury permissible to each class. For example, folk under the rank of a knight's eldest son were prohibited from wearing satin, damask, taffeta, and similar rich attire. Queen Elizabeth retained legislation to this end, but the power and wealth of the middle class increased during her reign to such a point that the previous regulations had to be relaxed; in a new statute of 1580 they were modified to allow a certain degree of finery to those who could afford it. A parallel may be seen in the attitudes of the Puritan elders of New England, who attempted to discourage the wearing of fine clothes by similar laws in the first decades of colonization. Eventually, however, they had to give up the effort because prosperity in their flocks stimulated an irrepressible desire for finery.

Whereas it had been true that any individual could be identified as belonging to a certain class by his apparel, there was much complaint during Queen Elizabeth's reign that it was increasingly difficult to do so. Hamlet's comment, "The age is grown so picked [refined] that the toe of the peasant comes so near the heel of the courtier he galls his kibe [irritates his sore heel]," is an exaggeration, of course. The country folk were relatively unaffected by changing fashions, and few had money enough to purchase urban finery, but they supplemented "hempen homespun" with satin and velvet whenever they had the means. On the whole, fashion's influence operated much as it does today. Rural areas showed the greatest faithfulness to tried and true articles of dress and were the last to feel the impact of novelty. The clothing of the yeoman farmers and their wives, for example, was simpler and more old-fashioned than that of city craftsmen who lived nearer the center of fashion.

The passion for dress and the tendency to dress above one's station in life were the subject of frequent attacks by satirists. With the rise of Puritanism the attack became a convention of Puritan criticism. Critics of various persuasions condemned the folly of enslavement to fantastic fashion and lamented the extravagance and waste of means incurred for finery. Indeed, the Church of England itself made an effort to curb the inordinate love of clothes in an official way by including a sermon "Against Excess of Apparel" in the *Second Tome of Homilies,* which was published by government authority in 1563. The contents were intended to be preached as sermons by all parsons not licensed to preach sermons of their own composition. This particular sermon was repeated in edition after edition of the *Homilies* during the reign of Queen Elizabeth and even after James I ascended the throne. The statement therein that fashions are "at these days so outrageous that neither Almighty God, by his word, can stay our proud curiosity in the same, neither yet godly and necessary laws, made by our princes and oft repeated with the penalties, can bridle this detestable abuse" applied to the sermon itself, which had little effect on the conduct of the English audience.

In their efforts to restrain extravagant dress both church and state were motivated by economic as well as ethical considerations. For example, silk, needed for the most luxurious fabrics, was not produced in England, and raw silk as well as some finished materials had to be imported from across the Channel. The cost of such luxuries sometimes caused an unfavorable trade balance and proved an economic embarrassment to the nation.

One sober observer, Philip Stubbes, complained that citizens were living beyond their incomes in a ridiculous effort to be as fine as their betters. "Everyone almost, though otherwise very poor, having scarce forty shillings of wages by the year, will be sure to have two or three pair of these silk netherstocks, or else of the finest yarn that may be got, though the price of them be a royal [approximately ten shillings] or twenty shillings, or more," he commented with disgust in his *Anatomy of Abuses* (1583). And as though that extravagance were not bad enough, over these elegant silk stockings went boot hose

of the finest cloth that may be got, yea, fine enough to make any band, ruff, or shirt needful to be worn . . . wrought all over, from the gartering place upward, with needlework, clogged with silk of all colors, fowls, beasts, and antics, portrayed all over in comely sort. So that I have known the very needlework of some one pair of these boot hose to stand, some in four pounds, six pounds, and some in ten pounds apiece. Besides this, they are made so wide to draw over all, and so long to reach up to the waist, that as little or less cloth would make one a reasonably large shirt.

Fashions, then as now, were rarely of English origin. Many observers expressed outraged national pride because English fads and fashions were derived from the Continent, and foreign travelers commented on the lack of a characteristically English style. The names of parts of the Elizabethan wardrobe indicate their foreign origins: French hose, French hood, Venetians, Spanish bonnet. The English showed less genius in designing new styles than in combining styles from many countries to create striking effects—though, indeed, the bizarre results of such combinations were the subject of much satirical comment by contemporary writers. Thomas Dekker in *The Seven Deadly Sins of London* (1606) declared that

an Englishman's suit is like a traitor's body that hath been hanged, drawn, and quartered, and is set up in several places: his codpiece is in Denmark; the color of his doublet and the belly in France; the wing and narrow sleeve in Italy; the short waist hangs over a Dutch botcher's [tailor's] stall in Utrecht; his huge slops [breeches] speak Spanish; Polonia [Poland] gives him the boots; the block for his head alters faster than the feltmaker can fit him, and thereupon we are called in scorn blockheads. And thus we that mock every nation for keeping one fashion, yet steal patches from every one of them to piece out our pride, are now laughing stocks to them because their cut so scurvily becomes us.

Portia's description of her noble English suitor is similar to other contemporary comments on the hybrid dress of fashionable young men who had traveled abroad: "I think he bought his doublet in Italy, his round hose in France, his bonnet in Germany, and his behavior everywhere."

An important factor in stimulating the English passion for dress was the enthusiasm of Queen Elizabeth herself for gorgeous clothes. Handsome costumes, besides satisfying her personal vanity, were evidence of her royalty and position and a symbol of England's power and pride. An inventory of her clothing in 1600 included almost three hundred gowns and several hundred other complete costumes, in addition to special apparel for state occasions. The Queen regarded richly ornamented stomachers, kirtles, and other articles of dress as highly acceptable gifts from her subjects. Such presents frequently appear in the annual inventories of New Year's gifts.

An indication of Elizabeth's influence on the tide of fashion in England is the extravagance of style near the end of her reign when her personal taste dictated a characteristic silhouette in which all the features of feminine attire were exaggerated almost to the point of caricature. In most of her late portraits she resembles a stuffed doll, with her tremendous ruffs, outlined against stiffened veils which are also of great size, sleeves distended, and skirts swelling out over equally big farthingales.

Stubbes aptly commented that "when they have all these goodly robes upon them, women seem to be the smallest part of themselves, not natural women, but artificial women; not women of flesh and blood, but rather puppets or mommets [dolls] of rags and cloths compact together."

Men looked equally artificial, since male and female fashion paralleled each other and corresponding parts of the dress of each swelled or shrank simultaneously. Thomas Middleton caricatured a male dandy in the early seventeenth century as follows:

. . . enters our young landlord, so metamorphosed into the shape of a French puppet that at the first we started and thought one of the baboons had marched in in man's apparel. His head was dressed up in white feathers like a shuttlecock. . . . His doublet was of a strange cut and to show the fury of his humor the collar of it rose up so high and sharp as if it would have cut his throat by daylight. His wings, according to the fashion now, were as little and diminutive as a Puritan's ruff. . . . His breeches . . . were full as deep as the middle of winter, or the roadway between London and Winchester, and so long and wide withal that I think within a twelvemonth he might very well put all his lands into them: and then you may imagine they were big enough, when they would outreach a thousand acres. . . . [He wore] a curious pair of boots of King Philip's leather, in such artificial wrinkles, sets and pleats, as if they had been starched lately and came new from the laundress'. . . . But that which struck us most into admiration, upon those fantastical boots stood such huge and wide tops, which so swallowed up his thighs, that had he sworn as other gallants did this common oath, "would I might sink as I stand," all his body might very well have sunk down and been damned in his boots. . . . Thus was our young landlord accoutered in such a strange and prodigal shape that it amounted to above two years' rent in apparel [*The Ant and the Nightingale, or Father Hubburd's Tales*, 1604].

Elizabethan men and women of the upper class dressed more for display than for comfort, and even their undergarments were designed to contribute to their appearance. The garment worn next to the skin by both sexes was a shirt, though in the case of women it was called a "smock" and was ankle-length. There is some evidence that men wore drawers called "trousers"; at least Ben Jonson refers to them in *The Staple of News* (1625). Women also wore several petticoats, to help the correct hang of their kirtles, and boned underbodices, the forerunners of corsets.

Nightgowns, frequently referred to in contemporary records, were apparently dressing gowns and were often so similar to the gowns worn publicly by men and women that they could be worn abroad at the owner's discretion. Though some of the wealthy had special garments for night wear, it is very likely that most people slept naked or in their shirts or smocks, perhaps the very ones they wore every day, since standards of cleanliness were not high. Conditions in this period made personal cleanliness more difficult to achieve than a handsome appearance. Soap was generally quite coarse, though fine perfumed soaps were also available, and hot water was not a ready convenience. Of course, the fine fabrics used for the dress of the upper classes were not washable. Perfumes and sweet-smelling herbs were necessary substitutes for regular bathing and freshly laundered garments.

Elizabethan clothing was very intricate, and the amount of time that must have been consumed in donning costumes with so many independent parts to be tied or pinned together is a marvel to the modern observer. The main feminine garment usually consisted of at least two parts: bodice and skirt (known as a kirtle or petticoat). The very name "bodice," a corruption of "bodies" (a pair of bodies), indicates that it was made in two pieces. A triangular piece known as a "stomacher" formed the front section and was joined to the bodice proper at the sides by ties, hooks, or pins. The bodice was stiff, reinforced with stays and sometimes padded, and came to a point below the natural waistline.

Necklines varied; if low, the smock or a briefer garment called a "partlet" filled in the space at the top of the bodice. In Elizabeth's later years and the early years of James I's reign the bosom was often immodestly bared with the neckline of the stomacher making a downward curve. High-necked bodices had standing collars, frills, or ruffs. Feminine versions of the male doublet had some popularity for a time, but these were distinguishable from the conventional bodices only by their center fastenings; even so they provoked a bellow of indignation from the satirists of the day.

Sleeves were separate and were fastened to the bodice at the shoulder line by ribbon bows or by hooks or pins concealed by decorative rolls of fabric known as "wings." The funnel-shaped sleeve common in the first half of the century went out of fashion about 1560 and sleeves thereafter might be gathered to fit closely all along the arm, tapered in a leg-of-mutton shape, or full. In any case they were tightly fitted at the wrists and finished in frills, wrist ruffs, or cuffs. Leg-of-mutton sleeves, known as "trunk" or "demi-cannon" sleeves, were shaped by stiffening or were padded. A more elaborate sleeve had a puff at the shoulder, with a change of fabric beginning just above the elbow, and might actually be made in two parts.

The skirt was not necessarily in one piece but might be opened in an inverted V in front to show a handsomely ornamented petticoat or a "forepart" of elegant design joined to the petticoat in front or fastened to the V opening.

Farthingales were usually worn to shape the full skirts. The Spanish farthingale, first introduced about the middle of the sixteenth century, became the fashion and was worn by all classes of women until about 1600. It consisted of an underskirt belled out by hoops of wood, wire, or whalebone, extending from the waist in circles which widened progressively as they neared floor level. The result was a cone-shaped skirt. The French farthingale was a padded roll worn around the hips which created a cylindrical skirt effect. The farthingale which produces the immense swell of skirts apparent in Queen Elizabeth's late portraits was a wheel or drum type. To conceal the hard line of the wheel, a "frounce" or ruffle was usually added to the skirt.

Over the kirtle and bodice a "gown" was also worn at times, mainly for added warmth or greater dignity on ceremonial occasions. This garment might be close-bodied or loose, with long sleeves or with short sleeves displaying the sleeves of the bodice below them. Sleeves which hung loosely from the shoulder were also common. The gown opened down the front but was often buttoned or fastened by bows at least to the waist. If designed for ceremonial wear the skirt might have a train.

In cold weather cloaks or cassocks would also be necessary for outdoor wear. For traveling or riding a cloak was usually worn, and the skirt was covered with a "safeguard," an outer skirt for protection against weather and dirt. A cassock was a loose coat reaching to the hips, usually having a small collar and sometimes a hood. Another outdoor garment was the gaberdine, a long, loose coat with wide sleeves.

Besides shoes and stockings (the latter held up by garters below the knee), girdles and other accessories were indispensable to the complete costume in the highest fashion. The girdle (belt), made of silk ribbon, gold chain, or the like, followed the pointed line of the bodice, and a pomander, jewel, or muff was usually suspended from it in front. A pomander was a globular metal container for some scented concoction. Originally designed to protect the wearer against the plague, pomanders served to shield a fine lady's nose from unpleasant odors. They were ornamental as well, being made of gold or silver and often set with jewels. Half-girdles, "demi-cents," were also worn; the back section of these was more austere than the conspicuous front part. Large feather fans, of round or semicircular design, often with a small mirror in the center, were popular accessories of the noble lady, and masks were frequently carried to shield the face from the sun and the public gaze.

Both young girls and married women often went hatless, even out of doors, but the feminine head was usually covered in some fashion. Simple white coifs of linen, which hid most of the hair, were the common head covering of many women who made no pretensions to being fashionable. One type was colloquially known as "cheeks and ears" because of the way it hugged the face, with the front border forming peaks. One of the most popular head coverings was the French hood, which was introduced into England about 1530 and survived the vagaries of fashion for almost a hundred years. This was a small hood, stiffened underneath, with a curved front border and folds of material falling below the shoulders in the back. Since they were usually of dark material, these hoods were often decorated with "biliments" (borders of silk, satin, or velvet, trimmed with gold or jewels). Queen Elizabeth in 1584 received as a gift a magnificent pair of biliments of gold set with pearls, rubies, and diamonds, but humbler women would be lucky to have simple silk trimmings, or at most gold. The Mary Stuart hood was similar to the French hood but was made of sheer cloth such as lawn, trimmed with a decorative fabric, and edged with lace. The front border made a characteristic V- or U-shaped curve above the middle of the forehead. Such hoods were sometimes made of black silk and accompanied by a falling back section to indicate widowhood.

Hair nets, made of gold mesh lined with silk, of silk thread, or even of human hair, were known as "cauls" and might be worn alone to hold the back hair in a coil, or a hat might be worn with one. Women's hats copied those of men but were smaller and were usually worn at less rakish angles. Among the most stylish hats in the late sixteenth century were the taffeta pipkin and the court bonnet. The pipkin was usually trimmed with ostrich feathers and decorated with jewels and had a moderate crown and a narrow, fairly flat brim. The court bonnet was a small pillbox hat of velvet, trimmed with jewels and feathers. Both were worn with cauls. Shawls of transparent fabric known as "rails" were worn over the head and shoulders by some women.

Hair, which early in the century had been modestly drawn back and was often completely covered, during Elizabeth's reign began to be treated more like woman's crowning glory. Women often curled and dyed their hair or supplemented it with false hair. During an audience with the Queen in 1602 a Venetian envoy's observant eye noted her "hair . . . of a light color never made by nature." There are many other comments similar to Shakespeare's reference to "crisped, snaky golden locks . . . often known to be the dowry of a second head." False hair was often needed for the elaborate headdresses which developed in the late sixteenth century, and whole wigs might be used. An Elizabethan woman could manage more easily the pearl strands and other ornaments if the whole coiffure was made on a wig stand. To set off the head, wired headrails of gauze were sometimes worn. Those worn by Queen Elizabeth arched in stiffened curves behind her head and shoulders and were generously trimmed with pearls.

Variety in materials, color, and ornaments characterized the Elizabethan woman's outer garments. Bodice and kirtle as often as not were of different fabrics. Sleeves might match some other garment, but not necessarily, and the forepart of the kirtle offered another opportunity for variety. Any part of the costume was likely to be decorated with braid, embroidery, pinking (pricking in patterns), slashing, or puffing, or it might be encrusted with pearls, jewels, or spangles or trimmed with lace or artificial flowers. The smock was usually embroidered and frilled at the neck. Partlets to fill in the top of the bodice were often as ornate.

Although all classes in the Elizabethan period began to dress better, for obvious reasons the clothing of wealthy and prominent people is more fully described and illustrated than that of humble folk. Most generalizations therefore, apply to people in court circles or to those exposed to the influence of the court. Conservative gentlewomen and the wives of prosperous merchants and officials had taffeta, satin, and velvet in their wardrobes, but on the whole their garments were more sober than those of court ladies, and durability was a factor to be considered in the fashioning of their apparel. Women of yeoman stock largely confined their selection of clothing to worsted, russet, and other nonluxurious woolens, though they might have velvet trim on their best kirtles and gowns. Clothing was sufficiently valued to be included as special bequests to friends and relatives when wills were made, especially garments "guarded" with velvet or trimmed with gold lace.

The favorite materials among the wealthy were silk, taffeta, velvet, and brocade. Bright colors were favored, particularly reds (Bristol red, flame, lusty gallant, sanguine, carnation, gingerline, maiden's blush, scarlet) and oranges (tawny, orange-tawny, horseflesh color [bronze]). Black set off by silver or gold was also frequently worn, and white was popular at court. Color symbolism was very important to the Elizabethans. Blue, symbolizing constancy, was conventionally associated with serving-men and apprentices, and because of this men and women of higher rank avoided shades of true blue, though they wore watchet (light blue with a greenish tinge) and azure (a lapis lazuli blue).

Elizabethan women delighted in gorgeous dress. But despite the richness of their attire, men frequently outshone them in complexity of costume and the variety of cuts that contemporary fashion provided. The capriciousness of masculine taste was ridiculed by Andrew Boorde in 1548 in his *First Book of the Introduction of Knowledge* by a woodcut of a man clothed only in a plumed hat and a breechclout, holding cloth and shears, with the explanatory verse:

> I am an Englishman, and naked I stand here
> Musing in my mind what raiment I shall wear,
> For now I will wear this, and now I will wear that;
> Now I will wear I cannot tell what.

The costume corresponding to a twentieth-century suit was basically doublet and hose, "hose" being composed of breeches and stockings made separately but sometimes sewn together. Under the doublet a shirt was worn and perhaps a waistcoat; the latter was an underdoublet usually padded and probably worn for added warmth. If the breeches were short, they might be supplemented by "canions," close-fitting cylinders of cloth resembling the knee breeches of a later period. Over the doublet a jerkin was also worn at times. The jerkin was often sleeveless and was a somewhat looser garment than the doublet, though following the same cut.

The doublet was a jacket, cut to fit the torso, though during most of the sixteenth century its waistline came to a point below the natural waistline. The skirts became so abbreviated in the late sixteenth century that they were mere borders just below the girdle line, but they still served to conceal the "points" which tied doublet and hose together. The front opening was fastened with decorative buttons or loops or tied with points. Stiffening and padding were usual, and many an Elizabethan gallant had, instead of padded shoulders, a padded chest. A Dutch fashion known as a peasecod belly became popular in the last quarter of the sixteenth century, and in consequence doublets were often so heavily padded near the point that they bulged and drooped below the girdle. Philip Stubbes describes them, perhaps exaggeratedly, as stuffed with four to six pounds of bombast.

Doublets sometimes had high standing collars, often finished with stiff tabs called "piccadills" to support the ruffs. The shirt collar was sometimes pulled over the doublet collar and spread below the ruff. Late in the century when deep collars called "falling bands" were more common, the neckline became flatter. The sleeves were separate and laced or hooked to the doublet, with the joint concealed by wings, often "wrought in piccadills." Sleeve styles were similar to those of women's dress.

Breeches generally took the form of "trunk hose"; these were puffed, often stuffed, rounded breeches reaching to mid-thigh, though the length varied greatly, some being almost concealed by the skirts of the doublet. The fabric of trunk hose was usually "paned"; that is, vertical strips of one fabric alternated with strips of another of a different pattern or color. "Venetians" were chiefly distinguished by their length, coming just below the knee, and were often padded to give a voluminous effect. These were not necessarily paned like trunk hose. "Galligaskins" were apparently similar to Venetians, but Stubbes differentiates between them, describing "gally-hosen" as coming only to the knee and Venetians below. "Open hose" were breeches that hung loose below the knee. They were cut straight across and were usually braided at the sides. This style made its appearance late in the sixteenth century and never became very popular until the mid-seventeenth century.

Over the doublet, and possibly over a jerkin as well, cloaks of various lengths were worn. Short cloaks were frequently made to match the trunk hose as a part of the ensemble and might be worn indoors as well as out. Three-quarter-length capes with sleeves, called "mandilions," were dashing versions of the cloak. Stylish gallants affected a fantastic mode of wearing mandilions turned around sideways so that the sleeves hung down in front and behind. Mandilions worn in this way were said to be "Collie-Westonward." The sleeves of these garments were so little used that tailors eventually made mock sleeves that could not be worn.

A long open-front gown over other clothing was worn by some men, but chiefly older men, particularly officials. Short gowns were popular with stylish young men until about 1570. Cassocks and gaberdines were also worn for warmth outdoors.

Men's clothing, like that of women, was gorgeous with color and ornamentation. The many parts of male attire contributed to the ornate and colorful effect of the ensemble. Trunk hose need not match the doublet, canions could be of another fabric or design, and the netherstocks might be still different. Ensembles of matching doublet and hose were not unknown, however.

The fashionable gallant's doublet and hose were commonly made of satin, taffeta, velvet, or some other rich fabric; they were decorated with slashing, pinking, embroidery, or any of the other types of ornamentation used on feminine apparel. Colored lining, or a colored shirt, might be drawn through slashes in puffs to ornament the doublet and sleeves. Cloaks and gowns were richly trimmed with fur or gold braid, and the stockings might be patterned or clocked in silver or gold. Men were as lavish as women in the wearing of jewelry, even to the wearing of earrings, though men usually wore a ring in only one ear at a time. Even the shirt, which was politely concealed under the doublet except for the collar, might be elaborately embroidered, perhaps with "black work," in which English embroiderers excelled.

Men of modest station dressed in more somber colors and fabrics of greater durability than fashionable men of higher rank. Yeomen might have in their wardrobes no fabric richer than fustian, an inexpensive substitute for velvet made of cotton or flax and wool. The traditional dress of countrymen is indicated in two quotations from Robert Greene. He describes "a plain country fellow well and cleanly appareled, either in a coat of homespun russet, or of frieze [a sturdy woolen with a heavy nap]" (*A Notable Discovery of Cozenage,* 1591). Elsewhere referring to a character in a pastoral, he pictures him as "tired in his russet jacket, his red sleeves of chamlet [a fine silk], his blue bonnet, and his round slop of country cloth" (*Menaphon,* 1589). Russet is not a color here but the name of a coarse woolen which varied in color from natural to reddish-brown.

Men wore hats even indoors, though they were doffed in the presence of royalty or as a courtesy to others of high degree. Male headgear hugged the head until the 1570's, when hats with high crowns became increasingly fashionable. The "copintank" or "copotain" hat, described by Stubbes as "sharp on the crown, perking up like a sphere or shaft of a steeple," was particularly popular. Feathers and jewels were typical ornaments. A small, flat cap like a beret with a narrow brim continued to be worn by craftsmen and many other citizens of London and was famous as the "City Flat Cap." This cap was almost a badge of London residence. With the object of assisting local industry, an Act of Parliament in 1571 required all citizens with the exception of the nobility, gentry, and officeholders to wear on Sundays and holidays knitted caps of wool manufactured in England. These "statute caps" were worn by many until the statute was repealed in 1597.

Masculine hair styles varied greatly. Sometimes the hair was cut closely at the sides, but it could be brushed up and held with gum, or it might be curled all over the head. From 1590 onward, long hair was more common and it was often worn curling to the shoulders, perhaps with a long curl at the left side called a "lovelock." Men in this period did not disdain to have their hair curled by artificial means if necessary. Most men also wore beards of a variety of cuts, ranging from a Vandyke style to a spade or full shape. Mustaches were an inevitable accompaniment but were rarely seen without beards.

Shoes for men and women were similar. They were made of many materials, usually luxurious ones: Spanish leather, called "cordwain" (Cordovan), silk, brocade, or velvet. In the sixteenth century they were generally flat-heeled, but toward the end of the period small heels began to appear. Scuffs known as "pantofles" were introduced about 1570 for the protection of dainty footgear outdoors, but the prevailing taste for luxury was such that the pantofles themselves soon were made of rich fabrics and in time they retreated indoors for use as house slippers. Cork soles raised the foot in pantofles from close contact with the ground, and some pantofles had excessively thick soles, a concession to fashion rather than utility. Shoes of stouter leather were also used for outdoor wear. Pattens, which had raised soles or were elevated from the ground by a ring of metal, were worn over elegant footgear to keep them from the mud. Boots, utilitarian or elegant, were also common for masculine wear.

Among other accessories of the male costume were gloves, sometimes perfumed, purses, worn slung from the belt or carried in the sleeve or hose, and fans, carried only by the more effeminate dandies. Swords or rapiers, and sometimes daggers, slung on chains or belts of elaborate design, were worn by many men. Steel collars, called "gorgets," actually a part of armor, were sometimes worn with ordinary civilian dress.

An extravagance of both masculine and feminine dress, and a theme for much satirical comment, was the ruff, which had grown to great size by the time Elizabeth began her reign in 1558. Starch was introduced into England about 1560, and its use made possible even larger and stiffer ruffs. Despite her own use of wide ruffs, Queen Elizabeth objected to the spread of the fashion, and her sumptuary statute of 1580 forbade the wearing of neckwear larger than a certain size. The citizens of London were ordered to enforce the observance of this restriction, and members of the Ironmongers' and Grocers' companies were stationed at Bishopsgate in London from morning till evening to stop any passerby entering the city with "monstrous ruffs" or swords or cloaks of excessive length. If offenders refused to reform their costume, they were subject to arrest. Despite the efforts to prohibit large ruffs, according to Stubbes, writing in 1583, they often measured nine inches or more from inner to outer edge.

Ruffs were shaped into tubular pleats by means of tools made of wood or bone called "setting sticks," but in the 1570's "poking sticks" of steel were introduced. The instruments were used in the same way as a curling iron on human hair. A newly laundered ruff or "band" was placed in a round box for protection; from this we get the expression "just stepped out of a bandbox" to indicate sartorial perfection. Despite elaborate efforts to shape and stiffen ruffs, they did not withstand bad weather gracefully, and Stubbes pictures them as going "flip-flap in the wind like rags flying abroad." The larger ruffs required wired props called "supportasses" to hold them erect. The open ruffs popular after 1570 were pinned to "rebatos," wired frames covered with linen.

Though neckwear was usually white, yellow ruffs and cuffs had a vogue for a time after Mrs. Turner, a dressmaker for the court during James I's time, brought from France the method of making yellow starch. Mrs. Turner was involved in the notorious Overbury poisoning case and was executed in 1615 for her part in it. To bring ridicule upon the fad of wearing yellow ruffs, which disgusted King James, Chief Justice Coke ordered that Mrs. Turner be sent to the gallows wearing the detested yellow bands. But apparently yellow retained some popularity, for there are references to yellow bands in the 1620's.

James I's accession to the throne in 1603 saw no immediate or drastic change in English style, but dress gradually assumed greater freedom in comparison with the stiffness that developed during Elizabeth's long reign. Ruffs were replaced by "whisks," standing collars supported by piccadills; a familiar example is the collar in the Droeshout engraving of William Shakespeare on the title-page of the First Folio edition of his plays.

Women's necklines became lower than before, frequently having only a narrow lace edging at the bosom without either ruff or collar. Both men and women wore their hair longer and allowed it to flow in curls. Farthingales narrowed and in time disappeared. Numerous petticoats provided a softer fullness for the skirts. The male doublet acquired a more natural waistline, and trunk hose were replaced by full, loose-fitting breeches without padding. Boots became more and more common with men of every class. Shoes acquired heels and were decorated with large rosettes. In general, both male and female dress drifted toward the "Cavalier" costume associated with the mid-seventeenth century.

English men and women of both the Elizabethan and Jacobean periods made dressing an art when their means permitted it. Though colors may have been brighter than is customary in modern dress, particularly masculine dress, the use of color was not always gaudy. Contemporary documents list subtle combinations such as peach-color cloth of silver, lined with ash-color unshorn velvet. Tasteful elegance was the ideal of the great, and the more sophisticated apparently realized that black and white, silver and gold, and similar combinations of contrasting colors could be used for costumes with striking effects, as is demonstrated by the costumes worn in many portraits of great personages including Sir Walter Raleigh, the Earl of Essex, the Earl of Leicester, Sir Christopher Hatton, and Queen Elizabeth herself. Indeed, the portrait of Raleigh in the National Portrait Gallery, in which he wears white silk and black velvet, decorated with silver, represents the very model of a fine Elizabethan gentleman at his handsomest.

SUGGESTED READING

The literature of the period is rich in references to contemporary clothing. An introduction to the subject will be found in the chapter on costume in Volume II of *Shakespeare's England* (2 vols., Oxford, 1916). Contemporary portraits constitute the most reliable guides to what English dress actually looked like.

An excellent general discussion is contained in the volume by Graham Reynolds in the series "Costume of the Western World," *Elizabethan and Jacobean, 1558–1625* (London, 1951), illustrated by carefully chosen contemporary portraits, some in color. Details of every part of male and female dress are described, with line illustrations taken from contemporary portraits and memorial brasses, in C. Willett and Phillis Cunnington, *Handbook of English Costume in the Sixteenth Century* (London, 1954) and *Handbook of English Costume in the Seventeenth Century* (London, 1955). Though it is poorly illustrated, much useful information about fabrics, colors (including color symbolism), and styles is given in M. Channing Linthicum, *Costume in the Drama of Shakespeare and His Contemporaries* (Oxford, 1936). Both the Cunningtons and Miss Linthicum give many quotations from contemporary documents to amplify their texts.

Information about undergarments is scanty, but C. Willett and Phillis Cunnington, *The History of Underclothes* (London, 1951) provides the most complete discussion of this aspect of the dress of Shakespeare's age.

Herbert Norris, *Costume and Fashion, Vol. III, The XVIth Century* (London, 1938) has many illustrations and is particularly good for pictures and discussion of details such as embroidery.

F. M. Kelly, *Shakesperian Costume for Stage and Screen* (London, 1938) is designed to foster accurate reproduction of the dress of this period for theatrical purposes and includes discussions of costuming most of the plays of Shakespeare. Details of costume are illustrated by line drawings after contemporary illustrations.

Also useful are F. M. Kelly and Randolph Schwabe, *Historic Costume, 1490–1790* (London, 1925) and Millia Davenport, *The Book of Costume* (2 vols., New York, 1948; 2 vols. in 1, New York, 1956), copiously illustrated with contemporary portraits, English and Continental, which provide an opportunity to compare English dress with that of other countries.

Iris Brooke, *A History of English Costume* (London, 1937), *English Costume in the Age of Elizabeth. The Sixteenth Century* (London, 1938), and *English Costume in the Seventeenth Century* (London, 1934), all illustrated by the author, are less accurate and should be used with care.

Elizabethan embroidery, which played such a large part in the decoration of dress, is pictured with a brief discussion in the Victoria and Albert Museum's Small Picture Book No. 5, *Elizabethan Embroidery* (1948 and 1956).

Two older standard works, Joseph Strutt, *A Complete View of the Dress and Habits of the People of England* (2 vols., London, 1796–1799) and J. R. Planché, *History of British Costume from the Earliest Period to the Close of the Eighteenth Century* (London, 1847), are rather outdated.

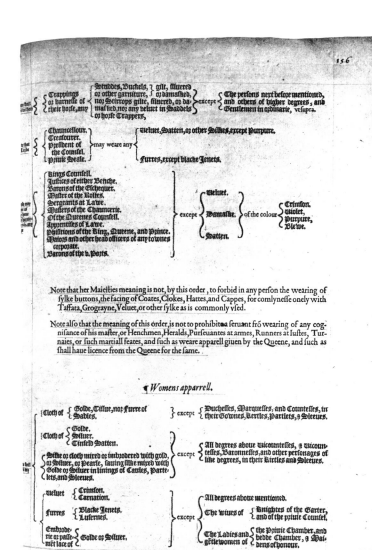

Note that her Maiesties meaning is not, by this order, to forbid in any person the wearing of sylke buttons, the facing of Coates, Clokes, Hattes, and Cappes, for comlynesse onely with Taffata, Grograyne, Veluet, or other sylke as is commonly vsed.

Note also that the meaning of this order, is not to prohibite a seruant frō wearing of any cognisance of his master, or Henchmen, Heralds, Purseuantes at armes, Runners at Iustes, Turnaies, or such martiall feates, and such as weare apparell giuen by the Queene, and such as shall haue licence from the Queene for the same.

❧ *Womens apparell.*

Plate 1. An excerpt from one of the proclamations concerning restrictions on the wearing of rich fabrics and expensive ornamentation. Throughout her reign Queen Elizabeth issued such proclamations, which often merely repeated the prohibitions decreed by her father, Henry VIII, and Mary Tudor.

405

Plate 2. Queen Elizabeth in the 1570's. Her dress is handsome and be-jeweled but less eccentric than it became in later years. (Portrait by an unknown artist; courtesy of the National Portrait Gallery, London.)

Are to be fould at ye popes head Alley at the white horse
by Iohn Sudbury and Georg Humble.

The most illustrious Prince Henry. Lord Darnly, King of Scotland, father
to our Soueraigne lord King Iames. He died at the age of 21. 1567.

The most excellent Princesse Marie. Queene of Scotland. mother to our Souer:
raigne lord King Iames. She died. 1586. and intombed at Westminster.

R. Elstrack
sculp:

Plate 3. Mary Queen of Scots and her second husband, Lord Darnley. Mary
wears an open ruff edged with lace, the hood to which she gave her name, and
a wired headrail. Her kirtle is open to show an ornate forepart, and her jeweled
girdle ends in a large jewel. Lord Darnley wears typical, paned trunk hose and
a cloak draped in a customary negligent manner. He holds a baton resting
against his right hip. Notice the ribbon bows on his flat-heeled shoes and the
ribboned garters. (An engraving by Renold Elstrack, executed 161–.)

Plate 4. The plain dress of unpretentious English folk is shown in this picture. The man wears a flat cap and a gown over a jerkin. The small frills showing above the collar of his jerkin and the bodice of the woman's dress later developed into the ruff. The soft folds of the woman's skirt probably indicate that she wears no farthingale. The child at the left still wears skirts, as did most children of both sexes. (*The Whole Book of Psalms in Four Parts*, 1563.)

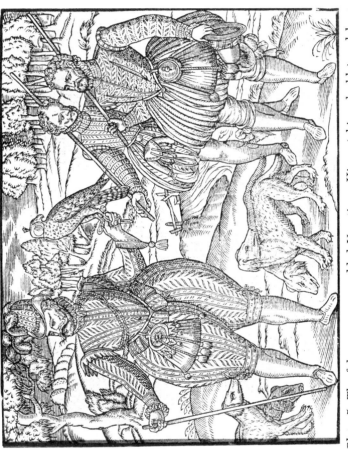

Plate 5. The falconer wears padded Venetians. His matching doublet and hose are slashed, as are the wings of his doublet. The other two men are wearing trunk hose, and the one in the foreground also wears canions and garters. (George Turberville, *The Book of Falconry*, 1575.)

Plate 6. This falconer wears padded trunk hose with less paning than usual. His canions and the wings of his sleeves are "wrought in piccadills," and his shoes are decorated with "razing" [slashing]. (George Turberville, *The Book of Falconry*, 1575.)

Plate 7. Mary Queen of Scots, whose taste for drama often dictated black and white dress. (Painting attributed to P. Oudry, 1578; courtesy of the National Portrait Gallery, London.)

Ein Engelische Fraw von Londen.

WANn ein Weib gehet auß dem Hauß
Ihre Geschäfft zu richten auß/
Zu Londen vber die Strassen/
Schmücket sie sich allermassen/

Wie dises Weib gemahlet ist/
Dem an schöne gar nichts gebrist/
So ist sie sonst stattlich geziert/
Am Leib wol proportionirt.

8a

Plate 8. An Englishwoman dressed for the street. She
wears a short cape and an open ruff. The skirt which she
lifts from the ground is probably a safeguard. Her girdle
has a pomander and a small purse suspended from it.
(Jost Amman, *Trachtenbuch*, 1586.)

Ein Fraw auß Engelland.

ẞJn Edelfraw in Engelland
    Jſt geſchmücket nach jhrem Stand/
Wann ſie alſo iſt angethan/
    Wie diſe Figur zeiget an.

Darinn hat ſie jhr recht Geſtalt/
    Auch jhrem Mann gar wol gefalt/
Vnd wann ſie ander Kleider trüg/
    Jhr Mann ſie zu dem Hauß außſchlüg.]

8z   L

Plate 9. Another Englishwoman pictured by a Dutch artist. She wears a bonnet, and the hood of her cloak hangs free behind. Her skirt demonstrates the effect of the Spanish farthingale. (Jost Amman, *Trachtenbuch,* 1586.)

Plate 10. Sir Walter Raleigh in black and silver. (Portrait by an unknown artist, 1588; courtesy of the National Portrait Gallery, London.)

Plate 11. Robert Dudley, Earl of Leicester. His costume includes a bonnet, a falling collar with matching cuffs, a short gown with fur facing, and paned trunk hose. The chain he wears is the collar of the Order of the Garter. (Engraving after a portrait by an unknown artist, 1588.)

Plate 12. Robert Devereux, Earl of Essex. He wears a lace ruff with "disordere[d] sets," a peasecod doublet, and brief, paned trunk hose with canions. (Engrav[v]ing after a portrait by Nicholas Hilliard.)

Plate 13. Queen Elizabeth dressed in the fashion of her later years. She wears a wired headrail decorated with pearls and jewels and a large drum farthingale. Notice the stiffness of her sleeves and the hanging sleeves which simulate a gown. (Portrait by an unknown artist, 1592; courtesy of the National Portrait Gallery, London.)

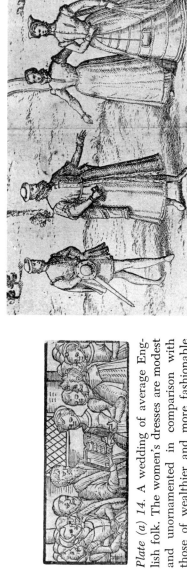

Plate (b) 14. Four Londoners. The young man carries a sword and a "target." (Braun and Hogenberg, *Map of London,* 1554–8.)

Plate (a) 14. A wedding of average English folk. The women's dresses are modest and unornamented in comparison with those of wealthier and more fashionable women. The head coverings are typical of women of their class. (Richard Day, *A Book of Christian Prayers,* 1590.)

Plate 15. A fashionable Frenchman. His short cloak has a contrasting lining, and he wears a peasecod doublet and Venetians. (Pierre Bertelli, *Diversarum Nationum Habitus,* 1594.)

Nobilis Gallicá ornatta

Plate 16. A highborn Frenchwoman wearing a Mary Stuart hood and veil stiffened behind her shoulders. Notice the point of the bodice, the unmatching sleeves, and the smock which fills in the space between ruff and bodice neck. (Pierre Bertelli, *Diversarum Nationum Habitus,* 1594.)

Plate 17. The man wears a short jerkin, trunk hose with canions, and a moderate ruff. The woman, in a larger ruff, is protected from dust and damp by a "chinclout" or muffler. Notice that the sleeves and stomacher are of different design. Her skirt appears to be shaped by a French farthingale. (John Speed, *Theatrum Imperii Magnae Britanniae,* 1616.)

A Citizen *A Citizens wife*

Plate 18. The man's gown obscures the rest of his attire, but note the hanging sleeve and his flat cap. His wife wears a large ruff and a drum or wheel farthingale. Her hair is wired into the fashionable horn-shaped headdress. (John Speed, *Theatrum Imperii Magnae Britanniae,* 1616.)

A Gentleman

A Gentle woman

Plate 19. The man is booted and spurred and wears a cloak draped
about him. His neckwear is a whisk or standing collar. The woman
also wears a whisk, and her hair is dressed in the high coiffure
fashionable after 1600. (John Speed, *Theatrum Imperii Magnae
Britanniae,* 1616.)

Plate 20. Francis Bacon wearing a long gown with hanging sleeves, decorate with braid. His neckwear is a falling band of lace. (After a portrait from th studio of Paul van Somer.)

Plate 21. Anne of Denmark, wife of James I. Her bodice shows the extreme decolletage popular with stylish women. She wears a wired collar and a frounced skirt. Notice the loveknots on her sleeve and at the edge of her bodice, and the deep lace cuffs. (Engraving by Simon van de Passe, 1616.)

Plate 22. William Herbert, Earl of Pembroke. He wears a Vandyke beard and an earring in the right ear. Notice the ring suspended from his bandstrings, the lace-edged falling band, and the decorative wing to his sleeve. (Engraving after a Daniel Mytens portrait, *ca.* 1620.)

English Sports and Recreations

By Lilly C. Stone

ALTHOUGH sports and pastimes in Shakespeare's age were far less highly organized than they are today, human nature was much the same, and Englishmen enjoyed many of the activities that still have a place in their recreations. To have an understanding of the social life and customs of a nation, a knowledge of its recreations is essential. The way a people spend their moments of leisure provides a clue to their personalities and qualities of character.

During the years when the Tudors and early Stuarts governed England, roads were poor, travel was difficult and sometimes dangerous, and ordinary folk usually did not go far beyond their parish limits for pleasure. Furthermore, life was hard for the ordinary citizen, and few had time for much leisure. Consequently, both time and opportunity were lacking for organized sports that could attract widespread attendance like a modern football match or modern horse racing. To working men and apprentices many sports were forbidden by statute except on such specified holidays as Christmas, but the laws were not always rigidly enforced.

Despite difficulties and handicaps, however, people of all classes enjoyed a variety of simple sports and amusements. If the Elizabethans had to work long hours at hard tasks, they nevertheless found time for play and gaiety. Fairs, festivals, and church wakes provided opportunities to villagers for many amusements. Everyone could look forward to the local fair, at which vendors of a variety of wares spread out their goods for sale. To the fairs came gleemen, jugglers, tumblers, acrobats, and animal trainers with their beasts: a dancing bear, monkeys, an exotic camel, and an "educated" horse. Traveling showmen also brought freaks, as in the "sideshow" at carnivals today, and sleight-of-hand artists were common. After the buying and selling were over, visitors to the fair, adults and children alike, joined in the activities. Women might dance for a prize, and the men engaged in foot races, bowling matches, wrestling, and other similar competitions. One of the most curious events, at which stout young men sought to show their worth and endurance, was the sport of shin kicking. Before this event the participants rubbed both their boots and shins with blue vitriol to harden them. At the close of the day many a young countryman must have been sore and sorry.

Festivals celebrated special occasions, such as the end of the harvest, sheepshearing, and the beginning of spring. Church wakes were held on a saint's day or the day of dedication of the church. A wake began with the vigil at the church and a service; then followed feasting, drinking, and contests of skill and strength like those at fairs. Originally these celebrations were held in the churchyard, but as the activities became more and more secular the churchyard was abandoned or forbidden. Many of the festivals stemmed from pagan rites, and the church thought to remove the taint of heathenism somewhat by acknowledging and modifying them. With the rise of the Puritans, however, objections grew louder, especially to such celebrations as church ales. On these occasions the church-wardens provided a quantity of malt, some from the church stock and the rest from parishioners. The malt was brewed into beer and ale and then sold to raise money for the church. This practice was condemned vociferously by Philip Stubbes, who complained in his *Anatomy of Abuses* (1583) of a situation in which profit to the church increased in proportion to the consumption of beer and the drunkenness that followed.

Pious Philip Stubbes also spoke out against the revelry that took place on May Day. On the eve of this holiday, or in the early morning hours of the day itself, people were accustomed to go into the forests to gather boughs and branches as decorations for their homes. A Maypole would be cut and drawn into the village by oxen. Each ox had flowers tied to its horns and the pole was decorated with herbs, flowers, and ribbons. When the pole was erected, the dancing began. The morris dance was traditional on May Day with a fiddler, Maid Marian, and ten men dressed with horns and bells. Maid Marian was queen of the May and mistress of the archery games. In later years Robin Hood was introduced, probably as king of the May. Upon such levity Stubbes frowned, but he deplored most the fact that the young men and girls "run gadding over night to the woods, groves, hills, and mountains" and there spend the night "in pleasant pastimes." He declared on "good authority" (one wonders if his own) that of a hundred maids going out scarcely a third returned in the state of virginity.

Archery occupied an important place in the May-Day activities, for it was virtually the national sport. Laws discouraged other physical exercises so that men would not be diverted from the practice of archery. From the time of Edward III when the value of the longbow was effectively demonstrated, it was thought wise to have all the men of England ready as trained archers in case of war. By the beginning of the seventeenth century the usefulness of archery in war was declining. As R. Barret says in *The Theory and Practice of Modern Wars* (1598) "they [archers] may serve to some sorts of service, but to no such effect as any of the fiery weapons," but the victories of the longbow at Crécy, Poitiers, and Agincourt were not quickly forgotten, and every man was expected to own a longbow and to practice regularly. Shooting contests were held to stimulate interest, and even churchwardens' accounts sometimes include expenses for making archery butts. Butts were mounds of earth, banked with turf. Against this mound was placed a white disk for a target. Shooting at these taught accuracy. To learn to "keep a length" the archers practiced "prick" or "clout" shooting, which meant shooting at a target eighteen inches in diameter, stuffed with straw. This mark was placed at a distance of 160 to 240 yards. "Roving" was to shoot in the open, at no mark, and at unknown distances.

Archery was praised as good for all men, great or poor. Gervase Markham in *The Art of Archery* (1634), dedicated to

Charles I, calls it an honest and wholesome sport, and much earlier, in *Toxophilus* (1545), Roger Ascham referred to archery as "the most honest pastime of all" and a cure of evil gaming. Ascham, who was at one time tutor to Elizabeth I, felt that a genuine effort should be made to teach archery because, truth to tell, the interest in archery was waning. He felt that many disobeyed the royal laws for lack of knowledge of how to shoot. Christina Hole suggests in *English Sports and Pastimes* that enthusiasm died out because laws commanded the practice of archery instead of leaving it to the pleasure of sportsmen.

An act passed in 1541 in the reign of Henry VIII shows us to what extent the government favored archery. After declaring that all able men under sixty must own a longbow and practice shooting, the act continues with a list of activities which are banned: "That no manner of person or persons . . . shall for his or their gain . . . keep . . . or maintain, any common house, alley, or place of bowling, quoiting, cloish, kayles, half-bowl, tennis, dicing, table, or carding, or any other manner of game prohibited by any statute heretofore made, or any unlawful new game now invented or made, or any other new unlawful game hereafter to be invented, found, had or made. . . ."

In spite of this act gaming houses were kept open, and the various sports flourished. Bowling was probably the most popular. Robert Crowley, printer and Puritan preacher as well as poet, testifies that bowling was not suppressed. In his *One and Thirty Epigrams* (1550), appeared this poem on bowling:

> Two sorts of alleys
> In London I find;
> The one against the law,
> And the other against kind.
> The first is where bowling
> Forbidden, men use,
> And wasting their goods,
> Do their labor refuse.
> But in London (alas!)
> Some men are devilishly
> Suffered to profess it
> As an art to live by. . . .

Two types of bowling were popular then as now. The favorite was played on bowling greens. Bowling in alleys, similar to the modern game, was also common. Bowling greens were often included as part of the gardens in the estates of the gentry, but bowling was not a sport for the rich alone. Besides having alleys in the supposedly illegal gaming houses, men also played at bowls in the open country, according to Gervase Markham's description in *Country Contentments* (1615): "There is another recreation . . . that is, bowling, in which a man shall find great art in choosing out his ground and preventing the winding, hanging, and many turning advantages of the same, whether it be in open wild places or in close alleys; and in this sport the choosing of the bowl is the greatest cunning; your flat bowls being the best for alleys, your round biased bowls for open grounds of advantage, and your round bowls like a ball for greenswards that are plain and level." Charles Cotton, who in the later seventeenth century wrote *The Complete Gamester* (1674), "borrowed" this passage from Markham. Cotton, however, does add a caution against gambling at a bowling match. In his advice on learning the game he states that "practice must be your best tutor . . . ; all that I shall say, have a care you are not in the first place rooked out of your money." Cotton's comments on the weird postures assumed by bowlers as the bowl is rolling down the alley, and the cries to go further or stop shorter, suggest that a bowler of the sixteenth century would not feel out of place in a twentieth-century bowling alley.

Many of the bowling terms, such as "rub," "jack," or "kiss," can be found in Shakespeare, and it appears probable that he was a knowledgeable bowler. A "rub" is anything that diverts the ball from its course (as in Hamlet's soliloquy: "Ay, there's the rub"); a "jack" (also "master" or "mistress") is a small bowl placed as a mark at which to aim; and a "kiss" occurs when one bowl touches another (as in *Cymbeline*, II.i.: "Was there ever man had such luck! When I kissed the jack, upon an up-cast to be hit away!").

Kayles, cloish, and loggats were all closely allied to bowling. In the game of kayles there were six or more pins set up in a straight row. Instead of bowling a ball at the pins, the object

433

was to knock the pins down by throwing a stick at them. Cloish also consisted of setting pins in a row, but a bowl was used to knock them down. In loggats, a game popular with boys and country folk, bones were substituted for the pins, and another bone was thrown at them. Shakespeare has a reference to this sport in the grave-digging scene where Hamlet comments: "Did these bones cost no more the breeding but to play at loggats with 'em?"

Men and boys of the sixteenth century, like their counterparts in other ages, enjoyed various forms of ball games. The variety of games played with balls was great, but often the same game appeared in different sections of the country under different names. As early as 1598 one finds a reference to cricket being played fifty years before. Cricket perhaps was an outgrowth of stoolball and clubball. In playing stoolball, a bowler tried to hit a stool with a ball. One player tried to defend the stool with his hand. In some localities a bat was used. In this game, however, there were no runs. Another game with overtones of cricket was trapball. A ball was placed in a spoon-shaped piece of wood. When the spoon was hit, the ball would rise and was hit into the field. Opponents tried to catch the ball, or to bowl the ball in to hit the trap.

Handball is probably the oldest form of ball game. Many games were derived from it, including fives and a form of tennis. Fives was played against a wall or church tower. This led to complaints from ministers against the delinquent boys who not only did not attend church but disturbed the service by playing ball against the church walls! Rules apparently differed in various geographical areas, as at Eton, where the buttresses from the wall formed two additional sides, and the game called "Eton Fives" developed.

Football was not unknown to the Elizabethan age, but it is hardly recognizable as the game we know today. The main similarity is that a ball, usually a bladder filled with air and encased in leather, was used, and the object was to get the ball across a goal line. What happened in between was nothing short of chaos or, as Sir Thomas Elyot says in *The Book Named the*

Governor (1531), "nothing but beastly fury and extreme violence." There were few if any rules, and each team could have an unlimited number of players. Often there were interparish contests, in which case much of the parish might be commandeered for the playing field, as one set of players tried to kick the ball into the opposing parish. On other occasions an open field or common was used. If the game was a parish affair, it was usually played on a holiday or feast day. At Chester a game was always played at Shrovetide, and legend has it that it commemorated the kicking about of the head of a captured Dane. Often it was a contest between two special groups of people, such as married men and bachelors. At Inverness, Scotland, an annual game was played between the married and the single women—and it is reported that the married women usually won!

Football was another sport prohibited by law to the working man as early as 1349 and as late as Elizabeth's reign. James I in *Basilicon Doron* (1599), a book of instructions for his son, forbids the prince to play football because he thought it "meeter for laming than making able the users thereof." Philip Stubbes gives us a vivid description in his *Anatomy of Abuses* of what happens during a game which he considers a "bloody and murdering practice."

For doth not everyone lie in wait for his adversary, seeking to overthrow him and to pick him on his nose, though it be upon hard stones, in ditch or dale, in valley or hill . . . he careth not so he have him down . . . so that by this means, sometimes their necks are broken, sometimes their backs . . . legs . . . arms. . . .

. . . They have the sleights to meet one betwixt two, to dash him against the heart with their elbows, to hit him under the shortribs with their gripped fists, and with their knees to catch him upon the hip and to pick him on his neck, with a hundred such murdering devices. . . .

Such a commentary suggests that Stubbes himself had been involved at least once in a friendly game of football.

Robert Burton in his *Anatomy of Melancholy* (1621) enumerates additional sports enjoyed by country folk and working people. They include quoits (similar to throwing horseshoes), pitching bars, hurling, wrestling (best done by those who knew the Cornish hug), leaping, running, fencing, swimming, football, balloon, and quintain. Balloon ball was, according to Markham's *Country Contentments,* "a strong and moving sport in the open fields, with a great ball of double leather filled with wind, and driven to and fro with the strength of a man's arm armed in a bracer of wood, either of which actions must be learned by the eye and practice." Quintain was at one time a knightly exercise. In the late sixteenth century it became a rustic pastime. The quintain was a post with a swinging shield attached. The object was to rush at the shield as if in a duel and then quickly to maneuver oneself out of the way as the shield swung around the post. The slow-footed were hit in the back of the head by the returning shield.

In the reign of James I the celebrated Cotswold Games, which exemplified many of the popular recreations of the day, grew into national importance. These games had begun in the reign of Elizabeth I, or perhaps even earlier, as a small local gathering, but they were taken over in the next reign by a man who had many of the qualities of a modern promoter, a certain "Captain" Robert Dover, who obtained from King James a royal sanction for the games and received from His Majesty as a further token of favor an old hat, a feather, and a ruff, which he wore with great pride. Information about the Cotswold Games is to be found in *Annalia Dubrensia* (1636), a volume edited by Matthew Walbancke, containing poems by Michael Drayton, Ben Jonson, and others in praise of Captain Dover and his activities. The Cotswold Games were compared by some to those held in classical times on Mt. Olympus. One poem by William Denny mentions foot racing, wrestling, bowling, chariot races, coursing with greyhounds, leaping, and throwing the sledge. Inside tents one could play chess; Irish, which resembles backgammon; and cent, a card game. Other activities included dancing and horse racing.

Elizabethan children had many ways of amusing themselves,

and some of their games are still familiar to juveniles. It would be impossible to list all the games at which children played, but a few will illustrate their characteristic amusements: put-die, blind egg, conquers, hoodman-blind, nine-men's morris, and top and scourge. Dice were needed to play put-die. Instead of numbers there were letters on each die—P, T, H, and L on the four sides, and A and D on the two ends. The dice were tossed in the air. Whatever letter turned up determined the number of marbles won or lost from the pool. Blind egg consisted of lining birds' eggs in a row. A blindfolded boy then tried to break the eggs with a stick. In one version of conquers the players took snail shells and pressed them together. The one whose shell did not break was the winner. Hoodman-blind, of course, is simply a variant form of blindman's buff. Nine-men's morris went by several names, one of which was merels. In this game each player had nine wooden pegs. A flat board with three squares and twenty-four holes was used, and the object was to capture the opponent's pegs and to get one's own pegs in three straight rows. This game was also played outdoors, using the ground for a board. Top and scourge was a seasonal game, connected with the Lenten season, in which a boy would whip a top to make it spin.

Recreation was obviously not restricted to any age group or class. Although the lower classes had certain handicaps, they found numerous ways of amusing themselves. The gentry and nobility naturally had few restrictions upon their recreations. Indeed, an ability in sports was an essential requirement for a young gentleman. One of the most noted books of instructions to young men of gentle breeding is Baldassare Castiglione's *The Courtier*, translated into English by Thomas Hoby in 1561. In this conduct book Castiglione lists among the chief qualifications of a courtier skill in martial exercises and in sports. The courtier must be able to fence with all kinds of weapons, to play tennis, to hunt, to hawk, and to ride well. Other activities suitable for young aristocrats were swimming, leaping, vaulting, wrestling, and casting stones or an iron bar. Here Castiglione gives an admonition "not to run, wrestle, leap, or cast the stone

437

or bar with men of the country, except he be sure to get the victory." It was not fitting for a gentleman to lose to someone of baser birth, and gentlemen engaged in these sports either alone or with their equals. On the other hand, one could tilt, ride in a tourney, and throw the spear or dart in public to delight the common people. Nicholas Faret in *The Honest Man,* translated by Edward Grimstone in 1632, gives virtually the same qualifications for proper gentlemanly behavior. Besides the foregoing skills a courtier was expected to have some knowledge of music and be able to play the lute or gittern and to carry a fair tune.

A courtier's life was devoted to following his prince, a life that provided in the Tudor age ample opportunity for a high-spirited young gentleman to develop his love of martial exercises. Henry VIII was fond of these sports and in his reign they flourished. Edward Hall's *Chronicle,* first published in 1548, describes the King's activities while on progress. Henry exercised himself with shooting, singing, dancing, wrestling, casting of the bar, jousts and tourneys, hunting and hawking. At times the King and another would issue a challenge to others to take part in some martial activity. On one occasion Henry and the Duke of Suffolk "were defenders at the tilt against all comers." Another time the King and two aides challenged all to fight "at the barriers with target and casting the spear of eight feet long." Then they challenged all to fight them for seven strokes with two-handed swords. To encourage further these manly sports, the King had built at Greenwich a place for the ladies to watch fights with battle-axes, because, Hall says, "the King [was] not minded to see young gentlemen unexpert in martial feats." To keep fit for these activities a man needed practice, and several hours a day might be devoted to riding at the tilt or ring. To tilt was to ride with a lance at a mark, or quintain. Although this later became a rustic pastime, it served as good exercise for aspiring knights. Another exercise was to ride with spear or lance and try to catch a ring hung from a pole, a feat that has survived to modern times.

Fencing became exceedingly popular in the reign of Henry

VIII, in part as a result of the King's own interest. By letters patent Henry VIII gave to the Masters of Defense a monopoly of teaching arms. In earlier years all free Englishmen carried arms, but fencing was looked down upon as being too subtle an activity and one that took away from true valor. To the medieval mind plain and simple hacking from left to right with sword and buckler was the mark of a man. It took some time for the English to learn new tactics and change their way of thinking. The gradual change was due largely to the Italian masters of arms who braved English criticism to teach their modern methods. The art of fencing developed in Italy, and Italian methods were far ahead of the English. The Italians discarded the buckler and added the poniard to the left hand. The poniard itself was finally discarded, and the sword was thenceforth used for both offense and defense. The "point" of the sword was rediscovered, and fencers learned the advantage of the thrust, called *stoccata* by the Italian fencing masters, over the side blows. In English tradition the use of the point was originally considered a dishonor.

In Elizabeth's reign the court went through an Italianate period, at which time the rapier was adopted. John Florio, an Italian naturalized in England, wrote in his *First Fruits* (1578) of the sword and buckler as "a clownish and dastardly weapon, and none for a gentleman." On the other hand, George Silver, an ardent Englishman, vigorously defended the short sword against the rapier and warned against Italian and other foreign methods. Shakespeare showed himself a loyal Englishman by satirizing the Italianate form of fencing in his plays. Silver practiced what he preached, for he was unaware of the lunge which was then being taught in Italy. His method of attack was to jump forward with both feet. He also advocated disarming and tripping, which apparently was not unsportsmanlike; at any rate, Castiglione recommended wrestling to young gentlemen because it was useful in the handling of weapons on foot. The rapier survived the Italianate period and passed on down to the middle class, and many Englishmen, despite Silver's warning, came to recognize it as a fine weapon. Joseph Swetnam, for ex-

ample, in his *School of the Noble . . . Science of Defense* (1616)
considered rapiers as the "finest and most comeliest weapons
that were used in England. The short sword against the rapier
is little better than a tobacco-pipe."

By 1639 a book called *Pallas Armata*, by G. A., introduced
new methods of fencing which were the forerunners of present-
day fencing techniques. The author advocates the single sword
or single rapier. The dagger, gauntlet, and buckler (formerly
used in the left hand as a means of defense) were no longer
considered fashionable.

For townspeople in this period one of the most popular spectacles was "playing a prize." To become a master of arms, the
aspirant had to challenge all masters within a certain radius.
These contests were held in public and were preceded by a
march through the town with drums to announce the coming
event. Municipal authorities usually frowned on these events
and often refused to give licenses, but outside the town
boundaries contestants could find places for these competitions.
Although blunted swords were used, the battles were lusty and
long. In fact they were as much a contest of endurance as of
skill, for the challenger had to fight each master with a certain
number of weapons for a prescribed length of time. Between
each event the challenger would parade around and exhort the
crowd to contribute money, for that is how he paid all his expenses. The weapons in which a master of arms had to be proficient were the two-handed sword, hand-and-one-half sword,
long sword, backsword, sword and buckler, sword and dagger,
pike, morris- or half-pike, halberd, quarterstaff, and battle-axe.
By 1605 most of these weapons were obsolete, but the English
teachers of arms clung tenaciously to all of them for many years.

A princely sport and one enjoyed by all the sovereigns of the
age was hunting. Deer, hare, and otter were the principal quar-
ries. Boars were hunted to a lesser degree than on the Continent because they were not so prevalent in England. Boar
hunting was a dangerous sport not only to the hunter but to his
hounds. Although the English loved the chase, English hunting
books for the most part followed the French originals, and the

customs were largely of French derivation. George Turberville in his *Noble Art of Venery or Hunting*, first printed about 1576, took much of his material directly from *La Venerie de Jacques du Fouilloux* and some from Gaston Phoebus. The English did not always observe fixed rules, but there was a certain pattern or ritual in their procedures, particularly in deer hunting.

This sport was engaged in not only for pleasure's sake, but for necessity as well. Killing a deer meant good meat, much needed in the winter, and therefore the choice of the deer was important. Before the hunt began huntsmen would go out early to locate a hart which would be good for hunting. There were many ways of doing this. A good huntsman would judge the age and size of the hart by the shape of the slots, or footprints. The droppings or "fewmets" provided other evidence of the age and state of the animal. The size of the animal's head and body could be guessed by the height and width of the space between twigs broken in passing. A huntsman would judge the hart's gait to see how long it could last in a chase; it was desirable to find a fat animal that would tire in a reasonable time. All of these signs might not be detectable on one hunting expedition but such information as a huntsman could gather was delivered to the prince or the master of game, who would then decide which animal was to be hunted.

After the deer was aroused from his lair, the chase was on. Old experienced hounds were the best, for they did not easily lose the scent. If the chase was a long one, the hounds were sent in in relays; that is, fresh hounds were brought in at intervals to continue the hunt. When the hart was caught, it was skinned and butchered immediately. Certain portions were given to special people: the participants of noblest birth and the huntsman in charge; even the hounds were allowed their bit. It was the prerogative of the prince to slit the throat and cut off the head. Often chafing dishes, coals, sauces, spices, and wines were brought along to heat and cook some of the delicacies, "caul, tongue, ears, doucets, tenderlings," reserved for the prince. Wine was also brought along for another purpose, for there was a superstition that the huntsman must take a drink of wine before breaking up the deer or the venison would putrify and stink.

When men wanted to exercise their cunning, show off the speed of their hounds, and pursue the chase for sheer pleasure, they usually chose the hare, for the hare was the swiftest of creatures. Sir Thomas Elyot in *The Book Named the Governor* commends this sport as suitable for scholars and women: "Hunting of the hare with greyhounds is a right good solace for men that be studious, or them to whom nature hath not given personage or courage apt for the wars. Also for gentlewomen which fear neither sun nor wind for appairing their beauty."

Although there were no hunting seasons such as we observe in this century, George Turberville recommends October and November as the best months, for in the summer the heat would be too great for the hounds, and in the spring the smell of the flowers and herbs would make them lose their scent.

In hunting otter a special spear or forked staff was used. The hounds would smell out the otter, but it was the huntsman's job to catch him if he went to the river. In this case a man would stand on each side of the river holding a line stretched across the stream. The line would be held slack so that it would sink under the water. The direction and whereabouts of the otter could be determined when it hit the line.

When boar hunting, Turberville suggests that dogs wear bells around their necks, for the boar will be frightened by the sound of bells and will flee instead of standing at bay or charging. Whether this was true or not, it was certainly wise to use the most experienced hounds in this dangerous sport. As in hunting a deer, the size of the boar could first be determined by his tracks or by seeing where he had rooted in a hedge. Another way was to find where the boar had rubbed against a tree after rolling in the mud. The weapon used in this sport was a long spear with a crosspiece. The crossbar was to prevent the spear from sticking too far into the boar as he charged against it.

Fox hunting as it is known today did not develop fully until the late seventeenth or early eighteenth century. Foxes as well as badgers were hunted as vermin and were dug out of their dens and killed. Terriers held the foxes or badgers in their burrows while the huntsman with spade or mattock dug them out. In addition to a supply of food and drink, Turberville advises a stout pair of boots, for, he laments, "I have lent a fox or a badger ere now, a piece of my hose, and the skin and flesh for company, which he never restored again." A hunt might last a long time, and Turberville recommends that a gentleman take along several mats to lie upon the ground. In some cases they even used inflated mattresses or "a windbed which is made of leather strongly sewn on all the four sides, and having a pipe at one of the corners to blow it as you would blow a bagpipe, and when it is blown full of wind, to stop it up and lie upon it on the ground."

Falcons were used for hunting of fowl and some game. Hawking, one of the oldest sports known, was expensive and therefore restricted to the aristocracy; it was greatly favored by the English nobility and gentry. Certain laws indicate the esteem in which falconry was held. One law stated that a lost hawk must be returned, or the finder would be charged with a felony, as would the stealer of a hawk's eggs. James I passed a law forbidding the shooting of game by guns, crossbows, or longbows, except to kill crows or smaller birds to feed the hawks. This is probably not so much an indication of James' love of hawking as it is an indication of his upbringing in Scotland, where shooting with gun and bow was considered thievish. James praised hawking sparingly in *Basilicon Doron* and thought that for Prince Henry hunting with hounds was better than hunting with hawks. Falconry is uncertain and more apt to stir up the emotions, the King observed.

The training of a hawk required patience and gentleness, but first a proper hawk had to be caught. Sometimes they were taken while they were just learning to hop from branch to branch, in which case they were known as branches. A soar hawk was taken wild in its first year, and an eyas was taken from the nest. Immediately after the hawks were caught, jesses, which were straps of leather, were attached to their feet and never removed. Rings of silver called vervels, to which the jesses were attached, were also put around the legs. Preparatory to training was seeling, in which a thread was drawn through the eyelids so that the eyes were partially closed to keep out daylight. This was supposed to help the hawk become adjusted to wearing a hood, which completely covered the head. A hawk was kept with a sharp appetite so as to respond to the bits fed her by the falconer. When the hawk learned to jump from the perch to the fist and to respond to the trainer's voice, it could be taught to come to the lure. The lure was a piece of meat, often a dead pigeon, used to get the falcon back to the owner. If a hawk remained wild and would not submit to training, then it was kept awake until fatigue tamed it.

There are many kinds of hawks, each with their special virtues, but they fall into two general classes: short-winged and long-winged hawks. The goshawk and sparrow hawk are short-winged and were used in woody areas or among shrubs. These hawks were flown from the hand, and they killed their prey on the ground with their beaks. Long-winged hawks include the gerfalcon, falcon, lanner, merlin, hobby, and kestrel. They were used in the open country. A hawk would hover above the falconer until the dogs stirred up the game, at which time the falcon would swoop down and kill its quarry in the air with a stroke of the claw. These hawks were brought back by the lure, and when flying they had bells attached to their legs so that the owner could find them again.

Fowling was popular with those people to whom hawking was denied because of class, time, or money. Since the Elizabethans, like many modern Europeans, enjoyed eating a variety of birds large and small, fowling was pursued primarily for food. Though some of the methods used to secure birds for the pot were ingenious and skillful, they were hardly sportsmanlike in the usual sense. Nets and snares of various kinds were common devices for catching birds. A snare of the springe type—a noose tied to the end of a pliant rod and triggered to tighten up when touched—was one of the most common. Also used were traps known as pitfalls.

444

Birdliming was another ingenious way of catching small birds. Small twigs from a willow were covered with birdlime, a sticky substance, and were scattered about a stale, or decoy. When the birds settled onto these twigs, they were unable to free themselves and the fowler could gather them in at his leisure. Dogs were sometimes used to retrieve any who managed to get loose; such dogs were trained to lie nearby and snatch up any bird which struggled free before it could fly away.

Somewhat more sport was involved in shooting birds, which was done with bird bolts (arrows with blunt heads) or stonebows (catapults which shot small pebbles). Firearms were beginning to come into use but were too clumsy as yet for shooting any but large game birds. Because birds are easily frightened, it was desirable to take them by surprise, and for this purpose a stalking-horse was used. This was originally a real cow, ox, or horse which had been trained to walk gently back and forth, while behind it the hunter drew a bead on his quarry. Dummy animals made of wood and canvas were also used in lieu of the living specimens. Even King Henry VIII used this method of hunting.

Fowling at night required different techniques—the two most popular being "lowbelling" and "batfowling." In the former the hunter carried a bell with a low, hollow sound which caused the birds to lie close. A large net was spread and then the birds were stirred up and caught in the net. Batfowling was a procedure in which the birds were confused by fires set in iron vessels. When the birds were caught in the light of the fires, they were batted down with broomlike poles.

Fishing was as popular with Tudor Englishmen as it is with men of the atomic age. These fishermen of old had just as much trouble catching fish as men of all centuries, although modern editors of Elizabethan fishing treatises contend that fish have grown craftier over the years. Methods and equipment were somewhat different then. Although fishing rods could be bought at the haberdasher's, the various books on the subject describe the rod and line with such care that it is evident that many Elizabethans were given to making their own. Rods were of three types, according to Markham's *Pleasures of Princes* (1614): of two pieces, the lower being nine to ten feet and the upper about a yard long; of one whole piece, which meant a short rod good only for narrow streams; of many pieces, usually made of cane, that fit into one another. The line was made of horsehair with threads of silk intertwined. Some years later Robert Venables in *The Experienced Angler* (1662) preferred a line of either horsehair or silk, but not a mixture.

Until the middle of the seventeenth century fishermen had no reels. Since the line was attached to a loop at the end of the rod, it was not possible to play the trout until it tired. Even when reels did appear, they were used more for salmon than for trout.

Elizabethan fishermen did not favor fishing upstream with a dry fly. Upstream angling was first mentioned by Venables and then with disapproval. He believed that in casting upstream one's line was more likely to hit the water before the fly, or at least the line would be visible, and in either case the fish would be frightened away—all of which argues the inexpertness of Venables as a fly-caster or the poor quality of the equipment then available.

Various baits were used, and Venables suggests that once a week a fisherman, if he had a special fishing spot, should cast in all sort of food, such as corn boiled soft, grain dipped in blood, or worms. Then the fish would be less suspicious of bait. Live baits consisted of such delicacies as red worms, maggots, flies, grasshoppers, hornets, wasps, and snails. Dried wasps, clotted blood of sheep, corn, seed, cheese, berries, cherries, or pastes were used as dead bait. For those who preferred fly-fishing, books told how to make one's own flies. According to Izaak Walton's classic, *The Compleat Angler,* "if he hit to make his fly right, and have the luck to hit, also, where there is store of trouts, a dark day, and a right wind, he will catch such store of them as will encourage him to grow more and more in love with the art of fly-making." This implies a big "if," but all writers on fishing stress the virtues a fisherman must have, the foremost being patience. As Markham writes: "Then he must be exceeding patient and neither vex nor excruciate himself with losses or mischances, as in losing the prey when it is almost in the hand, or by breaking his tools."

One unusual form of fishing was "tickling," in which a fisherman cautiously ran his arm under a bank until he touched a trout and then slowly tickled it until he was in a position to seize it.

Fishing was a sport sufficiently in favor to receive the blessing of university authorities in a day when sports had only a small place in university life. Sir Simonds D'Ewes mentions in a diary kept at Cambridge that angling was one of the pleasures that he enjoyed. D'Ewes also mentions a few other sports which served "as antidotes to disastrous diseases" and of course did not interfere with studies, unlike the experience of Sir Andrew Aguecheek in *Twelfth Night,* who laments: "I would I had bestowed that time in the tongues that I have in fencing, dancing, and bearbaiting."

Sports in which the students participated in their leisure time included tennis, shovegroat (shuffleboard), cards, bowling, jumping, and running. They seem to agree with Robert Crowley's idea of how a scholar should amuse himself.

> To fish, to fowl, to hunt, to hawk,
> Or on an instrument to play;
> And some whiles to commune and talk,
> No man is able to gainsay.
> To shoot, to bowl, or cast the bar,
> To play tennis, or toss the ball
> Or to run base, like men of war,
> Shall hurt thy study nought at all.
> For all these things do recreate,
> The mind, if thou canst hold the mean.

Scottish universities, somewhat more advanced than those below the border, included sports and exercises as a part of the official curriculum. On certain days the students were taken to the fields for organized exercises, and the University of Edinburgh had a tennis court on its grounds. James Melville, whose memoirs dating from the late sixteenth century were published in 1842, states that at school he was taught archery, golf, fencing, running, leaping, and wrestling, and at the University of St. Andrews he played golf and engaged in archery.

Golf was a great recreation in Scotland from early times, though it did not thrive in England until the Stuart kings popularized it there. The treasurer's records in the reign of James IV of Scotland included expenses for golf equipment:

1503, Feb. 3.   Item to the King to play at the
golf with the Earl of Bothwell . . . . xlii s
1503, Feb. 4.   Item to golf clubs and balls
to the King . . . . ix s
1503, Feb. 22.   Item, xii golf balls to the King . . . . iiii s
1506,   Item the 28th day of July for ii golf
clubs to the King . . . . ii s

Golf balls at this time were stuffed with feathers and covered with leather.

Tennis was played in both England and Scotland as well as on the Continent. In fact, it developed from the French *jeu de paume* or "palm play." In its early stages in the Middle Ages the palm of the hand was used instead of a racket. The hand was gloved, and later strings were stretched between the fingers of the glove. The next step was a crude racket with a handle. For a long time both the hand and the racket were used, but the racket had become sufficiently popular by Chaucer's day to be mentioned in his *Troilus and Criseyde*. The racket was oblong and strung diagonally with only a few strings.

The common people played some form of open-air tennis, but the game was largely the court tennis variety, played in an enclosed court. Because of the expense it was confined for the most part to the gentry and nobility, who could afford to build their own courts. Some public courts, however, were operated by the proprietors of gaming houses.

The actual size of the courts varied, but they all had the same features: the outer and inner walls, covered by a sloping roof called the penthouse; the dedans, a large opening at the end of the service side of the court; the grille, a small opening in the end corner of the hazard side; galleries along the side; and the lines in the court by which to mark a chase.

The object was to hit the ball back and forth, sometimes with the aid of the walls, until a point was won or lost, or a chase was made. A chase occurred when one player elected not to hit the ball, but to let it fall. Where it fell was marked, and the players changed sides, giving the opponent an opportunity to make a better chase—one that was further from the net. A point also was won if the ball was struck through the dedans or grille.

Tennis balls in the sixteenth century were stuffed with feathers or hair and encased in white leather. This made them stronger and more resilient than the earlier cloth balls. That hair was a popular stuffing is indicated by the many references to it in contemporary literature as in *Much Ado About Nothing*, III.ii:

Don Pedro.   Hath any man seen him at the barber's?
Claudio.   No, but the barber's man hath been seen with him, and the old ornament of his cheeks hath already stuffed tennis balls.

Tennis was a popular game with royalty. Most of the royal palaces had courts. Henry VII and his son Henry VIII were enthusiastic players, and Elizabeth apparently enjoyed the game, for there are reports of special games being played for her amusement while on progresses. The Stuart kings also regarded tennis with favor, and James I in *Basilicon Doron* included it in the list of approved sports for Prince Henry.

Proof that tennis was a gentleman's game is found in John Earle's *Microcosmography* (1628), where the character of a gentleman at the university is described thus: "The two marks of his seniority is the bare velvet of his gown and his proficiency at tennis, where when he can once play a set he is a freshman no more."

In a country of inclement weather indoor games were bound to be popular. Furthermore, even the most active could not always be running, leaping, or hitting balls, and there are always those who have no desire to engage in active sports. For moments of less activity there were cards and table games. The origin of card games dates far back in history. Cardplaying had spread over Europe before it crossed the Channel into England. By the fifteenth century card games were common in England, and Edward IV in 1463 forbade the importation of playing cards to protect local cardmakers. By 1496 cardplaying was added to the list of activities forbidden the laboring classes. Henry VII's law read that servants and apprentices could play at cards only during the Christmas holiday, and then only in their master's house. In 1628 a charter was granted the London Company of Makers of Playing Cards.

It is uncertain whether English cards were derived more from French or Spanish cards. They appear to have taken the names of their suits and the symbols from both. The Spanish suits were *espadas* (swords), *copas* (cups), *dineros* (coins), and *bastos* (clubs). In France the suits were *piques* (spears), *coeurs* (hearts), *carreaux* (squares or lozenges), and *trefles* (trefoils). The face cards on French cards were named after various emperors, queens, or famous knights. The knaves appeared in various dress, including armor, depending on the current events of a particular period. Samuel Rowlands in 1612, in his *Knave of Hearts*, indicated that the English jacks were dressed in the costume of Chaucer's time.

> We are abused in a great degree;
> For, there's no knaves so wronged as are we
> By those that chiefly should be our part-takers:
> And thus it is my masters, you cardmakers.
> All other knaves are at their own free will,
> To brave it out, and follow fashion still
> In any cut, according to the time:
> But we poor knaves (I know not for what crime)
> Are kept in piebald suits which we have worn
> Hundred of years; this hardly can be borne.
> The idle-headed French devised us first,
> Who of all fashion-mongers is the worst.

450

Cardplaying, as well as dicing, was condemned by many. Some claimed it to be an invention of the Devil, and because the cards were named, they described cardplaying as a form of idolatry. John Northbrooke in his *Treatise wherein Dicing, Dancing . . . Are Reproved*, published about 1577, felt that cardplaying was not so evil as dicing because there was less trust in chance. But since cardplaying furnished small training for the mind, he saw little good in it. According to him, cheating was prevalent, "either by pricking of a card, or pinching of it, cutting at the nick; either by a bum-card [i.e., a raised or marked card for cheating] finely, under, over, or in the middle, &c. and what not to deceive?" Although moralists condemned cardplaying and rogues cheated, the various games remained extremely popular through the years. Primero was played by Elizabeth I. It was a game at which two or three could play. In this the ace of spades was the best card, as it was always trump in "ombre," which succeeded "primero." Three players could participate in ombre, each receiving nine cards apiece. Trumps were named by the first player. James I liked "maw," which later became known as "five cards." In this game the five of trumps was the best card, the ace of hearts next, then the ace of trumps, and the knave. The ace of diamonds was the worst card unless diamonds were trumps. Two people could play this game—each receiving five cards. "Ruff" and "honor" required four players. Twelve cards apiece were dealt out, leaving four cards in the stack. The top card was turned up and its suit was named as trumps. The player with the ace of trumps could get the stack pile and discard four other cards. As in poker, the player bet on his hand in "post and pair." A poker face and a good bluff often won the game regardless of the cards held.

Dicing was popular and was more condemned even than cardplaying. Thomas Elyot's *Book Named the Governor* has little good to say of this form of play. "And I suppose there is not a more plain figure of idleness than playing at dice. For besides that therein is no manner of exercise of the body or mind, they which do play thereat must seem to have no portion of wit or cunning, if they will be called fair players." John

Northbrooke's treatise against dicing objects to it for similar reasons. To him only play which exercises the mind or body is permissible. He cites various laws against dicing but says that royalty sets a bad example, and certainly Henry VIII was an enthusiastic gambler. Nicholas Faret, giving instruction to young gentlemen in *The Honest Man,* indicated that they should know games at hazard, but they should not be gamblers, for as he says, "There are none but great princes (whose condition can never be miserable) which may abandon themselves boldly unto it [gambling]."

The most popular dice game was called hazard. In this game the thrower calls a number between five and nine before throwing. If he throws the number called or a number with a fixed correspondence to it, he "throws a nick" and wins. If he throws two aces or a deuce and ace he "throws out" and loses. If neither, he throws until the first number thrown (the chance) comes up and he wins, or the number first called (the main) comes up, in which case he loses.

Gambling took another form in betting, particularly on horse races. Public races were established by James I, and one of the famous races was the "Bell Course" race which had for a prize a silver bell.

There were other indoor games less harmful to the moral well-being of the participant. Among these was backgammon, called "tables" in Tudor times, probably because the board consisted of two tables hinged together. The ancient game of chess has been a favorite with contemplative men throughout the ages, though James I felt that, far from relaxing a person, chess filled his head with troubles. In England chess assumed its modern shape by Elizabeth's time, a little later than in Europe. Similar to chess was the philosopher's game in which the board was in the form of a parallelogram with squares marked. Instead of chessmen, the counters used had numbers on them. Each player had twenty-four counters, of which one was a king. The object was to take the opponent's king and make a triumph.

Shovelboard was played on a long table. The flat weights were shoved down the table to reach certain points. This is essentially the same as the shovelboard (or shuffleboard) played on board ship except for the use of the table.

Billiards in its modern form is not too different from the game known to the Elizabethans. The table was covered with a fine green cloth and had six pockets. One difference was that six-teenth-century players used a small ivory arch called a port which stood where the pyramid spot stands now; they also used an ivory peg called a king at the other end of the table. The players had two balls with which they tried to pass the port first and then gently to touch the king.

In the evening, for those men who preferred to pit their skill against the flashing eyes and nimble feet of a pretty girl, the music would sound and the dance would begin—either a "basse" dance in which the dancer's feet did not leave the ground or the "haute" dance which required hops, leaps, kicks, or stamps. A dance could be a dignified movement or a lively form of exer-cise. The pavan and allemande were stately dances, whereas the galliard and volta or lavolta were more lively. In many of the dances, as in the basse dance and the pavan, the man and woman danced side by side. The courante (sometimes spelled "coranto") presented another form, in which three couples in a straight line faced the onlookers, then each other, and finally turned around again to face the audience.

Dancing, however, was not approved by all. John North-brooke described dancing as one of the evils of the world. In his diatribe he called this amusement "the vilest vice of all" and then went on to say that "truly it cannot easily be said what mischiefs the sight and hearing do receive hereby . . . ; they dance with disordinant gestures, and with monstrous thumping of the feet, to pleasant sounds, to wanton songs, to dishonest verses."

All sports did not require active participation. One of the favorite pastimes for all was a bearbaiting match or a cock-fight. Cockfighting was an old sport. In the early days boys took a cock to their schoolmasters on Shrove Tuesday. Before the masters could claim the cocks, the boys were allowed to fight them in the yard. Or else they engaged in another pastime called

453

cockthrowing, which involved throwing sticks and stones at the cock until it was killed.

The first cockpit was not built until the time of Henry VIII. He liked the sport so much that he added a cockpit to his palace at Whitehall. Drury Lane (or the old Phoenix) Theatre began as a cockpit. Philip Stubbes tells us that houses were erected for the purpose of cockfighting, that flags and pennants would fly on the day of a fight, and that proclamations were sent to announce the coming event.

Bearbaitings were often announced by a parade with the bearward leading the bears through the street, probably accompanied by music and jesters. As early as 1526 Paris Garden in Southwark became a popular resort for bearbaiting and bullbaiting. There the bear or bull was chained to a stake and four or six mastiff dogs were turned loose. As one dog was killed another was set upon the bear. The sight of tearing flesh and spilling blood accompanied by the yelps of the dogs and the growls of the bear evidently gave the crowds great pleasure, for the events were largely attended. Robert Crowley in *One and Thirty Epigrams* gives us a good picture of the event.

> What folly is this, to keep with danger,
> A great mastiff dog and a foul ugly bear?
> And to this only end, to see them two fight,
> With terrible tearing, a full ugly sight.
> And yet me think those men be most fools of all
> Whose store of money is but very small,
> And yet every Sunday they will surely spend
> One penny or two the bearward's living to mend.
> At Paris Garden each Sunday a man shall not fail
> To find two or three hundreds for the bearward's vail.
> One halfpenny a piece they use for to give.
> When some have no more in their purse, I believe.

These brutal sports were favored by royalty, aristocrats, and the lower classes alike. Cockfighting was highly favored by James I, and Elizabeth entertained the French and Danish ambassadors on two different occasions by attending a bearbaiting. The Puritans and the city aldermen objected to this sport, not for humane reasons but because of the disorderliness of the crowds who attended. Bearbaitings were usually held on Sunday, a fact that increased the disfavor of the Puritans. The city aldermen were opposed to any large gathering, for the plague was a bitter enemy and spread easily in crowded areas. It was not until many years later, when the conditions of life improved for many people, that these sports came to be looked upon as brutal. But in the sixteenth and seventeenth centuries, when it was a common experience to see hangings, beheadings, and victims burned at the stake, the sight of dogs and bears tearing at one another must have been only a mild form of amusement.

SUGGESTED READING

General works covering various sports and recreations include Joseph Strutt. *The Sports and Pastimes of the People of England,* edited and enlarged by J. Charles Cox (London, 1903), which, although written in 1801, gives a comprehensive picture of most pastimes from medieval times; other general works are Christina Hole, *English Sports and Pastimes* (London, 1949) and Dodgson H. Madden, *The Diary of Master William Silence: A Study of Shakespeare and of Elizabethan Sport* (London, 1897; 1907). Volume II of *Shakespeare's England* (2 vols., Oxford, 1916) has several chapters on the subject, with special attention to Shakespeare's knowledge. Each chapter has a useful bibliography. A seventeenth-century work on games of chance and some sports is Charles Cotton, *The Complete Gamester: or, Instructions How to Play at Billiards, Trucks, Bowls, and Chess . . . To which is Added the Arts and Mysteries of Riding, Racing, Archery, and Cockfighting* (London, 1674; reprinted with the title *Games and Gamesters . . .* (London, 1930).

Thomas Frost, *The Old Showmen and the Old London Fairs* (London, 1874) has several chapters covering the Tudor and Stuart periods, and James H. Bloom, *Folk-Lore, Old Customs and Superstitions in Shakespeare's Land* (London, 1930) supplies information about fairs and festivals as well as children's games.

Edmund H. Burke, *The History of Archery* (London, 1958) has a good chapter on "The Yeomen Bowmen." Roger Ascham's *Toxophilus* (1545) was reprinted in an edition by Edward Arber in his series of English Reprints (London, 1869). For more titles see Clement C. Parker, *Compendium of Works on Archery* (Philadelphia, 1950).

General works on fencing include J. D. Aylward, *The English Master of Arms* (London, 1956) and Egerton Castle, *Schools and*

Masters of Fence (London, 1893), which surveys various works on the subject and contains illustrations from sixteenth- and seventeenth-century works. George Silver's defense of the English method, *Paradoxes of Defense* (1599), was reprinted with an introduction by J. Dover Wilson (Oxford, 1933).

Several contemporary works on hunting and hawking have been reprinted: George Turberville, *The Noble Art of Venery or Hunting* with the title *Turbervile's Booke of Hunting, 1576* (Oxford, 1908); Thomas Cokayne, *A Short Treatise of Hunting* (1591; London, 1932); Edmund Bert, *An Approved Treatise of Hawks and Hawking* (1619; London, 1891); and a section from Richard Blome, *The Gentleman's Recreation* (1686) under the title *Hawking or Faulconry by Richard Blome* (London, 1939).

Gerald E. Bentley has recently edited the anonymous *Art of Angling, 1577* (Princeton, 1958), which has particular interest because Mr. Bentley believes it to be the source for much of Izaak Walton's more famous *Compleat Angler*. Gervase Markham, *The Pleasures of Princes, or Good Men's Recreations* (1614) and Colonel Robert Venables, *The Experienced Angler* (1662) have been reprinted in one volume (London, 1927).

Information on dancing will be found in Mabel Dolmetsch, *Dances of England and France from 1450 to 1600* (London, 1949), which gives a good account of the dances and how to dance them, with music. Several contemporary works have been reprinted: Jehan Tabourot [Thoinot Arbeau, pseud.] *Orchesography* (1588), edited by Cyril Beaumont in an English translation (London, 1925); Sir John Davies, *Orchestra* (1596), edited by E. M. W. Tillyard (London, 1945); and Henry Peacham, *The Complete Gentleman* (1622; Oxford, 1906), which covers other accomplishments as well.

Julian Marshall, *The Annals of Tennis* (London, 1878) is a complete history of the game and gives a description of courts and the rules of play. Kenneth Matthews, *British Chess* (London, 1948) has a chapter on "The Early Game in Britain." For information on cards see Cotton's *Complete Gamester*, already cited, William G. Benham, *Playing Cards* (London, 1931), and Edward S. Taylor, *The History of Playing Cards* (London, 1865). A good contemporary description of bearbaiting is given in Robert Laneham's account of the entertainment of Queen Elizabeth at Kenilworth in 1575, reprinted by F. J. Furnivall under the title *Robert Laneham's Letter* . . . (New York, 1907).

Plate 1. Bowling. From *Le centre de l'amour* (*ca.* 1600).

Plate 2. Balloon ball and wrestling in the foreground, with other activities in the background. From Erasmo di Valvasone, *La caccia* (*ca.* 1602).

Plate 3. Frontispiece to Matthew Walbancke's *Annalia Dubrensia* (1636), showing some of the activities of the Cotswold Games.

461

Plate 4. Children's games, including a form of bowling, whipping the top, and walking on stilts. From Johann Amos Comenius, *Orbis sensualium pictus* (1685).

Plate 5. Children with hobby horse and tennis racket. From *Le centre de l'amour* (*ca.* 1600).

Plate 6. Ice skating. From *Le centre de l'amour* (*ca.* 1600).

Plate 7. Swimming. From Everard Digby, *De arte natandi* (1587).

465

Plate 8. A jousting match. From *Le centre de l'amour* (*ca.* 1600).

Plate 9. Fencing school. From Johann Amos Comenius, *Orbis sensualium pictus* (1685).

Plate 10. Tripping up the opponent. From Camillo Agrippa, *Trattato di scientia d'arme* (1568).

Plate 11. Queen Elizabeth being offered the knife to slit
the throat of the slain deer. From George Turberville, *The
Noble Art of Venery* (*ca.* 1576).

Plate 12. Hunting the deer with hounds. From George Turberville,
The Noble Art of Venery (*ca.* 1576).

Plate 13. Boar hunting with a spear
with a crossbar. From Guillaume de La
Perriere, *La morosophie* (1553).

Plate 14. Hawking. From Erasmo di Valvasone, *La caccia* (*ca.* 1602).

Plate 15. Falcons attacking in flight. From George Turberville, *The Book of Falconry* (1575).

Plate 16. Fishing. From *Stirpium, insignium nobilitatis* (*ca.* 1602).

474

Plate 17. A game of tennis. From *Le centre de l'amour* (*ca.* 1600).

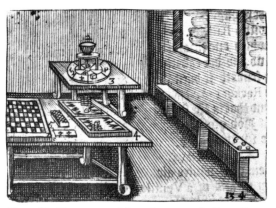

Plate 18. Games requiring the use of dice. From
Johann Amos Comenius, *Orbis sensualium pictus*
(1685).

Plate 19. Shovelboard. From *Le centre de l'amour* (*ca.* 1600).

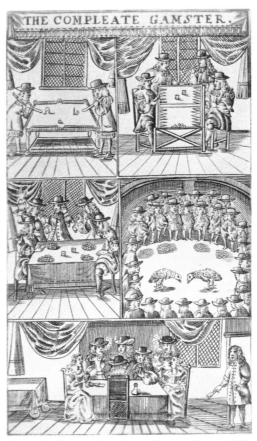

Plate 20. Frontispiece from Charles Cotton's *The Complete Gamester* (1680), showing billiards, tables, dicing, cockfighting, and cards.

THE

Commendation

of Cockes, and Cock-fighting.

Wherein is fhewed, that Cocke-
*fighting was before the com-
ming of Chrift.*

LONDON,
Printed for *Henrie Tomes,* and are
to be fold at his Shop ouer a-
gainft Graies Inne gate in Holburne,
1 6 o 7.

Plate 21. Title-page to George Wilson's *The Commendation of Cocks* (1607).

The Government of England
under Elizabeth

By Conyers Read

SOME five years after Elizabeth's accession to the throne Sir Thomas Smith wrote the first account of her government. Sir Thomas was a man of many parts, one of the distinguished Greek scholars of his time, Regius professor of civil law at Cambridge under Henry VIII, Principal Secretary to Henry's son Edward, Member of Parliament, Privy Councillor, Principal Secretary under Elizabeth. He had besides a facile pen. No man in England was better qualified to write of her government. His discourse, *De republica Anglorum,* was not published until 1583, six years after his death, but it ran through five editions before the end of the reign.

Smith adds very little to our knowledge of the subject. The value of his discourse is its revelation of how the government appeared to a contemporary.

The earlier chapters of Smith's book reflected his classical background and consisted of a classification of different types of government after the pattern of Aristotle's *Politics.* Like Aristotle, he singled out three main types, monarchy, aristocracy, democracy, and went on to say that perfect examples of any one type were rare. Most commonwealths were a mixture. Although he did not precisely say so, he evidently regarded the Elizabethan government as a mixture of monarchial and aristocratic elements.

His approach to the government was by a definition of the people governed. "We in England," he wrote, "divide our men commonly into five sorts: gentlemen, citizens, yeomen, artificers and laborers."

The first three sorts are those which one way or another participate in the government. The fourth group Smith defined more particularly as day laborers, poor husbandmen—those who had no free land—and all artificers not yeomen or citizens. "These," he wrote, "have no voice nor authority in our commonwealth and no account is made of them but only to be ruled, not to rule others." And yet, he went on to say that at the local level men of this poorer sort were sometimes utilized for jury duty, or as churchwardens and constables.

Smith, in short, recognized and accepted a society of classes. He accepted no doubt what was known as the great chain of being, the social implications of which were well set forth in the 1547 book of homilies as follows:

Every degree of people in their vocation, calling, and office hath appointed to them their duty and order. Some are in high degree, some in low; some kings and princes, some inferiors and subjects; priests and laymen, masters and servants, fathers and children, husbands and wives, rich and poor and every one have need of other so that in all things is to be lauded and praised the goodly order of God without the which no house, no city, no commonwealth, can continue and endure.

The classic expression of this pattern of society is the speech which Shakespeare put into Ulysses' mouth in *Troilus and Cressida*, "Take but degree away, untune that string, and hark what discord follows."

The important fact is the general endorsement and justification of political and social inequality. On the political side it was the negation of the democratic principle. Democratic rule was indeed generally discredited everywhere in the sixteenth century, in all governments and all creeds, and those who advocated it were regarded very much as we in the West today regard Communists; and everywhere democratic advocates were persecuted. Sir Thomas in one place insisted that the classes should be marked by their attire. "A gentleman," he wrote, "must go like a gentleman, a yeoman like a yeoman, a rascal like a rascal." By rascal he meant not a bad fellow but a base fellow. This explains in part the persistent efforts of the government to control apparel.

In the sixteenth century the social reformers, by and large, preached not equality but the due recognition by each class of its duties and responsibilities. This of course did not mean that the various classes were enclosed in watertight compartments. The class system was not breaking down, but there was a steady recruitment of the upper classes from the lower classes. The yeoman might, and often did, gather together enough property to enter the ranks of the gentry. What was more important, prosperous townsmen, aspiring to be gentry, were buying their way into the countryside. Sir Thomas pointed out: "As for gentlemen, they be made good cheap in England. For whosoever studieth the laws of the realm, who studieth in the universities, who professeth liberal sciences, and, to be short, who can live idly and without manual labor, and will bear the port, charge, and countenance of a gentleman, he shall be called Master . . . and shall be taken for a gentleman . . . and (if need be) a king of Heralds shall also give him for money arms newly made and invented." It was merely a matter of money or its equivalent; even the pedigree was a matter of money.

The same thing was true in the further ascent from the gentry to the nobility. Elizabeth herself was very chary about creating peers, but most of the great noblemen in her reign were recent upstarts. Of sixty-two peers in 1560, thirty-seven held titles conferred since the accession of her father. The Dudleys, the Sidneys, the Russells, the Wriothesleys, the Herberts, the Cecils, all belonged in that category. The Wars of the Roses had pretty well wiped out the old nobility. Their titles perhaps survived but often had been transferred to new men. If the bottles were old, the wine was new.

But there was a flow from class to class both ways. If some were climbing up, others were slipping down. The law of primogeniture which controlled the descent of the title and the real property, while providing for the first-born, made no provision at all for the younger son, who had more or less to shift for himself. Without real estate, the current coin of wealth and social prestige, he tended to go downwards, from nobility to gentry, from gentry to yeomanry, from yeomanry to something below. The result was a certain blurring of class levels, accentuated by a good deal of intermarriage. There was nothing hard and fast about English class lines, as there was for example in France under the old régime.

The process of change within the social pattern was quickened by the wholesale confiscation of church lands associated with the break from Rome. This land came into the real-estate market and a considerable part of it was purchased by the nouveaux riches who had made their fortunes in the city or in public office. Land, after all, in the days before stocks and bonds, provided one of the few opportunities for profitable investment. The purchasers brought to the countryside the attitudes and impulses of the market place, with little of the traditional and sentimental obligations recognized by the country gentlemen of the old school. For these newcomers, agriculture was not a way of life; it was a source of profit. They expected a yield upon their investments and presently discovered that rents might be raised and arable land enclosed and turned into pasture land to advantage. The social reformers of the time were constantly venting their spleen upon the encloser and the rack-renter. As Sir Thomas More put it, sheep were eating up men. The change was perhaps inevitable, but the death throes of a feudal, self-sustaining economy and the rise of a capitalist, profit-making economy were hard on the little man and brought about a great deal of distress and unrest. The sporadic riots which plagued the Elizabethan justices of the peace in almost every county in England were the fruits of this unrest; so was the marked increase in unemployment. One of the fears which constantly beset William Cecil in his forty-odd years of service as Elizabeth's chief counselor was that any foreign invader would find a great deal of domestic discontent to support him.

Queen Elizabeth at the age of twenty-five, without any overt opposition, ascended the English throne in November, 1558. She certainly had the best claim to it by inheritance, though her father, Henry VIII, repudiated his marriage to her mother and she had been declared a bastard by act of Parliament. The act still stood on the statute book at her accession, though Parliament had subsequently given to Henry the right to determine the succession, and Henry had named Elizabeth to succeed her half-sister Mary. There were those who maintained that Henry's will was a forgery. There were even those who asserted that Elizabeth's father was not Henry but her mother's paramour. But England at large accepted Elizabeth with enthusiasm.

She was unmarried, and until she did marry and have children she was the last of the direct Tudor line. Henry's will provided that, in default of offspring to Elizabeth, the succession should pass to the descendents of his younger sister Mary, the so-called Suffolk line, though actually the descendents of Henry's older sister Margaret, the so-called Stuart line, had the prior claim. There were other claimants as well.

At the time of Elizabeth's accession, the Suffolk line was represented by Catherine Grey, sister of the unfortunate Lady Jane Grey; the Stuart line by Mary Stuart, married to the Dauphin of France, already Queen of Scotland and presently to be Queen of France. English Protestants favored the Suffolk line, English Catholics the Stuart line. Elizabeth herself was noncommital. To the very end she remained noncommital.

The preferred solution of course was that she should marry and bear children. Until she was past childbearing age she was under constant pressure to marry, or if not to marry, to designate her successor. Parliament pressed her hard, particularly in the first decade of her reign, fearing that if she died, as she came near dying in 1562, the throne would pass to the Catholic Mary and the whole battle for the faith would have to be fought all over again. But neither Parliament nor the constant urgings of Lord Burghley, her most trusted counselor, prevailed. Elizabeth died unmarried. Indeed, she made a virtue of her spinsterhood. During the last twenty years of her reign, when everybody had abandoned hope of her marriage, they glorified her as the Virgin Queen.

She was without doubt the chief figure in her government, under God and under the law. And she could and did dispense with the application of the law in particular cases. The export trade of unfinished cloth, for example, was prohibited by law, and yet, by special license from the Crown, the export of unfinished cloth was the most important commodity in the English export trade. She could by proclamation come near to making the law, though it does not appear that she ever used the proclamation that way. She could and did assume the right to initiate legislation, though she did not always succeed in imposing her will upon the lawmaking body. She could exercise an absolute veto on laws passed by both Houses of Parliament. She had complete control over appointments to all offices under the Crown, including the judges of all the courts, even including the justices of the peace, and could at her pleasure dismiss any one of them. In fact, she delegated a considerable amount of patronage. In the administration of her finances, for example, Lord Burghley, her Lord Treasurer, appointed virtually all the officials having to do with the royal revenues, except those at the highest level, and he could generally influence the Queen to accept his choice in those.

In foreign affairs she was supreme and could make war or peace at her will. In practice she never declared war without the advice of her Council, though she often sought to make peace when her Councillors opposed it. The entire personnel in foreign affairs she herself appointed. It is to be observed however that throughout her reign she had a resident ambassador in only one country, France, though she generally had a representative in Scotland and, after 1584, in the Dutch Low Countries. In Spain she had no resident ambassador after Dr. John Man's recall in 1567. She did however finance a secret intelligence service overseas organized by her Principal Secretaries, first by William Cecil, later by Walsingham, and ultimately by Robert Cecil; and on occasion she talked in person with the agents themselves.

Financially she enjoyed a considerable revenue from the rentals of Crown lands and from feudal dues. She also received the customary grant of the customs revenue for life at the beginning of her reign. The import and export duties were for the most part ad valorem duties, the percentage fixed by statute, but the basis for calculation was provided by a book of rates prepared by royal officials. By the simple expedient of increasing the prices in the book of rates she could, within reason, automatically increase the customs revenues. At times she farmed out customs revenues in particular ports or on particular commodities to private individuals. Robert, Earl of Essex, for example, had the farm of the import duties on sweet wines and made a handsome thing of it. Elizabeth's refusal to renew the grant in 1601 was the turning point of his fate.

All these independent sources of revenue taken together were inadequate to meet the ordinary expenses of government. What was short had to be made up by taxes levied by Parliament on the laity and by Convocation on the clergy. Elizabeth did not like to ask her people for money and on occasion liquidated some of the Crown lands rather than call on Parliament for taxes. Nevertheless, as time went on, and particularly after the outburst of war in 1585, she had to depend more and more on Parliamentary grants. And the burden of taxation grew steadily heavier upon her subjects.

Elizabeth's chief instrument of administration was the Privy Council, all appointed by herself. Their numbers varied at different times, never exceeding twenty. Some who were nominally of the Council rarely attended. And the active members of the Council were less than a dozen. But if we may judge from the records kept of their proceedings, they were more concerned as a body with the details of administration than with the formulation of policy. In really important matters there was an inner circle upon which Elizabeth chiefly depended. Foremost among these was William Cecil, Principal Secretary during the first fourteen years of her reign, Lord Burghley and Lord High Treasurer for the next twenty-eight years. Whatever his title, he was her chief counselor. She almost never reached an important decision without consulting him. Even so she was always the dominating figure and he always the obedient servant. Next to him in point of influence probably was Robert Dudley, Earl of Leicester, who had, and retained till the end of his days, a unique hold upon the Queen's affections. He was far inferior to Cecil in ability, in diligence, and in disinterested love of country. During the first decade of the reign Leicester's one consuming objective was to marry Elizabeth. After twenty years he finally abandoned hope and took another wife. Yet he never lost his place in her regard. According to the historian William Camden, within a month of Leicester's death in August, 1588, Elizabeth seriously contemplated appointing him to be Lieutenant General of the kingdom. Leicester appealed to the woman in Elizabeth, Cecil to the Queen. Apart from the Queen's marriage, which Leicester always aimed to prevent and Cecil to promote, they were not widely at variance in matters of policy, except that Leicester subordinated policy to personal interest, and Cecil's principal objective was always the welfare of Queen and country.

The other Councillors who belonged to the inner ring were Nicholas Bacon, the Lord Keeper in the first decade; Sir Francis Walsingham, who succeeded Cecil as Principal Secretary; and Sir Christopher Hatton in the second and third decades; Robert, Earl of Essex, and Robert Cecil in the fourth decade. Hatton and Essex belonged among the Queen's favorites, but were both men of marked ability. Hatton became first the eloquent spokesman of the Queen in the House of Commons and later her Lord Chancellor. Essex was an able soldier and a clever politician, but was "of a nature not be ruled" and finally ended a brilliant career at the block.

It is to be noted that during Elizabeth's reign only one ecclesiastic was a member of the Privy Council, and that the important members were all commoners, or else, like Leicester and Burghley, peers of her own creation.

It has been said that Elizabeth, like her father, deliberately nourished factions in her Privy Council on the principle of divide and rule. Certainly factions developed—in the first decade the Cecilians vs. the Leicesterians, in the last decade the Cecilians vs. Essex. In the second and third decades, when the Puritans were strong in the Council, the division expressed itself chiefly in foreign policy, the Puritans aiming to subordinate national considerations to religious ones, the *politiques* aiming to subordinate religious to national interests. Leicester was the titular head of the Puritans, Burghley of the *politiques*. But the driving spirit in the Puritan faction was Francis Walsingham. After Leicester's death in 1588 and Walsingham's in 1590, the Puritan faction faded away and was in a sense displaced by a war party led by Essex and a peace party led by the Cecils, father and son. But it is easy to overemphasize these lines of cleavage. There was a great deal of the Puritan in Burghley, and when the wars came he was as stout a supporter of military and naval operations as anyone was.

The Privy Councillors were not all of one type, but those upon whom Elizabeth chiefly depended, with the exception of Leicester and Essex, were able and patriotic public servants. They were always subordinate to their mistress. The two who tried to coerce her, Norfolk halfheartedly, Essex belligerently, lost their heads—figuratively and literally lost their heads.

Generally speaking, those in the Queen's service were inadequately paid. But they were allowed to exploit their official positions to increase their income, by fees, by perquisites, by the sale of offices under their control, and by lucrative concessions of various sorts. Indeed, public officials from top to bottom sustained themselves by the practice of what we should call graft. Even Cecil himself, otherwise a model of integrity, grew rich from the sale of wardships under his control as Master of the Court of Wards. Elizabeth in this respect was penny-wise and pound-foolish. What she gave away was worth considerably more than what it would have cost her to provide adequate compensation for her servants. Her armies were shot through with corruption. Fortunately her navy was in honest and competent hands.

Next to herself, the most important part of Elizabeth's government was her Parliament, composed of two houses, the House of Lords and the House of Commons.

The Lords were made up of the hereditary lay peers and the spiritual peers, that is, the two archbishops and the twenty-odd bishops of the Anglican church. The lay peers outnumbered the spiritual peers two to one. Altogether there were some ninety members of the Upper House. The spiritual peers were appointed by the Queen and could be discharged by the Queen. On more than one occasion she threatened to "unfrock" them. Archbishop Grindal was in fact deprived of his office because he was too favorably inclined towards the Puritans. As for the lay peers, they might not be discharged but they might be outnumbered. The Queen might create as many new ones as she pleased. In point of fact she created very few new peers. They were not necessary to strengthen her position in the Lords. On one occasion when she proposed new creations, she discovered that her candidates were not disposed to accept title unless they were provided with estates to sustain it, and that the thrifty Queen was not willing to supply. Burghley himself refused promotion from a barony to an earldom on those grounds.

The Lords were indeed very tractable to the royal wishes. Their presiding officer was the Keeper of the Great Seal, or his equivalent, the Lord Chancellor. During the first decade of the reign Nicholas Bacon occupied that office. But after Cecil was raised to the peerage in 1571 he appears to have looked after the Queen's interests in the Upper House until he died twenty-seven years later. The Lords were called to the meeting of Parliament by writs directed to each one individually. If they were unable to attend, they might give their proxies to some other peer, a privilege denied to the members of the Lower House.

Bills might originate in either house, though it was generally recognized that money bills (i.e., those levying taxes) should originate in the Commons. On one occasion, when Burghley thought the taxes offered by the Lower House were inadequate to meet the royal needs and proposed to introduce a bill in the Lords supplying more, he had to accept rebuke from the Commons.

The more important and far more independent house was the House of Commons. It was elected. When the Parliament was summoned, royal writs went down to the sheriff of each county directing him to arrange for elections in the various constituencies. There were two types of constituency—first the counties, second the boroughs. The English counties elected two members each to represent them in the Commons; the boroughs generally sent two members. Boroughs were simply urban communities within the counties which had, one way or another, acquired the right to separate representation in the House of Commons. The Crown might create new boroughs at pleasure. It would have been an obvious way to strengthen the government position in the Lower House. Elizabeth indeed created or restored thirty-one boroughs, adding sixty-two members to the Commons. But there is no evidence that this action was taken to pack Parliament. The increase seems to have been due rather to local pressures than to government interest. At the end of the reign the House of Commons numbered 462.

County elections were held in the County Court, which met once a month and was made up of those freeholders within the county who held freehold land to the annual rental value of forty shillings. Generally the value of land was expressed in terms of annual rental. Since the usual price for land bought and sold was designated as twenty years' purchase, i.e., twenty times the annual rental, the county voter had to hold land by freehold tenure worth at least £40. This debarred smaller freeholders; it also debarred those whose land was held by some other tenure or was leased or rented.

Within boroughs the right of franchise varied. In the great majority of cases it seems to have been limited to a small oligarchy which controlled the town government. In all except a few cases the voters in the town were a small minority of its inhabitants.

The great majority of Englishmen had nothing to say about the election of M.P.'s. Nevertheless, as Sir Thomas Smith declared, "The consent of Parliament was taken to be every man's consent."

The borough members made up something like four-fifths of the House of Commons. It might have been presumed that urban interests would have dominated the assembly. But there is no evidence in the debates as recorded or in the ensuing legislation of any conflict of urban and rural interests. The reason for this is not far to seek. The boroughs preferred to be represented by the gentry. In only a few of the larger cities, in London, for example, were they represented by citizens. The consequence was that very much the same type of man sat for the county and for the borough within the county. Sometimes the poorer boroughs were moved by pecuniary considerations. They had to pay wages to their member, two shillings a day. But even the more important boroughs wanted a patron, a friend in high places, and the ambitious country gentlemen wanted an opportunity to spend some time in London, to visit the Court, perhaps even to kiss the hand of the Queen. The lawyers were particularly eager to sit, since Parliament usually met in term time and gave them an opportunity to pursue their legal business. The county seat offered them greater prestige, but failing a county the gentleman would settle for a borough. Contested elections in both county and borough reveal the fact that the issues at stake were not primarily political or even religious, but as to whether a Cecil or an Essex would win the place. Instead of one gentleman to four townsmen, Elizabeth's later Parliaments contained four gentlemen to every townsman.

Elizabeth generally summoned Parliament because she needed money. Altogether, in a reign of forty-four years, she called ten Parliaments, but the Parliament of 1563 sat again after a long prorogation in 1567, and the Parliament of 1572 sat again in 1576 and again in 1581. So there were really thirteen Parliaments. The largest interval between Parliaments was four years. Parliament was not regarded as part of the ordinary machinery of government. In only two cases—her first Parliament in 1559 to establish her religious settlement and her sixth Parliament in 1586 to deal with Mary Queen of Scots—can it be said that the purpose of calling them was not primarily fiscal. Cecil on more than one occasion when war was in question advised that Parliament should be consulted, but Elizabeth would not have it so.

She tried to manage her Parliaments, and always saw to it

that some of her Privy Councillors were present. During the first decade of her reign William Cecil was her spokesman in the Commons, and when he was elevated to the peerage in 1571 he occupied the same position in the Lords. Sir Christopher Hatton was elected to the Commons and he acted as spokesman for the Queen until his appointment to be Lord Chancellor in 1587. During the last decade of her reign Robert Cecil served in that position. All three of them were competent speakers—Hatton particularly so. It was part of their business also to maintain harmony between Crown and Commons. In this particular they were not altogether successful. Elizabeth did not get on well with her Parliaments. They were quite prepared to grant her the taxes she asked for, but they wanted things from her in return. They wanted a definite commitment from her on her marriage and on the succession in case her marriage should be fruitless. Above all they wanted reforms in the established church—in its vestments, its ritual, and its government. All of these demands she refused to entertain, on the grounds that they were her business, not theirs.

Parliamentary money grants took two forms, both of them inherited from earlier times. The first was the so-called fifteenth and tenth, which had a long history; the other was the subsidy. The fifteenth and tenth, originally a tax on movables, became a fixed amount in the fourteenth century, attached to lands rather than to movables and apportioned among the counties. There was no reassessment, each county paid what it had paid before. It amounted in the sixteenth century to £32,000. The subsidy, first introduced in Henry VIII's reign, attempted to tax income from wages and rents as well as movables. It too came to a fixed sum distributed among the counties. By the end of Elizabeth's reign it produced about £80,000. Action by Parliament in the matter was always in terms of these units. Grants were for fifteenths and tenths or a multiple of them and for subsidies or a multiple of them. In 1593, for example, Parliament granted six fifteenths and tenths and three subsidies. Usually payments were made in installments over a period of two or three years. During the last decade of Elizabeth's reign the average taxpayer paid some one of these installments annually.

The objection to this form of tax was that it laid the burden where it had been and made little or no attempt to relate the burden to the distribution of wealth. In the case of the fifteenth and tenth the burden was distributed as it had been in 1334. No reassessment was made. The burden was distributed by local assessors, appointed by the local M.P.'s, generally on the basis of land holdings, not personalty. All taxes in England tended to fall upon the land, because a man's land could not be concealed; his movable property could.

In the case of the subsidy, the commissioners in charge of collection were appointed by the Crown, though the actual assessing was by local committees appointed by the commissioners. A taxpayer's rating was recorded in what was known as a subsidy book. If his name appeared in that book he became "a subsidy man." It exposed him to all sorts of other local tax burdens; poor relief, musters, ship money, what not. So Elizabethans tried to keep their names out of the subsidy book or to keep their ratings as low as might be. The influential were outrageously under assessed, and the burden, both of the fifteenth and tenth and of the subsidy, fell disproportionately upon the less well to do. In 1593 Burghley observed that some of the richest landowners in England were not taxed above £80 in land, and in London, "where was the greatest part of the riches of the realm," none above £200 in goods, and but eight above £100.

He pointed out that one subsidy, honestly assessed, would yield as much as three subsidies as currently collected. But nothing effective was done about it. Even with the inequalities, the tax burden upon the English was far lighter than it was elsewhere. There were no excises, no profits taxes unless those profits found expression in increased receipts from rentals, in increased stocks of merchandise, or in increased luxuries in living. It is interesting to note that the rate of tax on jewelry in the subsidy bill of 1593 was higher than on other forms of property. But one doubts whether much or any of it found its way into the subsidy book.

Parliament was commonly referred to in the sixteenth century as the High Court, but such judicial functions as it actually exercised in that century were attached to the Lords, who occasionally heard appeals on writs of error from lower courts. It was primarily a lawmaking body, with no constitutional limit upon its legislative power except the royal veto.

In practice the superior courts in England were the Court of Queen's Bench, which heard criminal pleas, otherwise called pleas of the Crown; the Court of Common Pleas, which heard pleas on matters civil; the Court of Exchequer which dealt with cases arising out of the royal revenues; and the Court of Chancery, which dealt with cases in equity. All of these Courts met in Westminster Hall.

Twice a year between law terms, during Lent and midsummer, when the Queen's Bench and Common Pleas were not in session, the judges divided into couples and each couple went on circuit to the six different circuits into which England was divided. They held court for all pleas in each of the counties within their circuit, usually sitting from one to three days, at the county seat. The Sheriff of the county attended to local arrangements, submitted a panel of jurors, and had the defendants and the plaintiffs involved at hand. He was also expected to entertain the visiting judges. These local sessions were originally designed to maintain uniformity in the common law administration at Westminster and in the counties, and to curb local bias and prejudice. Like all the Elizabethan courts, their function was not confined to matters judicial. The justices on assize conveyed the royal purposes and the royal wishes to the county at large and kept the Crown informed of local conditions, local attitudes, local desires. They were indeed the vital connecting link between the Queen and her counties.

There were besides other courts established by the Tudor monarchs to try cases with which the royal courts for one reason or another appeared incompetent to deal. The most significant of these was the Court of Star Chamber, made up of the Queen's Privy Council with the Chief Justices of the Queen's Bench and the Common Pleas. Its procedure followed rather the pattern of the Roman civil law than of the common law. Testimony from witnesses was taken in writing. There was no jury. Star Chamber, named for the room in Westminster Hall where it sat, had been organized by Henry VII to deal with civil disorders. It was used for many other purposes, largely for dealing with disobedience to royal commands. On one occasion it tried William Davison, the Queen's Secretary, for indiscretion in the interpretation of royal orders. It dealt with forgery, slander, libel. Strangely enough, it became for a time the tribunal to which disputed elections for the House of Commons were referred.

It was regarded askance by the common lawyers but was not unpopular with the rank and file of the people, who looked to it for protection against powerful nobles in the country whom local juries did not dare find guilty. Later, under the Stuarts, when the issue was definitely joined between the Crown and Parliament, it was violently attacked, and like all the other so-called prerogative courts it was swept away in the Great Rebellion. Other prerogative courts were the Court of Requests, set up for dealing with poor men's cases, and the Court of Wards, which administered the royal wards of the Crown and contributed not a little to the royal revenues, to say nothing of the perquisites to its officials. Under Elizabeth, the Mastership of the Wards was regarded as the choicest plum in the gift of the Crown. Lord Burghley held that position during most of Elizabeth's reign and made a modest fortune out of it.

It was through the judiciary that the Queen maintained her contact with local government. And it was the local justices of the peace into whose hands by little and little the control of local government passed.

The justices were named by the Lord Chancellor in a Commission of the Peace which was issued at irregular intervals. Their term of office was not defined and in the majority of cases they served for life. But new names could be added and old ones dropped by the issue of a new Commission. Elizabeth herself kept a close eye upon the J.P.'s and revised the list from time to time. Their number varied from twenty to sixty in each county. In 1589 there were 1,738 all told.

The law provided that J.P.'s should have at least £20 income from lands. They were in fact of the gentry, including some noblemen, and were of course residents of the county in which they sat. This gave the county a comfortable sense of being ruled by one of their own and not by a "foreigner," an imposed outsider. The J.P.'s taken as a whole were in fact the natural leaders of the country. Unlike the French noblesse, they lived in the countryside which they governed and understood it, though more than once the Queen had to admonish them for flocking to London and the Court and to send them home. They were from the same class, by and large they were the same men, who sat in the House of Commons. It might almost be said that they made the law at Westminster, interpreted it, and enforced it in the county. Consequently, statute law became sometimes rather a register of good resolutions than an effective order, particularly if the enforcement of it ran counter to the interests of the gentry class. What they said in Westminster they could more or less gainsay in the counties. Their local autonomy was in fact very considerable.

Generally speaking, the office of justice of the peace was held by the great county families. The listing of them was a sort of local social register. Although the office was not hereditary, it often passed on from father to son. We have here indeed a sort of revived feudalism in which the local magistrate was the lord of the manor, supported by the traditional loyalties of the countryside. Very often he held the right of advowson to the village church; that is to say, he nominated the rector. As legislator in the Commons, he placed in his own hands the fixing of wages, the maintenance of the roads, and the care of the poor, and he applied all these in his own interest. As Kenneth Pickthorn observes in *Early Tudor Government: Henry VII* (Cambridge, Eng., 1934), what the gentry wanted done, the Crown could get done very easily; what they did not mind being done, it could get easily enough. What would happen if the Crown should want something which that class was determined should not be done, was a question still to be settled, even still to be raised.

The justice could act as magistrate, alone or with another, but his more extended powers were expressed in the assembly of the justices of the county, four times a year, in Quarter Sessions. For that meeting, as for the semiannual courts of the judge of assize, the Sheriff provided a panel for a grand jury of presentment and for trial juries, and saw to it that plaintiffs and defendants were on hand. It was a considerable company and came as near to a county assembly as England was to come. In this respect it had displaced the County Court, which had lost most of its significance and become little more than a gathering of voters for county members to Parliament. William Lambarde, the Kentish antiquary, in charging the grand jury at Kent Quarter Sessions, more than once pointed out with pride that the law was locally applied and enforced not by "foreign" officials but by kinsfolk and neighbors. They determined in a local grand jury who should be tried and by a local petty jury who were innocent and who were guilty. The trouble was, as Lambarde insisted, that, whether for fear or favor, the grand jury did not present and the trial jury would not condemn. That, he thought, was the reason why prerogative courts like Star Chamber were springing up and the liberties of Englishmen were by little and little diminished.

In the Commission of the Peace distinction was made between the ordinary judges and those specifically designated whose presence was essential for certain decisions. These special ones came to be known as "of the quorum." At the outset they were men learned in the law and served to prevent unlearned colleagues from acting counter to the law. The commission also provided for a *custos rotulorum*, keeper of the county records. He appointed the Clerk of the Peace and was, if any one was, the President Justice. The office had considerable local prestige and later was generally, though not always, conferred upon the Lord Lieutenant when that office was created.

The J.P., the Clerk of the Peace and even Shakespeare's "coram" and "custalorum" were often the butt of the dramatists. Too often they knew no law, and there was a flourishing book business in guides for the justices in the sixteenth and seventeenth centuries. But what they lacked in law, which could generally be supplied by their clerks, they more than made up by their acquaintance with the countryside. Their administrative duties were probably more important than their judicial duties, and the Crown looked largely to them in all local matters from the fixing of wages to the collection of taxes and the levy of troops.

The Sheriff was the old leader of Crown officials in the county and he still continued to function as the titular head of the county. His official duties were in part fiscal, in part judicial, in large measure social. He was in general responsible for the police of the county, the keeping of the jails, the execution of capital punishment. He held office for one year only and was annually selected by the Queen herself from a list of eligibles, in the ceremony known as "the pricking of the sheriffs." It was generally held that he should have some military experience, though when the wars came he was nudged aside and the military aspects of the county passed into the hands of the Lord Lieutenant and his deputies.

The Lord Lieutenant was usually a nobleman, very often a Privy Councillor. Quite frequently two or three counties were assigned to one Lord Lieutenant. And there were counties which had none. Generally speaking, the imminence of war quickened the royal interest in the office. That was so in 1569; it was so in 1588. The office conferred great social prestige. Burghley himself made a great point of it and felt abused when the Lord Lieutenantship of a county in which he had an interest went to someone else. He was indeed Lord Lieutenant of three counties: Lincolnshire, Herts, and Essex.

Being no soldier, Burghley functioned through Deputy Lieutenants. So did most of the others, generally appointing Deputies from the local gentry. It was felt that half-trained troops would serve better under officers selected from the natural leaders of their own counties. Actually there was an acute shortage of seasoned officers. What few there were with actual battle experience were in Ireland and the Low Countries. But they were fighting England's battles in both places and could not be too heavily drawn upon.

The army, such as it was, was based upon the musters of all the able-bodied men (sixteen to sixty) in the kingdom. Some part of them received a little training and were alluded to as the trained bands. Probably the most intensive effort to mobilize the military strength of the realm was made in 1588 to meet the approaching Spanish Armada. Walsingham, six months before the Armada came, asserted that he and Burghley between them had organized and trained 50,000 men for the defense of the kingdom and the Queen. These figures come close to a report two years later, which gave 42,000 trained men, 54,000 equipped but not trained, and 6,000 neither trained nor equipped.

If we estimate the trained bands at 50,000 men in the aggregate, we come as close to accuracy as the available figures support. It is worth noting, however, that of this array not more than 14,000 were mobilized when the Armada was actually in the Channel. This however does not include forces gathered in the North to guard the postern gate or in the maritime counties along the Channel to repel landings. One estimate puts the troops in the maritime counties at a little over 20,000.

Horsemen were furnished by the gentry in proportion to their means, by the clergy, and by the recusants. We have no complete figures of those forthcoming in 1588. Figures for the following year come to a little over 10,000.

Generally speaking, the trained bands were not used for military service outside England. For service in the Low Countries and in France troops were drafted, usually from the able-bodied unemployed, commonly known as rogues and vagabonds, or from the jails. William Lambarde pointed out that this accounted for the vagabond soldiers produced by the foreign wars. When they came back they had no jobs waiting for them; instead they joined the growing army of the unemployed and were a serious menace to peace because of the plundering habits developed in foreign service.

There was a good deal of corruption in the drafting of them by the local J.P's, who sometimes levied twice the number required and then allowed half of them to buy their way out. Sir John Falstaff made merry with the ragged regiments which were the fruits of this corruption. And yet the English soldier overseas turned out to be a good fighting man, even when he lacked pay and lacked food and went to battle in rags.

Shortly after Elizabeth ascended the throne she established a national church under royal supremacy. It was based upon the second Edwardian Prayer Book and on the Edwardian Articles of Faith, though with some conservative modifications. It was imposed upon the nation by an Act of Uniformity which provided severe punishment for those who administered or attended any other service. Those who refused to attend the established church were fined one shilling a Sunday and were subject to ecclesiastical censure. The fine was so small that it was not worth the expense of collecting it. Ecclesiastical censure might entail excommunication and unlimited imprisonment, though it rarely did. The choice was, indeed, between the established church and no church. Actually, the Act of Uniformity in its original form entailed very little physical hardship on the laity. And as for the clergy, though the Marian bishops with one exception refused to conform and were deprived, probably 95 per cent of the lower clergy accepted the new arrangements. Opposition to the Establishment came from the left and from the right—from the left by zealous Protestants who thought reform had not gone far enough; from the right from those who preferred the old faith. The radicals were a nuisance but not a menace; the Roman Catholics were at the start no more than passive resisters. We hear of them as recusants, refusers not rebels. In the remoter areas they often maintained old services and sheltered old priests. So long as they went no further the enforcement of the laws against them was languid. Without much doubt the old church steadily lost ground. There were no inquisitions, no martyrs, no stake. Elizabeth, as Francis Bacon observed, had no wish "to make windows into men's hearts and secret thoughts." So long as they behaved themselves, what they believed was their own affair. Her success, during the first decade of her reign, was the success of attrition, not of compulsion.

Later, when the Pope excommunicated the Queen, when missionaries from the Continent undertook to re-establish the old faith, and when discontented English Catholics supplied the background for numerous foreign plots against the Queen and the realm, the official attitude towards the recusants stiffened and the penalties for recusancy became crushingly heavy.

On the left, the radical Protestants, or Puritans as they came to be called, directed their efforts to the reform of the Establishment, attacking first the vestments of the clergy, then the ritual, ultimately the church government. They grew stronger as the reign progressed, not only among Englishmen at large but particularly among those in high places, in the House of Commons, even in Elizabeth's Privy Council. Many of them, through the instrumentality of the country gentry, found places in the church itself. Elizabeth was violently opposed to them because she regarded them as a dangerous menace, not only to her concept of church government but to the whole monarchial principle. But it was not until the last decade of her reign, when the defeat of the Spanish Armada had delivered her from the Roman Catholic menace, that she dealt vigorously with the Puritans. We hear little of them during the nineties. They had lost their old leaders and something of their old crusading zeal. They did not lose faith, but for the time being they stopped fighting.

The pattern of Anglican church government followed the Roman model. England was divided into two provinces, one with its headquarters at Canterbury, the other at York. Canterbury was much the larger, and the Archbishop of Canterbury was primate of England. He usually resided in London at

Lambeth Palace. The provinces were divided into dioceses under bishops, the dioceses into archdeaconries, and so down to the ultimate unit, the parish. The archbishop and bishops, though nominally elected, were actually appointed by the Crown. They were supported by what were called temporalities, that is to say, the revenues of lands held by the bishop in feudal tenure of the Queen. The income from temporalities varied. Durham, for example, and London, were much the richest sees in England. Others, like the Welsh bishoprics, were notoriously poor. Ambitious prelates always had their eyes on the rich sees, and sometimes spent more of their time promoting their interests at Court than was quite consistent with their ecclesiastical duties.

Elizabeth made systematic depredations upon episcopal temporalities. She not only kept offices vacant in order to enjoy the revenues, but she often drove hard bargains with new appointees. And she resorted to various other extortionate devices both for herself and her favorites. Sir Christopher Hatton and Sir Walter Raleigh both grew fat upon the ecclesiastical spoils.

What Elizabeth did at the top, the country gentry did at the bottom. In the parishes the rector was ordained by the bishop of the diocese, but was normally appointed by the lord of the manor who held the right of advowson, or by any other who had lawfully acquired the right either by purchase or by inheritance. Before the break from Rome the rector of the parish was normally supported by tithes, being one tenth of the annual produce of the soil. But in many cases the right to collect the tithes had passed, by way of the monasteries and the Crown, into the hands of lay impropriators, who assumed the obligation to supply religious services but generally managed to make a considerable profit out of the transaction. One way or another, either by the right of advowson or by impropriation of tithes, the parish clergy became creatures of the gentry, and that meant that the religious complexion of the parish often reflected the religious views of the lord of the manor or his equivalent. In the North he looked through his fingers at a scarcely disguised Roman Catholicism; in the South and East he often appointed a Puritan rector and nourished a Puritan congregation. It was one of these, in the next reign, that crossed the seas in the Mayflower and laid the foundations of New England.

The canon law of the medieval church and the ecclesiastical courts which administered it, except insofar as the papacy was concerned, survived the break from Rome and continued to have jurisdiction over those persons and in those cases which were recognized as its proper field.

It had jurisdiction, not only over all clergymen, but over those who could justify a claim to benefit of clergy. In the common law courts a man accused of felony could claim clergy and establish his claim by reading scripture, and so avoid capital punishment. Ben Jonson, the poet, escaped hanging by that appeal.

The church court also had jurisdiction over the laity in a variety of cases, such as marriage, kinship, testamentary inheritance, blasphemy, heresy, and other cases of the same sort. The line between what case belonged to the church courts and what to the courts of common law was an uncertain one and the cause of a good deal of dispute later.

So far as the average Englishman was concerned, his objection to the ecclesiastical courts was that they provided none of the safeguards for the defendant which he had come to regard as basic in English justice. There was no jury trial; the defendant could be forced to testify under oath against himself in matters incriminating. Legal or not, it was not British.

The chief offender in this regard was the so-called Court of High Commission, set up by the Queen in 1559 to implement the royal supremacy over the church. It was not primarily an ecclesiastical court but rather a prerogative court dealing particularly with offenses against the Acts of Supremacy and Uniformity. But it followed ecclesiastical procedure. In composition it was a mixed company of bishops, Privy Councillors, civilians, sergeants-at-law, and suchlike, nineteen all told in the original commission, of whom seven constituted a quorum. Later commissions enlarged the membership and reduced the number of the quorum, so that different sections could be sitting in different places at the same time. Archbishop Whitgift made use of it in his attack upon the Puritans and aroused a great deal of opposition among the friends of the Puritans in the House of Commons and the Privy Council. Lord Burghley wrote to Whitgift that though the canonists might defend it, it smacked too much of the Roman inquisition.

Whitgift stuck to his guns and with the help of the Queen rather more than held his own. But those who were arrayed against him, the Puritans and the common lawyers, carried on the fight and ultimately not only did away with the Court of High Commission but with the established church itself.

Elizabeth was not a reformer. She was innately a conservative, though a flexible one. No small part of her greatness lay in her ability to operate a government machine, already creaking in the joints, to the satisfaction of her people and the glory of her kingdom. What would happen when a less skilled hand was at the helm was a problem which she would not discuss or permit to be discussed.

SUGGESTED READING

The best life of Elizabeth is by Sir John Neale, *Queen Elizabeth* (London, 1934; reprinted in a paperback, New York, 1957). Although it lacks footnotes, it is based throughout on sound scholarship. Sir John comes near to idealizing Elizabeth and needs to be tempered by J. A. Froude's estimate, which is definitely iconoclastic, in his *History of England from the Fall of Wolsey to the Death of Elizabeth* (12 vols., London, 1856–70), see Volumes 7–12, *The Reign of Elizabeth*.

On the constitutional history of the reign, Sir David Lindsay Keir's chapters in his *Constitutional History of Modern Britain, 1485–1937* (London, 1938), are as good as any; and there is a good deal of pertinent documentary material, with significant introductory notes, in Joseph R. Tanner, *Tudor Constitutional Documents, 1485–1603* (Cambridge, Eng., 1922, 1948). The chapters in Edward P. Cheyney, *A History of England from the Defeat of the Armada to the Death of Elizabeth* (2 vols., New York, 1914, 1926, 1948), particularly Part i in Volume I on the Royal Administration and Part viii in Volume II on Local Administration, are models of careful scholarship and clear exposition, though needing perhaps to be supplemented by Neale's admirable discussion of corruption in high places and exploitation of official positions for private profit in *The Elizabethan Political Scene* in *Proceedings of the British Academy*, Volume XXIV, 1948; also printed separately (London, 1948). The pertinent chapters in Wallace Notestein, *The English People on the Eve of Colonization, 1603–1630* (New York, 1954) are admirable, though they are more relevant to the reign of Elizabeth's successor, James I.

There is no adequate book on the Privy Council under Elizabeth. Its actual role can best be followed in the biographies of her two great secretaries, William Cecil and Francis Walsingham: Conyers Read, *Mr. Secretary Cecil and Queen Elizabeth* (London, 1955) and *Mr. Secretary Walsingham and the Policy of Queen Elizabeth* (3 vols., Oxford, 1925).

Sir John Neale's three volumes on Parliament under Elizabeth are as learned as they are interesting, and they displace all earlier works on the subject: *The Elizabethan House of Commons* (London, 1949), and *Elizabeth I and Her Parliaments* (2 vols., London, 1953–57), which has chiefly to do with the House of Commons and its relation to the crown. For the House of Lords, available source material is relatively scanty. Luke O. Pike, *Constitutional History of the House of Lords* (London, 1894) is useful but inadequate.

On public finance F. C. Dietz, *English Public Finance, 1558–1641* (New York, 1932) is the only adequate account, though it calls for corrections in detail.

For local government, Cheyney, cited above, is the best, though Notestein throws a good deal of light upon local officials such as the churchwardens and the constables. In this connection William Lambarde's *Eirenarcha* (London, 1581), the standard sixteenth-century handbook for justices, though hard to come by, is very helpful on matters of detail. Two MSS. by Lambarde in the Folger Library, one, *Ephemeris,* his diary as a justice of the peace in Kent, the other his addresses to the grand jury in Kent, are very illuminating. *Ephemeris* has been published (*Huntington Library Quarterly,* XV [1952], 123–58); the addresses to the grand jury are being prepared for the press.

Elizabethan courts of justice can be best pursued in Sir William Holdsworth's monumental *History of English Law* (12 vols., London, 1903–38). Prerogative courts have been subject to special study. For Chancery, Star Chamber, and Court of Requests, Cheyney gives the most succinct account. For the Court of Wards, two excellent books have recently appeared: H. E. Bell, *Introduction to the History and Records of the Court of Wards and Liveries* (Cambridge, Eng., 1953) and Joel Hurstfield, *The Queen's Wards* (London, 1958).

In matters ecclesiastical, the best narrative history of the Elizabethan church is Walter H. Frere, *History of the Church of England, 1558–1625* (London 1904). Felix Makower, *Constitutional History and Constitution of the Church of England* (Berlin, 1884; English trans., London, 1895) is still the standard, though difficult to use. John H. Pollen, as far as he goes (to 1581), is the best history of the Roman Catholics under Elizabeth: *The English Catholics in the Reign of Queen Elizabeth* (London, 1920). A. O. Meyer gives the complete story, best used in the English translation: *England and the Catholic Church under Elizabeth* (trans. by J. R. McKee, London, 1916, and revised by the author). There is nothing better than Knappen on English Puritanism: Marshall M. Knappen, *Tudor Puritanism* (Chicago, 1939).

John Strype's voluminous works, written early in the eighteenth century, particularly his *Annals of the Reformation* and his *Life and Acts of John Whitgift, D.D.* (Oxford, 1820–40, 1832), are gold mines of pertinent documents on Anglican church history, based largely on the Burghley papers in the Lansdowne MSS., British Museum,which were at one time in Strype's possession.

On the social philosophy supporting the structure of English society, the classical account is A. O. Lovejoy, *The Great Chain of Being* (Cambridge, Mass., 1936). As applied specifically to England it is well set forth by E. M. W. Tillyard in *The Elizabethan World Picture* (London, 1943).

For a more detailed bibliography on all of these subjects, see Conyers Read, *Bibliography of British History, Tudor Period* (Oxford, 1933; 2nd ed., Oxford, 1959).

Plate 1. Queen Elizabeth dressed as for the opening of Parliament. Engraved by Crispin van de Passe (1603–4) after a drawing by Isaac Oliver. From Humphrey Dyson, *A Book Containing All Such Proclamations As Were Published during the Reign of the Late Queen Elizabeth* (1618).

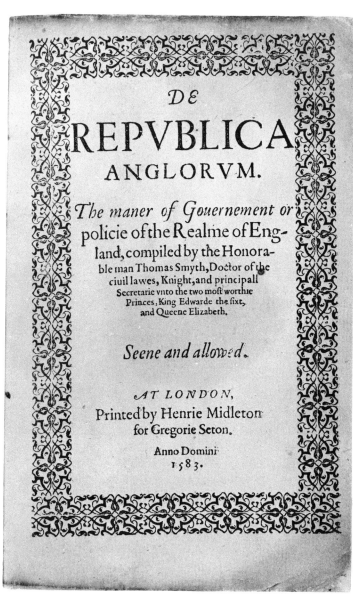

DE

REPVBLICA

ANGLORVM.

The maner of Gouernement or policie of the Realme of Eng-land, compiled by the Honora-ble man Thomas Smyth, Doctor of the ciuil lawes, Knight, and principall Secretarie vnto the two most worthie Princes, King Edwarde the sixt, and Queene Elizabeth.

Seene and allowed.

AT LONDON, Printed by Henrie Midleton for Gregorie Seton.

Anno Domini 1583.

Plate 2. The title page of Sir Thomas Smith, *De republica Anglorum* (1583).

Plate 3. The arms of England emblazoned by an anonymous artist. From Humphrey Dyson, *A Book Containing All Such Proclamations As Were Published during the Reign of the Late Queen Elizabeth* (1618).

Plate 4. Queen Elizabeth attended by three counselors. From a woodcut initial C in Gabriel Harvey, *Gratulationum valdinensium libri quatuor* (1578).

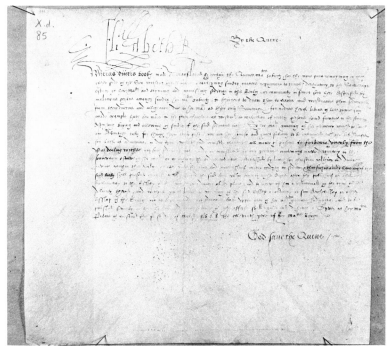

Plate 5. A proclamation against importing or possessing seditious books, March 1, 1568/69, printed for distribution the same date. The Queen's subjects are forbidden to have anything to do with books designed to corrupt their allegiance to the Queen and the established church, and are ordered to deliver up any such books in their possession to the bishop or other church official in their diocese within twenty-eight days after publication of the proclamation. Folger MS. X.d.85.

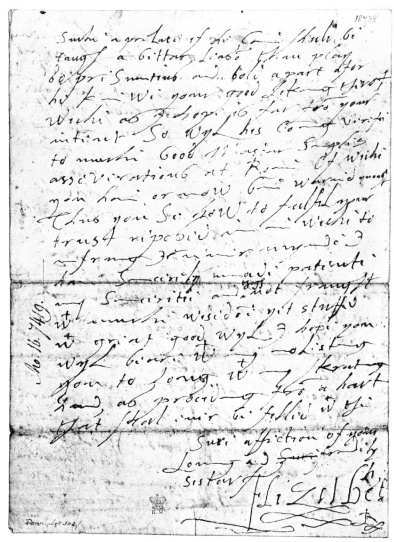

Plate 6. Part of a holograph letter of Elizabeth to James VI of Scotland, 5 January 1602/03. [BM Add. MS. 18738 f.39, courtesy of the British Museum.] The same letter is printed with variations in spelling from a copy in the library of Sir Peter Thompson in *Letters of Elizabeth and James VI*, ed. by John Bruce, Camden Society Publications, No. 46 (London, 1849.)

516

(The transcript below reproduces the spelling of the original except for the expansion of contractions such as wt and cõing.)

Suche a prelate if he come shuld be taugh a bettar leason than play so presumtius and bold a part afor he knewe your good liking therof wiche as I hope is far from your intent   So wyl his coming verefie to muche Good Mastar Simples asseverations at Rome òf wiche you haue or now bene warned ynough Thus you se how to fulfil your trust reposed in me wiche to infring I [ ] neuer mynde   I haue sincerely made patente my sinceritie and thogh not fraught with muche wisedome yet stuffed with great good wyl   I hope you wyl beare with my molesting you to long with my skrating hand, as prociding from a hart that shal euer be filled with the

sure affection of your
Louing and ~~sure~~ frindely
sistar
Elizabeth
R

Plate 7. William Cecil, first Baron Burghley, 1520–1598. Portrait by an unknown artist, courtesy of the National Portrait Gallery, London.

SERO, SED, SERIO

Plate 8. Robert Cecil, first Earl of Salisbury, 1563–1612. A portrait attributed to John De Critz, 1602, courtesy of the National Portrait Gallery, London.

Plate 9. Sir Francis Walsingham, 1536–1590. Portrait by an unknown artist, courtesy of the National Portrait Gallery, London.

Plate 10. Sir Christopher Hatton, 1540–1591. Portrait by an unknown artist, courtesy of the National Portrait Gallery, London.

Plate 11. Sir John Popham, 1531?–1607, Chief Justice and Speaker of the House of Commons. Portrait by an unknown artist, 1600, courtesy of the National Portrait Gallery, London.

Plate 12. Sir Nicholas Bacon, 1509–1579, Lord Keeper of the Great Seal. Portrait by an unknown artist, 1579, courtesy of the National Portrait Gallery.

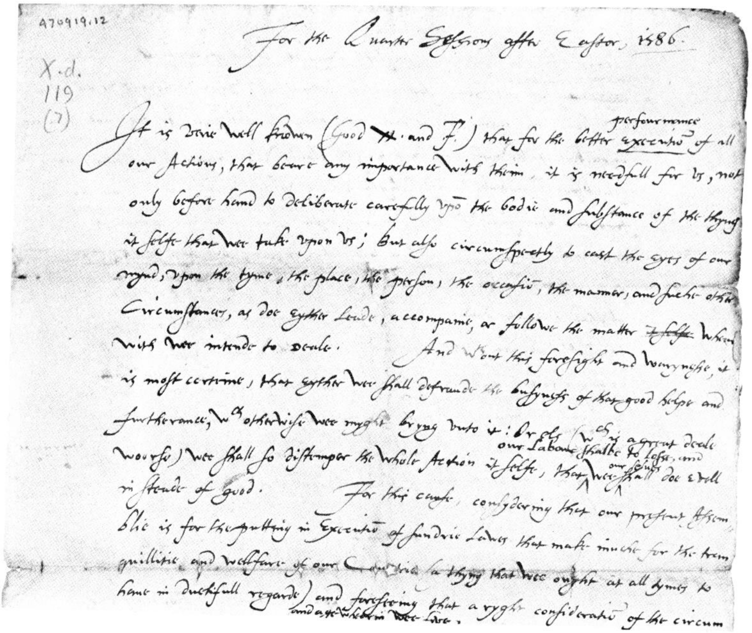
A70919.12

X.d. 119 (7)

For the Quarter Sessions after Easter, 1586.

It is verie well knowen (Good M. and F.) that for the better execution performance of all our Actions, that beare any importance with them, it is needfull for us, not only before hand to deliberate carefully upon the bodie and substance of the thing it selfe that wee take upon us; But also circumspectly to cast the eyes of our mynd, upon the tyme, the place, the person, the occasion, the manner, and suche other Circumstances, as doe eyther leade, accompanie, or followe the matter itselfe wherewith wee intende to deale. And wthout this foresight and warynesse, it is most certeine, that eyther wee shall defraude the busynesse of that good helpe and furtherance, wch otherwise wee might bryng unto it: Or els (wch is a great deale worse) wee shall so distemper the whole Action it selfe, that wee shall doe evell in steede of good. For this cause, consydering that our present Assemblie is for the putting in execution of sundrie Lawes that make muche for the tranquillitie and wellfare of our Countrie (a thyng that wee ought at all tymes to have in duetifull regarde) and foreseeing that a ryght consideration of the circum

Plate 13. One of William Lambarde's charges to the jury as a justice of the peace in Kent: "For the Quarter Sessions after Easter, 1586." Folger MS. X.d.119 (7).

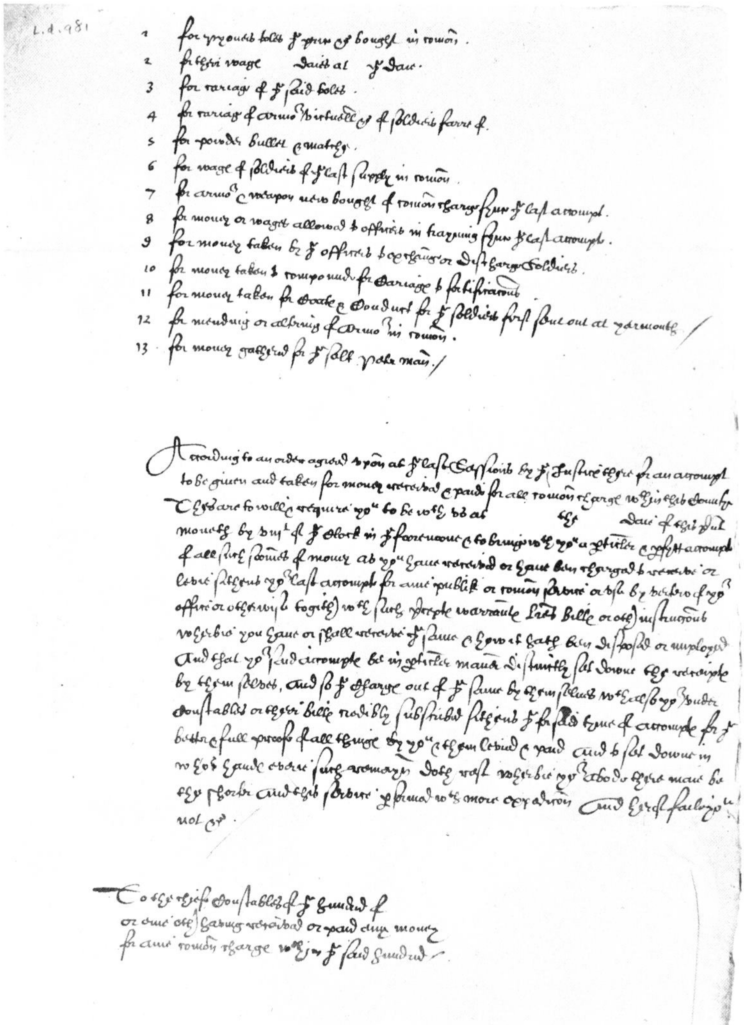

L.d.981

Plate 14. An order to the chief constables, probably of the county of Norfolk, regarding the rendering of accounts of expenses connected with their duties. From the Bacon-Townsend Papers, Folger MS. L.d.981.

Plate 15. The Queen opening a new Parliament in the White Chamber. From Robert Glover, *Nobilitas politica vel civilis* (1608).

Plate 16. The Parliament House, Westminster Hall, and Westminster Abbey engraved by Wenceslaus Hollar, 1647.

Plate 17. Burghley presiding over a meeting of the Court of Wards and Liveries, engraved by George Vertue. The painting from which Vertue made his engraving was probably not the original but an early copy still in the collection of the Duke of Richmond. The portrait of the presiding master at the far end of the table closely resembles a miniature of Lord Burghley, with the same kind of hat, in the possession of the Marquess of Salisbury.